Children's Multilingual Deve

The study of families and educators who successfully sustain children's linguistic resources is a novelty in current educational research, where focus has largely been on the development of students' English language skills. In this book, Alison Bailey and Anna Osipova provide a systematic examination of the beliefs and practices of parents and educators who share the common goal of improving educational and social outcomes for multilingual children. Giving voice to parents and educators, they explore the strategies being devised to foster multilingualism and support its development both at home and in the classroom. This book presents new research findings and combines these with compelling first-hand accounts of the successes and concerns of both families and educators, making its content pertinent to a wide audience of researchers and a range of higher education courses.

ALISON BAILEY is Professor of Human Development and Psychology in the Department of Education at UCLA and a faculty partner with the National Center for Research on Evaluation, Standards and Student Testing (CRESST).

ANNA OSIPOVA is a faculty member within the Division of Special Education and Counseling at California State University, Los Angeles.

Children's Multilingual Development and Education

Fostering Linguistic Resources in Home and School Contexts

Alison L. Bailey and Anna V. Osipova
With a Foreword by Fred Genesee

CAMBRIDGE
UNIVERSITY PRESS

CAMBRIDGE
UNIVERSITY PRESS

University Printing House, Cambridge CB2 8BS, United Kingdom

One Liberty Plaza, 20th Floor, New York, NY 10006, USA

477 Williamstown Road, Port Melbourne, VIC 3207, Australia

314-321, 3rd Floor, Plot 3, Splendor Forum, Jasola District Centre, New Delhi-110025, India

79 Anson Road, #06-04/06, Singapore 079906

Cambridge University Press is part of the University of Cambridge.

It furthers the University's mission by disseminating knowledge in the pursuit of
education, learning and research at the highest international levels of excellence.

www.cambridge.org
Information on this title: www.cambridge.org/9781108449274

First published 2016
First paperback edition 2017

A catalogue record for this publication is available from the British Library

Library of Congress Cataloging in Publication data
Bailey, Alison L.
Children's multilingual development and education : fostering linguistic resources
in home and school contexts / Alison L. Bailey, Anna V. Osipova; foreword by
Fred Genesee.
    pages   cm
Includes bibliographical references and index.
ISBN 978-1-107-04244-5 (hardback)
1. Multilingualism in children.   2. Bilingualism in children.   3. Multilingual
education.   4. Education, Bilingual.   I. Osipova, Anna V.   II. Title.
P115.2.B34   2015
404´.2083–dc23   2015028145

ISBN 978-1-107-04244-5 Hardback
ISBN 978-1-108-44927-4 Paperback

To our parents, those who continue to love and
support us
&
those whom we remember and miss dearly.

Contents

Figures

Tables

Foreword

It has been estimated that more children grow up speaking two or more languages than only one. While it is difficult to cite precise statistics that provide conclusive evidence for this, no one would disagree that there are a lot of bilingual individuals in the world, and many of them are children. Studies on alternative forms of bilingual education and second language instruction have enjoyed some popularity for some time – dating back to the 1960s with the inauguration of immersion programs in Canada and bilingual education in the United States (see Genesee and Lindholm-Leary, 2013, for a review). However, until recently, researchers in most other fields of inquiry have largely ignored issues related to multilingual acquisition. Fortunately, this has started to change. For example, in my own field of inquiry on second language and bilingual acquisition, or what some might broadly call cognitive neuroscience, studies on language learning, representation, and use in children and adults who are learning and using more than one language have become mainstream and highly respected as researchers realize how prevalent bi- and multilingualism is. Enhanced interest in bi- and multilingualism has also been motivated by the recognition that theories of language learning must include all types of language learners, not just monolinguals. We now have much more empirical evidence on many aspects of second language learning than ever before to inform decision making, although there is still much more to learn.

As valuable as current evidence on second language and bilingual acquisition is, it often exists in a contextual vacuum. That is the say, the empirical evidence is often abstracted from the actual lives of children who grow up bilingual and our understandings of empirical evidence often fails to consider the contexts in which acquisition actually takes place. Bailey and Osipova's book on *Children's Multilingual Development and Education: Fostering Linguistic Resources in Home and School Contexts* helps fill this vacuum. In a very useful and non-academic fashion, Bailey and Osipova review a great deal of what we know about raising and educating children bi- and multilingually in a uniquely contextualized way. At the same time, they extend our understanding of bi- and multilingual development by examining in detailed and intimate ways the contexts in which childhood bilingualism actually occurs.

Their story is about the "big picture" in which children actually grow up to become bi- or multilingual. They use the terms "multilingual" and "multilingualism" to include bilingual and bilingualism, so I will use these terms in the same way in this Foreword. Although they assert in the Preface that this book is not for parents but, rather, is *about* parents, there is nevertheless much in this very readable volume that will help guide and inform parents, as well as educators and other professionals who contribute to the development of these children.

At the core of this book is a detailed discussion of the results of an ambitious study of the beliefs, fears, motivations, practices, and challenges of parents who raised children to be competent in more than one language. Their study was conducted in the United States – predominantly California, and included 23 families with 39 children. Families selected for participation were raising and educating their children under very diverse circumstances. This was done deliberately to ensure that the families represented the wide range of circumstances in which children in the United States actually become bilingual. Although based on a sample from the United States and, thus, arguably limited in geographic scope, the authors also discuss studies conducted on bi- and multilingualism around the world.

While diversity among bilingual children and their families is often alluded to in other studies, it is seldom described or discussed in such intimate detail as in this book. As a result, one of the main conclusions to be drawn from their study and the book as a whole is that to really understand multilingual development and how to promote it requires an understanding of the diverse circumstances in which it occurs. While one could argue that this was an obvious and foregone conclusion, given the nature of their sample, the full diversity of circumstances in which children become multilingual is seldom highlighted in such insightful detail. More pointedly, the fact of such diversity and its critical relevance to multilingual development are seldom taken seriously by classroom educators, educational administrators, or policy-makers (let alone other professionals) who work with multilingual children. In fact, as the authors point out, most educators working with multilingual children in the United States are themselves monolingual and thus have no intuitive sense of such diversity; this is likely to be true in other communities around the world. In North America, teachers often do not even know what other languages their minority-language students know or the circumstances of their language development, critical information for appropriate differentiation of instruction. It is a truism in Western education that all children are different and that effective education takes individual differences into account, and, yet, when it comes to educating children who have minority language/cultural backgrounds, we often fail to delve into their individualities. By focusing on families raising children in diverse contexts, the authors sensitize readers to the critical importance of context in understanding multilingualism. By implication, they are also alerting researchers, educators, and parents around the world to this fact.

Their sample included children from minority groups who were acquiring English as a second language along with their birth language as well as majority group children in English-speaking families who were acquiring an additional language at home or in school; these groups in turn included recent and established immigrant families along with native-born American families; they included families who were acquiring foreign, heritage, or ancestral languages, which in some cases were similar and in other cases highly dissimilar (e.g., Chinese and English). While most children in the sample were acquiring one additional language, there were also children who were learning or had learned more than one additional languages – five in one case! The learners were toddlers, preschool-age, school-age, or young adults at the time of data collection. Data collection included face-to-face and semi structured telephone interviews with parents (mostly mothers) about family background, the context in which multilingualism occurred, the child's multilingual development, beliefs about bilingualism, strategies and practices for supporting multilingualism in the home, and perceived roadblocks to achieving multilingualism, among others.

The study also included 13 educators who encountered multilingual children in their day-to-day teaching, but had not necessarily taught the children of the parent participants in the study. Data were collected from the educators using individual and focus group discussions and semi structured interviews and touched on topics related to teacher interactions with multilingual students in their classrooms, their beliefs about multilingualism, challenges and rewards in working with multilingual students, strategies and practices they found effective in promoting multilingualism, among others. Including educators is an invaluable part of the study because it provides a broader and, thus, more realistic picture of what it means to raise children to be multilingual – while past studies have examined families or educators, few have examined both at the same time. To examine the lives of multilingual children taking family or school perspectives alone into account is to get only half the story. Much insight is to be gained from looking at the overlap and disjunctions in these two domains of multilingual children's lives. Taking such a broad perspective is critical if we are to move beyond a deficit or subtractive view of bilingual development to an additive one – ignorance of the complexities of multilingual children's lives is prone to oversimplifications and misunderstandings since it feeds a false dichotomy comprised of bilinguals versus monolinguals.

Bailey and Osipova adeptly use the information collected from the parents to identify salient beliefs they hold about multilingualism in general and in their families (Chapter 3) – beliefs that shape the decisions, practices, and strategies they adopt to support children's multilingualism. In fact, many of their beliefs reflect misunderstandings or fears about raising and educating children to be multilingual. Many of these fears are not supported by empirical evidence, but are nonetheless important in their lives. While some of the discussion in this chapter is quite specific to attitudes, beliefs, and policies surrounding multilingualism in the United States, there is still a great deal that will be of broad interest and relevance to those interested in individual multilingualism elsewhere. More specifically, the following topics of broad relevance are discussed and then challenged using available research evidence: learning more than one language is detrimental to children's development; multilinguals are late talkers and have limited language competencies; some children and, in particular, children with disabilities cannot learn additional languages; knowing other languages jeopardizes children's academic success and puts their social development at risk; and there are certain strategies for raising children bilingually that are more successful than others; and others. Discussing these widely held beliefs and concerns using first-hand expressions of the participants' beliefs and concerns grounds them in the day-to-day lives of parents and, thereby, validates them while raising awareness of the need to provide parents more information so that they can make better-informed decisions. Indeed, later in the book, the authors note that parents make a plea that educators provide them with more information about language learning in general and multilingualism in particular so they can make responsible decisions. It has been my experience that teachers themselves also need such information. The authors' coverage of these issues is refreshingly balanced and authentic precisely because it is embedded in the lived lives of their participants.

The richest part of the book is to be found in Chapters 5 and 6 on "Raising Multilingual Children" and "Fostering Multilingualism in Diverse Educational Contexts," respectively. It is in these chapters that the authors directly explore the expressed beliefs, fears, motivations, and challenges of raising and supporting multilingual children. In a section in Chapter 5 called "Pathways to Multilingualism," the authors sketch out the alternative and varied contexts in which parents support their children's multilingual development, and here we see the intense and complex reflections that parents engage in as they embark on and try to sustain their individual paths to multilingualism. They illustrate the diversity of contexts in which multilingual children grow up by describing the histories of different types of families – for example, English-dominant parents versus bilingual parents versus non-English-dominant parents. In this way, it becomes clear that there is not a single portrait of the multilingual family; there are many. It is these portraits that, in my opinion, are most revealing because it is here that we see how individual family practices and strategies for promoting their children's multilingualism is shaped in critical ways by their historical and present-day contexts as well as by their beliefs about multilingualism and their motivations for wanting their children to be multilingual.

Parents' concerns were not just about language but also about culture – how to maintain heritage cultures, fitting into mainstream cultures, being part of an interconnected and globalized culture, and connections with family and others. It is impossible to summarize here the full richness of understandings that emerge from the authors' discussions of the parent interviews in this chapter – readers will have to discover this on their own.

A useful and key construct to emerge from this chapter is the notion of investment. Bailey and Osipova point out that parents make multiple forms of investment – in time, money, emotion, education, friendships for themselves and their children, and in the family, to achieve their vision of multilingualism for their children. Investment is about commitment, taking charge, resilience, facing and overcoming challenges, and the future. It is here that another overarching theme emerged from my reading – the tremendous effort that is needed to raise and educate children to be multilingual in environments that do not support multilingualism and may even obstruct its achievement. It is also here that we see that the nature of the effort that parents must invest to achieve multilingualism changes with time as their children grow up. The authors devote a separate section to consider the challenges that parents perceive as obstacles to achieving their goals of multilingualism, including challenges linked to insecurities in the family, outside influences (e.g., monolingual peers), being different from monolingual families and children, and monolingual school systems. It is intriguing to speculate whether one would find the sample challenges and demands for effort and investment in other cultural-linguistic contexts – a topic of another book.

The authors continue their discussion of how context affects children's multilingual development in Chapter 6 as they review the interview data from the teacher participants. Here the authors consider the beliefs, challenges, practices, and strategies of educators who encounter multilingual students in their classrooms, even when the classroom and school function monolingually. It is interesting to note that even teachers working in programs that are designed to support multilingualism talked about the challenges they face supporting children's multilingual development despite the school's stated aims. More specifically, they talk about challenges related to instability in program design, lack of adequate resources in all languages used in the classroom, isolation from mainstream classrooms and teachers, and teachers' concerns about their own abilities to function in more than one language. Despite these evident challenges, the teacher participants expressed wholehearted enthusiasm for working with multilingual students. Aside from the importance of the details about educational contexts presented in this chapter, this chapter is important because it highlights the importance of taking a broad holistic view of multilingual development. In this chapter, the authors stress that is not only up to families to maintain, support, and protect the multilingual resources of their children; but schools and, by extension, the wider community also have a role to play. It is only by including educators in the study that their call for families and educators to work together is so clear.

In sum, Bailey and Osipova provide a refreshingly grounded, contextually rich discussion of the lives of children who grow up in families that want them to be multilingual. This volume is an important antidote to the often overly simplistic view that we have of the lives of multilingual children. It tells us that there are many ways for children to become multilingual; that forces in their families as well as in their schooling and communities at large play important roles; and that we need to work together to protect, foster, and celebrate children's multilingualism. This book should motivate parents, professionals, and researchers to reconceptualize how they think and work with these children.

Fred Genesee,
McGill University

Genesee, F., and Lindholm-Leary, K. (2013). Two case studies of content-based language education. *Journal of Immersion and Content-Based Language Education*, 1(1), 3–33.

Preface

Just like music is a language and you don't get confused when you listen to Bach versus, you know, jazz! You know, you can be exposed and understand that they are both completely different.

Tina, Taiwanese-English bilingual mother

We are inspired by these words from Tina, a bilingual mother aspiring to raise her young daughter with two languages. Her words remind us with simple aplomb how amazingly adaptable the human mind is. Of course we do not confuse Bach with jazz, and what is more we can appreciate and understand both with ease. A myriad of books on raising bi- and multilingual children have hit the bookshelves recently, both real and virtual, indicating the public's burgeoning interest and investment in multilingual parenting. These books offer parents guidance, recommendations, or the latest top 10 tips for providing children with a polyglot upbringing. This book differs from them all in one major respect: This is not a book *for* parents (although parents will undoubtedly find it of interest), rather it is a book *about* parents and the educators who partner with families to create and sustain the linguistic resources of children.

This volume came about as we reflected on the questions from an increasing number of parents we encounter in our professional and personal lives who are raising or preparing to raise their children with exposure to more than one language. The unique and compelling stories of successes and sometimes difficult dilemmas experienced by these parents motivated us to embark on a systematic look at U.S. families who speak two or more languages and their child-rearing practices, as well as the multifaceted roles of the educators who may support these endeavors.

In conducting this work, we quickly realized that there was a disjuncture between the popular image of the U.S. as a monolingual nation and the reality of the families we were interviewing. As quickly as the questions of our parent acquaintances gave us hope that multilingualism was a serious and determined part of their families' lives, we realized that their questions also revealed how pervasively certain myths and misinformation about multilingualism still abound in U.S. society. Consequently, this book tackles the beliefs of the participating parents and educators turning to the research literature for their verification.

The study of parents and educators that we report in this book should appeal to educational researchers, as well as to psychologists, applied linguists, sociologists, and anthropologists who study language, ethnicity, and multiculturalism in children, their families, and their wider communities. The volume counters many of the (low) expectations held by wider society for the linguistic prowess of the typical American. Our book explains how, through their interactions, planning, teaching, and mentoring, families and educators work hard, often facing difficult challenges but nevertheless making multilingualism part of the fabric of the daily lives of an increasing number of U.S. children.

Alison L. Bailey and Anna V. Osipova

Acknowledgments

Our biggest debt of gratitude is of course to the families and educators who gave their time for this work to become a reality and who shared all their hopes and not a few of their fears about children's acquisition of two or more languages. We also thank our tireless transcribers Rachel Zwass, Orlando Piña, and Janet Huynh. For financial assistance, we acknowledge the UCLA Graduate Division who made the research possible through a year-long Graduate Research Mentorship Award to Anna for which Alison served as mentor. We are indebted to Fred Genesee for his contribution of the Foreword. His remarks perceptively cut to the specific ways in which our research can hope to positively impact practice. We would also like to thank our colleagues at UCLA and CSULA for their encouragement and overwhelming enthusiasm for this enterprise, but we would especially like to acknowledge Shilpa Baweja, Frances Butler, Diane Klein, Jennifer McCormick, and Norma Silva for the special roles they have each played in our pursuit of a deeper understanding of the development of multilingualism. Frances's and Norma's generous feedback on early drafts and their constant encouragement of our efforts especially have made this book so much the stronger as a result. Anna would also like to thank Lucia Smith-Menzies for her tireless editorial support. Alison would like to thank Michael Rex Bailey for serving as Prof's PA again on the index, and, along with Jane Christianson, for providing warm places in which to write during the final push: the "blue room" writing desk did the trick. The arrival of William Ziolkowski on the scene undoubtedly gave rise to a very personal investment in what we have attempted to document here. He and his father suffered silently – and sometimes not so silently – with mummy living endless months in front of the computer. Alison would like to say thank you to Frank for his love and support. William, *espero que tú comprendas el propósito y nuestro compromiso con este esfuerzo y que un día en el futuro cercano tu sabrás que todo esto valió la pena.* Anna is grateful for the ceaseless support of her UCLA research group and CSULA friends and students who shared with us their stories of multilingual experiences and connected us with a rich network of families for whom multilingualism is a way of life. Anna would especially like to thank her mom and brother, Orlando, Suzan and Susie, who have never stopped listening, talking the ideas over, and offering great perspectives. "Эта книга посвящается моей маме и отцу, которые говоря со мной только по-русски, всё-таки вырастили из меня полиглота." Finally, we thank our thoughtful anonymous reviewers and editors at Cambridge University Press. We are especially grateful to Hetty Marx at Cambridge who helped us to develop the original proposal, and to Rebecca Taylor, Carrie Parkinson, Rob Wilkinson, and James Harrison for seeing the final manuscript to press. All errors herein remain our own.

Abbreviations

CAL	Center for Applied Linguistics
CCSS	Common Core State Standards
DBE	Developmental Bilingual Education
ELD	English Language Development
ELL	English Language Learner
ELP	English Language Proficiency
ESL	English as a Second Language
FEP	Fluent English Proficient
FLA	Foreign Language Learning Aptitude
HLS	Home Language Survey
LEA	Local Education Agency
LIEP	Language Instruction Educational Program
LD	Learning Disability
L1	First language
L2	Second language
NCELA	National Clearinghouse of English Language Acquisition
OTL	Opportunity to Learn
SEI	Structured English Immersion
SES	Socioeconomic Status
SIOP	Sheltered Instruction Observational Protocol
SLD	Spanish Language Development
SLI	Specific Language Impairment
SDAIE	Specially Designed Academic Instruction in English
TBE	Transitional Bilingual Education
TWI	Two-Way Immersion
TWIOP	Two-Way Immersion Observational Protocol
ZPD	Zone of Proximal Development

1 Multilingual Nations: Multilingualism in Context

In this chapter we provide an introduction to our research with families and educators on their practices of rearing bi- and multilingual children in the United States and comparatively in other parts of the world. We introduce the myth of monolingualism that pervades some societies as well as perhaps the equally mythic notion that "everywhere else" people acquire two or more languages quite routinely and with ease. We conclude with an overview of the remaining chapters.

Can you have a conversation in a language besides your mother tongue? Readers may have selected this book because they can indeed converse with others in more than one language and are keen to learn more about how families and educators can work together to create favorable conditions for multilingualism to flourish in children. This question, however, is intended to be more than just a rhetorical one. It is the actual question posed by the European Commission in a 2006 survey of Europe's inhabitants (Directorate General for Education and Culture, 2006). The number of affirmative respondents may surprise readers, and we will return to the result presently. First, we turn to a confluence of issues both professional and personal that define the content and central thesis of the book.

As we write this introduction, the first author has just finished making operational an online forum for a professional learning community (PLC) dedicated to the exchange of ideas by educators working in two-way immersion (TWI) and other forms of dual-language programs in the Southern California region. Nationally, TWI programming is increasing in the United States. The TWI model is a dual-language program in which two languages are partnered. Children who are native-English speakers acquire a second language (e.g., Spanish, Korean, or Mandarin) as they learn academic content alongside the native-speaking children of the second language. These children, in turn, learn English as their second language. The two sets of children in effect serve as models for one another's language learning. The "ticker" in the directory of programs that is maintained by the Center for Applied Linguistics (CAL) puts the number of TWI programs in the United States at 441 in 2014. The largest period of growth since CAL began keeping track in 1962 came in just the past 15 years. There were 280 programs newly registered between 1997 and 2011 alone, the last available year that CAL analyzed the TWI data by year (CAL, 2011). We know this number to be an underestimate: registry is entirely voluntary and none of the dozen or so TWI programs belonging to the new UCLA PLC is in fact registered with CAL. In 2013, the Foundation for Child Development put the estimate of programs closer to 2000 (Espinosa, 2013).

In just the past year or so, National Public Radio (NPR) has given a number of accounts of such programs. Closest to home for us, the annual address to administrators by the superintendent of the Los Angeles Unified School District was broadcast on NPR. To herald the start of a new school year, Nelson Henriquez, 11, was heard welcoming the school leaders in Spanish, English, and Mandarin. Nelson's multilingualism is the product of the City Terrace Elementary dual-language immersion program teaching not one but two additional languages. Incidentally, also in the past year, Dodger Stadium in Los Angeles was featured on NPR announcing that its baseball games have become trilingual – now televising in English, Spanish, and Korean.

Recently two reports have attempted to debunk the mainly negative myths surrounding multilingualism. The *Society for Research in Child Development's Social Policy Report* places an emphasis on high-quality language input to support the acquisition of each language a child has the opportunity to learn, and provides recommendations for early childhood education policy and practice (McCabe et al., 2013). A reprise of an earlier report from the Foundation for Child Development systemically reviews the common myths that early education program administrators and teachers encounter and counters these with results from the most recent research literature (Espinosa, 2013). While both policy reports also tackled the myths that surround multilingualism, particularly around the early education of multilingual students, this study differs from them in an important way: the myths arise from our conversations with parents and educators directly and reveal many more misconceptions of multilingual development and education than we could have anticipated from previous reviews. We take each of these myths and examine them from the parents' or educators' perspectives and contextualize them with what is known in the research literature.

While the efficacy of TWI programs in particular has been questioned for children speaking the partnered minority language (e.g., Valdés, 1997), such programs have become one of the fastest growing forms of language instruction. One of the concerns has been whether pedagogies used in TWI can effectively teach minority language children and reduce the prejudice and discrimination toward the minority language and its speakers witnessed in society more broadly (Genesee and Gándara, 1999). The increase in popularity has occurred during an era when the bilingual education of language-minority children has been scaled back in the face of state-level initiatives like the ones in California, Arizona, and Massachusetts that sponsored the almost exclusive development of and education through English (Lindholm-Leary and Howard, 2008). However, these initiatives may have had their day with revisions made to ballot initiative Question 2 in Massachusetts to make TWI more readily available to families, and a ballot initiative now afoot in California to repeal its restrictive language instruction policies that came about with Proposition 227 in 1998 (Ash, 2014).

Ironically, the growth in TWI programming may be attributed to this less-than-auspicious climate for the bilingual education of language-minority students. Despite the best efforts of 27 states that have declared English to be their official language (de Jong, 2011), we have personally seen principals become explicit about the fact that TWI programming provides a mechanism by which to continue to offer non-English language instruction to language-minority students so that they may access academic content in their primary language; all the while acquiring English in order to meet Federal Government English-language progress and proficiency mandates under the No Child Left Behind Act of 2001 (NCLB) (Mayer, 2007).

For the parents of children who are already proficient in English or for whom English is initially their only language, a range of issues may motivate their increased enrollment in TWI programs across the nation. Parents may value the personal benefits of multilingualism for their children (i.e., linguistic and academic advantages) as well as see dual-language immersion as a signal commitment to social justice efforts in the United States with the belief that exposure of their children to more than one language and culture will promote greater cross-cultural understanding. Of course much multilingualism in the United States is achieved by families without a child's enrollment in a TWI program. Children acquire additional languages in other contexts, both through formal instructional settings such as transitional bilingual education programs, one-way immersion programs, heritage language programming, and English language development classes, as well as through informal interactions with siblings (perhaps ones who are already being schooled in an additional language), with peers, and with parents, grandparents, or other adult caregivers.

While the new work that we report in the book was conducted in the United States, findings from studies with multilingual families and educators in others countries are woven throughout the discussion. These include studies conducted in countries with wholly different languages in contact with one another. For example, we examine situations in European countries that have a tradition of playing host to "guest workers" who by now have multiple generations of European-born children. These include Turkish-origin families settled in Germany (Razakowski et al., 2013) and the Netherlands (Prevoo et al., 2013). Studies of European, African, and Asian linguistic contexts are also included to illuminate cases of trilingual development (e.g., Hoffmann, and Ytsma, 2004).

We also discuss studies conducted in English-speaking countries other than the United States. These studies have examined both indigenous and immigrant languages in contact with English, for example, the attempts to revive the Welsh language against overwhelming odds of language attrition in the face of English-language dominance (Gathercole and Thomas, 2009), the situation of Asian and Eastern European immigrant families in Britain where languages such as Bengali (Pagett, 2006) and Polish (see, e.g., BI-SLI Poland Studies) increasingly come into contact with English.

Two seminal language contact situations that have been extensively researched are those found in Francophone Canada (Genesee, 1998; Wright, 1996) with its special dynamic created by French-English bilingualism in an otherwise English-dominant North America, and Castilian (Spanish)-dominant Spain that has seen the survival – even revival – of Catalan, Galician, and Basque (DePalma and Teasley, 2013; Wright, 1996). Studies of trilingualism in Switzerland (Chevalier, 2013) and Poland (Gabryś-Barker and Otwinowska, 2012) reveal that English is often the "third" language in the linguistic mix, and where countries are joining together in formal trade or political networks they are also choosing English as their lingua franca (e.g., The Association of Southeast Asian Nations, Kirkpatrick, 2008).

While the large number of different languages spoken in close proximity to one another in the European context would certainly seem to offer ready opportunities for multilingualism (Ortega, 2013a), the result of the European Commission survey we referenced earlier was surprising. A mere 56% of Europeans reported the ability to converse in a language other than their mother tongue. This certainly calls into question the widely held belief that most people around the world with the exception of North Americans can speak more than one language. Indeed, Erard (2012), writing in *The New York Times*, publicized this reversal of multilingualism's fortune both questioning whether the United States is really as monolingual as people believe it to be and indeed whether the rest of the world is as predominantly multilingual as commonly proclaimed.

Given the ubiquitous dominance of English in so many of these contexts, let us turn briefly to the projected fate of the English language worldwide. Although it will apparently be so for the foreseeable future, English cannot remain dominant. Its maximum spread as a first language has apparently already peaked (Ostler, 2005) and a Chinese language variant may eventually take over the hegemony that British English once held and that the American variety currently enjoys at home and abroad, or else one of the ascending varieties of the world's Englishes, such as an East Indian variant.

Undoubtedly, raising multilingual children can be difficult. Parenting children who will be (and educating children who are) multilingual is not without serious challenges. Parents face many daunting obstacles to their attempts to provide exposure to two or more languages either in the home or through enlisting the support of educators and others in their milieux. Unbeknownst to many families, one of the most potent forces to undermine their best intentions lives right in their midst. Research has found that the presence of an older sibling, the child who first goes out into the wider society, is in actual fact the proverbial Trojan horse of the multilingual aspirations of many families. Their contact with the majority or dominant societal language when they enter school brings the majority language into the home. Their preference for the majority language may overwhelm parental attempts at controlling input of the linguistic minority language – the family's heritage language, in this case the children's first language (L1) – and the majority language, in this case the children's second language (L2).

The erosion caused by older siblings on the younger siblings' L1 is quite astounding such that within one household there may be parents who are monolingual in a language that has the minority status in a community, older children who are bilingual in both the parent's L1 and the majority language, and then subsequent younger children who are almost entirely monolingual in the majority language of the wider society. Gathercole (2014) recently provided commentary on a number of factors that have been found to influence the course and attainment of bilingualism, including the quantity, quality and contexts of exposure. These factors included findings replicated in a number of studies that coming later in birth order predicts a greater degree of development of English and less utterance sophistication and lower vocabulary scores in L1. Gathercole concludes that "The majority language wins out; the minority language is threatened. Because of the dominance of the majority language in the community, children seem to achieve parity in that language regardless of the patterns of exposure, e.g., in the home. This contrasts sharply with the fate of the minority language. We have seen over and over again ... that the minority language can suffer in comparison" (p. 364).

But for all the ease by which children with a minority language background may seem to acquire the majority language as their L2, there are still many children who face a major undertaking to become proficient speakers, readers, and writers in that target language (e.g., testing as fluent English proficient [FEP] in U.S. public schools, Slama, 2012). Given that in most cases, proficiency in the majority language is a prerequisite for school achievement, educators face different but equally complex issues when teaching multilingual children. Faced with the challenge, educators must be vigilant not to view students whose L2 is still emergent as any less capable, any less smart, nor any less possessing of the potential to achieve at the very highest levels of performance in school. Moreover, educators face difficult choices about the kinds of instructional approaches to language and content teaching that will best suit their students' linguistic needs, not just in one language, but taking into account two or even more languages.

In the past five years or so, much has been made in the popular press of the potentially protective neurocognitive effects of bilingualism on aging (along with learning to play a musical instrument – another symbolic representational system like language). This positive influence is believed to be due to the buffer that bilingualism provides during the decline of executive functioning and control (e.g., selective attention, organizational skills, and problem-solving abilities). It seems that the science behind these claims is a lot more nuanced and a lot less conclusive than the simple optimistic portrayal that has made it into the public discourse thus far. Bilingualism may not have the retarding effects on the onset of diseases like dementia that it is currently touted to have. Baum and Titone (2014), in a review of bilingualism and the effects of aging, conclude that science would best be served by a notion of "neuroplasticity" that individuals may have in different degrees rather than simplistically pitting bilingual brains against monolingual brains and making claims about group differences in favor of bilinguals. In fact, Morton (2014) in his commentary on this review takes child language researchers and others to task for painting far too "sunny" a picture of the lifetime effects of bilingualism on executive functioning without properly testing meaningful hypotheses. Rather, he sees "The whole story to be an insufferable mixture of excessive claims and weak evidence" (p. 931). Moreover, claims of enhanced executive functioning amongst healthy bilinguals more generally have been viewed as a publication bias toward accepting and disseminating studies that report positive findings (de Bruin, Treccani, and Della Sala, 2015) and, as a consequence, further call into question the cognitive benefits of bilingualism.

But no matter! Parents and educators are not investing in children's multilingualism solely for the protective effects it may have on the diseases of old age. Nor do too many rationalize their support of multilingualism because of the supposed greater executive control that comes from the mental exercise of constant selection between two or more languages. Rather, parents are rationalizing their support of multilingualism because it can serve as an important conduit to participation in their families' daily lives, knowledge of their histories, extended family, and the linguistic communities they either belong to or aspire to belong to. The languages children acquire are part and parcel of their identity, their self-esteem, and their attitudes toward their own and others' ethnic and cultural ties. Educators support multilingualism in children because they see the opportunities it affords children academically and socially in an increasingly diverse society at home and a globalized world beyond. Many may even see the connections between knowing two or more languages and the metalinguistic and metacognitive abilities of their students. And, because it is the right thing to do: where is the social justice in replacing a child's language with a different one if maintaining two is well within the pedagogical capabilities of teachers, schools, and states when the will-power is there?

We conclude this section with a little levity; a joke told to us on different occasions by both a parent and an educator who took part in our research. The joke "works" because it relies on that widely held belief that the United States is a monolingual nation. We found a recount of the same joke in an essay by Mary Louise Pratt (2003) and so include it here verbatim but caution that it is our chief intent with this volume to debunk this belief as myth and replace it with arguments for the United States as a thriving multilingual nation:

> What do you call a person who knows three languages?
> Trilingual.
> What do you call a person who knows two languages?
> Bilingual.
> What do you call a person who knows only one language?
> An American. (p.111)

Overview of the Chapters

Chapter 2 reviews the research showing the importance and impact of multilingualism for children, their parents and teachers, and society at large. We attempt to establish the size of the population with the potential to develop multilingual practices in the United States, especially the elusive under-5-year-old group, whose language abilities and exposures are not accounted for in U.S. Census surveys. We also examine teacher demographics in the areas of reported language knowledge and ethnicity in an even more challenging attempt to ascertain the nation's ability to meet the diverse needs of multilingual students. We highlight findings on the linguistic, cognitive, academic, and social developments of children and then consider the impact of multilingualism from local and global perspectives.

Chapter 3 treats in some depth the wide range of beliefs and understandings of multilingualism that we encountered in the interviews with both the parents and educators. Using extensive quotes from the participants in our research, we first thematically group the different beliefs they hold about how language is acquired and sustained through various types of exposure and instruction. In the case of the parents, we also examine their perceptions of the role multilingualism plays in their families' lives. We then connect these beliefs and understandings to the extant research literature and discuss how they are frequently revealed as myths and misconceptions of the effects of speaking two or more languages.

Chapter 4 introduces the families and educators whose lives and work are the focus of the research reported in this book. The chapter provides details of the methods we used, including the descriptions of the participant families and educators, the research procedures and related analyses. The families were chosen systematically to represent a wide range of different circumstances under which multilingualism can occur, including recent and more established immigrant families, mixed race/ethnicity families, families reviving a heritage or ancestral language, and monolingual families adding a foreign language as enrichment for aesthetic, instrumental, or social justice reasons.

We deliberately included families whose members speak Spanish, numerically the most prevalent language spoken in the United States after English, as well as additional widely spoken languages in the contemporary United States, such as Farsi, Mandarin, Armenian, and Arabic. We also included families who have chosen to raise their children speaking languages that are no longer as commonly heard among minority groups in the United States but play a role in the global context (German, Russian, and French). These families provide us with a representation of children from birth to adulthood (toddlers, preschoolers, kindergarteners, elementary, middle/high school students, young adults). We also included couples who aspire to raise their future children as multilingual members of society.

The educators we studied have all encountered multilingual children in their classrooms. They were chosen to represent a wide variety of teaching settings. Dual-language settings include two-way or dual-immersion programs, one-way immersion programs, developmental (maintenance) bilingual programs, and heritage language programs. English-only settings include English-as-a-second-Language (ESL) and English language development (ELD) programs and general education English-only classrooms that are increasingly the educational environment encountered by many children with languages other than English.

Our research procedures included face-to-face and telephone semi structured interviews with one parent representing a family or, in the case of three couples, with both parents interviewed together. We also conducted semi structured interviews with educators alone, in pairs, or, on one occasion, in a group of three. These procedures are particularly effective for generating personal narrative data. Stories can provide first-hand accounts of daily family routines and activities, as well as the critical or "telling" experiences that can reveal the meaning-making processes, values, and beliefs of participants (e.g., Barth, 2003; Bruner, 1990). Verbatim transcripts of these data were then systematically coded for themes that were identified in the research literature introduced in Chapters 2 and 3, as well as closely read for new themes revealed in the interviews. These new themes were systematically noted and then the data analyzed to see if these additional themes also emerged across other families or educators. High-contrast cases and "telling" cases among the families and educators are selected to illustrate prominent themes in greater detail, and to bring the educators' personal perspectives to bear on the review of educational programs in later chapters.

Chapter 5 presents the findings from the interviews with families raising children as multilingual speakers. We meet, for example, Linda Harrison-Beltran's family who deploy their "Spanish Channel" – a fun yet effective way to encourage their children to speak Spanish in their home[1], the teenage boys of Monica Perez who are motivated to maintain Spanish through their common love of "música folklórica" with their grandfather who still resides in Mexico, and the various families who speak of "infusing" their children with their L1 by taking them on trips to visit family members who reside round the United States and in their home countries.

The findings of this chapter help to illuminate the beliefs and practices of individual families as well as explore the themes that are common across families raising children in very different contexts. We also discuss the fears of parents as their children move into puberty, start to take on the views and language of their peers, and show a waning interest in maintaining their linguistic heritage. We hear how hard it is to support more than one language and how parents have to strike a balance so that the parent-child and sibling relationships do not suffer even if parents insist on using two or more languages. Parents also talk of making investments in multilingualism, along with trade-offs and sacrifices, both financial and, surprisingly, linguistic. For example, one father consciously knew he was not going to be able to acquire English to the same degree as his children as a result of his efforts to exclusively support Spanish in the home. We conclude this chapter with a discussion of how the findings from the parents' narratives can help the education field understand first-hand their motivations, challenges, and successes.

Chapter 6 surveys the range of formal Language Instruction Educational Programs (LIEPs, Faulkner-Bond et al., 2012) and informal approaches (e.g., parochial schools and church groups, private language schools, play-dates with peers, "Mommy and Me" classes, multilingual caregiving arrangements, daily interactions with siblings) to fostering multilingualism that are available to parents. Interviews with the educators reveal their beliefs about multilingualism in the classroom, in the homes of their students, and in the wider U.S. society. These participants either have experience in teaching in multilingual classrooms or they teach multilingual students in an otherwise English-only environment. We garnered information from them about the rewards and challenges of teaching in their respective programs, and the practices they have adopted that have been successful in fostering positive linguistic, academic, and social outcomes for students. These practices include a wide array of approaches from the simple celebration of children's

cultural holiday ... c training they need t ... ing for
the recognition ... school
administrations.

In the seventh ... ... search,
specifically mal ... ... ectives
in order to info ... ... ight be
more systematic ... ... than is
currently the ca ... ... or educators and vice ... ... d practices for fosterir ... ... nentary
experiences rep ... ... ifferent
contexts or for (... ... s (e.g.,
searching for o ... ... ig) that
unwittingly may unite parents (e.g., the immigrant Spanish-speaking parent
with the English-dominant TWI program parent) can provide the impetus
toward a collectivist approach to multilingualism in the future – an approach
that is part of the systematicity we argue is needed to effectively sustain
multilingualism. Requisite further research to build this argument is also
highlighted.

A key theoretical lens we explore to make sense of the findings overall is the notion of "investment" in multilingualism (Norton Pierce, 1995;
Potowski, 2001). Attempts to maintain a first, second, or more languages
are viewed as multi-year (possibly life-long), often multi-generational commitments that include making financial, psychological, sociological, and
educational investments. Such investments it turns out can have important
implications for children's personal, familial, and public identities, their
academic standing, and most definitely for their future position in our global
society.

NOTE

[1] Pseudonyms are used throughout the book for the names of the participating parents and educators, and for the names of their children, students, friends, and family
members.

2 The Importance and Impact of Multilingualism

In this chapter we review research on the importance of multilingualism for children, their parents, educators and society at large. We begin by attempting to gauge the potential for multilingualism among children in the United States, as well as how many educators are prepared to teach them. From these basic demographics and a brief review of theoretical underpinnings, we switch to a child development perspective to highlight findings from research on the linguistic, cognitive, academic, and social developments of children reared with two or more languages. We consider the central myth of monolingualism, and conclude by considering the impact of multilingualism from local and global perspectives.

The importance of multilingualism cannot be overstated. Even leaving aside the contested cognitive outcomes, for children, the importance lies in the increasingly documented advantages that multilingualism has for their development and well-being in the areas of language development, academic achievement, employment opportunities, and socio-affective outcomes. For parents, the importance is in maintaining family ties to heritage and culture, generational connections, and seeing their children better prepared for the new demands of globalization. For educators, the importance is in having diverse and pluralistic classrooms, rich with multiple perspectives and experiences. For society, the importance is in better understanding and mutual acceptance of people from diverse backgrounds. Multilingualism allows societies to move beyond simple tolerance toward a more peaceful coexistence and mutual respect.

Multilingualism is the more inclusive term we use for ease of reference throughout the remainder of this book to characterize a variety of situations in which languages are acquired and used.[1] We use the term to include bilingualism, or the acquisition of two languages, but also to encompass complex circumstances in which multiple languages may be in contact – households in which each parent speaks a different language neither of which may be English, and households in which all members of the family may use English alongside an additional language or two or even more.

Once in school, children may be expected to set aside the language or languages they have acquired in their homes and their local communities and use only English in the classroom. Other educational settings, however, may allow them to use their existing language resources to either transition to proficiency in English or continue their acquisition of a home language alongside English. In some circumstances, children who start out as speaking only English will begin the task of acquiring an additional language once they enter formal schooling. Increasingly, classrooms may contain an array of different languages spoken by children as a first or additional language. Multilingualism, consequently, is the overarching term we utilize to signal both the variety and complexity of language learning situations that are experienced by individuals who speak two or more languages.

Our interest in studying this topic is further promoted by the vulnerability of multilingualism: the delicate balance that sustains it as children's social environments change as they grow older and transition from home to school, and then move on into the workforce or post-secondary settings. At the heart of the book lies a potent myth – a false belief that the United States is a monolingual, English-only speaking nation – a place where in the public discourse immigrants arrive and within one or two generations lose their ancestral languages in favor of English. Relatedly, and perhaps equally mythically, are the frequent claims that much of the rest of the world is multilingual.

Based on our research described in detail in later chapters, we argue, to the contrary of the myth of monolingualism, that the United States is home to an increasing number of individuals who are part of family networks that support the acquisition of two or more languages. It is this private and personalized multilingualism and how it is achieved by individual families that inspired the book – one family at a time, the United States is proving to be a multilingual nation. However, one important intention of reporting on the studies included in this book is to make the case for a necessary shift from a frequently piecemeal or fragmented approach to multilingualism to one that highlights an attempt to systematically coordinate the forms of support across the contexts in which multilingualism is being fostered, including arguing for the development of a collectivist outlook amongst families with quite different backgrounds and motivations. While we do not collect data with families and educators outside the United States, we do review the current literature on multilingualism in other countries, and report on how families fare in other parts of the world in comparable circumstances where appropriate throughout the book. Moreover, we examine the parent and educator participants' perspectives on multilingualism more globally through the comparisons they frequently made to the language-learning contexts in their countries of origin, to the countries of their ancestors, or to the countries in which they once temporarily lived. Indeed, about a third of our participants had acquired their additional languages globally, as they worked, traveled, or studied abroad. The participants fostered new or continued existing global connections through their travels, by their prolonged stays abroad, and by hosting family members and friends from other countries.

Demographic trends in the United States reveal a dramatic increase in the numbers of children who come from families that speak more than one language. The findings of the National Center for Education Statistics (NCES, 2012) indicate that between the years of 1980 and 2009, the percentage of U.S. school-age children (officially children aged 5–17) who spoke a language other than English at home increased from 4.7 to 11.2 million, or from 10% to 21% of children. This trend of growing numbers of children who will learn English as their second or third or more language, has grown exponentially over the past decades. According to Crawford (2002), the population that speaks languages other than English increases by roughly 40% every ten years in the United States. Additionally, the profile of languages spoken by these children is extremely diverse. Goldenberg (2008) reported that 400 various languages make up these children's linguistic backgrounds.

The U.S. Census Bureau (2011) reports that more than 60.5 million U.S. residents over 5 years of age speak a language other than English at home. In fact 17.9 million, or a quarter of all millennials (young adults aged 18–34), speak a language other than English at home. In California that proportion reaches one in two (U.S. Census Bureau, 2014). In the 2011–2012 school year, the most recent year available, 4.4 million kindergarten (K)-grade 12 U.S. students were identified as English language learners (ELL students) receiving English language support services in public schools (9.1% of the U.S. school-age population) (NCES, 2014). (See also Pandya, McHugh, and Batalova, 2011, for additional demographic trends for ELL students in the United States).

These numbers do not take into consideration the nearly 30 million children under 5 years of age who may be candidates for multilingual education. Current estimates suggest more than 50% of preschool children (i.e., 4-year-olds) come from families who do not speak English at home (Espinosa, 2008). Nor do these numbers include the children whose parents foster multilingualism without being foreign born or without any foreign language skills/background of their own. Indeed, CAL (2011) reports that the fastest growing form of bilingual programming has adopted the TWI model in which English and a partner language are both fostered. This may be capturing an increasing interest among parents of English-dominant backgrounds in the additive aspects of multilingualism. Enrollment may be for reasons related to an instrumental motivation, such as broadening the future career opportunities of their children, or to developing a global orientation, or to instilling a social justice commitment in the education of their children.

These statistics translate into millions of children who enter the U.S. school system with the potential to become bilingual or multilingual participants of the educational process. U.S. schools are already teaching steadily increasing numbers of students, many of whom already speak more than one language. Researchers, the faculty of teacher preparation programs, educators, and our society as a whole must also be ready to greet this new multilingual student population.

The importance and timeliness of turning society's attention to the topic of multilingualism cannot be underestimated. Despite the rapidly growing numbers of children who speak two or more languages, educational approaches maximizing the positive impact of multilingualism on children's cognitive and social development are understudied (Bjork-Willen, 2008). On a societal level, multilingual competence can engender more positive attitudes toward other cultures and languages (e.g., Genesee, 2008), and on a personal level, it may hone metalinguistic and executive functioning abilities linked to academic success (e.g., Adesope, Lavin, Thompson, and Ungerleider, 2010; Luk and Bialystok, 2008) and stave off dementia in old age (Baum and Titone, 2014), although there are challenges to the claimed cognitive benefits to which we will return (e.g., de Bruin et al., 2015). It is ironic that while multilingual speakers possibly outnumber English-only speakers (Grosjean, 1982, as cited in Hoff, 2009, although note the number of multilingual individuals is difficult to verify), at many levels of the U.S. educational infrastructure (within preschool, elementary, and secondary school settings) multilingual children are taught in the classrooms of monolingual, English-speaking teachers.

Educating Multilingual Children

While race and ethnicity are not determinants of linguistic background, they have been used as likely proxies of teacher language knowledge. During the 2011–2012 school year, 82% of public school teachers across the nation were non-Hispanic White, 7% were non-Hispanic Black, and 8% were Hispanic (Goldring, Gray, and Bitterman, 2013). Bunch also points out that "Even in states that have more diverse overall populations and with large numbers of ELs [English learners] and other linguistic minority students, the teaching force is predominantly White. In California, for example, 72% of teachers are identified as White, 16% Hispanic, 7% Asian American, 5% African American, 1% American Indian/Alaska Native, and 1% "multiple races" (Commission on Teacher Credentialing, 2008)" (p. 331, 2013).

While the match between student ethnicity and that of their teachers is important in its own right as a predictor of linguistic minority students' college enrollment (e.g., Gándara et al., 2013), we, nevertheless, feel it is unsatisfactory to rely on teacher ethnicity alone as an indication of their language backgrounds. This cannot reveal much about their potential to meet and effectively support the language needs of multilingual students, especially those students still in the process of acquiring English in order to access the academic content areas taught in English. Absent national surveys of the language backgrounds of teachers, we offer the following demographics from two small-scale surveys of teachers. The teachers were asked to report their knowledge of languages other than English along with responses to questions about their science instruction with English language learners (unpublished data, *Evaluating the Validity of English Language Proficiency Assessments* project, Bailey, 2011). In one state, the survey was administered to 236 teachers and revealed that 79% did not speak a language in addition to English. Of those who did, most (16%) spoke Spanish in addition to English. One percent of all teachers in the survey spoke Russian and 8% reported speaking different additional languages (most reported that the additional language was German, with at least one respondent each for Italian, French, Korean, Filipino, and Hebrew).

The survey was administered to 153 teachers in a second state with quite different results. Twenty-five percent reported not speaking a language in addition to than English, whereas 65% reported speaking Spanish as well as English. Cantonese and Russian were each spoken by 1% of the teachers and 15% reported speaking different additional languages (most reported French as an additional language, followed by a smattering of Arabic and Polish). The differences between the linguistic acumen of the teachers surveyed in the two states may have its roots in the fact that the second state has historically serviced far greater numbers of ELL students and moreover has a demonstrated commitment to bilingual education by financially supporting it when several states were attempting to reduce the amount of dual-language programming through their various ballot initiatives. These factors have two key repercussions: teachers are given greater preparation in order to teach using at least Spanish and English, and teachers may themselves be the former graduates of the bilingual programs being offered to families in this state. However, even in this scenario, a full quarter of teachers who were charged with teaching science with ELL students in their classrooms reported not speaking their students' first language.

The discrepancies between both the ethnic and potential linguistic profiles of educators and the students they teach make the endeavor of supporting multilingual development appear almost insurmountable. Much as parents encounter myths about the positive and negative aspects of multilingualism (e.g., multilingualism makes children smarter; learning more than one language confuses children) so too do educators encounter myths about the right l wrong pedagogical approaches to use with multilingual students. They combating ideas that would suggest teaching two languages will cause confusion and delay in one of the student's languages, or, for example, that full language immersion is the best way students can successfully acquire an L2 (Espinosa, 2013). At the same time, a number of studies and research syntheses suggest that the task of educating children from diverse ethnic backgrounds with different kinds of linguistic resources is quite possible and manageable (Schwarzer, Haywood, and Lorenzen, 2003; Dixon et al., 2012). In this volume, we present and critique the programs that either explicitly or implicitly foster multilingualism and the accompanying strategies that the educators implement to support the academic and social successes of multilingual children.

The Loss of Linguistic Resources

Instructors' lack of familiarity with effective ways to support multilingual children and parental concerns that children must master the majority language of their society often have detrimental consequences for children's multilingual development. Research shows the extreme vulnerability of children's home languages. Worthy and Rodríguez-Galindo (2006) report that by the time children enter elementary school, their L1 already shows signs of decay. This phenomenon of L1 loss before L2 is developed, known as subtractive bilingualism (Lambert, 1975), can result in a diminished sense of connectedness to one's roots, including disrupted communication within the family and wider language-minority community. These detrimental effects can then impede the formation of self-concept and self-esteem (Lambert, 1987; Puig, 2010; Wong Fillmore, 2000).

The moment for turning attention to the narratives of families who speak more than one language is ripe: academic, political, and public discourse around multilingualism is changing. As an example of this zeitgeist, a recent policy statement of Head Start, a federally supported preschool program for low-income families, endorsed the creation of effective programs that would promote "continued development of the first language while the acquisition of English is facilitated" (Head Start, 2010). After decades of viewing children's first languages that differed from English as challenges that needed to be overcome, society is showing signs of now beginning to view these languages as resources to be valued and nurtured. *However, how can multilingualism be sustained most effectively?* The studies described in this book turn to families and educators to document and better understand potential solutions.

Theoretical Perspectives on Language Development and Teaching

There are a number of different accounts of the manner in which languages are developed and/or learned by children. They range from nativist arguments at one end of the spectrum (i.e., the rules that govern language are largely innate, highly specialized to the language learning task and require minimal amounts of exposure to trigger acquisition) to general learning principles at the other end (e.g., memory, pattern analysis, analogy) that can apply to a variety of different learning situations, not only language learning (see also Dixon et al., 2012, for a review of contrasting perspectives on L2 acquisition more specifically). We adopt a social interactionist account of language learning, one that is grounded in the support children receive from others they converse with and the predictability of the routines they regularly participate in (i.e., the language structures and vocabulary they will hear and will need to produce). This description of the mechanisms by which we assume language development and learning take place is important for motivating the interview questions we devised for the parents and teachers (see Chapter 4).

The social interactionist account of language development has its roots in Vygotsky's (1978) view of learning as inherently social. A key concept in Vygotsky's theory is the *Zone of Proximal Development* (ZPD) – the distance between independent achievements and what can be achieved with assistance from more expert interactants. Language experiences that take place within the ZPD are thought to be most effective for moving children's development forward. The social interactionist account can explain how the general learning mechanisms mentioned above are tailored to the child's task of language learning by the modeling, scaffolding (i.e., graduated assistance), and routinized exchanges with expert others (Bruner, 1985). Parents, caregivers, siblings, educators, and more knowledgeable peers typically engage in these behaviors when they are conversing with a more novice language learner (Bailey, Osipova, and Kelly, 2015).

Within theories of L2 acquisition specifically, a *common underlying language proficiency* has been posited to account for the interdependence between languages and the transfer of knowledge from L1 to L2 and vice versa (Cummins, 2000; Genesee, Lindholm-Leary, Saunders, and Christian, 2006). Most recently, a view of language learning as a *complex adaptive system* has gained traction in the field of L2 acquisition (Larsen-Freeman, 2011; Churchill, 2008). Language structures are argued to emerge from experience, social interaction, and cognitive mechanisms to explain both L1 and L2 acquisition (e.g., Ellis and Larsen-Freeman, 2009). Children are seen as learning language by responding to "affordances" (i.e., verbal supports; tailored tasks and activities) emerging from dynamic communicative situations (e.g., van Lier and Walqui, 2012).

The Benefits of Multilingualism to Children

Linguistic and Metalinguistic Competence

Research over the last two decades provides plentiful evidence of the benefits of multilingualism to the individual. Children who speak more than one language demonstrate greater linguistic competence than their monolingual counterparts. This becomes apparent at early stages of language development. Multilingual children exposed to several languages have shown a heightened sensitivity to phonemes in both L1 and L2 (Puig, 2010), which contributes to their ease of acquisition of L2 phonology and native-like pronunciation. Successful and highly flexible word learning abilities are another strength exhibited by multilingual children in the early stages of language development (Yoshida, 2008). Unlike monolingual young children, who often demonstrate difficulty learning adjectives and words with similar meanings, children who are learning more than one language acquire words with overlapping meanings with greater ease. Additionally, young children learning to speak more than one language often demonstrate a rapid mastery of communicative structures (Puig, 2010). These children are capable of carrying on basic minimal conversational exchanges (such as greetings, expression of gratitude, etc.) in more than one language, at the same time as their monolingual peers do so in just one language.

Similarly to the heightened linguistic competence outlined above, multilingual children demonstrate greater metalinguistic awareness, an understanding of how languages are used systematically to convey meaning (Adesope et al., 2010). Mora (2008) suggests that multilingual children's metalinguistic awareness features a unique ability to compare and contrast the different languages and their subsystems, as well as recognize commonalities and differences between the languages that they speak.

Metalinguistic awareness in multilingual children includes a wide array of skills, including the recognition of sound/letter similarities and differences across their languages, awareness of the differences in sentence structures, and accurate adherence to cultural and linguistic norms which require switching between their languages, if needed. These unique multilingual capabilities fit well within the framework of the *interdependence model* that suggests the two-way transfer of linguistic/literacy knowledge and skills (Cummins, 1979; 2000).

Superior metalinguistic awareness and its gradual emergence over time in bilingual children were explored by Bialystok, Peets, and Moreno (2014). Their study examined metalinguistic skills of second- and fifth-grade Canadian students who spoke English at home and attended French immersion programs. The results of the study extend the findings about excellent metalinguistic abilities demonstrated by simultaneous bilinguals and indicate that even a relatively brief period of immersion leads to metalinguistic advantages (i.e., ease of manipulation of linguistic rules). Second graders in the immersion program surpassed their monolingual peers and demonstrated metalinguistic gains comparable to those shown by fully bilingual children. After five years in the immersion program, bilingual children continued to outperform their monolingual counterparts in the domain of metalinguistic awareness and completely caught up with them on verbal fluency tasks. Their performance on English proficiency tasks was sustained despite the fact that French was the language of instruction. Within this context, it is not surprising that several studies have linked keen metalinguistic awareness in bilinguals with greater academic success and literacy acquisition (Bialystok, 2001; Bialystok, Luk, and Kwan, 2005; Luk and Bialystok, 2008; Malakoff and Hakuta, 1991).

Children who speak more than one language frequently tap into their knowledge of L1 for tasks in L2. For example, children who have developed literacy in their home language transfer their literacy awareness skills into new languages. Additionally, in the cases of languages with shared origins children can often rely on cognates (e.g., words with common roots) when speaking L1 and L2. Finally, tapping into the home language can be clearly evidenced by children's codeswitching between their L1 and L2 in diglossic situations (Vu, Bailey, and Howes, 2010). Diglossia can occur situationally when some activities and events routinely take place in one language (e.g., home life) and other activities and events take place in a different language (e.g., schooling). Another form of diglossia is the parallel use of two languages within one dyad, when a parent may only use Korean, for example, and the child always responds in English, showing at least receptive understanding of Korean. A final behavior connected to metalinguistic awareness is the documented tendency of multilingual children toward linguistic risk taking (Puig, 2010), which includes frequent trial and error application of the rules and the structures of L1 to the child's L2.

The Contested Impact of Bilingualism on Cognition

Multilingual children have demonstrated overall greater mental flexibility that goes beyond the linguistic and literacy domains to include cognitive functioning as well (Bialystok, Craik, Green, and Gollan, 2009). Mental flexibility developed due to bilingualism is manifested in better problem solving skills, better concept formation, acute pattern recognition, and creativity frequently demonstrated by children who speak more than one language (Bialystok, 1991; Hoff, 2014; Martin-Rhee and Bialystok, 2008; Rodríguez, 2010). A variable that has received a lot of attention recently and is related to academic success is heightened executive functioning (Barkley, 1997; Friedman et al., 2007). Studies have noted that multilingualism positively affects children's attention, organizational skills, and problem-solving abilities, commonly united under the umbrella of executive functioning (e.g., Bialystok and Peets, 2010; Hoff, 2014; Yoshida, 2008). Children who speak more than one language have demonstrated better ability to inhibit preferred response patterns and show "developmentally advanced executive control" (Yoshida, 2008, p. 27). Despite the large number and seemingly robust studies of cognitive advantages to bilingualism (Kroll, 2009), studies have surfaced that show no bilingual advantage over monolingual speakers on some measures of executive functioning for instance (e.g., Esposito, Baker-Ward, and Mueller, 2013). Moreover, recent criticisms have been leveled at the body of work claiming a bilingual cognitive advantage, including research showing that fewer studies reporting no effects or negative effects of bilingualism are published despite their strong representation amongst conference abstracts (de Bruin et al., 2015). Also, as mentioned, studies that have favorably compared bilingual speakers to monolingual speakers on cognitive functioning have also come under attack for the rigor of the research (Morton, 2014; cf. Kroll, 2009). The controversy over the robustness of study designs and publication biases paints a complex and far from conclusive picture of the impacts of multilingualism on cognition. However, the positive findings from studies of the linguistic and metalinguistic development of multilingual children at least suggest that children's abilities to speak more than one language can still be a viable resource – a resource that may help enhance their interactions with others and ultimately their academic successes.

Enhanced Socio-affective Development

If the quality of cognitive research with multilingual children is being questioned, there are additional domains of child development that are still thought to benefit from a multilingual start in life. Research that focuses on the social and emotional development of multilingual children has shown promising positive effects of multilingualism on this population. In fact, some studies reveal an interesting link between the socio-affective development of multilingual children and their linguistic abilities. For instance, Puig's study (2010) indicates that unlike their monolingual peers, children and adolescents who speak more than one language often demonstrate low affective filters, which are characterized by lower anxiety and greater self-confidence when speaking their L2. These low affective filters allow multilingual speakers to engage in more conversational exchanges in L1 and L2, as such speakers tend to be less inhibited by shyness and self-consciousness (Krashen, 1981). Studies of young children's socio-affective development indicate that children exposed to and learning several languages develop diverse communication styles, form secure attachments with family members and caregivers across languages and cultures, and demonstrate greater positive attitudes and tolerance toward other culture, languages, and/or peers (Dubiner, 2010; Genesee, 2008; Puig, 2010; Bailey, Zwass, and Mistry, 2013). Oh and Fuligni (2010) found that proficiency in L1 may even help immigrant-background Latino and Asian American students better cope with the stresses of adolescence.

Studies of switching back and forth between the languages they speak when they serve as interpreter for family (e.g., being a language broker), or when they codeswitch as part of their discourse repertoire (e.g., to signal affiliation with the listener), show that even very young children can have sophisticated bilinguality (e.g., Martínez, 2010). Moreover, bilinguals must have socio-pragmatic sensibilities to successfully participate in these highly interactive social practices (e.g., Orellana, Reynolds, Dorner, and Meza, 2003; Reyes, 2004; Vu et al., 2010). Bailey and Orellana (2015) review this literature and speculate that codeswitching and serving as language brokers for their families may positively affect children's metacognitive and metalinguistic skill sets. These aspects of multilingualism can be viewed as assets that educators may leverage for language and other types of learning in their classrooms. These practices allow children to hone their pragmatic skills in two languages which can be used in academic tasks, especially those linked to the increased communicative and collaborative demands of the new U.S. college and career ready standards such as the Common Core State Standards (CCSS) (Council of Chief State School Officers [CCSSO], 2010a; 2010b) and the Next Generation Science Standards (NGSS Lead States, 2013; see Bailey and Orellana, 2015, for review).

Effects on Multicultural Awareness

In addition to the enhanced socio-affective development, multilingual children have been shown to demonstrate a finely tuned multicultural awareness. Multilingual and minority language families feature unique cultural characteristics that are often very different from the mainstream family structure of the dominant culture within society. These families have their own idiosyncratic rules and traditions. Many multilingual families greatly value the preservation of family culture, and nurture the sense of belonging to the unique microcosm of one's family. Language is often seen as the critical medium for participation in the activities, values, beliefs, and dispositions of the cultural group and parents have shown strenuous efforts to maintain the language of the cultural group, for example, by funding heritage-language schools, promoting peer and other social groupings, preserving the language through and for religious practices, and maintaining connections to the parents' country of origin (Imbens-Bailey, 2000).

Efforts to preserve a minority culture within the macrocosm of the dominant culture can foster a sense of ethnic pride (Worthy and Rodríguez-Galindo, 2006). Moreover, speaking more than one language and frequently serving as interpreters for their families, multilingual children demonstrate an ability to adopt differing cultural norms and communicate within and across the home/dominant cultures (Mushi, 2002; Rodríguez, 2010). Growing up acutely conscious of the differences and similarities between the home culture and wider societal cultures contributes to multilingual children's heightened awareness of pragmatic nuances and allows them to successfully navigate a host of cultural contexts.

Multilingualism: Global and Local Perspectives

Having discussed the effects of multilingualism on children's linguistic, cognitive, academic, and socio-affective development, we come to a discussion of the benefits to raising multilingual children within the context of modern society. Multilingualism has never been more crucial a skill, given educational, economic, and cultural globalization. Linguistic competence in more than one language allows for multicultural and global awareness while at the same time promoting academic success and broadening career perspectives. Multilingualism promotes the blurring or softening of barriers between the members of different linguistic groups which, one may hope, can help lead to a more peaceful global coexistence (Wan and Ramsey, 2014). From a more local perspective, multilingualism allows for the preservation of unique cultures and traditions within a multicultural society. It strengthens the bonds within families and can help unite minority communities across generations (Imbens-Bailey, 1996; 2000). For individuals, multilingualism can boost personal earning power in a labor market that serves an increasingly multilingual society, as Rumbaut (2014) recently found for fluent bilinguals living in Southern California.

However, despite its obvious benefits, multilingualism remains a pedagogical puzzle for many researchers, as well as for the parents and educators of multilingual children. This mystery is both profound and ironic because the United States is a multilingual nation even if it is rarely perceived that way domestically or internationally. Multilingualism is achieved at the intensely personal or local level by American families, one family at a time, going about their busy daily lives, and by educators who recognize the potential and encourage multilingualism in their students. The successes, as well as the dilemmas connected to raising and teaching children who speak multiple languages are at the core of this volume which aims to unveil the environments and practices that allow multilingualism to flourish in the United States despite the myth of monolingualism in public discourse.

We see studies of multilingualism that examine it at its roots – within home and school environments – as critical and timely contributions to the education and social science literatures. This research will allow for a closer examination of multilingual contexts of development from early childhood into adulthood. Such examination raises researchers' and others' awareness of this group of individuals with distinctive linguistic, academic, cognitive, and social profiles, who make up the majority of the next generation of students. This awareness should serve to promote future research on the ways in which multilingual children develop and preserve their unique skills. Research of the kind presented here has helped to reveal commonalities across different contexts of multilingualism that may prove useful in fostering a systematic approach to sustaining multilingualism (e.g., promoting closer home-school connections; promoting a collectivist approach amongst families with disparate backgrounds and reasons for sustaining multilingualism; identifying effective language instruction methods; encouraging second/foreign language programming from the start of elementary schools). Such a coordinated approach to sustaining multilingualism also has the potential to change the image of the United States as a monolingual country.

The following chapter examines parent and educator beliefs and understandings of multilingualism. It is important to give these beliefs and understandings an extensive treatment because the research base frequently reveals them as myths and misconceptions that can stymy the efforts of families and educators in their support of children's multilingualism.

NOTE

[1] We retain use of the terms "bilingualism" and "trilingualism" where a contrast in the number of languages spoken is deliberately being drawn by our study participants or by researchers of other studies.

3   Debunking Myths about Multilingualism

In this chapter we turn to the common misconceptions of raising and teaching children as multilingual speakers. We discuss beliefs about multilingualism that persist among parents and educators but that are frequently revealed as myths in the empirical research. The discussion is informed by the interviews with the parents and educators of multilingual children who participated in our study. While their experiences are shared in detail in the later chapters on the findings of the study, we include here examples of the parents' and educators' commonly held beliefs of the potential ills and positive outcomes associated with multilingualism and compare and contrast these beliefs with the current research literature on the benefits and challenges of acquiring two or more languages.

Searching for the Causes of Myths about Multilingualism

While reading through the parent and educator interviews we first attempted to understand the causes of the many myths surrounding multilingualism: myths about language learning and the multilingual upbringing of children. One of the persistent themes in the parent participants' interviews was the theme of needing to constantly "nurture" children's languages. This was done for fear that their children's language would "wilt," "get worse," "die," and/or "deteriorate" if not actively used or nourished. This theme arose out of the advice that the parents of multilingual children in our study offered to other potential parents trying to raise children speaking multiple languages. It can be illustrated by a recommendation made by Miko, a prospective father, one of many parents concerned with preservation of Spanish within the family: "Nurture that language so that they can continue speaking it when they come out of the school and pass it on to their children."

Several educators in multilingual settings also spoke of the vulnerability of language due to lack of use, fearing that languages will be "lost," "eventually die" without "dedication and an effort." As Alejandro, an elementary school teacher in a Spanish-English TWI program explains, "It's kind of sad to me. I mean I don't know about multilinguals per se. I can only speak to children who did learn Spanish at one point in their lives.... students who come through here that always say, 'I remember learning Spanish three, four, five, six years and I don't remember and I don't speak it.'"

We also found that the concepts of bilingualism and multilingualism appear to be vaguely defined in the public discourse, and that there is a wide and paradoxical range of speakers of more than one language. The participants of our study had self-reported linguistic abilities that fell along a continuum, the extreme ends of which could include speakers who readily defined themselves as multilingual when they merely knew "menu Spanish" and those who used a language other than English daily in their homes and at their jobs, but were still not sure whether or not they could describe themselves as "truly bilingual."

Similarly, the developmental stages of multilingualism appear to be perplexing in popular discourse. For instance, our participants wondered about the multilingual abilities of very young children. Take, for example, a 28-month old child who clearly understands two languages but speaks only one. Can he be described as being a bilingual? What if he also speaks some words in a third language? Would that warrant him a trilingual status? The further linguistic development of multilingual children was also puzzling for many parents and educators. Many of them noted the developmental periods when their children stopped using two or more languages and overtly preferred communicating in one language only. Danielle and Ultan, who speak French and English to their children, experienced this rejection in both languages, as they changed their country of residence when their children were nearing adolescence. Danielle recalls, "There is a passage which is difficult ... when they didn't want Ultan to come and talk to them in English at the end of school [day]. They would want just to speak French coming out ... And there was one moment when we moved here [to the United States] that Sylvie [their daughter] told me that I should speak English too, like everybody else."

The trend of choosing one language over another appeared to be the prerogative of most of the participants' children. Meanwhile, parents and educators wondered what the outcome would be for these youngsters' multilingual abilities and whether they could still be considered bilingual or multilingual. Finally, many participants provided chronological accounts of their own multilingual abilities that developed, peaked and deteriorated due to the lack of consistent use. One of the participants, Lilian, a prospective mother of multilingual children who grew up bilingual, confessed: "If I am not speaking it, I am losing it. I feel like I lost a lot of vocabulary that I used to have. And I am thinking, I learned Spanish while I was at home growing up. When I was 18, I wasn't home anymore, I went off to college, and from that age on I feel like it's gotten worse. I have a loss of language, a loss of learned Spanish."

The motto "use it or lose it" was prevalent in parents' accounts. These personal reports as well as the questions and doubts raised by the participants led us to hypothesize that the plethora of myths surrounding multilingualism may stem from the multifaceted nature of these two phenomena and the fleeting, hard-to-pinpoint set of characteristics that make one truly bi- or multilingual. We feel that examining these myths and putting them to the test by providing current research on the issues and illustrating them with stories of our participants will allow us to further uncover and clarify the rich yet vulnerable nature of multilingualism.

America as a Monolingual Nation

It is not that I don't think Spanish is a good language, it is not that. My thing is that we are in a country that primarily speaks English. (Nora, a Salvadorian-American mother of three bilingual daughters, ages 7–25)

... you know languages are great, but in this country they are not as essential. You know you don't almost need any other language ... It doesn't actually have as much of a merit ... for everyday life, for I mean you almost don't come across people who don't speak English. (Hediyeh, an Iranian-American mother of a bilingual daughter and son, ages 30 and 33)

The theme "America is a monolingual nation" surfaced in over 30% of participating parent interviews. While not all of them firmly believed in this notion, participants spoke about their perceptions, the attitudes of others, and the sociopolitical discourse within the country. The speakers were mothers and fathers of bi- and multilingual children from different home language backgrounds (Spanish, French, Russian, Farsi, Portuguese, and English). They had varying professional occupations and diverse SES. Among them were Nora, an office assistant, and Dulce, a preschool teacher, both from El Salvador and both currently working as house cleaners in the United States; Danielle, a foreign language teacher of French-Russian origin, and her husband, Ultan, a retired film critic whose family came from Ireland; Hediyeh and Ghodrat, a home designer and a professor of engineering from Iran; and Kevin, a Euro-American medical professional, born and raised in Los Angeles. The parent participants represented and reported their impressions of living in several American states that range from highly to moderately culturally and linguistically diverse: California, Florida, Maryland, and Wisconsin. Some of them recently came to the United States, while others have lived there for over 30 years, and some were born in the United States. But all of them spoke of their perception of the United States as a country where communication in English is predominant, and where the value of other languages is primarily recognized within the family only, as Dulce, the Salvadorian-American mother of 5-year-old José, explains:

Porque aquí el idioma que se habla más es el inglés. Prácticamente es la familia la que habla Español, pero fuera de esto solamente el inglés. Entonces es necesario para el que tenía que aprender los dos idiomas, el Español para mí y el inglés para el afuera.

[Translation: The language that is most spoken here is English. Practically, it is the family that speaks Spanish, but outside of that there is only English. Therefore, it is necessary for him [son] to learn both languages; Spanish for me and English for the outside world].[1]

Interestingly, none of the participating educators touched upon the theme of America as a monolingual nation. While this may be understandable with the educators who worked in the different forms of dual-language programming we included, it is surprising of the educators who are themselves monolingual English speakers and who worked in predominantly English-only school contexts. However, on closer reflection, it makes sense that they would not necessarily adopt a mythical view of America as monolingual when they are working daily to address the very real linguistic needs of the growing population of students who come from families speaking a variety of different languages.

Three educators did however convey a belief that other parts of the world enjoy multilingual utopian societies which by contrast implies a less than optimal monolingual situation in American society. Elena, a middle-school ESL specialist and a Spanish-English bilingual, for example, saw students from European and Asian countries as having a "broader perspective of the world and the issues and people and culture." In addition to mentioning Europe and Asia, Alejandro adds, "even Latin America these days, there's more of this global view that is instilled early on."

The parent participants saw the United States as a nation where knowledge of another language is stereotypically expected from a recent immigrant, but not from a person born and raised in the United States. The experiences of Nora and Kevin, two Spanish-English bilinguals who are very different from each other in every respect – a middle-aged Latina woman and a Euro-American man in his twenties – complement each other's narratives in confirming these stereotypes. Nora, currently a graduate student in a master's program, tells how the people that she encounters decide for her what her primary language is: "A lot of the times people tend to say, 'No, you are not English, you are Spanish.' And I say, 'No, no,' I say, 'My primary language is English.'" On the other hand, Kevin shared that throughout his life people were surprised to learn that he is fluent in Spanish: "Then they wanted to learn why [I could speak Spanish so well]. Like I said, I was a white boy from the suburbs. There was never a reason I should speak any Spanish at all, let alone any good Spanish."

America then is viewed as the proverbial "melting pot" where English is the language of the nation, and where the heritage languages spoken within the families are akin to family traditions: important to keep within the family, but rather useless, "not essential," using Hediyeh's determinant, for the rest of its citizens. The languages spoken within the families are something that makes us diverse and different from each other, and not something that brings us together. In the eyes of several participants, the monolingual America myth presents the United States as a country which finds "no merit" in knowing languages other than English, and where the political discourse, bitterly identified by Ultan, states that "America is wonderful and the language here is English, and we expect the [immigrants] to only speak [English] – why don't you learn English for crying out loud?"

Sociopolitical Discourse and the Myth of Monolingual America

Research on historical events in U.S. politics and legislation points to the possible roots of the "monolingual nation" myth. Despite the fact that America is a country where over fifty million immigrants speak numerous languages (Camarota, 2012), it is also a country where, according to the popular discourse, these languages get quickly forgotten and thrown away, thus giving the United States a reputation of being a *Cementerio de Lenguas* (language graveyard) (Pratt, 2003). Pratt (2003) and Trimbur (2006) examined the unique linguistic culture of the United States with the goal of understanding the paradoxical nature of this phenomenon: a country rich in languages where public discourse emphasizes monolingualism. Linguistic culture as defined by Schiffman (1996) is "a set of behaviors, assumptions, prejudices, folk belief systems, attitudes, stereotypes, ways of thinking about language, and religio-historical circumstances associated with a particular language" (p. 5). This set of behaviors and beliefs, throughout the centuries, has shaped the U.S. sociopolitical discourse which reveals an ongoing dichotomy between America's monolingual self-identity and the multilingual reality of the nation.

Some of the scholars who are in search of the origins behind the feeble preservation and apparent demise of native and immigrant languages engage in historical analysis of U.S. language policies (Crawford, 2003; Ovando, 2003; Pratt, 2003; Skutnabb-Kangas, `Phillipson, and Rannut, 1994; Trimbur, 2006). In their work, Pratt (2003) and Trimbur (2006) dismiss the view that monolingual policies are a sign (or a result) of general hostility toward other languages. As a country of immigrants, America is not specifically hostile to its inhabitants and their tongues. Instead of hostility, these authors identify centuries-old national ambivalence toward other-than-English language mastery and preservation, the longstanding fear and mistrust of those who speak languages other than English, as well as the fears of learning another language as potential causes of largely monolingual policies in the United States (Pratt, 2003; Trimbur, 2006).

The Roots of Ambivalence toward Languages Other Than English

America's persistent self-perception as a monolingual society, as well as its ambivalence toward the learning of other languages, has a long history. In his article "Linguistic Memory and the Politics of U.S. English" John Trimbur (2006) traces the roots of this ambivalence to the times of the Founding Fathers, who, following the laissez-faire political philosophy of the time, chose not to select a national language for the United States, leaving matters of language learning to the "private domain" (p. 576). This laissez-faire approach to the national language agenda, Trimbur believes, inaugurated the lag in recognition and respect of linguistic rights of America's diverse population groups that has continued up to this day. In order for languages other than English to survive and be not only respected but also nourished in a multilingual society, there needed to be a clear language policy that would have protected and promoted multilingualism. In the absence of such policy, English received its de facto status of the language of the dominant group that exercised power within the colonies. Due to this status, English not only survived but was also recognized as the language of the privileged class, which used it "for government, work, education, religion and commerce" (Trimbur, 2006, p. 577). It was seen as the language of the newly independent nation, the language that needed to be prioritized over any other language that could create a potential threat to America's identity, and, particularly, its linguistic identity. In Franklin's words, "Why should Pennsylvania, founded by the English, become a colony of Aliens?" (Franklin, 1959, as cited in Trimbur, 2006). This agenda became further entrenched as the linguistic diversity of colonists from non-English speaking countries, Native Americans, and people brought into the country as slaves went unrecognized or purposefully ignored in the public discourse.

Early Notions of Bilingualism in the United States

Curiously, during the Colonial Period and Revolutionary Era and the time of the Early Republic (1640s through early 1800s) the notion of bilingualism developed in the context of the juxtaposition of British English and American English. However, this further contributed to the image of English as the central language within the country, with superiority assigned to the American English dialect. No other prominent language in America at that time, whether German, Dutch, or Spanish, was considered important enough to breach the binary opposition of the two English variants. While many other languages that were present in the private domain continued to be spoken, it is American

English that enjoyed public attention and the exceptional status. Trimbur (2006) cites Webster, who pointed out that while in Great Britain, residents of distant counties may have had difficulty understanding each other due to the regional variance of dialects, the citizens of the United States did not face such a challenge when speaking the American English that united its speakers and that was thought to be free of local dialects (Trimbur, 2006). Webster's words, in which the multitude of languages present within the country during his time is simply ignored, serve as a good illustration of the long-term ambivalence toward languages other than English that has dominated the American linguistic culture since the 1700s. This special "chosen" status of American English and the absence of political recognition and regulation of the United States' numerous languages from the nation's inception are the backdrop to a severe neglect of non-English languages in U.S. linguistic culture and contributed to a continued disregard and ambivalence for the multilingual richness of the nation.

Fear and Mistrust at the Root of Monolingual Policies

The roots of fear and mistrust toward those who speak languages other than English can similarly be traced back to the earliest period of U.S. history. During that time the newly established and rapidly expanding nation faced the threat of rebellions coming from slaves, Native Americans, whose territories were being taken away, and other European immigrants arriving to establish new communities within the United States. The private domain and state policies established at the time targeted the languages other than English as the source of potential coalition building and emergence of a diverse national identity other than the monolithic one based on American English. To avoid the threats of defiance and noncompliance, slave traders strategically separated the speakers of the same African languages as a means of control and suppression of rebellious tendencies. Brutal penalties, such as the cutting out of slaves' tongues for speaking their mother tongues and teaching their children to speak ancestral languages, are also at the root of the U.S. English-only linguistic tradition (Trimbur, 2006).

The harsh history of Native American language eradication is also linked to fear and mistrust of the use of languages other than English within the United States. In the State of California alone, only half of nearly 100 indigenous languages that were spoken by Native Americans survive, and virtually none of them are being learned by children today (Hornberger, 1998). An additional blow to the preservation of Native American languages was the establishment in 1879 of a system of boarding schools for Native American children that were located far from the reservations. This policy cut children off from exposure to their heritage language and contributed to the extinction of a multitude of unique indigenous languages. While many tribes and their languages were completely eradicated during the western expansion of the United States, some tribes, including the Cherokee, Choctaw, and Seneca, were able to open schools where the indigenous languages were taught alongside English (Skutnabb-Kangas et al., 1994). The Curtis Act of 1898 eliminated these practices, pushing the Native American languages further into the private and hidden domain, contributing to the monolingual myth of America. These policies of social and political pressure led to rapid and sustained eradication of languages other than English.

Speakers of African and Native American languages were not the only linguistically diverse groups that experienced political and cultural pressure to give up their mother tongues. The events of the 19th–mid 20th centuries illustrate the tensions in political discourse toward languages spoken by immigrants from non-English speaking countries. In the late 1880s, a number of states proposed laws that would restrict or ban bilingual education and teaching in languages other than English. When the United States joined World War I, the state Councils of Defense prohibited the use of German in schools, churches, and media. The ban was extended to the use of German in the workplace and on the telephone (Trimbur, 2006). Similarly, in the 1920s, the Hawaiian territorial legislature passed anti-foreign-language press legislation, resembling an Oregon State press law that had passed before it (Tamura, 1993). While these measures may appear to be an extreme reaction in line with the war-time sentiments in the early twentieth century, similar and far more recent legislation reveals a broader trend. In 1996, a federal bill that established English as the sole language of official business, as well as the anti-bilingual education legislation passed in several states in the late 1990s (Ovando, 2003), illustrate the continued mistrust toward languages other than English and the uncertainty of the public regarding whether bilingual education results in academic success. We found evidence of the oppression experienced by the families of speakers of languages other than English in the interviews of our participants. They spoke of their great-grandparents and grandparents prohibiting their relatives from speaking the family language out of a cautious desire not to be seen as outsiders. Tina, a second generation Chinese-American and mother of 19-month-old Lilia, recalls the story of her family:

When my mom came to this country she was first generation. My parents met in Taiwan, they got married there and then they came over here and had kids. They came over here right after the Vietnam War and moved to Oregon. And my paternal grandmother instructed my mother to never speak anything but English to us, because we live in America ...

Unfortunately, fear continues to be one of the strongest sentiments dominating the subject of speaking other languages. The theme of xenophobic attitudes toward foreign languages in dominant U.S. society came up in several interviews with our participants. The following quote from Tina, a mother teaching her daughter three languages, sums it up: "I think Americans are scared of foreigners sometimes ... even in the business world I've found that they're scared of people that they don't understand, that they can't understand their language." This fear is multifaceted and penetrates both public and private domains in the linguistic culture of the United States. Despite a monolingual self-image, there was a recharged federal and public interest in learning foreign languages critical for the country's security in the aftermath of 9/11 (Pratt, 2003). In these circumstances however, the motivating force behind the government's call for learning another language remains fear. The processes of globalization and the prospects of facing increased economic competition in a multilingual global market compound the incentive to learn other languages from fear of a foreign economic threat. On a personal level, a monolingual self-identity creates a mental block for many Americans to learning another language (Stein-Smith, 2013). This fear of being unable to learn new tongues promotes the creation of multiple myths about bi- and multilingualism that we address further in this chapter.

Debunking the Monolingual Myth

The parent interviews revealed that the "monolingual nation" myth is still present in public discourse and rooted in longstanding cultural practices and language policies of the United States. With educators, we infer that at least some hold this myth given they held up "abroad" as a place where multilingualism was the norm in implicit contrast with the U.S. situation. However, many facts debunk this myth. Despite many policies and public beliefs that limit multilingualism, numerous languages have survived and continue to develop in the United States in the private domain of speakers' homes and in many schools, both public and private. The first fact that debunks this myth is statistical. For example, the number of people who live in the United States and speak languages other than English is very high. According to the U.S. Census of 2011, over sixty million people in the country speak more than 300 different languages (Ryan, 2013). This trend cuts across the generational differences of speakers from adults to preschool children. Among the latter, as mentioned, over 50% speak a language other than English (Espinosa, 2008). Further evidence that debunks the myth was frequently present in participant interviews. While 31% of the parent participants reported having experienced or come across opinions that languages other than English do not matter, 69% of the parents and all but one of the 13 educators noted examples of the importance and usefulness of multilingual skills and abilities. As Tina, the mother of 19-month-old trilingual Lilia, put it, "It's important ... to be able to learn many different languages. The world is just becoming a smaller and smaller place."

When asked about their motivation to raise their children multilingually, between them the parents listed over fifty different reasons. Many of these reasons debunked the myth that the United States is a monolingual nation. While we address those reasons further in Chapter 5, it is pertinent to outline a few trends in participants' motivation to raise their children multilingually. The categories of reasons that we identified include the value of international and global connections. One parent participant stated: "I think the world is getting smaller and it's shrinking, and so I just think that the cultural boundaries are fading, and I think that knowing multiple languages will just give you access to so many resources and experiences in life" (Taani, an Indian-American mother of two young sons). One of the educators put it simply as "A lot of parents are thinking ahead. Like if you want a better job or if you want a job in China, the official language is Mandarin so you have to speak the language" (Jake, director of an after-school Mandarin-language program). Reasons also include the respect for other languages and cultures and going beyond simply accepting the differences to also include friendships with people regardless of their background: "I would like him to have a wide set of friends and not to distinguish based on culture or race or religion and I think that language-wise that is helpful too" (Veronica, a mother of a 2-year-old son, raising him to speak English, German, and Hebrew). Furthermore, the association of bi- and multilingualism with professional success ("... and if you are a doctor that means your cliental has just broadened because of your ability to interact [in both languages]. So if you are a doctor you can have ... twice the patients because of that," Monica, a mother of two teenage sons, speaking Spanish and English), and acknowledgment of community building by learning each other's languages ("I think that there is a sense of community that's built based on not just only the culture ... via the language," Lilian, prospective bilingual mother). The final reason is the appreciation for foreign and heritage languages ("Understanding of foreign languages is empowering," Tina, a Chinese-American mother). These trends in motivation for raising children as multilingual speakers reveal a qualitative shift in public understanding of the role that multiple language knowledge plays in the current social, economic, and cultural context and were echoed by educator participants such as Elena: "if you look at the world economy, and the global economy, if they want to be twentieth century employable people, you have to be multilingual."

The participants' comments also revealed the changing discourse around multilingualism and the U.S. self-identity. In their opinion, America needs to now be recognized as no longer monolingual: "We live in a multicultural society, and even though we are in the United States, there's people that don't speak English ... and even though I think it is beneficial for them to speak English, I think it is also beneficial for me to understand their language as well. It breaks down barriers" (Tina, a Chinese-American mother). The ability to speak English does not bring the feeling of superiority that is characteristic of the monolingual myth paradigm. Instead, many of the participants reveal a desire to speak more than one language and identify the missed opportunities to become multilingual during their own upbringing. Tricia, a mother of three children, confessed: "[My mom] speaks five languages … She is incredibly good at languages so I am very annoyed that she never taught us any languages." Melanie, a middle-school ESL specialist who learned to speak several languages in adulthood, addressed her own mother in person during her interview with a very similar reproach: "You started us with English and then tried to introduce Spanish and German later. It was challenging for us and we got frustrated." This yearning for speaking several languages translated to parent determination to raise their children as multilingual speakers. Additionally, perception of English as the sole language for business and economic success was not evident. The participants were ready to share stories in which the ability to speak another language was more important than English for their careers. Tina, who speaks Chinese, English, and Spanish, reported: "It's beneficial in business. You know I've been in many business situations where the person across the table, they've only spoken Chinese and I don't look like I can speak Chinese and I've understood every word that they've said." Tricia reinforces this sentiment: "I was a Latin sales rep, and they told me I had to speak Brazilian Portuguese to continue working, so I went there for work and took initiative and kind of picked it up…." Her statement shows a monolingual American taking up a challenge of learning another language in adulthood, a life-changing experience that would lead her to teach her own children to speak Brazilian Portuguese.

As we revealed in the introductory chapter, the popular press has also scrutinized the belief that America is a monolingual nation (Erard, 2012), and has further debunked the myth that most other places in the world are de facto multilingual societies. This would suggest that the small group of educators in our study who cited the multilingual state of other nations in contrast with the United States have perhaps a rather optimistic view of the linguistic affairs of the rest of the world.

Many participants' valued multilingual abilities and actively searched for ways to join a community of multilingual speakers. They strived to be global citizens establishing worldwide connections and building international community through learning multiple languages and raising and teaching multilingual children to make the world a better, friendlier place. Alejandro speaks for several educators in the study when he eloquently states,

Of course, in the future it opens up more possibilities economically speaking, but I think primarily it really does open up the world to you as I see it…. When I speak to the parents of these children, one of the things that they tell me is that they truly believe that being multilingual also enriches their children's lives. That they're able to get to know the world better because of it.

In the concluding discussion of the myth of a monolingual America, it is important to note the crucial role that multilingual children play in facilitating change in attitudes toward non-native English speakers. Parent participants unanimously reported the overwhelmingly positive reactions of others toward multilingual children and their linguistic abilities. Even though the public sometimes exhibited surprise when their children spoke multiple languages, this surprise came from amazement at these children's unique abilities. Linda, a mother of two bilingual daughters, shared a sentiment that was reported by many parents:

When we are [out], people may not expect one or the other language, and so it is always fun to get that "Oh my gosh! Your kids speak Spanish! That is amazing!" People probably say that more when they are with me. And then the flip side is when Ubaldo [the girls' father] is with them and they are like "Oh they speak English!" You know, now I think being here people expect them to speak English but it is kind of fun when we get an "Oh that is neat your kids speak Spanish!"

Thus, multilingual children growing up today, the focus of this book, bring the promise of a change to the linguistic culture of the United States where bi- and multilingualism will become the norm and speaking several languages will be customary of U.S. citizens.

We now turn to additional myths reported in the literature and that can be richly illustrated by the study participants.

Learning More than One Language is Detrimental to Children

It is possible to hypothesize that the deep-rooted fear of multilingualism described in the section above translates into a number of apprehensive beliefs about multilingual development. Since the first half of the twentieth century, when learning another language or growing up multilingual was viewed as a "burden to a child" (Schiffman, 1996), the effects that learning more than one language has on children's linguistic, cognitive, academic, and social development have been questioned and surrounded by parental dread. The fear of the negative impact of learning more than one language often results in families giving up attempts to raise their children multilingually (See Table 3.1). In fact, in our study seven out of eight families whose children's language development seemed to be negatively affected by multilingual environments reported giving up additional languages and focusing all their efforts and their attention on their children's progress in just one particular language. This language for most of the participants was English. Mayda's comment illustrates

Table 3.1 *Components of the broad myth* learning more than one language is detrimental to children

Specific misconceptions and beliefs	Component myths	Broader myth
Bi- and multilingual children are late talkers They will never speak without an accent Their vocabularies will be smaller than those of their peers They will have difficulties with grammar Some children (especially those with disabilities) may not learn a 2nd language	Overall language development is slower and/or different in bilingual and multilingual children	Learning more than one language is detrimental to children
If they do not focus on learning English they will not succeed English is the language of academics	Academic success is at risk	
They will not have any friends They will have difficulty communicating They will not be experts in either culture	Social development is at risk	

that this decision is common for many families: "I pushed more English at home. I stopped talking to him in Armenian. I tell everyone around us, you know, 'Please, let's concentrate on one language with Raffi. I just want him to open up [in English].'" Table 3.1 reflects the more specific misconceptions and beliefs that we found in participants' interviews.

The participants' responses in our study yielded a considerable number of myths and misconceptions that surround raising children multilingually. These included the beliefs that a multilingual upbringing leads to overall deceleration of language development, flawed language development in all languages that the child is trying to learn, and negative impacts of multilingualism on specific aspects of language, such as vocabulary and phonology, all of which ultimately result in struggles with academic achievement in school. Additionally, we came across the widespread misconception of the linguistic "haves and have-nots": several parents spoke of children who were "made for learning many languages" and children who were not able or should not be learning more than one language. Children who were late talkers and especially children with disabilities fell into the latter category. Finally, we discovered a worry about multilinguals' social development and parents' fear that multilingual children would have trouble making friends. In this section, we gathered these misconceptions under the umbrella of a larger myth that *learning more than one language is detrimental to children's development.* We examined the participants' stories and strived to debunk the myths that give multilingualism a bad reputation with parents and educators alike.

Children Who Learn More Than One Language Are All Late Talkers

He did not pick up language all that quickly ... but he had a couple of words around his 1st birthday. [It is only] in the last 3–4 months that his vocabulary really skyrocketed. [Before that] I know Rajeev [husband] was definitely worried that he was a little slower than many kids around his age.... (Taani, mother of 2½-year-old Mihir who speaks Hindi and English and is exposed to more)

It is just that they would be late speakers because everyone said that's how it would be. (Tricia, mother of 5-year-old Gabriela, 4-year-old Paolo, and 1½-year-old Jessica who speak Brazilian Portuguese and English)

Ten out of 26 parent participants brought up the theme of multilingual children beginning to talk later than they were expected to begin. Nine of the parent participants (eight families) were in fact parents of children who started talking later than expected. These parents shared with us their personal experiences and reactions of their friends and family members. Table 3.2 presents a summary of the details about participants who brought up this theme in their interviews, including details of their children and families.

Debunking the Myth

It is important to note that parents from the eight families of late talkers above are fairly homogeneous in their SES. All of the parents in this subgroup held higher than bachelors' degrees and represented two-parent households of middle-class income. While their professions differed, they were similar in holding white collar occupations: five respondents were working in academia in the field of humanities, one had a background in mathematics, and the remaining two worked in business. In six of the eight families, one of the spouses was born outside of the United States, in one family both parents were immigrants, and in one family both parents were the first generation to be born and raised in the United States. Each family had at least one parent who was a native speaker of a language other than English. Upon

Table 3.2 *Multilingualism and the characteristics of late talkers*

Participant	Number of languages spoken within the family, examples of languages	Child reported as late talker, name and age	Child's gender	Birth order	Age of language onset and any language differences	Complications at birth, diagnosed disability, or language delay (yes/no)	Gender and age of other siblings	Methods parents used to promote language development
Taani	4, English, Spanish, Hindi, Bengali, (American sign language)	Mihir, 2½ years old	M	1st child	Onset at 12 months, slow vocabulary development until 24 months	No	None	The parents switched to 2/3 English and 1/3 Hindi
Larisa	1, Russian	Boris, 23 years old	M	1st child	4 years old	Yes	None	The parents continued speaking Russian at home and enrolled the child in many playgroups, some of which were bilingual
Danielle and Ultan	2, French, English	Georges, 33 years old	M	1st child	Approx. 24 months	Yes	Brother, 30 years old, sisters, 28 and 26 years old	The parents switched to English during the time in language therapy; took the language of the country of residence
Mayda	3, Arabic, English, Armenian	Raffi, 6 years old	M	2nd child	3 years old	Yes	An older sister, 9 years old	The parents switched to English

Victor	2, English, Japanese	Sakina, 14 years old	F	1st child	Unknown, but the parent mentions late language onset	No	A younger sister, 12 years old	The parents switched to English
Kimberly	2, Korean, English	Tamer, 5 years old	M	1st child	Unknown, but the parent mentions late language onset	Yes	A younger sister, 3 years old	The family designated a focal person for each language and stopped using Korean for 1–5 months
Leonid	2, English, Russian	Luis, 11 years old	M	3rd child, the second of the 2 twins	Unknown, but the parent mentions late language onset	Yes	An older sister, 25 years old, from the 1st marriage, and two brothers from the same family: one older brother, 13 years old, and a twin brother, 11 years old	The father stopped speaking Russian until the language delay diagnosis was reversed
Veronica	2, English and German	Andrew, 2 years old	M	1st child	The mother reports that the child still says just a few words in both languages	Yes	None	The parents continued bilingual communication

Table 3.3 *Comments from parent participants debunking the myth*

Kimberly, a mother of 5-year-old son who acquired language slower than his younger sister	"Well, with my daughter there's a very different experience. Now I see like she has no issues, so with my daughter we're making very different choices [the family did not stop bilingual exposure] than for my son because he was a first child and we were worried …"
Leonid, a father of a 25-year-old daughter, 13-year-old son, and 11-year-old twins	"My daughter started speaking early, and then one of the twins and my oldest son, they were fine …"
Danielle, a mother of 33-year-old son, who started speaking later than expected, 28-year-old son, and 26- and 24-year-old daughters	"I think each child is different … with our first child who has learning difficulties, we first started worrying about him when he was a year and a half, maybe 2, when he had hearing difficulties or so we assumed … The one who spoke fastest and used complete sentences, and you know 3, 4 word sentences really fast was Adele at the age of 2. At the age of 2 she was fluent basically, you know. She had a little lisp, it was funny but it was fluent and bubbly. And Andre and Sylvie were probably about the same …"

closer examination, a few additional common threads stand out from this table. First, six out of eight participants' "late talker" children either had complications at birth or were diagnosed with a disability or language delay. Their siblings who did not have a disability factor were not recognized as late talkers. In fact, many of the participants spoke of the siblings' language development as having an early onset and being difficulty-free. Table 3.3 presents three comments from the families in which only one of the children had delayed language development.

These comments once again underscore that even within the families where one child started using language later than expected other children might have different language development trajectories.

A range of disabilities (including congenital language disorders) or birth complications that result in temporary or long-lasting health problems, but not multilingual practices, are likely to have served as contributing factors for language delay (Vukelich, Christie, and Enz, 2008). Second, seven out of the eight children who were discussed were boys. Though research on gender differences remains controversial, a few studies indicate that boys' early language development is slower than that of girls (Fenson et al., 1994; Leaper, Anderson, and Sanders, 1998). One educator, David, a high school ESL specialist even made this point based on his own observations of his students' interactions in class:

DAVID: ... in general, girls are much more diligent at learning English than their boy counterparts.

ANNA: Well, let me ask you this, do you think it's because girls are also more talkative and, you know, there's this other stereotype in terms of ...

DAVID: They're much more verbal.

ANNA: More verbal. So do you think that comes into play or do you think it's just something, you know, just about girls being studious or do you think ...

DAVID: It's interesting. Actually, I think girls are much more verbal and they do better verbally.

Third, nearly all of the late-talking children were first-born children in the family. Research on this issue points out that first-borns have qualitatively different language development experiences. Hoff (2006) suggests two key differences in early language development of first-born and later-born children: while first-born children might have larger vocabularies and more complex syntactic structures than later-born children, they tend to engage in "analyze-first, speak-later" communication, while later-born children are more likely to speak first and then analyze and have advantage in "the development of conversational skills" (p. 55).

The myth is probably based on the fact that infants exposed to more than one language exhibit a slightly slower linguistic development than that of their monolingual peers (Espinosa, 2008). Also, the language abilities in L1 and L2 of these children do not match (Cheatham, Santos, and Ro, 2007). These phenomena are not indicative of any detrimental effects of exposure to multiple languages, but rather likely result from an inaccurate assessment of children's communication abilities (Cobo-Lewis, Pearson, Eilers, and Umbel, 2002) or indicate the typical development of multilingual children whose language skills develop according to the contexts of language exposure (Cheatham et al., 2007). Given that the vocabulary of multilingual children is more complex to measure (Espinosa, 2013), it is possible that parents cannot accurately judge the actual size of their children's lexicons, since it should be taken as a measure of all the lexical components of all the languages that a child speaks or understands. Notably, a theme that did not become apparent in the course of the interviews, yet is present in multilingual language development research, is that the speed of language acquisition and development depends considerably on the similarity of languages being learned (Oller and Jarmulowicz, 2009). Languages that have similar phonology and syntax tend to be acquired more quickly because the skills acquired in one language are applicable to the other language(s). In situations where languages are very different, the linguistic transfer is problematic and can even create interference. This interference may lead to a slower pace of language learning. Thus, there seems to be a multitude of contextual factors that might go unnoticed and be masked by the blanket misconception that all children who acquire more than one language develop language later than peers.

Even though our study yielded a fairly large subgroup of parents who brought up the myth of multilingualism leading to delay in language development, it is important to note that the majority of parents (remaining 15 participants) either did not mention late-talking as a worry or an experience. On the contrary, many interviewees debunked this myth in their comments. All of their children started speaking within the expected time or even earlier, despite their expectations. In fact, for the entire study, out of 114 children referenced in parent participants' narratives, only 8 started talking late. Tricia, the mother of three children raised speaking Brazilian Portuguese, who expected her children to begin talking a bit later, recalled: "that wasn't the case ... all three. They were really early. I can get dates when they said their first words but [while] other kids wouldn't even be talking and they would be saying words in both languages. They all were very early speakers. Gabriela is the oldest. She was amazing." Tina, who introduced her daughter Lilia to Mandarin, Taiwanese, and English from birth, as well as introducing American Sign Language, told us of her little girl's extraordinary early language development:

She did her first sign at five months. She did the sign for milk, which was amazing. And then she did the sign for more, and she was able to start signing at a very, very early age, which was just wonderful.... [Now at 19 months] she already is able to translate.... And she said, "grandma said, 'okay go ask grandpa for some water.'" Grandpa only speaks English, but my mom asked her in Chinese. She went over to grandpa and asked him in English.

The comments of the parents of numerous multilingual children who met all the expected benchmarks developing multiple languages conveyed the sense of wonder and amazement at their children's unique linguistic abilities. The progress their children made in more than one language at once served as an inspiration and reassurance for the parents/families to continue their efforts in fostering bi- and multilingualism.

Educators also spoke overtly of the speed of language acquisition, some concerned with the unrealistic expectations of parents and others speaking of the rapid acquisition they had witnessed in young children especially. We might account for these contradictory points of view in educators by the population of students they were teaching. Paola teaches in a Spanish-English TWI program at the elementary level. Her students include English dominant students who are acquiring Spanish as a second language alongside Spanish-dominant students acquiring English. Her conservative perspective on the rate of language acquisition is in reaction to desires of parents that their children become speakers of Spanish after just one year in school:

They do have expectations that are a little bit skewed though. They don't necessarily take into account developmental stages of acquiring a second language. So once they're in the bilingual program, by the end of that first year when they're 4 years old, they want them to be speaking in full sentences, you know and it's like it doesn't really work that way.

In contrast, Sandra in her French one-way immersion kindergarten reports "how much they can change and learn quickly in a year." Other educators whose ELL students are in English language development classes reported and applauded the frequently rapid English development of many of their students. For example, Elena says of her middle school newcomer ELL students, "I'm thinking language acquisition. I would say they're more open to learning the new language. So their comfort level is, I guess slower or increases faster, is what I'm trying to say. The affective filter is lower because they are used to change. And therefore because they are used to change, their comfort level increases faster and by that they learn the second, third, fourth language faster."

Do Multilinguals Have Accents, Limited Vocabularies, and Struggle with Grammar?

Well, sometimes when he'll say some Armenian words, it's so funny like as if I'm asking you to repeat a word after me in Armenian. He [would] say a couple words and we just start laughing, you know, totally very heavy accent. (Mayda, a mother of simultaneous trilingual 9-year-old Vana and 6-year-old Raffi)

Their vocabulary, the number of words that they know in English is far less than someone who's only speaking English and has had the same kind of you know level of school. (Ultan, a father of four multilingual children, Georges (33), Andre (28), Adele (28), and Sylvie (26), simultaneous bilinguals in French and English who later learned at least one more language)

And even now ... she says things and I know she hears that they're awkward ... the best way to say it is it's an incomplete sentence. It's always missing, it's either constructed strange or missing something. And I let it go because I just know she's wired differently and I'm not gonna stress her. (Victor, a father of two daughters (14 and 12 years old) who are simultaneously bilingual in Japanese and English and who later acquired Korean and Russian)

Besides general dread of delayed language development, a few parents had some very specific concerns about language development. The top three worries were about accents, vocabularies that are smaller than those of their peers, and struggles with grammar that multilingual children might have.

Accents. While most of the parents commented that their children sounded like native speakers in both languages, a handful of parents brought up multilingual children speaking with an accent in one or two of their languages. Lilian and Miko, prospective Spanish-English bilingual parents, recounted accent patterns in their Spanish-English sequential bilingual niece's language:

LILIAN: When she was younger, she was in a daycare, just a friend of a family who took care of children ... she was two or three when she went. And the woman was trying to teach her "Twinkle, Twinkle, Little Star." That lady had an accent and she would say "diamont" [with a Spanish accent], and my niece would say "diamont" too.

MIKO: She also says "brokkoli" [also with a Spanish accent].

LILIAN: Yes, I know that one comes from my mom. She says "brokkoli" and so my niece says that too.

MIKO: I assume that eventually she will separate the words that are pronounced in Spanish from English pronunciation ...

Research on phonological development suggests that phonological processing and production skills develop differently in bilingual and multilingual children in comparison to their monolingual counterparts (Hoff, 2006). In some children, this development results in acquisition of a single phonological system (Werker, Weikum, and Yoshida, 2006), while other children develop separate phonological systems distinct for each language (Hoff, 2006). These children might appear to have a slight accent in both or all languages. Grosjean (2011) pointed out that even the most fluent and balanced bilinguals at times have an accent in one of the languages they speak, and sometimes, less fluent bilinguals do not have an accent. Our parent participants who brought up the theme of accents spoke of children whose ages ranged from roughly 24 months to late adolescence. At least one ESL teacher, David, overtly mentioned the sensitive period to perceiving sounds that made it difficult for second language learners to produce the sounds of a language that are not in their native language. Indeed, existing studies examining sensitive periods for phonological acquisition suggest that there exists a wide window from eighteen months to puberty for the age of exposure to sequential languages that may result in an accent-free or native-like sound production (Oyama, 1976; Au, Oh, Knightly, Jun, and Romo, 2008). Additionally, research on the subject of accents indicates a wide range in mastery of several phonological systems for multilingual children (from accent-free to accents in both or all languages) depending on the age, the extent of naturalistic exposure and the intensity of contact with different languages (Bialystok, 1997). This justifies the concerns of some parents who strive to bring up their children sounding like native speakers in all their languages.

Vocabulary. The theme of limited vocabulary resulting from exposure to more than one language also appeared among the specific concerns that parents had about their multilingual children's language development. Worrying about vocabulary size of their children, parents seemed to be preoccupied with two distinct worries: the overall size of their children's lexicons and especially the size of their English vocabulary that is needed for school success. Ultan's remark illustrates the common misconception that children who speak more than one language have "smaller" vocabularies than their monolingual counterparts: "Their vocabulary, the number of words that they know in English is far less than someone who's only speaking English and has had the same kind of you know level of school." Ultan, a retired film critic and a writer with a well-developed native English vocabulary, perceived the size of the lexicons of his four children, who grew up speaking French and English, and each of whom later picked up Italian, or Spanish, or Japanese, as less developed than those of their peers. With his children now grown up and in their twenties and early thirties, he reports still noticing gaps in their English vocabulary. Another participant, Monica, an administrator of an elementary school with a Spanish-English TWI program and a mother of two Spanish-English teenage bilingual sons, now regrets having not spoken "enough" Spanish to them as they were growing up: "… And it is like 'I don't think I did enough!' And 'But I wish that I would do it more often.' I think there is always a little bit of guilt with not having enough Spanish in the home."

However, speaking of her reasons for speaking to her sons in English more than in Spanish while they were in school, she confided, "Yeah that was a little bit of [the worry about vocabulary development] too. That there had to be some English too. And I went all the other way which was unfortunate but that is an honest answer. That is still within me. It is like you still have to develop vocabulary and all of that stuff in English as well." The worry that if a language other than English was spoken at home the children would not have gained sufficient English vocabulary was a frequent theme in the parent participant interviews. Multiple parents spoke of sacrificing speaking the home language for the fear that the children would have limited vocabularies in English. Sandra, an elementary teacher in a French one-way immersion program, was the only educator to speak directly to this point, stating, "I think sometimes the more languages you know, the less you are – your vocabulary can only be like – you have so much vocabulary split between two languages that the vocabulary from one language is never as big as someone who only speaks one language, maybe."

Grammar. Another concern related to language development that was voiced by parents of multilingual children was difficulties with grammar. The parent participants were concerned about their children's grammar in both or all languages they spoke. Victor is the father of 14-year-old Sakina, who speaks English and Japanese and studied Russian and Korean. Victor noted that Sakina's sentences are "awkward … the best way to say it is it's an incomplete sentence. It's always missing, it's either constructed strange or missing something." Sonia, the mother of a Russian-English bilingual son named Alex in his early twenties, expressed concerns about her son's difficulty with spelling, grammar, and what she called "академический язык" (the language of schooling). Sonia states:

Я все ещё замечаю это. Он допускает ошибки, хотя и нечасто, но во многих русских словах. Я чувствую, что у него пробелы в русском. Как будто он не доучил это в школе – академический язык у него не устоялся. Ограниченный словарный запас. Он не знает, где ставить запятые, и от этого предложения получаются не совсем правильные. Он мне посылает электронную почту, и я ему правлю пунктуацию. Она у него не совсем сложившаяся.

[Translated: This is something I still notice. He misspells, though infrequently, many Russian words. I feel that there are gaps in his language development. It's like he did not get it all – his language of schooling is incomplete. His lexicon is limited. He does not know where to put commas or makes sentences that are not quite correct. He sends me e-mails and I correct his punctuation. It remains incomplete.]

The languages used in both these families' homes are grammatically very different from English. In Japanese, the majority of the sentences end with a verb and subjects in the sentences are commonly omitted. Different grammatical nuances may have led Victor to perceive an "incompleteness" in Sakina's sentences. In Russian, the alphabet (33 letters in Cyrillic script compared with 26 letters of Latin script in English), the sound system (10 vowels, 21 consonants, and two pronunciation signs that rule over soft and hard pronunciation, nearly doubling the number of consonant sounds), and the punctuation rules are vastly different from English. This has likely made it difficult for Alex to spell and punctuate his sentences correctly. His mother reported that although Alex eventually mastered essay writing, he still needs his essays proofread.

Debunking the Myth

Research offers an alternative take on the limits to multilingual children's vocabularies. While studies of lexical development confirm that children who speak more than one language are likely to have smaller (up to one standard deviation in difference) vocabularies in each language than their monolingual peers (Oller and Eilers, 2002), they emphasize the differences in patterns of vocabulary, not the limited size of vocabularies. Researchers point out that the summative vocabulary or conceptual vocabulary (words in both or all languages that they have for particular concepts) of multilingual children is often equal to or larger than the single language vocabulary of their monolingual counterparts (Pearson, Fernández, Lewedeg, and Oller, 1997). Responses from several of our participants reflect these findings. Taani, the mother of a two-and-a-half-year-old, Mihir, recalls him learning the names of the animals:

The babysitter who would speak to him only in English, she would try to teach him different animals, and I had been teaching him the same kind of animals in Hindi. And so what happened was that for some reason he picked up a couple of them in English and a couple of them in Hindi. So for the word elephant, he would only say the word "elephant" in Hindi … I did not tell her initially that he had learned it in Hindi already, and she would try to get him to say that word but he would be giving her this [other] random word. And she could not understand. He would be learning other words, like cow and sheep, but why is this random word for this one particular animal? And I was like, "No, no, no, he actually is recognizing it correctly, and he does understand. He is saying it correctly. He is just saying it in Hindi."

Additionally, the size of individual vocabularies in each language that the child speaks depends on the amount of exposure to that language (Pearson et al., 1997). Furthermore, in bilingual and multilingual children of school age, the size of individual vocabulary becomes a function of exposure to the dominant language and the language(s) spoken at home (Oller and Eilers, 2002). Studies also recognize domain-specific vocabularies characteristic of children who speak more than one language. Hoff (2006) attributes it to the fact that multilingual children are usually exposed to a particular language in a particular setting and, therefore, they might have vocabulary for different activities in each language. We found evidence for this in participant interviews. Mayda, a mother of two children who speak English, Arabic, and Armenian, describes using English for school and politics because she earned her bachelor's degree in History at a U.S. university. Ethnically Armenian, she uses Arabic for cooking because she grew up in the Middle East speaking Arabic with her mother and learning how to cook, and she speaks Armenian with friends and family because she has found a close circle of Armenian friends in Los Angeles. Taani, describing her 2½-year-old son's language practices, stated,

Seventy-five percent of the time he speaks English. But I would say that the words that he uses to say that he is tired or sleepy he says always in Hindi. He does not say them in English at all. And that's I think because that ever since he was a baby those words we taught to him. And I would say that.... milk ... because it was a fundamental word that he always says in Hindi. He says some other words [in Hindi], they are more words to describe food – like the temperature of food or the taste of food, lots of words associated with food because he eats a lot of Indian food, but not just the names of the food, but also words used to describe the food. And water, he usually asks for it in Hindi.

These personal narratives echo research findings that multilingual vocabulary acquisition and development are complex and different but not considered limited in comparison to that of monolingual speakers.

Oller and Jarmulowicz (2009) find the differences in syntactic principles of the languages the child speaks as sources of interference and as a potential source of erroneous carryover from one language grammar to the other(s). David, an ESL teacher in our study, reminds us of the large number of irregularities found in the English verb system (e.g., buy-bought, fly-flew). These exceptions to the rules of English in his experience have been one of the biggest challenges for his Spanish- Chinese- and Korean-dominant high school ELL students.

Additionally, Hoff (2006) views bilingual situations where one language is primarily spoken as a special case. Alex's struggle with spelling and punctuation is an example of language development where one of the languages is spoken but not written. Alex's parents speak only Russian at home, and he prides himself on being fluent in that language. However, when it comes to writing, the proficiency of Alex's Russian is not sufficient for him to always use correct spelling and punctuation. Although Alex's parents insisted that he reads books and even writes essays in Russian, they did not have enough materials or time to perfect his grammar and spelling in both languages. Emily, a high school Spanish-English teacher in a dual-language program predominantly for Spanish-dominant students, echoes this concern more generally at the classroom level when she laments the lack of bilingual materials including textbooks and other literacy materials at the middle and high school levels even in a common partner language such as Spanish. Research on this issue stresses the need for a balanced exposure to both (or multiple) languages (Hoff, 2006). If the goal is not only bi- or multilingualism, but also biliteracy and even multiliteracy, it is important to provide children with plentiful opportunities to practice reading and writing in all their languages and support their out-of-school literacy activities (i.e., journaling, e-mailing, and writing letters to relatives and friends). However, due to the informal contexts of writing practice in a minority language, spelling and grammar often go unstressed. Yet, to support the multiliterate abilities of multilingual children it is important to encourage and value their engagement in literacy activities in any language and their use of the skills as a foundation for further instruction (Yi, 2007).

Some Children May Never Be Able to Learn Another Language

We found evidence in the participants' interviews of the common misconception that there are people who are unable to learn another language. There is much research on the subject, which acknowledges a wide range of beliefs and misunderstandings about aptitude for learning languages (Horwitz, 1999). In our study, cause of the inability to learn a language was a misconception that was prevalent in participants' accounts of their children learning two languages. This occurred particularly in instances of sequential bilingualism, when another language was being learned after the child started to acquire the dominant family language, typically English. Parents raising several children multilingually occasionally commented that even within the same family one of the siblings unfortunately would not be able to master the second language. For example, Nicole, who is raising two sons bilingually in English and German, stated, "I feel that my older son is not a big language person.

I think some people are made for foreign languages. I don't know if he is." This quote poignantly illustrates a misconception that has long-dating roots that can be traced to the controversial construct of foreign language learning aptitude (FLA) that was particularly popular in the middle of the twentieth century. It is one that is still alive in some quarters as the comment by Jake, the director of an afterschool Chinese program, reveals: "When I talk to people who speak one language, like parents, and they say 'Oh! He tried to study Spanish. He is just not good at languages.' No, it is not true. The kids pick up really fast if you encourage it."

Debunking the Myth

Research findings debunk the myth of an inherent inability for individuals to learn a second language. The idea of FLA goes back to the 1950s, when the Modern Language Aptitude Test was created (Carroll and Sapon, 1959). At that time, foreign language aptitude was seen as comprising four key components, including phonemic coding ability (an ability to identify the L2 sounds and tie phonetic symbols), sensitivity to grammatical functions, ability to learn inductively from language samples, and ability for rote vocabulary learning (Carroll, 1962). In the past decade, understanding of FLA has changed. Current research refutes the non-malleability of FLA, underscoring the role of language learning skill development in the acquisition of a second/foreign language (Wen, 2012). Sparks and Ganschow (2001) proposed the Linguistic Coding Difference Hypothesis, which postulates existence of a wide range of learners who process L2 information differently, but not insufficiently. Some individuals within this range may be experiencing difficulties learning a new language, especially if the teaching methods are not rigorous enough to address and provide adequate support for their challenges. Sparks (2006) continued this research and proposed a wide continuum of language learning abilities, decidedly dismantling the concept of a "foreign language disability," a so-called condition, that (if it existed) would have impeded some people from learning additional languages. Wen (2012) states that this research marks a shift in understanding of FLA, from being perceived as a non-malleable trait that prevents language learning to a set of dynamic and malleable abilities that can be developed in any individual if specific difficulties experienced by learners are matched with targeted intervention. Thus, current research challenges the common misconception that some people will never be able to learn a language other than their first language. Interestingly, none of the families whose first language was not English doubted their children's ultimate ability to master English. While they had worries about their children's school readiness, vocabulary, and grammar, these parents never expressed a belief that their children had no aptitude for language learning.

Children with Disabilities May Not Be Able to Learn/Should Not Be Taught Additional Languages

In our discussion of this myth, it is important to note that the subgroup of parents who brought up disabilities as an obstacle to multiple language learning was largely different from the subgroup of parents who actually had children with disabilities and who successfully raised their children bi- or multilingually. The subgroups practically did not overlap, except for one parent, Leonid, whose son Luis was diagnosed with language delay in early childhood. A total of five parents in our sample (approximately a fifth of our study participants), including Leonid, spoke of disabilities as a potential obstacle for learning another language – either as their belief or as an opinion that they had come across. Among the former was Kelly, a prospective mother who planned to raise her children speaking English and Cantonese, and an aunt to 9-year-old Josh, who had autism. Kelly's sister's experience in raising Josh convinced her that raising a child bilingually is "very challenging when your kid has a disability." Once a special education teacher, Kelly saw having a disability as a roadblock to successfully learning more than one language. Similarly, Tina, a mother of a nearly 2-year-old daughter, growing up in a trilingual household where Spanish, English, and Taiwanese were spoken, was adamant that a child can learn as many languages as she is exposed to, but did not see such a possibility for a child with a disability. In her interview, Tina stated, "You know children are gifted. And capable … Unless there is a learning disability there, they speak a language, and they can speak multiple languages."

Taani, whose young son's story of learning animals in Hindi and English we introduced earlier in this chapter, recalled her son's language delay and being tempted to blame it on "exposure to four different languages when he was just starting to formulate language … I am still curious to know if that was in any way involved in his language delay. You know again, language delay not clinically speaking, but just I think he is at one end of that bell curve …" As a result, Taani and her family stopped speaking multiple languages to her son: "So I think what happened was that because we really wanted his language to develop quicker, we wanted him to catch up, because he was a little bit behind his peers … we did not push Hindi that much …" Veronica, a mother of a 2-year-old, Andrew, bilingual in German and English, recalled her son's cousin's language delay. The cousin's parents were advised that their child should not be learning Hebrew and English and stopped his multilingual upbringing because of the language delay.

These stories illustrate parent participant beliefs that disabilities might preclude a child from learning another language and that a combination of a disability and exposure to more than one language can be detrimental to a child's overall language development. The solution to these concerns was similar in each case: cease multilingual exposure for children with disabilities. Apart from Leonid, the parents who considered that disability prevents one from learning multiple languages did not have first-hand experiences with the issue. They observed it through friends and relatives with children with disabilities who had given up the idea of teaching their children multiple languages. This hearsay characteristic of the narratives contributes to the myth status of this misconception. The participants' responses also pointed to potential sources of this myth to which we now turn.

One of the overarching themes in participant responses was the advice of experts to stop the multilingual upbringing of children with disabilities. The expert advice came from multiple sources, including schools that the children of the participants' friends/families attended and the numerous specialists working with children with disabilities. When asked about potential roadblocks to raising children while speaking more than one language, Kelly recalled the experience of her friend speaking of disabilities as the only obstacle that she saw on the way to raising her daughter bilingually: "Unless she has a disability of some sort. Because a friend of mine, her first baby has a speech and language impairment. A lot of times the schools tell them to focus just on one language and English is usually the language." Reflecting on her nephew's story, Veronica referred to the advice of pediatricians: "That's what the doctors told my sister. To stop speaking Hebrew ... I think it [was] because her son was language delayed." Leonid remembered taking his son to a neuropsychologist:

Early on when he was diagnosed with speech processing and linguistic development problems we talked to a neuropsychologist and we said, "You know, we're trying to raise them bilingual," and she said, "In his particular case you may want just to sit back a little bit and make sure that at least his English, or his development in English is as advanced as possible."

Even Danielle (whose son Georges has high-functioning autism but nevertheless grew up speaking French, English, Spanish, and some Japanese) did not see a disability as a roadblock. She never completely gave up speaking French and English to her children, although recalled getting such advice from a speech pathologist:

Actually there was one point when we started going to ... the speech therapist in Canada, I think he was only like two, two and a half. When she started making him talk ... that was the only passage then when [following her advice] for a while I started not speaking exclusively in French so that I could repeat those English things to him so that I could see how he responded.

Many parents of children with disabilities took the "expert advice" when their children were not progressing in any language learning as quickly as expected.

Even among the educators we heard similar stories in which they discouraged families from enrolling children in programs fostering two languages if the student presented with a disability. In one instance, Alejandro explained how he and the parents of a Mandarin-English bilingual boy decided they would postpone his enrollment in the TWI program and the introduction of Spanish as a third language because the boy was having difficulties acquiring language. Sandra, the French one-way immersion teacher echoes this decision with her comment, "I also think for children who have language difficulties in the first place, I don't know if going to school trying to learn two languages is good for children who already have a problem with one language on their own."

We now turn to research and stories told by parents of children with disabilities that debunk this myth.

Debunking the Myth

Research on language and social development of children with disabilities confirms the widespread apprehension and confusion about the possibility of a bi- and multilingual upbringing for this population of children and their outcomes (Hambly and Fombonne, 2012; Chen, Klein, and Osipova, 2012). One participant, Danielle, reported that she also "pushed for more English" when her son initially struggled with language production. However, she reflected on the advice by professionals to give up on her son's multilingualism and concentrate on just one language as "the practice of the past." But to this day, many families of children with disabilities receive similar professional advice from physicians, speech and language pathologists, educators, family members, and friends and are cautioned to promote only one language (Wharton, Levine, Miller, Breslau, and Greenspan, 2000). Disabilities, such as autism spectrum disorder (ASD), intellectual disabilities, and language and communication disorders often result in delayed language development and production, which cause great distress and anxiety for parents. Feeling anxious to see their children develop language and the pressure to get their children school-ready, many multilingual families, much like the families in our study, abandon their home language(s) and devote all their attention to English, the language of schools (Paradis, Genesee, and Crago, 2011; Kremer-Sadlik, 2005). However, a decision to abandon the home language or stop exposure to an additional language (spoken by at least one of the parents) not only disrupts children's home language development and interaction within family, it also precludes them from acquiring the significant benefits that a multilingual upbringing can provide for all children and from the additional benefits often touted for children with disabilities.

The maintenance of home language practices positively affects children's self-identity, sense of belonging, and ultimately social development (Genesee, 2008; Puig, 2010; Wong Fillmore, 2000). Additionally, when parents are confident in the language in which they communicate with their children, they provide extensive language interaction, freely express their affection, and create more nurturing linguistic contacts than parents communicating in a non-native language (Kremer-Sadlik, 2005). Meanwhile, nurturing and extensive linguistic input is critical for language development of children with disabilities (McCormick, Loeb, and Schiefelbusch, 2003).

Studies that looked at the effects of dual-language exposure for children with specific disabilities unanimously report encouraging findings that debunk the myth of a negative impact of multilingualism on children with disabilities. First, research underscores that there is no evidence of detrimental effects or language learning inhibition due to bi- and multilingual exposure for children with disabilities (Kohnert and Medina, 2009). Research by Bird et al. (2005) compared language profiles of monolingual and bilingual children with Down syndrome and did not see any significant differences between the language abilities of participants. Edgin, Kumar, Spanò, and Nadel (2011) compared cognitive profiles of bilingual and monolingual children with Down syndrome and did not discover any differences in neuropsychological functioning of the study participants.

Other studies emphasize the positive impact of a multilingual upbringing for children with disabilities. Wharton et al. (2000) list increased linguistic competence and stronger emotional attachment as positive effects of bilingualism on preschoolers with ASD. Research by Kremer-Sadlik (2005) suggested that extensive interactions in the home language aided understanding of speech acts for young children with ASD. Studies by Gutierrez-Clellen, Simon-Cereijido and Wagner (2008) and Gutierrez-Clellen, Simon-Cereijido and Sweet (2012) focused on children with specific language impairment (SLI) and discovered evidence of the home language supporting the development of English. Similarly, Seung, Elder, and Siddiqi (2006) examined language development of a preschooler with ASD whose home language was Korean and found out that the child's understanding and production of early word combinations facilitated production of English words. These studies debunk the myth that calls for abandoning second and multiple language exposure for children with disabilities and suggest that children with disabilities can learn more than one language and, moreover, they benefit from it.

Finally, while none of the educator participants made comments to dispel the myth that children with disabilities may not be able to learn more than one language, findings from the parents in our study largely support the potential of children with disabilities to successfully acquire more than one language. The range of disabilities was very diverse. Two of the participants had sons with autism, one of whom had additional intellectual disability. Three parents informed us that their children were diagnosed with language delay and speech disorders; two others talked about their children having emotional difficulties. One of the parents had a son with visual impairments and a learning disability and another had a son with a health impairment that significantly affects his daily life. Despite having disabilities, seven of these children are successfully bilingual and two are multilingual and speak three or four languages. We would like to finish debunking this myth with Georges' story. A multilingual adult with high-functioning autism whose first language was French, Georges' path to speaking four languages was recounted by his father, Ultan:

Georges had started [learning English] in France just before we left and then he continued here. Then he did some two or three years of Spanish then he took Japanese at [name of community college]. And he did fairly well because there was no way we could even help him or read along with him or anything, yeah. So he managed to be okay ... He's always liked Spanish, so he continued that too. And he went a few times to Spain before and after, so he's always been really interested for Spanish. And he has more Spanish than we ever realized. Well, he came to Morocco with me on this one picture [film production]. And I got him a job with the wardrobe department that was entirely Spanish. And this woman whom I had known 20 years before said, "Your son speaks very good Spanish!" What?

Learning More than One Language Will Lower Children's Chances of Academic Success

Another myth that falls under the category of myths about the detrimental effects of multilingualism is the myth that multilingualism prevents academic achievement in school.

"If they do not focus on learning English they will not succeed." Several parents shared this belief that a multilingual upbringing may hinder their children's chances of academic success. Explaining her choice to speak English to her daughters even though it might have caused discontent among her Spanish-speaking relatives and friends, Nora commented,

We are in a country where they don't use Spanish in academic [settings], unless it is a second choice when they are in high school. English is your academic language. So it is very hard for some kids to have both [languages for] academics at the same time. Personally, I think it is hard for them, so you always have to choose, even though a lot of parents have criticized me why I don't believe in bilingual education. If you want the kids to succeed, you have to give the tools for them to be able to succeed, and if everything is in English that is what they have to learn. As a parent you have to make a conscious call, I think.

Nora illustrates the reality of much current mainstream education in which the children are not given credit for their knowledge of a subject, unless it is communicated in English.

"English is the language of academics." Many parents who decided to give up their home language or place greater emphasis on English when communicating with their children as they approached school age, were driven by the fear of a possibility of their children's academic failure. Even parents who persevered and sent their children to school after speaking to them only in a language other than English at home reported having serious worries that their children would not be able to learn and ultimately switched to speaking English during their children's school years. Tricia, who raised her three children speaking exclusively Brazilian Portuguese at home, recalls the fears she had when her children went to kindergarten and how these fears were eventually alleviated. Tricia's dread of the transition to school was double-edged: she was worried that her children would not be able to comprehend the curriculum and that they would lose their ability to speak their home language once school started. After her older children successfully completed kindergarten, and her fears subsided, Tricia, who used to prohibit any other language than Portuguese in her household, switched to speaking more English with her children: "It is easier when they get older ... because now I just speak English. I am [also] not so worried that they are not going to learn and they went through that first year of school. Before I worried a lot that they were going to go to school and lose everything."

While Tricia's worries represent a widely acknowledged parental concern about the effects of home language practices on overall learning, other parents feared home language-specific effects on specific academic subjects. Nicole, bilingual in German and English, is raising her two sons to be bilingual. She hypothesized about the potential negative effects that German might have on children's language arts success: "Their language development in English, in reading and comprehension might be different than kids who only speak one language because the grammar, the sentence structure is different in German than in English and somebody who only really speaks German at home possibly could mix up both things and make more mistakes or different mistakes. So I am thinking there would be an English language art where they would have issues." Even some of the educators in our study have questioned the potential for negative outcomes as a result of their students' being schooled in or maintaining two languages. For example, Paola questioned at some earlier point in her career whether bilingual education was a viable instructional model: "And I remember thinking at one point in my career early on, gosh maybe I did study the wrong thing, maybe it's not good to teach the kids two languages at the same time, maybe it is confusing for them. Even though that was going against everything

I had learned…." So does a multilingual upbringing affect academic achievement? We turn to research and other participants' stories to debunk this myth.

Debunking the Myth

Research examining the effects of multilingualism on academic achievement recognizes the common worry that learning two or more languages may interfere with a child's overall linguistic and social development (Genesee, 2008) and, as a result, with school achievement (van Goor and Heyting, 2008). Multiple factors contribute to this misconception. For example, children who easily navigate casual conversations in the L1 and L2 may have insufficient academic language skills to succeed in classes taught exclusively in the L2 (Puig, 2010). Additionally, an early switch from L1 to L2, when the child's L1 is not quite developed, may lead to difficulty developing the L2 (Espinosa, 2008). However, research on balanced or native bilingual children disproves the link between multilingualism and low academic achievement, showing that, on the contrary, these children show academic success if they are exposed to both languages in systematic and rigorous ways (Espinosa, 2008). A research synthesis conducted by Collier (1992) examined the use of minority language for instruction and has shown its positive impact on minority students' academic performance, especially if it is combined with balanced and rigorous English support. More recently, a study by Ardasheva, Tretter, and Kinny (2012) that examined the predictive strength of English proficiency on academic achievement in 17,470 middle school students has shown that redesignated fluent English proficient students outperformed native English speakers and current ELL students on reading tasks. A study of risk factors affecting performance of Mexican-American students by Roosa and colleagues (2012) dismissed bilingualism as negatively affecting academic success. Bailey, Moughamian, and Dingle (2008), in a study that used a broad definition of success and a comprehensive array of measures of efficacy in dual-language programming, found that Spanish L1 students with stronger Spanish language skills (including extended discourse skills such as oral narrative abilities) also showed stronger academic achievement as well as heightened metalinguistic skills and more positive feelings toward school and academic content areas such as reading and mathematics.

In our study, we had families raising children whose L1 is a minority language within the dominant English culture and those whose native language is English and whose parents decided to add one or more languages to it to raise a bi- or multilingual child. However, for both groups of children research does not find evidence of any detrimental effects of learning multiple languages on academic achievement (Collier and Thomas, 2004; Cooper, 1987; Thomas, Collier, and Abbott, 1993). On the contrary, studies point out its advantages, specifically in regards to schooling. These include heightened problem solving abilities and enhanced creativity (Bialystok and Martin, 2004), access to greater number of information sources in multiple languages via internet media, and overall strong cognitive abilities when compared to monolingual peers (Genesee, 2008). Most of the educators in the current study recognized such abilities in their students, even those who were supporting English language development potentially at the cost of their students' L1, although studies reveal that bilingual children whose L1 has been substantially supported in schools perform on par or outperform their monolingual counterparts within five to seven years of schooling (Fitzgerald, 1995; Oller and Jarmulowicz, 2009). From the educators supporting the acquisition and maintenance of two languages we heard such positive outcomes as "They think in different ways" (Paola), and "They're more open to different kinds of learning ... And I think that multilingual kids are a little more motivated in some ways, and I'm not sure why but they're a little more motivated to learn" (Alejandro). Pablo, a Spanish-English teacher in a high school dual-language program, also speaks to the motivational advantages of his students' multilingualism: "Another benefit is that more than anything the kids in this program, they tend to be more self-motivated and more in tune with the education and the goals in the future."

Jake provided us with the story of a specific former student, Bobby, to make his point about the academic advantages of multilingualism: "In a way I think the more languages you speak I think the kids are more smarter ... You know what, down the line he [Bobby, now at an Ivy League institution] was able to read Chinese and because of that hard work I think translate to other things it would be easier.... So I can see the correlation between learning Chinese and being able to take that into a different subject."

From educators who were supporting the English language development of ELL students we heard very similar observations. For example, Camila, a middle school ESL specialist, claims, "A student who comes in with more than one language is already more ahead because they can use what they know from either language to help solve any issues that they maybe are confronted with in school.... As a teacher, I find that I can assist students in making stronger connections to their studies if they have two backgrounds, two languages."

As is well known, success in literacy is linked to overall academic success (McWayne, Fantuzzo, and McDermott, 2004). Research specific to academic achievement in literacy also points out that bilingual students outperform their monolingual peers on a number of language and literacy tasks (Oller and Eilers, 2002), which include verbal reasoning (Ben-Zeev, 1977), thinking in original ways, and making metalinguistic comparisons (Bialystok, 2001). This is especially true if the languages spoken by the child are similar, allowing the child to benefit from positive transfer and perform just as well or surpass monolingual children on tasks such as decoding (Oller and Jarmulowicz, 2009; Verhoeven, 2000). Additionally, children who have had literacy experiences in L1 develop L2 literacy with greater ease as they can draw on literacy skills in L1 (Genesee, 2006). Fitzgerald (1995) suggested that proficiency with more than one language leads to the "common underlying proficiency" that is useful in a wide array of academic tasks.

So what then is at the root of the myth of negative effects of growing up learning more than one language? We hypothesize that the statistics which portray ELL students as underachieving are one cause for this myth. Research underscores that the initial lag in certain tasks and skills, such as vocabulary learning, demonstrated by ELL students (Carlo et al., 2008), can be attributed not to bilingual abilities but to the following four major causes. The first cause is the abrupt abandonment of the children's L1 that leads to lower linguistic and academic competence (Espinosa, 2008; Genesee, 2008). According to Genesee (2006), bilingual Hispanic students had higher achievement scores, GPA, and academic expectations than their Hispanic peers who only spoke English. Second, the differences between children's L1 and L2 may contribute to literacy difficulties (Oller and Jarmulowicz, 2009). Third, children's vocabulary which is often seen as a predictor of academic achievement is the domain for which the language transfer is most limited (Oller, Cobo-Lewis, and Pearson, 2004). Bilinguals' often wide cumulative lexicon is hard to measure and is frequently assessed, erroneously, in only one of the child's languages (Oller and Jarmulowicz, 2009). Finally, many multilingual children have difficulty achieving academically not only because of a language gap but because of being raised in low SES circumstances that are often associated with limited linguistic and academic experiences (Hoff, 2006). A study by Krashen and Brown (2005) for example, showed that ELL students from high SES backgrounds performed significantly better on reading and math tasks than their low SES counterparts. All of these factors are likely to contribute to the myth of the negative impact of knowing more than one language on academic success.

Our final argument in debunking this myth is supported by participants of our study who persevered in raising their children multilingually and saw positive effects. Danielle, a mother of four multilingual children who started their schooling in France and completed it in the United States, reflected on their school functioning:

[Their] language [was] pretty good for English, you know it's a lot of vocabulary and all that. I think they knew quite a lot without even knowing it. The other thing is all the funny words that you see in SATs [an academic assessment] or whatever are really French, Latin, you know it's all. So that I'm sure helped them too. You know, look at the base, look at the root, it comes from there ... they don't have less [language] than their friends. They have as much as their peers.

Her husband, Ultan, continued Danielle's thought, "Children who speak two languages are better off than children who speak one, and three languages are [even] better. It's a mental exercise that is I think very very beneficial intellectually. Beyond the communication and the social aspect of it, I think it affects their learning, their ability to learn anything." All of the older children of the participants who continued their multilingual upbringing successfully completed high school and went to college. Many of them acquired additional languages or continued to master their home language(s). Seven adult children from six participant families found fulfilling employment in which they can use their multilingual skills.

Learning More than One Language Puts Children's Social Development at Risk

"They will not have any friends." In addition to previously mentioned myths about the harmful effects of multilingualism, a few parents shared with us their apprehension regarding the impact of growing up speaking more than one language on children's social development. This apprehension appeared as another reason due to which some parents in our study switched to only speaking English with their children. Bianca, the mother of two English-Spanish bilingual teenagers, recalled her husband's worry about their sons not having friends. She states,

Since I speak only Spanish to them all day because they are with me, my husband said, "You should speak a little more English because when they go to school they are going to be lost with their friends." And I think about it maybe he was right, but the school they went to – there were so many different kids [and they made friends]. That is why I think I should have never changed it to English because he speaks the language to them and they should have both of the same type. But no, we changed it completely 100% in English.

Abandoning the home language in order for children to enjoy a shared culture with their friends was a common theme throughout the interviews. The degree to which the parents attempted this differed greatly, including switching to English when friends were around or changing the entire family's preferred language of interaction.

"They will have difficulty communicating." Another concern related to the myth of impeded social development expressed by parents was that their children would not communicate with their peers. Bianca, who came from Mexico over two decades ago, is in touch with many other parents in her neighborhood and makes a point of welcoming new families who move in, especially if they are also immigrants. She shares her story and the stories of her sons with them in an effort to alleviate their school-related worries. In her interview, Bianca recalls one of her neighbors who was concerned about her son's communication skills:

My neighbor, she has just moved five months ago, she is very worried that her son only speaks Chinese and she is looking for an only English school … and I said, "Why do you worry?" and she said, "I want him to communicate in English." And I said, "Don't worry about it … He will learn it in the school, trust me! In five months from now you will be amazed at how much he knows because of all his friends." And she looks at me and says, "But I worry about him that he will not communicate!"

Parental concern about their children's inability to communicate compels them to take extreme measures such as enrolling their very young children who hardly speak English in English-only programs or abandoning the home language altogether in order to promote communication in English.

"They will not be experts within either culture." An additional concern expressed by parents regarding multilingual social development was that multilingual children will not truly know the culture of the languages that they speak. Veronica, a mother of a German-English speaking Andrew and a member of informal German-speaking "mommy-groups," spoke of the "third-culture kids," children whose parents came from cultures that differ from the U.S. culture: "I think as these kids get older, because they don't have a cultural home because their parents aren't at home in their dominant culture, it can be very problematic …" Parents who are raising children multilingually spoke of their constant search for authentic materials, including genuine books by native-speaking authors, children's literature from countries speaking the target language, educational supplies, cartoons, and music – all designed to enrich and enhance their children's understanding, enjoyment, and familiarity with the cultures of the languages they speak.

   While several parents reported going to cultural festivals, providing toys and playing games, and tapping into other non-U.S. cultural resources, some were acutely aware that their children's culture was different from both the U.S. mainstream and the linguistic minority cultures. Betty, a mother of adult Spanish-English bilingual sons who is an administrator in higher education, recalled an eye opening discussion with a colleague:

I interviewed the woman who is the lead teacher at the [name] school for kindergarten and first grade. I talked with her about what kind of books did she want and I was all focused up on books that were originally written in Mexico or Spain, actually probably more Latin [America]. That was what was needed and she said, "Well, yes and no, Betty, because they are also of this culture. So things that are of this culture translated into Spanish are also equally appropriate because they are living here. They are not living in Mexico and so they see the other things around also."

Presumably a balance is warranted between authentic texts that can reflect the linguistic traditions of the minority culture in a rich and educative way that Betty was envisioning, and popular children's books and other texts that may appeal most to children being raised and schooled in the United States. While some parents worried about the lack of authenticity of available books, realia, and traditions related to the target language, a few parents, especially those who are second-generation in the United States, seemed to be more comfortable with how their minority cultures have evolved and adapted within the United States and embraced what is still available, hoping to ignite the same respect and sense of value in their children. Miko, a Spanish-English bilingual prospective parent, spoke more specifically of the generational differences in attitude to immigrant cultures within the United States:

I've never as a child ... my parents were never interested in celebrating El Dia de Los Muertos. And Lilian and me, we started going to celebrate it in the past couple years at the Hollywood Forever Cemetery, which is a big deal here in Los Angeles. And that's been very interesting for us and that could be something we will do for our child to teach them about our culture.

In contrast to Miko and Lilian who could easily find a rich Mexican-American cultural milieu, some parents, especially those who live outside the linguistic minority diasporas and who less frequently encounter languages other than English in their neighborhoods, spoke of their awareness that the mainstream U.S. culture does not always accept children who come from minority cultures. Ghodrat, an Iranian-American father, decided to stop speaking Farsi to his son and daughter, so they would not have difficulty with being accepted at school. He recalled the reasons for his decision, stating,

Also the child [who does not come from the majority culture] has a problem, [and it] is in a society ... That society, his small society does not accept the other culture and so on. Who am I to add more burden to that, you know? That was a time that I decided to just also speak with them in English, even my English is still broken English. So it is a just more or less for the benefit of the children in my point of view to just, as long as we have the control, to adjust to the culture and the environment that they are growing in.

Concerns about children's cultural competence, that is, what it is and how it plays out for different families, were reoccurring themes throughout the participant interviews. Participant interviews reveal an important construct of vulnerability of multilingual children's cultural identity and the need for the society as a whole to be accepting and supportive. They also show the serious sacrifice that parents sometimes decide to make, giving up their own language and culture in order for their children to feel accepted and welcome, helping them navigate the world outside of the family home. We question whether the fears of parents are warranted or not. Was Bianca right telling her neighbor not to worry and that "the kids will learn it all at school"? Research offers a positive outlook on the social development of bi- and multilingual children.

Debunking the Myth

Research recognizes that multilingual children face extra challenges in communication, especially when they must navigate a more complex world of interpersonal communication compared to their monolingual peers. Children who are learning more than one language must choose which language to use with their different interlocutors, decide whether code-mixing is appropriate, and track for potential breakdowns in communication (Genesee, 2008). However, even when language development in very young children is at the one- or two-word stages, they can successfully use their languages with family members who speak different languages as well as with unknown interlocutors (Paradis et al., 2011). Therefore, bilingual and multilingual children are completely capable of successfully managing communication in more than one language (Genesee, 2008).

Research also recognizes the significant role that parents and community play in social development of their children (Lanza, 2001; Zhou and Kim, 2006). It is parental practices of codeswitching and other home language practices that set the model of socialization for children, even if these practices are different from the majority language and culture (Döpke, 1992). Studies also recognize the protective factors at child, family, and neighborhood levels for multilingual children's mental health and social adjustment. Zhou et al. (2012) find maintenance of heritage culture, bilingualism, parental support, and residing in an ethnic community as protective factors for multilingual Asian American children. Several studies indicate that it is not multilingualism that has detrimental effects on one's social development, but the abandonment of the home language and differences in parent-child heritage cultural orientation that are associated with negative outcomes for social development, including conflict within family and higher rates of depression in school-age children coming from immigrant families (Costigan and Dokis, 2006; Ong and Phinney, 2002; Weaver and Kim, 2008). Zhou and Kim's research (2006) showed that residing in ethnic communities offers valuable and academic support for children from Asian American immigrant families. Research also offers an answer to the worries of the parents who are concerned that their children will not be able to fit in the culture outside of their home. Harris (1995) suggests that it is "intra- and inter-group processes, not dyadic relationships" that transmit culture (p. 458). In other words, culture is not transmitted solely from parent(s) to child, but is absorbed by the child as he/she engages in and observes his/her family interactions with other families and individuals, as well as the community's interactions with the larger societal culture. Therefore, socialization within the family (as a social group) and within the groups of peers at school would be sufficient for the children to become familiar and successfully navigate both cultures.

In addition to disputing the negative impact of speaking more than one language on children's social development, a number of studies discuss the benefits related to multilingual children's social development. The positive influence of multilingualism on children's socio-emotional development, as discussed in Chapter 2, includes greater self-confidence, lower affective filters for communicative risk taking, multicultural awareness, tolerance, and positive attitudes toward other cultures. These findings are reinforced by research that also identifies bi- and multicultural competence and efficacy, knowledge, and successful navigation of multiple cultural norms, positive attitudes toward both minority and majority cultures, and a wider range of culturally or situationally appropriate behaviors as frequently observed in individuals who speak more than one language (Genesee, 2008; LaFromboise, Coleman, and Gerton, 1993). Indeed educators in the study reported on the positive outcomes for the social interactions of their students. For example, Elena notes that the ELL middle school students she teaches "had to adapt quickly to other cultures and languages. And so they're actually, I would say, socially advanced because they have to deal with changes in their lives that usually most kids don't have to deal with until they leave home." Even though many studies emphasize that additional research, especially longitudinal studies, are needed to obtain further evidence of successful social adjustment and functioning for multilingual children of different ages and ethnic and linguistic backgrounds, the overall findings of existing studies debunk the myth that a multilingual upbringing may potentially harm children's social development, suggesting quite the opposite.

Myths of Successful Methods for Raising Multilingual Children: Certain Language Acquisition Methods Must Be Strictly Adhered to

Another group of myths that prevailed in parent interviews was the cluster of myths pertaining to *certain language acquisition methods must be strictly adhered to*. Participants of the study brought up numerous beliefs regarding some of the best methods for their children's multilingual development and education. These beliefs included not only methods, but also specific tools, optimal age ranges, and means by which language(s) could or could not be acquired. These strict regulations had been recommended by the participants' friends and families as the indubitable language acquisition principles. In this section we discuss each of these principles and put them to the test by research and our participants' narratives.

One-Parent-One-Language Method

[The belief at the time was that] if you had a parent that spoke always English with you and a parent who always spoke Spanish, you would develop as a true bilingual and the worst thing was to mix up the languages and the people and all of that. So I really focused up, we structured it in a way that was like that. (Betty, a mother of four adult children, two of whom continue to use Spanish in their daily lives)

Many of our participants held the belief that the one-parent-one-language method is the most desirable and most successful method for raising multilingual children. Many of them were also convinced that this had to be a predominant approach used in many families where parents aspired to raise simultaneous bilingual or multilingual children. One-parent-one-language is a method in which each family member commits to using just one language consistently in communicating with the children within the household. Thus, for example, a mother may decide to speak strictly only Spanish to the children, while the father would use only English. The name of the method was coined by a French linguist Maurice Grammont in 1902 (Barron-Hauwaert, 2004).

The approach has been recommended for families raising multilingual children for over a hundred years as means of avoiding codeswitching, which at the time was considered to be a sign of confusion. Even though the research of the late 1980s and the 1990s deemed codeswitching to be a natural part of bilingual development (Cheng and Butler, 1989; Genesee et al., 1995), the myth of one-parent-one-language persists among the parents. Monica, the mother of two teenage English-Spanish bilingual sons and administrator at a school with a TWI program, reflected on her own beliefs regarding raising children bilingually,

[Bilingualism] was something that I knew that I wanted. I just think that we could have done much better in terms of [consistency]. It would have been good for Gonzalo [her husband] to speak in English and me to just speak in Spanish. But then when you start to look at the amount of time one person spends versus the other and then you think, 'Are they going to get this?' There is too much second guessing that I did and even knowing, having that kind of information I still second guessed and I can imagine what parents go through too.

Monica is joined in her reflections of what might have been by Melanie, an ESL specialist in the study, who as we reported above is still taking her own mother to task for not raising her using the one-parent-one-language model. Melanie claims to have seen the model successfully implemented with her cousins and friends' offspring,

My cousin, Tina, is bilingual perfectly because one parent always spoke Spanish and the other always spoke English. I think it's important to always have a division. I lived with a family that was half, well he was from South Sudan and she was from Canada. Their son, until he was two years old, couldn't speak because they were speaking four different languages in the house.... It helped when they took a step back and every parent had a certain language only instead of speaking different ones.... The problem that we had in our family, we didn't do simultaneous alphabetization. I think that's really important.

The results of a belief in the one-parent-one-language model may have negative consequences however: like Monica, other parent participants in the study also reported "second-guessing," "worrying," and "being unsure" about this rather rigid approach. These feelings at times result in parents giving up or feeling unsuccessful. Therefore, it is important to closely examine this potential misconception of how language input should be provided or more accurately embodied and to share research findings on this well-known approach.

Debunking the Myth

The last few decades brought significant change in the outlook on what works and what does not work in bringing up children multilingually (Bain and Yu, 1980). During this time the principle of one-parent-one-language has been heavily critiqued, as "elitist", "atypical" and "highly unrealistic" (Döpke, 1998). Since the 1990s, multiple studies found that the one-parent-one-language approach is not a guarantee of successful multilingualism in children (Döpke, 1992; Gutierrez-Clellen, 1999). Moreover, strict adherence to this principle does not warrant that children will not codeswitch (Genesee, Nicoladis, and Paradis, 1995; Lanza, 1997). The studies also uncovered a number of additional factors that interfered with perfect outcomes of this method. A study by De Houwer (2007) that examined varying rates of bilingual success in 1,899 Belgian families of children 6 to 10 years of age suggests that the balance between minority and majority language plays a significant role in bilingual outcomes. The study showed that the households where both parents used the minority language and the families where no more than one member spoke the majority language had the highest rates of success for successful bilingual development of their children. The same study revealed that the one-parent-one-language approach provided "neither a necessary nor a sufficient condition" (De Houwer, 2007, p. 420). Additionally, the one-parent-one-language approach does not provide an environment where the languages are truly balanced, because besides addressing the child, the parents also interact with each other, other members of the family, and the community, thus creating a higher frequency, and therefore imbalance, for the use of one of the languages within the family.

Finally, ethnographic research of various methods of raising children multi-lingually debunks the superiority of the one-parent-one-language method suggesting that there are numerous methods that are contingent on a myriad of factors. In her book *Growing Up Bilingual,* based on her qualitative study of a predominantly Puerto Rican neighborhood in New York, Ana Cecilia Zentella (1997) suggests that "ultimately there were almost as many language patterns as families because of the unique configuration of several variables, including the number of caregivers and children, and differences in language proficiency, education, bilingual literacy skills, years in the US, gender and age of each speaker" (p. 58). We conclude debunking the myth with an opinion of one of our participants, Linda, a doctoral student, who studies child development while bringing up two young daughters speaking Spanish and English. Linda and her husband decided long ago to raise their children bilingually. Initially, they also were convinced that they would have to adhere to the one-parent-one-language approach, but they soon became disillusioned. Here is Linda, providing her take on the issue:

I guess there is some misinformation out there. I think until recently I thought it was "Well, if one person speaks [one] language to the kid that is the model to go with." And then there is the context specific [approach], so always in one context speak one [language]. And I think language ... is such a fluid piece ... Kids from a young age that language is used [speak] so freely and interchangeably and they are mixing and switching and it is a different language. It is not being an English speaker and a Spanish speaker, it is having both at the same time at your fingertips that makes it a different kind of thing but ... it is so different for every situation, and kid, and family.

Complete Immersion Is Needed for L2 Acquisition

Another myth about successful bi- and multilingual language development methods encountered in the participant stories was the myth that complete immersion is needed for the acquisition of additional languages. Eight out of the 26 parent participants (nearly one-third of the parents that we interviewed) believed that full immersion is the optimal way to support language acquisition. When asked about the strategies that she believes are successful and that she is planning to implement with her children, Lilian, a prospective mother and a teacher in a bilingual program, responded, "Full immersion. If some people ask, 'Why are you speaking Spanish?' keeping it very clear to our families and friends or wherever we go that we are making a conscious effort in raising the child bilingually." Given her profession, Lilian's comment represents beliefs of both parents and educators. Our participants spoke of different ways in which they envisioned complete immersion. Some planned to go on vacations to the L2 countries ("21 days in Mexico was our longest span of time but it was during that time that we also tried to immerse them in Spanish,"

Monica), others hoped to live outside of the United States for a while, some planned to send their children to immersion schools ("They are sending them to an English-only speaking school because they want [the kids] to learn English ... They need to get immersed," Tricia), some created full immersion households where only one language was permitted ("In our house that is the only language we speak [Brazilian Portuguese]," Tricia), and others hoped to perfect the seemingly imperfect bilingual abilities by sending them to a college in a different country ("If they were to do a study abroad hopefully it would be ... in an immersion context," Linda). Certainly there are educators who would support this point of view as we have previously heard with Melanie and her wish that her parents had started young with her exposure to Spanish, German, and English in the home. But most educators, rather than touting full immersion, instead speak of the need for "constant exposure," and "having consistency" for language acquisition to be successful, or else articulated this through the stated worry that there was not enough exposure to the target language(s). But is full immersion even all that necessary?

Debunking the Myth

Research findings regarding the effects of complete immersion on successful acquisition of more than one language are controversial. While some studies recognize a number of positive effects of complete immersion for language learning and learners, others uncover potential drawbacks (Cummins, 1998; Feuer, 2009; de Jong and Howard, 2009). A study by Feuer (2009) that examined children's L2 learning in complete immersion Chinese and Hebrew language summer camps reported learners' positive attitudes to language learning and positive social outcomes. On the other hand, de Jong and Howard (2009) examined TWI programs and found that programs originally designed to equalize the benefits of immersion for both majority and minority-language speakers, in fact may be failing "to optimize language learning opportunities for all students, particularly for language minority students and in the minority language" (p. 81). Researchers also caution against withdrawing L1 support too abruptly, since it may work against successful acquisition of L2 (McLaughlin, 1992). Another important argument in this context is made by studies that have shown that it is not the length of time and the amount of exposure that is important for language learning, but rather time on task (the time when language learners are engaged in rigorous and engaging language learning activities) that makes the difference in successful L2 acquisition (McLaughlin, 1992). Thus, even though a larger number of parents in our study were convinced of the benefits of immersion and its necessity for L2 language acquisition, research does not unequivocally endorse it as the best way to promote children's multilingual abilities.

Effortless Multilingualism

ANNA: Is it difficult or easy to raise multilingual children?
MIKO: I think it's easy! I see it as an easy process.

(Miko, Spanish-English bilingual, prospective father
hoping to raise his children as bi- or trilinguals)

On the other end of the continuum about the methods that work for successful upbringing of multilingual children lies the belief in effortless multilingualism. This myth appeared in several parent interviews. It appeared to be a bipartite myth based on the responses of the participants. Many participants reported having an impression that parents who are engaged in raising multilingual children do not necessarily have to teach children these languages. Another similar and persistent idea that became apparent in the interviews was that languages come easily to children, and the younger those children are, the less effort they need put into language learning.

"Parents do not teach languages to the children." As might be expected, the parents who wished to raise their children multilingually, but have not yet done so, did not consider this kind of upbringing to be difficult. The quote from Miko's interview illustrates this position based on the "effortless multilingualism" myth. In other words, the process of raising children who speak more than one language appeared easy as the prospective parents or parents who have not yet embarked on this mission observed their family members and acquaintances do so. In total, six participants with first-hand experience in raising multilingual children also reported this process to be an easy one. We now turn to some of their stories in order to identify what lies at the root of the "effortless multilingualism" belief.

In the study, three mothers stated that they did not see the process of raising children speaking more than one language as particularly difficult. These women come from very different backgrounds. Their similar opinions present three possible scenarios that shed light on why many believe that raising children speaking more than one language is not difficult. Betty, an English-Spanish bilingual mother of grown-up children, had hired a Spanish-speaking housekeeper to help with her household and her children when two of them were young. Betty's sons' pediatrician commented that given that one of the boys was spending a lot of time with a native Spanish speaker he could learn that language. The housekeeper spoke Spanish with the boy for the duration of her hire, over multiple years. As a result, Betty's son grew up bilingual in English and Spanish. In her interview, Betty commented, "Well, it wasn't hard for me because I was off working and someone else was speaking Spanish with him all day and on the weekend." This quote from Betty's story, if taken without the entire context, illustrates a common misconception when not all participants in the immediate linguistic environment of a child are taken into consideration.

It is often overlooked that housekeepers, grandparents, uncles, and aunts who may also spend a lot of time with the child have a significant impact on the child's language development.

Tricia is the mother of three children under the age of ten, all of whom speak English and Brazilian Portuguese. She is a stay-at-home mom who has invested considerable effort in the bilingual upbringing of her three children. For example, she initially banned all other languages from her household (including English) to avoid "contamination" of her children's Portuguese. However, she did not consider her ongoing vigilant efforts of keeping out all languages but Portuguese as a strenuous effort: "No ... no ... I am not working and it is like a huge stress off of my shoulders. All I have to do is make sure they speak Portuguese. It is really not that hard but I am good with languages." Tricia's quote illustrates that certain efforts that might be considered very weighty by an outsider are not recognized as such by the parent for whom this is daily life.

Mayda, a graduate student and a mother of two trilingual children, was the third parent who did not consider the process of multilingual upbringing hard: "No it's easy. And I find it very interesting actually, very interesting. Because if we're in a restaurant or a market ... and I want to tell them that something, [I can do it in English, Arabic, or Armenian] ... We find it interesting and fun, actually." In her approach to multilingual upbringing, Mayda is using a domain-specific approach. She and the other members of her family use English when the kids study, Arabic when Mayda cooks, and Armenian when the relatives who speak this language are present. We can hypothesize that in Mayda's case, both factors that we mentioned above make multiple language maintenance seem effortless: the presence of different speakers of the household languages (similar to Betty) and the routine/habitual use of the language(s) (similar to Tricia).

"It is easy for children to learn another language." The second belief that forms the myth of effortless multilingualism was the misconception that younger children learn languages with ease. Linda reflecting on her daughters' experiences with Spanish and English, commented, "They just learn it when they are young and it is so much easier and it is effortless ... Little kids, they just soak it up." Seven out of 26 parent participants and one educator participant brought up the belief that it is much easier for young children to learn a new language. Many of the parents compared their young daughters and sons to themselves, seemingly unable to learn another language without an effort. Hediyeh, a mother of two bilingual adult children in their 30s, shared her beliefs about the ease with which her children acquired the Persian (Farsi) language: "It's easier for them [to] learn our language than us, you know at the older time." It is possible to suppose that the roots of this misconception lie in the fact that parents may not take into consideration the hard work that each adult in their family is doing when raising multilingual children. Imagine having several instructors working with an adult on his/her language skills daily, carefully scaffolding the language input. It could also be that the parents who recognize their own efforts in teaching children several languages, do not notice the work that is done by the young learners. With the exception of two educators (Alejandro in elementary TWI, and Emily in a high school dual-language classroom) who both said it was easy or easier to teach their Spanish-English bilingual students, the educators in the study did not claim that teaching students' languages was without challenges for them and nor that language learning was without effort for their students. Students were expected to have to "practice" and "do their work." They needed "strict" teachers to "push" them. They needed to stay motivated and needed the support from their parents at home. On this latter point of parent commitment especially, Gael, a district administrator of dual-language programming, states,

It requires a big commitment from the students, from the parents, for the district office, for the school site. The other thing also that many of the parents in our district, they want children to continue to develop and learn their primary language, so that's why I offer the dual program.... Also the fact that, in regards to our parents, obviously these parents have selected our program because they believe in the program and they want certain outcomes of the program. And many of our parents you know, not only do they want their child to know English, but also to be able to be biliterate...."

With this in mind, we now turn to research examining the nature and origins of the myth of effortless multilingualism.

Debunking the Myth

Research on the subject highlights some controversial points in this belief. While many young children may do well with acquisition of L2 phonology, other language domains are more demanding of them (Hoff, 2009). Moreover, research shows that older learners demonstrate advantages over young learners in pattern recognition, construction of syntactic structures, application of memory techniques, acquiring vocabulary, and learning rules of grammar (Brown, 2000; McLaughlin, 1992). Additionally, children's communicative constructions are simpler in structure and shorter in the length of utterance, which may be erroneously interpreted as an ease in language acquisition (McLaughlin, 1992).

And as far as debunking the misconception that parents do not directly teach their children the languages spoken in the household, we quote Linda, who works on her daughters' Spanish and English daily, and reports hearing from time to time, " 'Well, moms don't teach their children language.' Where have people been?! Elia [Linda's daughter], she mixes up. She often says 'dos' [instead of does]. 'She dos,' and I am like 'It is does! It is does!' You know, some of the irregulars are now regulars, and I am like 'That is went not goed.' "

It is important to address the myth of effortless multilingualism because the notion can be misleading. In fact it could be one of the factors that is indirectly contributing to the lack of success with multilingualism among the families who tried teaching children additional languages and eventually gave up having discovered that the process requires a great deal of work. In reality, children do not learn foreign languages effortlessly. Multilingualism does not always come naturally, and everyone – parents, other children, family, and friends – put forth great effort to maintain children's multilingual abilities.

Conclusion: Myths as a Source of Abandoned Dreams

In this chapter we hypothesized about the causes of the numerous myths surrounding multilingualism. As we examined and attempted to debunk these myths, we first identified the fleeting nature of multilingualism among these causes, due to the wide range of language abilities of individuals who are considered or who call themselves bi- or multilingual. The interviews with participants further revealed the complexity of multilingualism. They illuminated a multidimensional nature of multilingualism that ranges not only along the continuum of present abilities (from "comprehend but do not really speak" to "speak like a native"), but also in time (from "used to know it in childhood" to "now fully bi- and multilingual"), and across contexts ("kitchen Spanish," "English for politics," "Russian for soccer," "German for nursery rhymes"). The fleeting target of multilingualism and the impatient desire to see perfect multilingual abilities across all language domains lead to overly critical evaluation of self and others and inevitable discouragement which has negative consequences for language learning (Grosjean, 2002).

We also noted the vulnerability characteristic of bi- and multilingualism. It is something that vanishes if it is not nurtured. Having examined the myths presented in this chapter, we can further postulate that the myths themselves contribute to this vulnerability of the concept. For example, the *monolingual nation* myth may be stifling families' intentions to preserve and use their home language(s) or preventing monolingual families from venturing to learn new languages. Some educators were also not entirely immune from the romantic notion that the rest of the world somehow had the right approach to multilingualism. Furthermore, fears surrounding the unknown behind multilingual abilities are either not conducive to mastering languages other than English, or lead to learning a language as a form of defense (Pratt, 2003). Learning a language out of phobia is not a motivation used by parents in this study. However, those who are subject to fears caused by monolingual nation myths abandon dreams of multilingualism.

We have shown that misconceptions stemming from another central myth that *learning another language is detrimental to children* instill several fears in parents of multilingual children. These fears of linguistic, academic, and social failure often lead to parents' giving up on bi- and multilingual upbringing, unknowingly disrupting children's language development. Even the myths from the cluster of *certain methods must be adhered to for successful multilingual upbringing* may discourage families. These strict, often absolute and idealistic approaches ("one-parent-one-language," "full emersion," etc.) are hard to come across in pure form and are likely not necessary, as research and parent and educator participant responses have shown. However, the myths suggesting that only these methods work make the task of raising multilingual children appear very daunting and almost impossible to carry out. As a result, many families may give up their aspirations due to possible challenges of the methods that they mistakenly think they must adhere to. The myths of extreme methods for fostering multilingualism may also serve as rationale not to foster multilingualism within the family. Additionally, even the apparently benign myths from the *effortless multilingualism* cluster may threaten successful multilingual practices. Families who believe in that myth might not put sufficient effort into raising children to speak more than one language. Myths about a multilingual upbringing portray it at its extremes: either very difficult or very easy. They obstruct the true nature of multilingual practices, disguising the realities of challenges and preventing families from addressing these challenges perhaps as effectively as they might otherwise do. Thus, we see myths about bi- and multilingualism as factors posing a very real threat to the success of multilingualism.

Expectations of equally strong language abilities in all of the language domains ("speak without an accent," "speak like a native") are possibly rooted in the erroneous comparisons of bi- and multilingual children to monolingual peers. Such comparisons are unwarranted (Grosjean, 2009). Bi- and multilingual children demonstrate unique patterns of language development that are qualitatively different from monolingual children and their abilities should be measured in comparison to children of comparable linguistic profiles (Valdés and Figueroa, 1995). Even then the comparisons might be inaccurate and disappointing. The great "multidimensional" variability in language abilities discussed earlier make the comparison among bi- and multilingual children very difficult. Bi- and multilingual children do not learn the same way or meet developmental linguistic milestones in a uniform way (McLaughlin, 1992). In further chapters we turn to participants' narratives to examine multilingualism as a continuum of skills and a continuum of practices, unique to different children, families, and educational programs. From these narratives, leaving the myths in Chapter 3, we build a collective comprehensive portrait

of multilingual children, a unique population that debunks the myths by its
very presence.

NOTE

1 Only the first interview excerpt from each of the three non-English interviews is
given in the language used by the participants. All subsequent excerpts are provided
in English only and indicate from which language they are translated.

4   Introducing Families and Educators of Multilingual Children

This chapter introduces the 23 families and 13 educators whose lives and work are the focus of the research reported in this book. The chapter first provides details of the research methods we used, including definitions of key terminology, descriptions of the participant selection procedures, development of the interview protocols and the nature of the qualitative analyses we conducted. We provide details about the "linguistic" histories and circumstances of each of the families and the educational experiences, practices and programs represented by the study educators.

The 23 families (26 individual parents), with 39 children amongst them, were chosen systematically to represent a wide range of different circumstances under which learning more than a single language can occur in the United States. The details of these circumstances emerged from the narratives of recent and more established immigrant families, multiracial/multiethnic families, families reviving a heritage or ancestral language, and monolingual families adding a foreign language to the family linguistic repertoire as enrichment for aesthetic, instrumental, integrative, or social justice reasons. We included families who were raising infants, toddlers, preschoolers, kindergarteners, elementary/middle/high school students and young adults, as well as couples who were expectant or prospective parents intending to raise their future children within a multilingual environment.

The 13 educators we studied have all encountered multilingual children in their day-to-day teaching. They have experience with a wide array of different languages spoken by their students. Selected educators have taught in a variety of different educational settings including those that are specially designed to support the development of more than one language in different ways at the preschool, elementary, middle, and high school levels. The educators were chosen to ensure at least one individual (and sometimes more) had experience teaching in each of the language programs we review in Chapter 6.

Defining Multilingualism

As mentioned, we have adopted the use of the term multilingualism throughout the book. It is intended to encompass the full range of language knowledge and experience of the families, from just some exposure to two languages to productive use of several different languages. We can consider this range as it falls on a continuum. In Chapter 5, we expand on the notion of a continuum for the increasing number of languages acquired and used by the families (see Figure 5.1). For our purposes of introducing the families in this chapter, it is important to explain that at one end of the continuum, children may be predominantly speakers of a language other than English and are acquiring English as a second or additional language, or they may be predominantly speakers of English and are being exposed to additional languages. Such additional languages may be the heritage language or ancestral language spoken by one or both parents or perhaps by grandparents or even by a more remote ancestor. Alternatively, the family may have no connection to the additional language being acquired and the language may not be spoken by any other family members than the child who is being schooled in some type of language enrichment situation such as a one-way or two-way immersion program.

Next on the continuum are children whom the literature has traditionally referred to as bilingual and more recently as emergent bilinguals or dual-language learners. These children know and use two languages with some degree of proficiency in both. However, even children who are considered fairly proficient in both their languages are unlikely to be "balanced" bilinguals. This terminology has largely been discredited, with "native bilingual" now seemingly preferred to refer to children who are acquiring two languages simultaneously without overt teaching or training in either language – in effect acquiring two languages as their native language. The deemphasizing of "balanced" is important here because the sociolinguistic reality of bilingual individuals is that they rarely acquire equal proficiency in their two languages (Baker, 2011). This reflects the fact that they may use their two languages for very different experiences and thus there will be non-overlapping word knowledge in the two languages and possibly non-overlapping pragmatic skills if situations calling for certain competencies are encountered in one of the languages but never in the other. For example, a child may be required to give a formal presentation in English at school but never required to do so in his/her other language. In turn, that language may be used exclusively for expressing intimacy with close friends and family, something that the child may feel less able to do using English.

Moving along the multilingual continuum, we next place children who are trilingual. These children may be exposed to three languages as a result of both parents speaking different first languages and society at large being dominant in yet another language. In some cases, a third language is introduced by parents motivated to foster trilingualism using a non-familial caregiver such as a nanny who speaks a language that differs from that of one or both parents and/ or the wider society (Chevalier, 2012). As with bilinguals, a child's abilities in the three languages may differ and be the result of the different degrees and manners of exposure.

Finally, on the opposing extreme of the continuum, are families who have exposed their children to four or even more languages. Life circumstances such as sojourns in foreign countries on route to immigration to the United States, or life in a diaspora before migration, may have required parents to acquire several languages to survive in these different milieux. Once again, marriage or unions across racial/ethnic and linguistic grounds will add an even greater number of languages to the family mix. Interestingly, as later chapters will reveal, in some circumstances trilingual and polyglot families in the study fostered additional languages to which they had no historical or geographic connection "simply" as a form of even greater linguistic enrichment, having committed to the multifaceted linguistic lives of their children already.

Defining Second Language

Throughout the book we frequently use the term *second language* or L2 to refer to a child's additional language but this term differs in meaning depending on the language acquisition circumstances of the child. Where we use L2 for some children, it may be arbitrary which language is considered their first and which their second, or third for that matter. Strict chronology may not be useful because a child may have been exposed to two or more languages from birth. Alternatively the language a child technically learned first may no longer be a language they speak regularly or at all. Rather than try to convey which language is learned first, greater proficiency in one language may be the reason some families refer to their child's languages as L1 and L2.

Where we can be more specific for individual families in the study, we make it clear whether a child is acquiring their family's *heritage language* as a first, second, or additional language (i.e., whether a child is undergoing a second language acquisition process rather than acquiring the heritage language as an L1). In other instances, children are acquiring an additional language with no familial-cultural ties to the language and for these cases we refer to the child's additional language simply as their L2. On occasion, it is clearer to refer to an additional language as the *target language* (especially when a number of different languages are in the family mix and we attempt to focus on one), and in others as the *majority language* when the L2 is the language spoken by the broader society (i.e., English in the United States) and in contrast with the child's L1 that is spoken by a linguistic minority community within the broader society.

Study Methods

In this section, we first explain our motives for the choice of research design and methods, and then describe the process of participant recruitment and the representativeness of the sample on a number of key factors. Next, we detail the data collection procedures and conclude with data coding and analytical approaches.

Choice of Methods

Our research included face-to-face and telephone semi structured interviews with parents, as well as individual and focus group discussions and semi structured interviews with educators to generate two corpora of data. These procedures were particularly effective not only for generating specific answers to our questions and related follow-up questions, but also for generating opportunities to gather personal narrative data from which to learn about the parents' and educators' lived experiences and their unique perspectives on multilingualism. Narratives can provide first-hand accounts of daily family routines and classroom events and activities, as well as the critical or "telling" experiences that can reveal the meaning-making processes, values, and beliefs of participants (e.g., Barth, 2003; Bruner, 1990). Several of these narratives are integrated into the presentation of the results in Chapters 5 and 6. Obviously, another research method, for example ethnography, for observing family practices or witnessing classroom discourse may have revealed different aspects of the multilingual experience such as students' experiences of their parents' and educators' efforts. We leave this, however, to future research.

Participant Recruitment and Representativeness

Two main types of recruitment were used: (1) purposeful selection through approaching our professional contacts for specific family and educator nominations, and (2) the participants' own nominations of additional families or educators. Recruitment was deliberately contained to 23 families and 13 educators once we met our goals for representativeness (see below) so we could focus on in-depth interviews and analyses. We had no shortage of people who, upon hearing about the study, wanted to take part. No one who we approached for recruitment refused participation. Eventually we had to inform interested potential participants and participants who had additional nominations that we had sufficient recruitment of families and educators. However, we found the latter phenomenon quite telling; it appeared that study participants had greatly valued the opportunity to overtly articulate their understandings and beliefs about children and multilingualism, sufficiently so that most spontaneously referred family and friends to the study.

The 23 participant families represented the wide range of multilingual circumstances under which children are being raised in the contemporary United States. We also aimed to have a wide variety of bilingual/multilingual family profiles based on the ways English was acquired by children in the family. We deliberately included families whose members speak Spanish, the numerically most prevalent language spoken in the United States after English, as well as additional widely spoken languages in the contemporary United States, such as Mandarin, Armenian, and Arabic. We also included families who have chosen to raise their children speaking languages that are no longer as commonly heard among minority groups in the United States but play a role in the global context (German, Russian, and French). Overall, these families provide us with a representation of children from the first year of life to adulthood, including children who were infants, toddlers, preschoolers, kindergarteners, and elementary, middle, and high school students, as well as young adults some beginning families of their own. We also included three families (four interviewees) who aspire to raise their future children as multilingual members of society.

A total of 13 educators took part in semi structured interviews and focus groups. When selecting participants we attempted to ensure that we had educators teaching in a variety of language program types, with students across grade levels (preschool through high school), and working in schools that featured diverse language profiles (e.g., English language learners, multiple different languages within and across their schools). The educators we studied have all encountered multilingual children in their classrooms. However, they were not necessarily the teachers of the participant families' children. In fact, just one educator participant had taught the two sons of one parent participant. Two educators taught in the same school where the daughter of another participant family was enrolled.

We deliberately uncoupled the selection of educators from the selection of families so we could meet the criteria of representativeness in the two samples. With participating educators, we particularly wanted to achieve broad representation of language program type. Moreover, as already mentioned, some of the families had no school-age children and thus no one for us to match educators to; either the children were still too young or they were already grown beyond the school-age years.

Specifically, the educators were selected to represent the following educational settings: within dual-language programming we had educators who taught in TWI programs in which approximately equal numbers of majority-language students (e.g., English-dominant speakers) acquire a partner language (e.g.,

Spanish or Mandarin) as an L2 and the partner-language students acquire English as an L2; one-way immersion programs in which all children are schooled entirely in an L2 (e.g., French for English-speaking students), and bilingual programs in which English language learners are taught content in their L1 (i.e., Spanish) to enable access to content while they are acquiring English. Within English-language programs: we include English language development/English-as-a-second-language (ELD/ESL) programs in which English language learners (sometimes with a variety of L1 backgrounds) are taught English collectively and general education classrooms that teach ELL students alongside their monolingual or English proficient peers. In addition, we included interviews with a heritage language after-school program director tutoring predominantly English language learners with Chinese-language backgrounds, and a school district ELL administrator who provided additional insights into the educational experiences of multilingual students in a developmental bilingual education program. In Chapter 6 we provide extensive discussion of the characteristics of the different language program types.

Data Collection Procedures and Instruments

Our research procedures included 16 in-person and 7 telephone semi structured interviews with parents (i.e., guided by the same schedule of questions with the freedom to ask follow-up questions based on responses). These interviews were conducted by one or both of the authors. The opportunity to conduct interviews in the dominant language of the parents was provided. One interview was conducted in Spanish by one of the authors, who is a Spanish-English bilingual and long-time bilingual high school teacher, with the additional assistance of an interpreter. Two interviews were conducted in Russian by the same author whose L1 is Russian and who is still a fluent Russian speaker. All non-English interviews were transcribed and translated by native speakers of Spanish and Russian into English for further analyses.

The interviews lasted between 40 and 90 minutes each. While 23 families participated, 26 parents were interviewed. That is, in three families, both parents wished to participate in the study. In our description of the findings in Chapter 5 sometimes there were "family-wide" practices and views and sometimes the parents within the same family had different views or a theme came up specific to one of the parents' responses.

We also conducted six individual semi structured interviews with educators lasting between 45 and 75 minutes, as well as two paired interviews lasting 53 and 90 minutes each, and one group interview comprising three educators, which lasted 100 minutes. These multi-participant interviews also had a discursive element between the participants that meant these particular sessions functioned as small focus groups with participants addressing each other or referring to each other's answers on occasion as well as answering the schedule of educator questions.

The interview schedules included questions organized by broad topics. In the case of parents these topics included: family background along with a description of the context within which multilingualism took root; the child(ren)'s multilingual language development; and the parents' beliefs about multilingualism (e.g., anticipated and actual benefits, investment of parental and family efforts and resources, aspects of multilingual upbringing perceived as rewarding and/or challenging). Further topics included family strategies and practices used for fostering multilingualism, individual and societal factors perceived as roadblocks to multilingual development, and maintenance of multilingual abilities. Finally, the interview schedules also addressed the topic of gaps in parents' knowledge of multilingual practices, parents' needs as they promote multilingualism, and the questions that families have posed throughout the journey of multilingual parenting (see Appendix A).

In the case of the educators, the questions were organized around teacher–student interactions within specific educational contexts (i.e., dual-language programs, ESL classrooms, etc.) and included: topics related to educators' beliefs about multilingualism (e.g., perceived benefits, values, and challenges); the challenges and rewards they encounter in their respective educational settings in terms of supporting the education of multilingual students; their understanding of and experience with multilingual language development trajectories; the strategies and practices that they found effective in fostering multilingualism; their suggestions to parents to foster student development; and their continuing needs as educators that might be best addressed by educational research and policy in the future (see Appendix B).

Coding and Analyses

The audio-recorded responses of each participant were transcribed by graduate student researchers and the authors to assist with later reading and coding of the data. These electronic transcript files were then used to log the different codes alongside corresponding verbatim responses. Throughout the coding process, we continued to listen to the audio-recorded responses in combination with transcripts so we could be sure to capture any affective nuances in tone of voice, such as sarcasm, annoyance, humor, or anything not to be taken literally.

We coded the data using a combination of *a priori* themes that we identified in the research literature and reviewed at length in Chapters 2 and 3, as well as adopting a grounded theory approach that involved "open-coding" the data for new ideas and information revealed by the participants (Strauss and Corbin,

1990). These additional codes were then applied across all the interviews thus establishing new themes that cut across the data.

In the case of the parents, *a priori* themes included parental beliefs about multilingualism; the notion of making an investment in multilingualism (using investment as both an extended metaphor for the emotional and future-oriented commitment to multilingualism by families and literally as a financial cost to implementing and sustaining multilingualism); different myths about multi-lingualism, the linguistic, academic, and cognitive benefits of multilingual-ism, the various obstacles to parental fostering of multilingualism; strategies and methods used within families during multilingual upbringing; and paren-tal motivation for multilingual practices. The parent interviews also yielded themes that extended the ones we found mentioned in the literature. The theme of motivation in parent participant responses appeared to be composed of two main categories of child-centered and parent-centered motives, with each cat-egory having numerous subtypes, some of which were well documented in literature (i.e., school and career readiness), while others were specific to our study (i.e., the theme of access to resources). (See Chapter 5, Table 5.8 for detailed examples of motivation subtypes.)

Additionally, the open-coding of participant interviews yielded themes that were entirely new, not as frequently noted in the reviewed literature, or spe-cific to the focus of our study. These included the theme of obstacles, which embraced subthemes of practical dilemmas of inter- and intra-family commu-nication and dynamics and time constraints, such notions as "parent sacrifice," "tradeoffs in raising multilingual children," and "uniqueness of multilingual children," as well as the theme of "advice" that parents wanted to provide to educators who are working with multilingual children and families like theirs. Appendix C provides the final coding scheme created for analysis of the parent interview data. In this appendix, we list the thematic categories or meta-themes (i.e., "Parental Beliefs about Multilingualism") that were mentioned in the lit-erature and those that emerged from our open-coding of the transcripts, along with the examples of subthemes or individual codes and excerpts from the participant interviews.

The themes that were identified in the literature on educators and multilin-gualism were also systematically coded in the transcribed data. These themes included beliefs that multilingualism can be an aid to academic learning, has a positive impact on social development, and has a role in the home, local com-munity/culture, and wider U.S. society. In addition, themes about challenges and rewards encountered in the respective programs (i.e., difficulties with and benefits to children, parents, and administrators), issues with educational resources, and instructional strategies and practices that foster the growth of multilingualism were noted (See Appendix D).

The open-coding phase of reading educator transcripts revealed themes in the interviews and small-scale focus group discussions that had not necessarily been anticipated before the study. The themes generated by the educator data included concerns with "instability" of different elements within instructional programs, and the notion of "isolation" that the educators could apply, either to themselves, feeling distant from other educators, or could apply to their students who were perceived to be socially isolated from their frequently monolingual, English-speaking peers.

Using axial coding, we noted how the themes in the transcripts were related (i.e., if certain themes were antecedent to others or subcategories of a more common theme) (Strauss and Corbin, 1990). Collectively, these procedures allowed us to generate new hypotheses of how both parents and educators perceive multilingualism to supplement the notion of investment already suggested by the literature.

All transcripts were also read for information directly answering questions on the parent and educator interview schedules. These responses were used not only in the report of the main findings in Chapters 5 and 6 but also to illustrate myths held by parents and educators about multilingual development and education already reported in Chapter 3. Due to the informal semi-structured nature of the interviews, participants often brought up additional details in their narratives. For example, all prospective parents in our study provided thorough descriptions of their own childhood and their own parents' strategies for raising them multilingually. These stories were combined into a category of "Portraits of Multilingual Children." Another common deviation from the course of the interview schedule was when parents and educators provided stories (whether similar or contrasting) about other families' and educators' experiences. Key content was extracted from such digressions as well.

Once the interviews were coded and interrelated themes were established, the interviews underwent one last review to identify participants' quotes that could illustrate the generalizations derived from the thematic analysis. For example, additional analysis was performed to select vignettes used to introduce the families in Chapter 5. For this selection, the participants were grouped into four distinct groups based on the parents' own language skill sets: English-dominant parents (n=3), Non-English-dominant parents (n=3), Bilingual parents (n=13) and Multilingual parents (n=7). Within each group, we selected contrasting cases that complemented each other. (For a more detailed discussion of parents' and family profiles refer to Chapter 5). Additionally, high-contrast cases and "telling" cases among the families were selected to illustrate prominent themes in greater detail in Chapter 5. In Chapter 6, the educators' experiences are primarily organized around discussion of the different types of language program.

The self-reported data in the individual interviews and small-scale focus groups were informally triangulated in the following ways: In a few cases, we interviewed several members or multiple generations of the families: husbands and wives who reflected on each other's opinions, grown children whose parents had aimed to raise them multilingually and who are now either working in multilingual settings using linguistic skills they acquired through their families' efforts, or are themselves prospective multilingual parents. Having access to additional family members allowed us to compare and contrast narratives of multilingualism within the same family. We used the advantage of availability of adult children in some instances to hear their perspectives on the outcomes of their upbringing, and thus we were able to gauge some parents' reported success of raising their children multilingually. Similarly, we were able to compare and contrast the experiences of different educators where we interviewed educators from the same programs, either individually or during the small-scale focus groups. We also had a chance to interview educators who were administrators in these programs. While our sample of educators is small, such overlap among participants allowed us to gather multiple perspectives on key educational programs as well.

The Families

The sample of 26 parent participants representing 23 families included 20 mothers and 6 fathers of multilingual children (See Table 4.1). Two female and two male participants were prospective parents (i.e., individuals who volunteered to participate in the study due to the fact that they were planning to raise their expectant or prospective future children multilingually). It is important to make a distinction here between family, parent, and child language profiles. The majority of parents spoke either the same two languages (i.e., Spanish and English, Russian and English), or one of the parents was a monolingual English speaker and the other one was bilingual. For the purposes of the study, in all the cases described above, the families as a household were categorized as being bilingual. There were even initial monolingual household environments in which either English or a language other than English (LOTE) was the only language and the environments became bilingual over time as the children added an L2. There were also cases in which each parent spoke their own native language and English, thus creating a trilingual family environment for children. One last family profile was created if each parent spoke a different set or pair of languages (i.e., French-Russian-English and Spanish-English). In such cases, the family profiles were coded as polyglot because the children were exposed to more than three languages.

The assortment of languages represented by parent participants included 14 different languages which were strategically selected to represent languages frequently spoken within U.S. multilingual families. The majority of parents spoke Spanish (n=9), other languages included Mandarin, Korean, German, Russian, French, Portuguese, Farsi, Hindi, Bengali, Armenian, Arabic, Italian, and Japanese. An indication of the socioeconomic status of the families can be gauged by the parents' educational levels and occupations. In the majority of families (n=13) parents had an undergraduate degree and a professional occupation. In an additional seven families, the parents had a graduate degree and a professional occupation, and three families had parents with a high school or lower education and a manual occupation. (See Appendix E for further details of the parent occupations represented in the sample).

The age range of children within the families was another factor that we considered when sampling. Within the 23 sample families, there were 6 infants/toddlers, 6 preschool-aged children, 6 elementary school children, 2 children of middle school age, 6 high school children, and 13 adult children. The majority of the 39 children were school-aged, which was important for our study that aimed to examine the schooling experiences of multilingual children, among many other factors. Seven out of 23 families reported having a child with special needs. The range of disabilities (in a few cases co-morbid) included speech/language delay (n=3), visual impairments (n=1), ASD (n=3), behavioral challenges (n=1), and intellectual disabilities (n=1).

Parent interviews were also coded for the level of perceived success with multilingual practices (i.e., their responses to questions about achieving their goal of raising multilingual children). Three categories of perceived success in fostering multilingualism (high, medium, and low) were established. The codes that described levels of success included codes of "fluency," "confidence," and "comfort," as well as "bilingual," "biliterate," "multilingual," and "multiliterate," combined with markers of "completely," "not at all," "somewhat," and "in certain contexts." The majority of parents (n=11) perceived that their multilingual efforts were highly successful, while six and five parents evaluated their success as medium and low, respectively. Four paticipants (in three families) were not applicable for this and other characterizations of children because they were still prospective parents. Finally, we coded the context/sequence in which English and other languages were acquired by children in the participants' families. For the majority of families (n=14), English was not the L1 of their children, rather English was acquired as either a second language in the United States or children began acquisition of English outside of the United States as a foreign language. Just one family had English as L1 initially with parents who were monolingual English speakers at the time their children were born. In five families, children were exposed to multiple languages from birth.

We also documented in the interviews the number of children whose reported experiences served as a basis of our analyses. We first calculated the numbers of specific or "named" children (n=113) who were mentioned

Table 4.1 *Summary of the parent participants' personal and family profiles*

Participant's role (n=26)	Family language profile (n=23)	Home languages (in addition to English)	Parent education and occupation (n=26)	Age groupings of children (n=39)	Families with children with special needs	Parent's perception of success in multilingualism (n=26)	Family context of children's English acquisition (n=23)
Mother n=20	Bilingual* n=17	Spanish n=9	Undergraduate degree/ professional occupation n=13	Infants/ toddlers (6–36 mos) n=6	Children with special needs n=7	N/A n=4	ESL n=11
Father n=6	Trilingual n=3	Mandarin n=2	Graduate degree/ professional occupation n=7	Preschool (<5 yrs) n=6		High n=11	EFL n=3
	Polyglot (4 or more languages) n=3	Korean n=2	High school or lower/manual occupation n=3	Elementary (5–10 yrs) n=7		Medium n=6	English and other language(s) from birth n=5
		German n=3		Middle (11–13 yrs) n=2		Low n=5	English L1 n=1
		Russian n=4		High school (14–18 yrs) n=6			N/A n=3
		French n=1		Adults (18+yrs) n=13			
		Portuguese n=2					
		Farsi n=1					
		Hindi n=1					
		Bengali n=1					
		Armenian n=1					
		Arabic n=1					
		Italian n=1					
		Japanese n=1					

* Including initially monolingual in English (n=1) or in a language other than English (n=1); N/A: Not applicable for prospective families.

in the interviews (these were either the children of the parent participants or other children who were named and/or whose detailed stories the participants chose to include, e.g., "Really paying attention to Beatriz's language development, I am just seeing how much more English words she has"). We also calculated the number of "generic" children (n=52). These children did not have a name or a detailed story connected to them, but they were mentioned within the context of parents' making a particular point (e.g., "A lot of kids speaking Spanish," "A classmate"). We took note of groups of children mentioned by parents (n=78) (e.g., "The multilingual children ..."), and of all the languages that parents mentioned in their interviews (n=21). Table 4.2 illustrates the results of this analysis of the parent interview transcripts. The mere count of the children within the interviews inspired us to recognize the cumulative magnitude of the personal narratives represented in this book. Behind 26 parent narratives (and similarly behind the 13 educator narratives) are the life stories of several hundred different children who are growing up multilingually.

The Educators

The 13 educators were generous with their time and courageous with their willingness to talk about the challenges as well as the rewards of teaching multilingual students. They have a myriad of teaching experiences, and language experience and exposure especially. The seven women and six men in the study held a number of different roles. Six educators were current classroom teachers, four were ESL specialists, and one was a classroom teacher also currently involved in graduate research. One educator was the ELL program administrator for a school district and one was an after-school program tutor and director (See Table 4.3). In terms of the grades they taught in, five educators had elementary level teaching experience, six had middle school level experience, and four had high school level experience. In addition, two classroom teachers had experience with pre-kindergarten teaching as well as teaching at either the elementary or middle-school level. Finally, one educator had experience across the full range of the K-12 educational system.

Three educators in the study spoke English only but nevertheless taught multilingual students. Importantly, one of these educators spoke of being the parent to two children who have Latino heritage through his wife and are exposed to Spanish. Five of the educators taught multilingual students and were multilingual themselves. Beyond English they also spoke Spanish, Mandarin/Taiwanese, French, and German, and one educator spoke two African languages (Pulaar, spoken in Senegal, and Kinyarwanda, spoken in Rwanda) in addition to French, Spanish, and English. A further five educators taught multilingual students and were not only multilingual themselves but were also the

Table 4.2 *Number and languages of children mentioned by participating parents (n=26)*

Name of parent	Individually named children	Generic references to child(ren)	Specific groups (e.g., "bilingual children," "third culture children")	Languages spoken by children in parent interviews
Linda	3	0	2	Spanish, English, French
Monica	3	0	2	Spanish, English
Betty	7	1	2	Spanish, English
Kevin	3	1	1	English, Spanish
Nora	4	1	2	Spanish, English
Bianca	4	1	3	English, Chinese, Spanish, French
Lilian	3	2	5	Spanish, English
Miko	3	3	2	Spanish, English
Dulce	1	3	3	Spanish, English
Veronica	2	3	4	English, German, Hebrew, Tagalog
Nicole	4	2	2	German, English, Farsi, Russian
Tina	3	0	3	Mandarin, Taiwanese, American Sign Language, English, Spanish
Kelly	5	2	2	Russian, Ukrainian, English, Cantonese, Spanish
Kimberly	6	10	3	Korean, English, Spanish, Mandarin
Ghodrat	2	2	3	Farsi, English, Latin
Hediyeh	5	2	4	Farsi, English
Sonia	5	2	3	Russian, English, French
Larisa	5	2	4	Russian, English
Leonid	7	0	3	Russian, English, French, Spanish
Mayda	7	2	3	Armenian, English, Arabic
Danielle	4	0	2	English, French, Russian, Italian, Spanish
Ultan	6	4	5	English, French, Russian, Italian, Spanish
Tricia	7	2	3	Portuguese, English, French, German
Taani	2	2	4	English, Hindi, Spanish, Bengali
Victor	4	3	4	Japanese, English, Spanish, Korean, Russian, Latin
Tilda	8	2	4	Swedish, English, Portuguese, Spanish, Mandarin, French
Totals:	**113**	**52**	**78**	21 different languages

Table 4.3 *Background information on participating educators and their programs (n=13)*

Name of educator	Role	Program type and languages	Grade level experience	Languages spoken by participants	Parenting multilingual children
Paola	Classroom teacher	TWI: Spanish-English	Elementary	Spanish/English	Yes
Alejandro	Classroom teacher	TWI: Spanish-English	Elementary	Spanish/English	Yes
Sarah	Science researcher/ classroom teacher	TWI: Spanish-English	Elementary–middle	English	No
Sandra	Classroom teacher	One-way immersion: French	Pre-kindergarten–elementary	French/English	No
Jake	Director and tutor	Heritage language program: Mandarin-English	Elementary	Mandarin/Taiwanese/ English	Yes
Pablo	Classroom teacher	Dual-language: Spanish-English	Middle	Spanish/English	No
Emily	Classroom teacher	Dual-language: Spanish-English	High school	Spanish/English	No
Gael	District administrator	Dual-language: Spanish-English	Elementary–high	Spanish/English	No
Melanie	ESL specialist	ELD	Pre-kindergarten–middle	Spanish/English/ French/Pulaar/ Kinyarwanda	No
Camila	ESL specialist	ELD	Middle	Spanish/English/ German	Yes
Elena	ESL specialist	ELD	Middle–high	Spanish/English	Yes
David	ESL specialist	ESL*	High	English	No
Thomas	Classroom teacher	General education: history and government	Middle–high	English	No

* ESL is the term participants used in the high school setting for English-language instruction rather than ELD.

Table 4.4 *Number and languages of students mentioned by participating educators (n=13)*

Name of educator	Individual named students	Generic references to student(s)	Specific student groups (e.g., "bilingual students" "eighth graders")	First languages spoken by students in teacher interviews
Paola	5	7	21	Spanish, English, Hindi, Farsi, French, Japanese, Chinese (not specified)
Alejandro	10	1	4	Spanish, English, French, Dutch, Hindi, Korean, Mandarin, Farsi
Sarah	3	2	5	Spanish, English
Sandra	5	4	5	French, English, Korean, Russian, Arabic, Spanish
Jake	7	9	12	Mandarin, Cantonese, Taiwanese, Vietnamese, English
Pablo	0	1	3	Spanish, English
Emily	0	1	6	Spanish, English
Gael	1	6	8	Spanish, English
Melanie	8	2	4	Spanish, Sri Lankan, (others not specified)
Camila	8	10	9	Spanish, Tagalog, French, Georgian, Arabic, Mandarin, Korean, Hindi
Elena	5	4	4	Spanish, Chinese (not specified), Korean, Farsi, Sri Lankan, East Indian language (not specified)
David	15	1	2	Spanish, Chinese (not specified), Korean
Thomas	8	18	6	Spanish, Turkish, Arabic, Armenian, Pashto
Totals:	**68**	**48**	**83**	**22** different languages

parents of children who spoke English and at least one additional language (Spanish, Mandarin/Taiwanese, or Spanish/German).

As with the sample of families, we also documented the number of children mentioned during the educators' interviews in order to get a sense of on whom the educators based their responses. Again, we calculated the numbers of specific "named" students (n=68) mentioned in the interviews (these were students whose detailed stories and experiences the educators included and were introduced by name, e.g., "I knew this kid Kyle"). There were 48 "generic students" who did not have a name or a story connected to them, but were mentioned within the context of educators' making a particular point (e.g., "A student who comes in with more than one language"). We also noted the different groups of students mentioned by educators (n=83) (e.g., "They were kids who wanted to get to college."), and the number of different languages that educators reported the students spoke (n=22). Table 4.4 illustrates the results of this analysis with the transcripts of the educators' interviews.

With a sense of who the participants were in terms of their first-hand experiences with raising and educating multilingual children, as well as how we went about extracting meaning from their interviews, we now move to reporting the findings. In the next chapter, we provide the results of our analyses that help to illuminate the beliefs and practices of individual families, as well as report common themes that emerged across families raising children in very different contexts.

5   Raising Multilingual Children: One Family at a Time

In this chapter, we turn to the findings generated by the parent participants' interviews. We begin with a brief description of the sample and showcase select families in order to give the reader a better sense of the individual families, their multilingual contexts, and how the participants viewed multilingualism and their children's language abilities. We then examine the participants' beliefs regarding multilingualism and the wide and complex range of motivations that propel parents to foster multilingualism. The metaphor of investment that we found in the interviews is revealed as an integral yet many-faceted component of the multilingual child-rearing experience. We conclude with the challenges and successes experienced by the families in the process of raising a child who speaks more than one language.

Pathways to Multilingualism

The 23 families who participated in the study presented us with a range of parental multilingual abilities and a kaleidoscope of narratives of how multilingualism and multilingual practices developed within their families. Figure 5.1 presents a continuum of the sample families' multilingual contexts by the number of languages they were able to foster in their children. Some of the parents and children had initially begun their family lives together as either English-only speaking or speaking only a minority language, and later on they had added an additional language to the mix: a language other than English (LOTE) for the English-only family, and English for the three families with a LOTE as their home language.

The largest number of families in the study were living in bilingual contexts with the additional language provided by one (n=2) or both parents (n=11). A small number of families were raising children in trilingual homes and in some cases children were raised in contexts where they were regularly getting exposure to four or more languages.

Thus, even though the number of families who took part in our study was relatively small (n=23), it represents a fairly diverse range of multilingual contexts. The linguistic capital (total number of languages spoken around the child) in many families was not simply equal to the languages spoken by

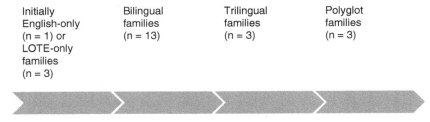

| Initially English-only (n = 1) or LOTE-only families (n = 3) | Bilingual families (n = 13) | Trilingual families (n = 3) | Polyglot families (n = 3) |

Figure 5.1 Continuum of multilingual contexts within participating families (n=23)

the parent (or parents) we interviewed. Instead, any given family's linguistic capital was a combination of languages that both parents' spoke, and, in some families, this combination was supplemented by languages spoken by the children's caretakers, household helpers, extended family, and teachers from daycare through high school.

The roads that the participant families took toward multilingualism also differed greatly. Over two-thirds of the participants knew that their children would be growing up multilingually even before the children were born. Others did not plan on it at all, but the life changes that the family experienced (e.g., parents temporarily obtained jobs in other countries or the family had to relocate to a different country) or the meaningful encounters throughout the parents' lives (e.g., inspirational experiences of friends raising their children multilingually, advice received from professionals, etc.) altered the course of the children's upbringing, brought in new linguistic experiences, and at times changed the language(s) spoken within the family. Another way of categorizing the data is by initial language dominance of parents. In this process of categorizing the range of our participants' language abilities, we clearly see four distinct groups of parents within the study's sample: 1) Initial English-dominant parents who have managed to raise bi- or multilingual children due to new circumstances in their lives, 2) non-English-dominant parents who did not plan to teach their children English (and other languages) but faced this necessity as they relocated to an English-speaking environment, 3) bilingual parents who are raising their children bi- or multilingually, and 4) multilingual parents who are fostering multilingualism in their families.

Showcasing Families

We now turn to specific families who shared how they decided to raise their children bi- or multilingually. This section aims to examine the different contexts in which multilingualism emerges and takes root. Below, we showcase two families from each of the distinct parent subgroups just identified. We purposefully chose, if not contrasting, then at least diverse narratives to display the plethora of contexts in which multilingualism is being fostered even if the families' linguistic profiles may seem similar. Other families' experiences are highlighted throughout the chapter.

English-dominant Parent Participants: Betty and Victor

There were three English-dominant parent participants in our sample. Among the three was Betty, who, while she had learned some Spanish in school, did not raise children bilingually until she could rely on a bilingual household assistant; Kelly, a prospective mother, whose in-laws speak Taiwanese and Mandarin, and who planned to have them spend most of the time with the baby she was expecting at the time of the interview; and Victor, a father of two multilingual teenage daughters, whose wife speaks Japanese and learned English while their daughters were growing up. Despite the difference of contexts, there were also convergent patterns in their beliefs and values. These parents did not take on the full responsibility for the children's language acquisition. They also firmly believed in the benefits of multilingualism and saw it as an attainable goal. These parents saw multilingualism as a product of joint efforts of the immediate and extended families and speakers of other languages who came into contact with the family. With this in mind, we now turn to the narratives of Betty and Victor to showcase development of multilingualism in two very different families where one or both parents were English-dominant.

My younger son is not bilingual but he is pretty competent in Spanish and he did speak Spanish when he was young. (Betty, a mother of four adult children, two of whom continue to use Spanish in their daily lives)

As mentioned in Chapter 3, in Betty's experience a circumstantial, seemingly random trigger changed the language spoken within her initially monolingual "WASP-y" (Betty's terminology) family and resulted not only in some of Betty's children having strong Spanish skills, but also in their continuing the bilingual tradition through the upbringing of Betty's grandchildren. Once a monolingual English-speaking household, Betty's is now a blended family with varying but extensive contacts with bilingualism. In her interview, Betty, provided a detailed account of how the multilingual practices came about in her household when the youngest of her four children was still a toddler. She related the following:

My younger son Kevin ... had a babysitter who started when he was 2–3 months old and was with him continually while I worked until he finished kindergarten. When he was about three months old, I took her with me when we went to see the pediatrician.... the pediatrician when we finished the exam looked at her and he said, "Well, do you speak any language other than English?" And she said, "Why yes, I speak Spanish because my mother only spoke Spanish, and my father only spoke English, so I learned to speak both." So my pediatrician said, "Why don't you speak Spanish to this child? Just Spanish." So that is how it started. I didn't even do it! And it was really nervy of the pediatrician, don't you think?! ... So I thought it was a good idea. I have studied it in graduate school, language development and bilingualism and all that, so I knew if she only spoke Spanish to my son that would be really good for my child. So I agreed and then after we started, she said, "Well, if I am going to speak Spanish to him, you can only speak Spanish to me when you are around because we have to always speak Spanish." So then I had to get better [at] Spanish ... I had some Spanish already ... So anyway, I was enthusiastic about it. She made me speak Spanish. She corrected my Spanish. I studied Spanish more, and he spoke only Spanish with her through kindergarten. Then I spoke Spanish with him too ...

Several mechanisms that allowed multilingualism to flourish in an initially monolingual family are illustrated in Betty's narrative. First, we should not underestimate the effect of the "expert opinion" in the jump start of the multilingual upbringing. Betty's pediatrician was the catalyst that propelled the family into exploring multilingualism. In this book, we have addressed the power that experts (pediatricians, speech and language pathologists, teachers, etc.) have over families contemplating or pursuing multilingualism (see Chapter 3). In Betty's case, an expert's opinion created a favorable impetus for their multilingual venture. Second, Betty's story illustrates that at times it is not always the parent who introduces the child to additional language(s) and carries on multilingual practices. In our study, over one-fifth of parent participants talked about the influence of their children's babysitters, housekeepers, and other household members on language development. These individuals brought an extra language into the child's linguistic repertoire. With the support of others, even initially monolingual parents can foster multilingualism in their homes. Third, Betty's success in raising her son bilingually had probably a lot to do with her own commitment and enthusiasm about developing Spanish as an additional language in her household. As Betty's son's babysitter compelled her to speak and study Spanish, Betty became a model of an enthusiastic bilingual language learner for her son, whose language success in turn served as positive reinforcement for Betty to continue multilingual practices in her household. Finally, as one more critical point in Betty's story: her son continued to use Spanish in later life:

[He] went to a school where they only taught in English and all the kids spoke English until high school, when he took Spanish. And then he took some Spanish in college, and then he got a job being a nurse where a high proportion of the patients spoke Spanish. So he went back to using it and it turned out that he could converse with them, and people used him as a translator ...

While we do not know for sure what led to this commitment to Spanish on Kevin's part, we hypothesize that he saw Spanish used by his babysitter as part of her job, as well as by his mother who found it a beneficial tool, which likely contributed to his fondness for Spanish as a useful language that also became part of his linguistic identity and his own professional life.⁕

Turning now to Victor, he told us:

My oldest, Sakina, is 14 years … My youngest, Emma, is 12 years old … My wife Rehiko, she is Japanese. Born and raised in Japan, so the children converse with her … not at a fluent level, but they understand a lot of what they're saying. But they will generally respond in English to Rehiko in the household. I speak very, very, very little [Japanese]. So the predominant language in our family is English … (Victor, a father of two teenage daughters, raising them within a Japanese-English bilingual household)

In addition to Japanese and English, Victor is adding additional languages to his daughters' linguistic repertoire through school and tutors. As a pastor who works with numerous multilingual parishioners, Victor witnessed multilingual-ism in action in his work environment as well as at home and recognized its benefits and values. Victor's story offers a scenario of raising children multilin-gually that is different from Betty's. Another parent from the subgroup of par-ents who see themselves as (initially) monolingual rather than multilingual, he reported studying a few languages, such as Spanish, Italian, and Korean, some time ago. The longest engagement with a language was his study of Spanish: "I took two years of Spanish, and I grew up in Los Angeles, so you kind of by osmosis […] know Spanish." Victor's wife, Rehiko, is Japanese. She grew up in Japan and took some English courses while attending a school there, but learned most of her English when she married Victor and moved to the United States. The family has two daughters, Sakina and Emma, who are growing up multilingually, speaking three languages on a regular basis (English, Japanese, and Spanish). They also have studied three more languages for several years (Russian, Korean, and Latin). Having heard about a father who considered himself a monolingual English speaker, but whose daughters were multilingual and planned on learning more languages, we met with Victor for an interview, in which he told us about the multilingual practices within his family and his perspectives on multilingualism:

I actually … speak very, very, very little [Japanese]. So the predominant language in our family is English. I would say between mother and child, it's 80% English. So it means mom is adapting to English because she learned English when she met me … But still there's about, I would say, about 20% between mother and daughter where she's really trying to make a point and really teaching, she'll use her native language to explain concepts. The Japanese part is all in [my wife's] control. I honestly had hoped that they would speak more. But she chose to be more dominant in English and in a way sacrifice herself … for the sake of just family cohesion. And … I appreciated Rehiko where I can be part of the mother-daughter stuff.

[The daughters] do not speak Japanese to each other. [But] my wife reports [that they] both understand what she's saying … My eldest will come back in English, but probably knows how to come back in Japanese, but doesn't ... My youngest though ... maybe half of the time will come back in Japanese, will reciprocate.... I think a lot of it is just her personality. She's just ... more comfortable in her own skin naturally. And I think that the other one is more sensitive and [...] maybe wants to say the right words so she picks [carefully], you know [...]. I think the pattern that I just described about how they respond back and whatnot is fairly consistent since early years. I would say maybe [since] age 4 or 5, really.

As my kids have developed in English, they have [come to] understand their mother's limitations in English. So they're able to adjust themselves to mom's understanding of English. And adjust to say concepts differently. Where they understand a certain concept, they have to say it a certain way or choose certain words to break it down to a simpler structure, where they'll get it all the time. They're very understanding of mom.

While Rehiko was responsible for the two main languages that the girls speak at home, Victor's philosophy was the driving force behind their learning of additional languages:

... if they're gonna be world citizens, they need to understand the world. And they can't understand every language, but they need to be, think beyond their own context ... if you look at the world that way, what practical things can I do to help my kids?... In our family we just kind of chose languages as a way to break open that door, that, and it's not multilingual, it's not like multicultural, it's almost a common culture of a connection ... So I had a very practical motive. I think what happened when they did Spanish, Latin, Japanese, in my mind, maybe 5 years ago, I made a list. I made a list of languages that I had prayed that they would take an interest in ... I knew that French was an international language. I knew Italian was near Spanish, so that could be easy ... Russian I picked because we knew [the girls' tutor who speaks Russian]. And then Mandarin I put on the list because, just its overall practicality. [And] you have to use the resources you have, from my experience. From friends, from a shared passion, some fit, some kind of natural fit ... because with kids you can only present choices where they really have some exposure to ... [and there has to be] a love for something. So trying to piggyback on a passion, on a love. And the love can be anime, it could be people they know, it could be, you know, somebody's grandma they love and they like to, you know there could be any hook.

Out of Victor's list, his daughters first picked Russian because they loved their multilingual tutor who had helped them earlier to become proficient in Spanish and then taught them Russian. They also planned to take Japanese once they entered high school.

In our sample, Victor also represents a group of parents whose spouses spoke a language they did not share. Several themes found in this group emerged in Victor's narrative. Like Victor, a number of initial monolingual parents recalled learning languages other than English, but not the language that their spouse spoke. However, language learning experiences for them were usually a familiar and positive memory that left them wanting to learn additional languages.

Although not speaking the language spoken by their spouses, the monolingual parents were devoted to promoting multilingualism within their homes. Similar to Victor, monolingual parents within multilingual households appeared to be just as enthusiastic about teaching their children additional languages and frequently expressed the wish that their L2-savvy spouses would do even more in terms of children's language development. Without the knowledge of the spouse's language, monolingual parents could not help teach their children first-hand. Their commitment to multilingualism took the form of trust and gratitude for the spouse's efforts. They also reported often sacrificing complete understanding of the conversations within their home in the name of multilingualism.

Betty and Victor's narratives show the contexts of children's multilingual upbringing by English-dominant parents. The contexts in focus present two different scenarios for fostering multilingual practices. Betty designated a focal person, Kevin's babysitter, as a Spanish language/bilingual model for her son. She also took the responsibility for developing bilingualism in her family into her own hands, learning along with Kevin and in a way modeling language acquisition for him, and creating a Spanish-speaking environment within her home. Victor, on the other hand, put the responsibility of speaking languages other than English onto others: his spouse, tutors, and foreign language teachers at his daughters' school. However, through his respect and enthusiasm toward languages and for multilingual speakers, he managed to ignite in his daughters a similar interest and commitment to learning other tongues. A lesson learned from Betty and Victor's stories is that even monolingual or English-dominant parents can find ways to foster multilingualism.

Non-English Dominant Parent Participants: Sonia and Dulce

Our collection of multilingual family portraits would not be complete if we did not take a closer look at the group of non-English dominant parents who spoke the language of home almost exclusively. These were the parents who emigrated from their countries of origin to the United States as adults, and whose English skills were significantly less well developed than their L1 skills. Despite having different paths that led them to the United States, from scientists who obtained a green card (documentation for legal residency) to lower skilled workers who emigrated to provide safety and a better future for their children, they are all determined to preserve their family language, at the same time wanting their children to succeed in English. Among a few families in our sample that were primarily monolingual, we chose to spotlight the two families of Sonia and Dulce, two mothers raising their sons multilingually despite their own unfamiliarity with English.

When I go back to Russia, mothers of Alex's peers ask me in disbelief, "Does he speak perfect English?" and I say, "Of course! He went to school there." They want to know if he speaks English better than I do. And I say, "Of course! He writes essays in English, and I do not think I could do that." [Translated from Russian] (Sonia, the Russian-dominant mother of 25-year-old Alex, initially an English language learner)

Sonia's family relocated to the United States when her husband, Sergey, was hired by one of the American universities. Political and economic changes in Sonia's home country in the 1990s that allowed this move were so sudden that the family did not have enough time to learn English. Their son, Alex, a sixth grader at the time, knew more English than his parents:

While we lived in Russia, we spoke only Russian in our family ... Sergey and I knew some French, but did not know a word of English. Not a word ... This is why it was so stressful when we came to U.S. In Russia, Alex studied English. Just at a regular school. So he started in 4th grade. But when Sergey left for America, I understood that we will also leave in about 6 months, that's when I hired a tutor. [When we got here, Alex] went to middle school. [Translated from Russian]

Sonia's story is typical for many families in which parents come to the United States without knowing English. The children in immigrant families are often the first and only ones who have some ability to communicate in the new language. However, the stress and anxiety felt by parents are often experienced by children:

[That year my] main priorities [were] to conquer the fear. We had a lot of fear. Alex was afraid. I still remember meeting him when he got back from school that day. A yellow school bus brought him back. He would get out from the bus and be very, very quiet and not say anything. I tried to talk with him, but he would not talk. This was going on for a month or two. It was clear that he was extremely stressed, but he could not, would not tell me. I think it was too hard for him. So hard and stressful that he would not talk about it. He was only 12 years old, even 11 at first ... and the situation was unfamiliar to him ... He was like an astronaut with nowhere to go. So he had to stick with it. This lasted two months. [Translated from Russian]

In the excerpt above, Sonia's interview introduces the new theme of loneliness experienced by some children whose heritage language is not only different from the majority language of wider society but is also a minority language within the languages spoken by other children in ESL classrooms. This nuance is important for educators to recognize, as the children who come from a relatively uncommon language background might be an especially vulnerable population of students. In her interview, Sonia put a lot of emphasis on the emotional strain that getting used to a new country and a new educational system has put on the family:

He was put in just regular ESL classes ... He never left ESL [until he graduated from high school] ... Everyone knew [his first language was Russian]. I never came across any negative reactions. All teachers stressed their subject and that was all that mattered to them. They did not care what languages he spoke …

[In high school] Alex was taking courses in absentia at one of the Russian universities in Moscow. He took courses there for 9–11th grade…. He liked it. [At that time] we lived knowing that we are going back. So we could not afford for him to lose his first language. [Translated from Russian]

The above excerpt from Sonia's interview illustrates themes common for the non-English dominant parents in our sample of participants. The theme of stress of their children not understanding aspects of life around them and in school stands out in Sonia's narrative. This theme was common for many parents who were not born and raised in the United States. While many of the children of our participants attended school not able to speak English, the stress parents felt over it was far more pronounced among parents who could not easily navigate the unfamiliar school system. Parents also spoke of their children's stress. Just as Tricia's young children did not speak for a while after beginning preschool, 11-year-old Alex went through a period of silence where he could not tell his parents about his time at school. While Sonia supposed that he did not want to upset her, we can hypothesize that Alex was going through the period of adjustment to a new environment. A third theme in Sonia's story that echoes the narratives of other parents who did not speak English well was the theme of investing in the child's acquisition of English through tutors, after-school programs, or through other means, despite not having time or financial means to learn English themselves. The final theme that we found was the parent's perception of home-school connection. In Sonia's opinion, Alex's teachers never gave special attention to his heritage language. Parents in our sample had very different perspectives on this issue that are discussed later in more detail. We now turn to Dulce, who is raising a much younger son. In her narrative we find themes similar to those of Sonia but also other themes that are particular to Dulce and her situation.

. . . It is necessary for him to learn both languages; Spanish for me and English for the outside world. [Translated from Spanish] (Dulce, the Spanish-dominant mother of 4-year-old José)

Dulce is a single mother from El Salvador. She arrived to the United States before José was born. While in her home country Dulce worked with preschool-aged children. She works hard on making sure that José masters English. She not only takes him to preschool and tries to do all his homework with him, she also takes him to speech and language sessions, as she worries about his phonological skills. Raising José bilingually is a high priority for Dulce,

I only have one [son]. He is four years old. His name is José. He just started school last year and there he began to speak English. He began to be multilingual when he was three. At school they only speak English. His teacher is Chinese and he has also gotten a lot of it from television. [Translated from Spanish]

Describing José's linguistic experiences, Dulce told us that José and she speak "entirely Spanish at home." When asked whether José has any exposure to other bilingual role models, Dulce responded that there were some multilingual members in her family, but they were outside her home:

DULCE: They are my cousins, my siblings. They live here in America, in Los Angeles. We see my cousins every day at church, except for Mondays. Sometimes we go out for dinner or sometimes we stay a while and chat at the church.
ANNA: Do you speak Spanish at church?
DULCE: Spanish, yes, but with children his own age ... It's good because perhaps in the future I will return to my country, El Salvador, and it will be good for him since he'll have more work opportunities in the future with both English and Spanish, two languages. Since I was pregnant I would have him listen to music in Spanish and English so that he would start listening not only to Spanish but also to English, since during my pregnancy I was alone. [Translated from Spanish]

When asked why she decided to raise José bilingually, Dulce pointed out that "the language that is most spoken here is English." She saw the following benefits in learning English:

Firstly, for ... work. Secondly, it helps him a great deal for communication and for socialization above all because in this country we can't just spend time with our peers from our native country. There are many other people that you can build relationships with, and it is necessary to go shopping, to go eat, even at a hospital. Therefore, it is very important. [Translated from Spanish]

Besides emphasizing importance of English and her efforts to make sure that José is successful in his learning, Dulce focused on José's educational experiences. One of the themes that emerged from her narrative was the theme of uneasiness felt by a parent when unable to help a child navigate the unfamiliar routines of school. While English-only instruction was definitely her first choice, Dulce felt both satisfaction that José was becoming more advanced than she was in English as well as frustration over her own inadequate English skills. She recalled that when José went to school, "... he got confused" because all of the communication at his school "was completely in English":

He got confused and he would say, "Mama, the teacher babababa. Mami, they aydadadada ... he would make fun." In other words, he did not understand what he would hear and he would tell me, "Mama, I don't understand." He would say, "Mama, the teacher sang something and she would say, what would she say?" [Translated from Spanish]

Despite José's frustration and Dulce's feeling of being unable to help him, she was adamant that English-only instruction was the best approach to teaching José even though we poignantly learn from her narrative that this has led over time to difficulties in communication between them:

DULCE: There was no choice, but if they had asked me, I would have decided on English. English, because at home there is only Spanish; it's only Spanish. So I couldn't decide for Spanish at school because then he would not learn English, and I can't really have everything in English because then he won't learn Spanish. So then I have Spanish at home and English at school ... His first words [in English] were "Hi now, mami!" "Mami, hi now!" And I would say, "What does 'hi now' mean?" "Now!" and he would go like this. "Mami, quickly," "easy, mami, easy." I could notice the difference. The first words that he learned he put into practice ...

ANNA: What's rewarding about bringing up your son bilingually?

DULCE: ... his ability to communicate with his friends. I take him to the park with my work friends. Even though I can't understand, he can communicate with them. So it pleases me.... Now that he is spending more time at school he wants to speak more to me in English than Spanish. He wants me to [sing in English] too but ... it's impossible for me ... There are some things he says that I don't understand. He does not want to speak to me in Spanish. I tell him, "What are you saying?" But with his language difficulties and with his English, I don't understand and he tells me, "It's okay" ... He is impatient, and there have been times when he cries. I told the teacher last time that he cries because there are things that I ask him about what he did in school and I don't understand him on account of the two issues, English and his [difficulty with articulation] ... I see myself in the future with him and in some three or four years his schoolwork will be totally in English. If I am not able to understand English I will not be able to show, teach or help him much. Then it will be difficult. Therefore, my goal is to learn English. [Translated from Spanish]

In comparison to Sonia's experiences, Dulce's interview presents a different story of a non-English-dominant parent raising her young son in the United States. We hypothesize that one of the main differences between Alex and José is the fact that José was born in the United States and had access to an English-speaking environment outside of his home. Even though his first language is Spanish, José is rapidly learning English and would like to speak English to his mother. Dulce would like to keep their home as a Spanish-speaking environment. In contrast to Sonia, Dulce has very well defined aims for José's acquisition of English. Unlike Sonia and her husband, who have found a niche within the international community of scientists, Dulce is very much aware of English as a key to opportunities in work and career in the United States and this is what she wants to bestow on her son.

Dulce and Sonia, however, do share a number of similarities. We also found views in their interviews similar to those of the other non-English-dominant parents. The first commonality is the theme of family practices. Many of the non-English-dominant parents chose to speak their heritage language at home in an effort to preserve it. Closely connected to this is the fear of loss of the heritage language. Many of the parents in this group, including both Sonia and Dulce, thought about returning to their home countries. This was an additional reason for heritage language preservation distinct from other motives shared with other groups of parent participants. Another common theme that was very prominent among this group of parents was the pride that they felt about their children's English abilities. Both Sonia and Dulce felt that their children clearly surpassed their own English language skills and they both are pleased and impressed with this. Two more intertwined themes were the parents' frustration at their own inability to help their children with schoolwork and the theme of using language learning as a form of defense. Both Sonia and Dulce saw that it was their responsibility to assist their children in learning. The two mothers did this in two different ways. Dulce decided to learn English along with José while Sonia was providing Alex with help in all the subjects she could, except for English. Both mothers felt that by learning English their sons were gaining tools of defense in a world where their parents could not come to their rescue.

Bilingual Parent Participants: Lilian and Miko versus Tricia

The subgroup of bilingual parent participants was the largest in our sample. We chose to spotlight two different families, one (Lilian and Miko's family) where bilingualism is a family practice for two generations and the other (Tricia's family) where parents who grew up in monolingual households made a conscious decision to raise their children bilingually.

"Of course, they will grow up bilingual!" "There was never a doubt that they won't ..." (Lilian and Miko, prospective parents of multilingual children)

Lilian and Miko are prospective parents, both part-time graduate students in their mid-twenties. They are second generation Mexican-Americans. Lilian and Miko were raised bilingually by their parents who were initially monolingual Spanish speakers when they emigrated to the United States. Bilingualism is a norm and a family practice for both Lilian's and Miko's extended families. When discussing the children they hope to have in the future, Lilian and Miko reported that they would like to start raising them bilingually from birth:

MIKO: When I [heard] the question [whether they are planning to raise their children speaking one or two languages], I thought immediately, "Of course, they will grow up bilingual!"

LILIAN: There was never a doubt that they won't ...

MIKO: How I think it would be is what I have seen from experience. It will probably happen like this: we speak English to our baby and we speak English to each other and our child will see that and learn English ... And our parents/their grandparents ... will speak Spanish and the child will see that and learn Spanish ...

LILIAN: I think I am going to make a conscious effort to speak Spanish too ... because that's what we did to our very first niece. I do not know why, but I would talk to her more in Spanish than in English in the beginning, when she was a baby ...

Lilian and Miko recalled their own childhood and how they grew up bilingually. Miko commented, "When I was a child I took it for granted. I do not think I even realized that I spoke 2 languages. You know what I mean. But now – yes, it is extremely important to speak at least 2 languages. And definitely Spanish, living here in Los Angeles."

Despite having similar experiences growing up as bilinguals, Lilian and Miko had slightly different expectations of this process. Lilian saw the potential for difficulties ahead:

I just want to say that [...] if I am not speaking it, I am losing it. I feel like I lost a lot of vocabulary that I used to have. And I am thinking, I learned Spanish while I was at home growing up. When I was 18, I wasn't home anymore, I went off to college, and from that age on I feel like it's gotten worse. I have a loss of language, a loss of learned Spanish ... [and] then it means that that's a challenge. That means that we will have to make an effort to speak Spanish. If we are saying that we are speaking to each other in English, and then if we are raising a child, we would have to make a conscious effort. We will have to speak Spanish to each other to speak it as long as we can. I would see it as challenging for me.

Meanwhile, Miko thought it would not be a difficult task. Both Lilian and Miko plan on teaching their children not only to speak Spanish, but also to have them read and write in that language. Miko remarked that they "would definitely want to see [their] child to read, write and speak Spanish very well ... I would like to see our child in college, being able to read and write definitely at least English and Spanish really well. To be literate in both. I think it will be a help for them."

Lilian also emphasized that staying connected to Spanish-speaking culture was something that she wanted to instill in her future children:

I would like them to ... certainly [learn] beyond reading and writing and communication. I see language as closely related or tied to their culture. So through the language, you are passing on that culture. To me it means that through the language you are valuing your culture, your heritage. I feel that as generations go by, we are more and more detached ... I would say that our parents are the first generation of that culture, that language here ... My fear is that as we go on, generation after generation, that [culture] gets kind of lost. And so it would be very important to me to foster that love of the language and what it means is not only being able to read, write and speak in Spanish, that would mean that their culture is also engraved in them too, and the appreciation of the language too. So that would be my goal. So ... our children ... could pass all of it on.

In their parenting plans, Lilian and Miko planned to go further than their parents who raised them bilingually. They talked about instilling the culture in their children and cultural pride and assertiveness. Miko commented:

That's very different for our generation, for me and Lilian's generation, because obviously, our parents did not exactly give us that. I am not saying that our parents were bad, but they were in a very different situation. They were only Spanish speakers when they came over. They came to this country when they were already adults, so they did not have all the opportunities that we have [as] educated Spanish and English speakers. And I think there are a lot of people in our situation who should take advantage of our ability to speak English and Spanish, and really pass that on to our children and make them really strong Spanish and English speakers, stronger than us even. Definitely … and of course, I will encourage the child to learn a third or a fourth language when they are older, maybe high school … the more languages you can learn the better.

In our sample of participants, Miko and Lilian represent a family where bilingualism has been a natural phenomenon for their generation and an aspiration for the ones to follow. For this reason, Miko did not realize that he was speaking two languages while growing up. In their eyes, bilingualism is expected and not questioned as a practice that may or may not work. Even before becoming parents, Lilian and Miko have experience with planning how to raise bilingual children. This experience is multifaceted. It is comprised partly of their own bilingual upbringing, watching their family and community members bring up multilingual children, as well as first-hand experiences communicating with their nieces and nephews. One of the distinguishing themes that came up in Lilian and Miko's interview (and in the interviews of parents with similar backgrounds) is the sense of connectedness to a bilingual community. These participants saw bilingual upbringing as a communal effort in which parents, grandparents, uncles and aunts, as well as younger generations all participate and mutually reinforce multilingual practices. Another central theme for this group of parents is seeing language and culture as interconnected entities. By teaching their future children to speak Spanish, Lilian and Miko hope to establish roots for future generations. Finally, another theme within the group of bilingual participants was the hope that their children would go further in language learning than they themselves had. While there was no question that they will master the family language, the parents hoped that their children would also learn additional languages and perfect their knowledge in reading and writing in the heritage language, surpassing the norm of conversational (oral) bilingualism.

In our house [Portuguese] is the only language we speak. (Tricia, an English and Portuguese bilingual mother of 5-year-old Gabriela, 4-year-old Paolo, and 17-month-old Jessica)

We chose to offset Miko and Lilian's story of bilingual prospective parents who dream about raising their children bilingually with Tricia's narrative of being a bilingual mother who grew up as a monolingual and who was able to create a rich non-English environment within her home. Tricia, presently a mother of three young children, learned Spanish at 15, and lived in Spain for a year and a half. She also spent some time living in Central America. As an adult, Tricia worked in Brazil, where she learned Brazilian Portuguese and met her husband. Her husband spoke English because he had previously studied as an exchange student in English-speaking countries. The family now lives in the United States and speaks only Portuguese within their household. In her interview, Tricia spoke of how she came to the decision to raise her children bilingually and the challenges that she has had to overcome in this process. Growing up in a military family that had been stationed in Germany, she had older siblings who

… went to a daycare and they were speaking German and English before they were three. They used to speak both languages, and then my parents moved back here and they didn't hear any more German, so they didn't speak [it]. [Our parents] never worked on their languages … [When] I went to Columbia, and I saw, [the people there] would watch all the movies … in English and just read the subtitles … I don't think I was jealous but just thinking that that was such a great idea. They were exposed [to multiple languages]. We were never even exposed …

Having studied overseas and having seen school students there routinely speak more than one language, Tricia became determined to raise her children to speak at least two languages. She decided that long before she was married, "Probably when I was in Spain or Columbia." And now,

I am a stay-at-home mom and I talk to them nonstop. I am always explaining what I am doing…. It is fun. It is not like a chore, and they like it, so I can't believe it worked. I thought by the time they started preschool it would be all over. It is not…. I don't let any English in the house. We don't watch TV in English. They get DVDs from Brazil or we watch TV in Spanish and then when I am around anybody I am always speaking Portuguese…. The kids went to school and they couldn't speak. They didn't know any English when they went to school … Gabriela was three … and then Gabriela did not speak until April … Paolo started when he was three and a half … and then he didn't speak [English] either…. It is really hard for my family because they can't communicate with the kids, or I'll be telling the kids what to do and they [other family members] don't understand what I am saying. So they are like, "Every now and then you could let in a few English words. It wouldn't kill them. It would make other people feel more welcome…." But I am really a diehard about the languages.

Tricia was able to create a purely Portuguese speaking environment in her household, and she carefully eliminated any non-Portuguese influences that could "contaminate" her children's knowledge of that language:

Our neighbors, they adopted a baby from Guatemala … So when the [neighbor] child finally learned how to talk, he was like, "I am not speaking that Spanish. We are not doing that. Don't talk to me in Spanish anymore." And then he comes into our house and he is like, "Quit talking Portuguese." So we don't really invite him over, but he does come in our house sometimes. It's going to be a battle. They look up to him. He is older and they just think he is great. I am like, "No. Years of effort, you are not going to ruin this…!"

Tricia represents a group of bilingual participants who acquired their second language through school or college. Some of these participants, like Tricia, were married to the native speakers of languages other than English, while others had spouses who were monolingual in English or had also studied another language in school settings. Many of these parents wished they had learned a second language within a family context, during their childhood. Parent participants strived to create a non-English-speaking environment within their homes. In contrast to Miko and Lilian, who saw bilingualism as a communal practice, Tricia represents a group of parents who have created a more isolated model of bilingualism, where a single parent or both parents are the primary (and often sole) speakers of languages other than English. This is typical for families where at least one parent is a first generation immigrant, but the family does not live within the linguistic community spoken by the family. It is also characteristic of families whose heritage language is less common within the area in which the family resides. Resulting from this was a theme about the fragility of language in the face of outside influences throughout the interviews. Awareness of this fragility could lead to "avoiding contamination" of the language spoken inside the home by outside influences including the wider family circle and friends.

In contrast to Lilian and Miko, who accept that their children will be exposed to both languages but hope to preserve Spanish through family practices and contact with numerous Spanish speakers, Tricia sees herself as a vigilant guard protecting her children's L1 environment from the outside influences. While Lilian and Miko rely on human resources within their family and community, given the absence of Portuguese speakers outside the immediate family, Tricia relies on an abundance of technology that provides children with access to their extended family in Brazil and uses DVDs in Portuguese for entertainment. Despite the differences between models of bilingual practices within households, common themes still emerged from the interviews. One was the hope that the children would grow up proudly and assertively speaking languages other than English. Overall bilingual parents hoped that their children would be free of the stigma of speaking a non-dominant language that had been felt by some amongst the first generation immigrants or the insecurities of parents who had learned additional languages through school and never achieved the sense of being a native speaker.

Multilingual Parents: Tilda and Tina

Our sample included five families who spoke more than two languages. Three households were trilingual and two polyglot families reported four or more languages spoken in their household. While we had several more multilingual parent participants, many of them were not able to foster more than two languages within their family. Two mothers amongst the multilingual families, Tilda and Tina, exhibited a similar commitment to teaching their children more than four languages. While Tilda fearlessly introduced Bryan to six languages (English, Swedish, Portuguese, Spanish, and Mandarin, and French) by the age of three, Tina worked on developing 19-month-old Lilia's three spoken languages (English, Taiwanese, and Mandarin) as well as American Sign Language, and planned to introduce Lilia to Spanish next. These mothers shared a common belief in a children's limitless ability for learning languages and were inspired by their young children's success. Having witnessed first-hand their children's confident multilingual linguistic development, Tilda and Tina both plan to persist with multilingual practices within their households.

I am the only one who ever left Sweden, so nobody else in my family speaks anything else except Swedish ... My parents barely speak English. I've always known that he would have to speak Swedish. (Tilda, the Swedish-English bilingual mother of 3-year-old Bryan who speaks six languages)

Tilda grew up in Sweden and moved to the U.S. in her twenties. At that time, she spoke Swedish and English and knew some Mandarin, which she took in college. Her husband speaks a different set of languages. He is fluent in Portuguese as well as in Spanish and English. This creates at minimum a quadrilingual environment within their household. Recognizing the value of multilingualism as a vehicle for future educational and career success, Tilda also decided to introduce her son, Bryan, to additional languages through children's play groups. Tilda's interview details her endeavors:

Fabio's [husband] family speaks nothing but Portuguese. Mine speaks nothing but Swedish, and the daycare I had chosen was Spanish. So [my son] never had a choice. Bryan will be four years old in May. I always spoke Swedish to him ... When he started to talk, his first words were in Spanish ... He was a very late speaker. So he was probably, maybe ... well over a year before he really started saying anything and it was mostly Spanish and Swedish.

Tilda pointed out that Bryan had "no choice" but to learn several languages from the start. This theme of "inevitability" of multilingualism was common in several families where the parents were multilingual and saw multilingualism as a "natural," "instinctive" phenomenon.

He was at the daycare and there was primarily Spanish ... So I know he was learning a lot of Spanish from the teachers and, of course, the other kids. He was the only non-native Spanish speaker ... All the other kids spoke fluent Spanish, but most of them chose to speak English ... My husband is fluent in Spanish... So [he] can always keep track of him, of what he is saying....

In many participant families daycare turned into a vehicle for additional language acquisition. In Bryan's case, the fact that his father knew Spanish contributed to his active use of Spanish across environments. The family also allows Bryan to be the "expert" in some languages and "teach" them to his parents. Such fostering of linguistic confidence by taking the child's lead was popular in several families where one parent spoke a language unknown to the other parent.

Bryan is learning Swedish, English, Portuguese, Spanish and Mandarin, and for a year he was also learning French because the daycare he was going to was teaching French … but it wasn't something I was going to pursue beyond just having the opportunity at the time … Mandarin, [on the other hand] when I was going to college, I knew that Mandarin was the number one language for business, and I always knew that if I had any kids they would have to learn Mandarin … I wanted to give him the foundation … It would be nice if he could start speaking enough Mandarin and maybe get a good job that takes him around the country and around the world.

When asked about people's reaction when they learn that Bryan speaks six languages, Tilda responded,

Most of the time I don't say anything … Because people don't really understand it. I mean four [languages] he would get immediately by being born and the Mandarin I [had] always known I would add. If you talk to an American-American, they only speak English. A lot of people don't understand that he has four [languages] at birth and I add Mandarin and he was taking French at school. Very few people I tell that. I guess they think it is weird. I don't know. It seems like they are kind of judging something, that something is wrong. So I am not really saying anything. So a lot of people only think he speaks three…. I hope that he will fit in in many places.

Multilingualism within Tilda's household illustrates a unique situation of a child being exposed to several languages from birth. Despite the small number of these families represented in our study, this context is typical for families where both parents speak different non-dominant languages. The number of languages at birth might range from a minimum of three (mother's first language, father's first language, and the dominant language) up to five or more depending on the languages spoken by the extended family, caregivers, daycare staff and children, etc. These so called "third culture kids" represent a linguistically rich but vulnerable population for whom fitting in with the mainstream culture might be difficult (Pollock, Van Ruth, and Van Reken, 2009). Tilda's narrative illustrates four themes that were found in all the interviews of multilingual parent participants. One theme gives a great deal of credit to outside influences. Tilda and the other participants who are raising children who speak three or more languages stated that their children easily learn languages that they come into contact with outside the family. Parents recognized and accepted the profound influence of caretakers' and daycare providers' language.

Another theme was the abrupt transition between language environments that multilingual children undergo. These children navigate multiple language environments throughout their daily routines, and as Tilda noticed, they do not complain. Additionally, all of the parents of multilingual children recogni[...] the fact that their sons and daughters exceeded the number of languages kno[...] by parents. Another frequently occurring theme is the hope that their children will teach additional languages to their parents. In Tilda's case, Bryan is already teaching Swedish to his Portuguese-speaking father. Orellana and colleagues (2012) examined this phenomenon, coining the process as "dynamic teaching and learning," a process in which children take on the role of being their parent's teacher and becoming linguistic go-betweens (cf. Vygotsky, 1978). This is a curious trend common in multilingual families where the more traditional practice of parent facilitating child growth is shifting and taking forms of mutual facilitation of learning on behalf of parents and children. Tilda still has reservations about making Bryan's multilingual abilities known to people who come in contact with him. This perhaps illustrates the state of U.S. society in which knowing more than just two or three languages might be considered an aberration.

In contrast to Tilda's multilingual family where both parents are first-generation immigrants with different first languages, the second family that illustrates the context of fostering more than three languages is a household where both parents were born and raised in the United States. Tina, a mother to a young multilingual daughter, challenges the myth of the monolingual nation in her interview.

We feel it's important for her to be able to learn many different languages. The world is just becoming a smaller and smaller place.... (Tina, the multilingual mother of 19-month-old Lilia)

Tina, a daughter of Taiwanese immigrants, grew up in the United States. She mastered Taiwanese in her teens by traveling to visit her family and learned other languages in school and college. She traveled extensively and witnessed multilingualism around the world. She is keen to learn languages and is adamant in her decision to bring up her daughter, Lilia, speaking multiple languages.

I am half Taiwanese, so Lilia is a quarter Taiwanese ... so we are speaking with her in Chinese [Mandarin], in Taiwanese, in sign language, English, and then also Spanish ... I learned [sign language] through videos, through YouTube, through books ... I started when I was pregnant. I would teach [my husband] the words. She did her first sign at 5 months. She did the sign for 'milk,' which was amazing. And then she did the sign for 'more,' and she was able to start signing at a very, very early age, which was just wonderful. [The words] kind of all started coming all at the same time. [She said] "Mama," and then they just accelerated. You know from about 9 months she started saying mama and then dada, and then she did signs for more, thank you.... And then you know she started saying "Ama" which is grandma in Taiwanese. That was like her 3rd or 4th spoken word. "Mao," she started saying cat in Chinese ... I want her to be fluent. And I want her to have, and I've read that a child can have unlimited native languages. So I want to expose her to as many native languages as possible ... So then I figure, okay

I've got 5 languages I can use ... I kinda mix both [sic] languages with her, sometimes I'll do Chinese, sometimes I'll do English. We have our part time helper that basically only speaks Chinese. And she also can speak some Taiwanese. And so she only speaks Chinese and Taiwanese to her. So it's, that's kind of how we're doing it ... And then I'm gonna be introducing her to more Spanish later on. We're actually changing helpers, and our new helper's only going to speak Spanish to her. And so when that comes about, I'm only gonna speak Chinese to her. And really, and I've been trying to really only do Chinese, but it's hard when my husband is around because then you know then he'll speak English.

In her interview, Tina demonstrates a truly global perspective on multilingualism and its usefulness. In contrast to Tilda's household where three to four languages were readily available through Tilda's and her husband's non-English speaking backgrounds, Tina's household became multilingual due to Tina's conscious efforts to recruit language input from others. Despite growing up in a somewhat bilingual household in which English took precedence over both Taiwanese and the more formal Mandarin, and the fact that her husband is a monolingual English speaker, Tina is determined to provide her daughter with an opportunity for an early start with multiple languages. Of course the question remains whether these languages, the use of which started so early, will be maintained. While time will tell, Tina was certain that she would be able to continue talking to Lilia in Mandarin (which she studied in college), the grandmother would continue to talk to her in Taiwanese and Mandarin, and as for the sign language, in Tina's family it was a vehicle for communication while Lilia grappled with multiple language acquisition:

Well the interesting thing is, is that she already is able to translate. Like my mom, like we were at my parents' house over the weekend. My mom [speaks] only in Chinese [Mandarin] and Taiwanese to her. And my mom said, [Lilia] wanted some water, she asked grandma for some water. And [my mom] said, "Okay, go ask grandpa for some water." Grandpa only speaks English, but my mom asked her in Chinese. She went over to grandpa and asked him in English ... it's reinforced my desire to speak to her. Because ... I've truly realized she doesn't get confused. You know she understands everything. She's not slowed down because of it and it's only enhanced her.... Just like music is a language and you don't get confused when you listen to Bach versus, you know, jazz! You know, you can be exposed and understand that they are both completely different. You know, language is just another music. It's really given me much more determination to look for more ways to enhance her language and exposure to more languages.

The defining characteristic of Tina's approach to multilingualism is her "experimenter's attitude" to the whole process. Her dream of teaching Lilia "unlimited languages" resembles a linguistic experiment where the final number of languages is undefined. Another experimental quality is added by the fact that Tina is trying a variety of languages of different modalities, such as sign language. Unlike Tilda, who puts a great deal of effort in providing Bryan with a variety of different language environments outside the family, Tina generates this type of environment within her family and household. She learns new languages, for example American Sign Language, and practices others, such as Spanish and French, along with her daughter. Tina has given a good deal of thought to multilingual upbringing and she has read popular literature that has a positive outlook on multilingual practices. The theme of reading published positive accounts of the benefits of multilingualism came up repeatedly in our participants' interviews, especially of those who were raising young children. Along with reliance on discussion of multilingual benefits in the press, Tina's motivation appears to be kindled by several additional factors: her own positive attitude and fearlessness to trying different languages and Lilia's early linguistic successes that dismissed initial worries Tina had. Lilia was neither confused nor did she demonstrate delayed language acquisition. Lilia's triumph over the common myths about growing up multilingually has added to Tina's determination for her multilingual upbringing.

The accounts presented in this chapter provide a first-hand look at how multilingual practices take root in different contexts, allowing for a better understanding of various participant subgroups identified in our sample of 23 families. In the rest of the chapter we present in fuller detail the range of themes that emerged from all the parent interviews. We examine their beliefs and motivations for the laborious but rewarding process of raising multilingual children.

Parental Beliefs

I think bilingual children are in a unique place where they are a step ahead of children who are not bilingual ... (Miko, a Spanish-English bilingual prospective father)

It probably depends on where you live in this country, but in [my children's] school there are a lot of bilingual kids. There are a lot of kids who speak Spanish, Russian or Farsi, so it is fairly normal I think that kids speak another language somehow. (Nicole, a German-English bilingual mother of two sons, 5 and 3 years old)

Parents' responses to questions that focused on the history of multilingual practices in their families often drew out two distinct themes of a) parents' beliefs about multilingual children and their abilities and b) their beliefs about multilingualism as a phenomenon within family and school life. Overall, the responses took on two positions: one of seeing multilingual children and the multilingualism trend as "unique" or seeing them as "normal" and "not unusual." *Are multilingual children unique or not?* We begin the discussion of parents' beliefs with the theme of the unique nature of multilingual children.

The dichotomy of "unique" vs. "typical"/"ordinary" held true here for all the families. The participants were divided into two groups: 16 out of 26 parents thought their children who were learning more than one language were unique, while 10 considered their children's language abilities quite ordinary. Curiously, opinions differed within the same family. The assumption of uniqueness was particularly characteristic of parents who were not multilingual themselves or who had recently learned another language (in college, while traveling, or working abroad) and who were observing their young children easily acquire more than one language.

One parent who grew up monolingual and mastered German in college, Veronica, whose 2½-year-old son Andrew was making steady progress speaking German and English and learning some Hebrew, proudly commented, "I know that my kid will have the skill that is unique ... and a unique set of languages!" The literature has documented the unique linguistic abilities of multilingual children (e.g., Ball, 2008). However, the parents in our sample defined uniqueness very broadly, recognizing linguistic, social, metacognitive, and academic abilities suggesting multilingual children are a distinct population of children who are qualitatively different from their monolingual peers.

For parents who were multilingual themselves since childhood or who grew up surrounded by multilingual family members within a multilingual community, children who spoke more than one language seemed quite "normal" and "typical." When we asked Miko and Lilian, Spanish-English bilingual prospective parent participants in our study, if they were certain that their future children would speak more than one language, Lilian confirmed: "There was never a doubt that they won't ..." Within Lilian and Miko's family, it is not bilingualism but monolingualism that is unusual. "It would be very strange to have one of my nieces or nephews speak only English ..." commented Miko.

Meet the Multilingual Children: A Collective Portrait

Using parent sentiments, we created a collective portrait of multilingual children. This portrait highlights characteristics that the parents deemed unique in comparison to monolingual children and at the same time typical for multilingual children. We also included the features of multilingual children that parents thought were similar to their monolingual peers. The portrait is comprised of themes that emerged when parents told their stories of multilingualism in their families. We structured the portrait chronologically, from early childhood to adulthood. Several linguistic and social development characteristics of multilingual children in general were discussed in earlier chapters and we revisit these for the specific children of the families in our study to complete the collective portrait.

Robust non-verbal communication in early childhood. Several parents raising young children talked about specific characteristics of multilingual children in early childhood. According to these parents, while having individual and unique trajectories and varied rates of multiple language acquisition, multilingual babies demonstrated common patterns in non-verbal communication. One pattern was the liveliness of their non-verbal communication. Table 5.1 illustrates parent observations of their children's non-verbal behaviors.

Research links non-verbal communication and language development (Mayberry and Nicoladis, 2000). Studies show that more robust non-verbal communication continues in multilingual children and adults in comparison to their monolingual counterparts. In bilingual children 2 to 3½ years of age, gestures have been shown to facilitate production of longer utterances (Nicoladis et al., 1999). In a more recent study by Nicoladis, Pika, and Marentette (2009) French-English bilingual preschoolers engaged in more active use of gestures than their monolingual peers. The authors attributed this higher rate of gestures to the cross-linguistic transfer of gestures and to the use of gestures as an aide to formulate verbal messages. Some studies show non-verbal communication as a moderately strong predictor of expressive language and social cognition (Mundy, Kasari, Sigman, and Ruskin, 1995). Therefore, active non-verbal communication observed by our study parent participants in their multilingual children is a phenomenon confirmed in research and could be reflective of children's active linguistic and socio cognitive development in more than one language.

The robust non-verbal communication and lively socialization that the parents noticed in multilingual infants could also be the precursors of the common social nature and low affective filter demonstrated by multilingual children in the literature and noted by many of the parents in the current study. When asked if she noticed any common characteristics of bilingual children that she knows, Lilian, a bilingual elementary school teacher and a prospective mother, stated, "Maybe they are more social?" She spoke from her own experience of growing up bilingual: "I was put in the position where I had to translate a lot ... so it's you have to be more social. You have to be okay with talking to adults ..." Additionally, we can hypothesize that high engagement in non-verbal communication from early on in life later translates into "ease with languages" in both social and linguistic domains noted by many participants. Kevin, a prospective parent bilingual in English and Spanish, reflected on his own experiences from childhood to adulthood:

I have a greater facility [with language] ... I have a greater ... knowledge or understanding of the public life around me. Many people around here are Spanish speakers and from that culture ... So it sort of helps to know a little bit more about those sorts of

Table 5.1 *Robust non-verbal communication of multilingual children in early childhood*

Parent	Non-verbal behaviors of children
Tina, the mother of 19-month-old Lilia	"Lilia did her first sign at 5 months. She did the sign for milk, which was amazing. And then she did the sign for more, and she was able to start signing at a very, very early age, which was just wonderful. And so now sometimes she'll do the sign along with the word … Early on they um, and sign language is actually considered a language for them as well."
Veronica, the mother of 2½-year-old Andrew	"Language wise, it is interesting that he's using a lot of non-verbal communication. I don't know what other kids do because he is my only kid but he is pointing a lot more [than his peers seem to point] and shaking his head yes and no instead of crying …"
Mayda, the mother of 8-year-old Vana and 6-year-old Raffi	"Before Vana was verbalizing her words, she would point to stuff a lot. And that showed me that she understood all of my languages. I would tell her, 'Let's say what's this, what's that color, what's that shape?' and in three different languages."

things … I love the fact that I have that facility with language. If I don't know a word and I can take a guess at it or I can decipher it more easily.

Danielle and Ultan, who speak French, English, Spanish, and Russian, talked about a similar fearlessness and enthusiasm for learning languages that they observed in their four multilingual children:

All our children had abilities similar to Georges' [their older brother] facility and desire to learn languages. Adele took Spanish because everybody takes Spanish here, but not seriously … but she's fluent and she read Cervantes in the original. She made her level of Spanish impress her friends rather than the fact that she speaks French because she has the [French-speaking] mother. Sylvie at university took Russian first. Because she said, "Okay, I'm gonna learn Russian." And then she switched because they had a trip to Italy and so she switched to Italian and she really got into Italian too. They have their mother's fearless attitude of throwing themselves into a language, which is great.

It is probable that being more social, having a facility with learning languages, and fearlessness noticed by several participants can be attributed to the low affective filter typical for multilingual children (Krashen, 1981) that we discussed among other benefits of multilingualism in Chapter 2.

Accents and frustration at being misunderstood. Parent opinions were divided when they talked about their young children's idiosyncratic linguistic characteristics once they started using language. In Chapter 3, we discussed the apprehension and worry that some parents felt about their multilingual children speaking with a "foreign" accent or an accent characteristic of a non-dominant language as one of the many myths that may stop parents from raising their children multilingually. Here, we turn to a wide variety of accents that the parents noticed in their children, and not necessarily as a phonological limitation, but as hallmark of a multilingual speaker. A few parents noticed that their children spoke with an accent that resembled their own or another caregivers' accent. Victor, a monolingual father of two multilingual daughters, mentioned that in their early childhood they spoke in the same manner as their mother. This was a typical observation for families in which one or both parent(s) were not native speakers of a particular language. Other parents described that their children spoke with an accent close to that which an American child would have. Tilda, whose 3-year-old son Bryan is growing up regularly exposed to four languages and with the opportunity to learn two additional ones, spoke of his American accent, which she detects when he speaks her native Swedish, her husband's native Portuguese, and Spanish:

Bryan does have an accent. An American accent. He doesn't say too much in Portuguese, and I asked my husband, "Does he have an accent?" and he is like, "Oh, not too much." But … I can hear it is not perfect, but maybe his ear will be better for Portuguese. I don't know? In Swedish he's got a pretty strong accent. In Spanish I am pretty sure he has an accent too because he kind of feels very stiff so far. For Swedish I think he would need to be more exposed to Swedish to lose his accent and who knows, he may never lose it.

These observations are consistent with the research findings discussed previously in Chapter 3 (Hoff, 2006). Parent observations of a variety of accents that their children have can be indicative of their development of a single phonological system (Grosjean, 2011; Werker et al., 2006).

Another characteristic that parents reported about their children's language development was the marked frustration that multilingual children experience when their interlocutors do not understand them due to accents or occasional codeswitching. Tilda recalls the tantrums Bryan occasionally had out of irritation at not being understood:

Bryan has trouble saying "r". His speech is not the clearest, but the fact is that he has always had four or five languages. You kind of have to think which language he is speaking. He has said words to me in Swedish that he butchers so hard that I don't know what he is saying, and I feel bad about that. There was the longest time we could not speak while driving because I could not understand what he was trying to tell me and I would be asking him what he said. He'd be getting furious and I couldn't turn to look at him because if you look at somebody you might better understand what they are saying … but I was driving.

Parents observed similar frustration in multilingual children when they did not understand other speakers. Nicole, a German-English bilingual mother, recalled her son being visibly annoyed when he did not understand what she was saying:

At one point I even was wondering if my older son was kind of standoff-ish against the German language because I would try to keep speaking German and he sounded a little frustrated at times because sometimes he wouldn't understand what I was saying and I think there were misunderstandings … I would be frustrated if I told him to do something and he didn't. I would get upset, not really upset but "I just told you to do this!" and then I realized that sometimes he just didn't really understand what I was saying. I think once I realized I have to make sure that he knows what I am saying to him so that we don't misunderstand each other it got better and now I noticed that he is trying more.

Parent comments illuminate important discoveries about the linguistic and social behaviors of multilingual children who are actively learning more than one language. They contain observations critical for other parents and educators: acquiring multiple languages can lead to difficulties with immediate understanding of what is being said by interlocutors. This, along with unique accents and difficulties with particular sounds in a particular language, is a part of a natural course of multilingual development. Understanding this natural process might ease the frustration on the parts of both the child and the adult, who also wants to be understood.

Do multilingual children know that they speak more than one language? The children's overall awareness of the fact that they speak more than one language is a common theme in parent interviews, particularly those who had young children. This awareness generally fell along the continuum of "my child does not know that she/he speaks two (several) different languages," to "my child is very aware that she/he speaks two (several) different languages," and "my child thinks (or pretends) she/he speaks some other languages besides the languages she/he *really* speaks." Table 5.2 illustrates this continuum.

It is possible that the early "pretense" of knowing more languages than the child really speaks later develops into the desire to acquire additional languages that no one in the family speaks. Several parents informed us that once in school their bilingual children chose to study languages that were different from languages spoken within the family, even if the schools were offering the languages familiar to them. For example, Rudy, who is bilingual in English and Russian, chose to study Latin. Tim, who speaks Spanish and English, took Mandarin in high school, and Georges and his sister Sylvie, who speak French and English, studied Spanish and Italian. These stories possibly uncover a developmental trajectory of establishing multilingual identities as a speaker of many languages. In early childhood these children believe that they speak multiple languages beyond the ones spoken by parents and siblings and later implement this desire as they enter high school or college.

The sense of comfort and confidence when speaking language(s) other than English. Another theme, closely related to the theme of children's

Table 5.2 *The continuum of multilingual children's awareness of the fact that they speak more than one language*

Category within the continuum	Children's awareness of multilingualism
My child does not know that she/he speaks two (several) different languages	"The little one doesn't understand. He will actually argue with me if I point out something in a book and use the German word and then he is like, 'No, it is this!' and then he'll say the English word and then I am like, 'Yeah, it is the same thing.' He doesn't get that there are two languages. I think that is not until school age that they understand that those are two different things." Nicole, a German-English bilingual mother of 5-year-old Michael and 3-year-old Tristan
My child is very aware that she/he speaks two (several) different languages	"The interesting thing is, is that she already is able to translate [at 19 months] … We were at my parents' house over the weekend. My mom [speaks] only in Chinese and Taiwanese to her. And [Lilia] wanted some water, she asked grandma for some water. And grandma said, 'Okay, go ask grandpa for some water.' Grandpa only speaks English, and so but my mom asked her in Chinese. She went over to grandpa and asked him in English … She translated it because she knows who speaks what language, and she already knows to talk, speak that language to that person." Tina, a Chinese-English bilingual mother of 19-month-old Lilia
My child thinks she/he speaks some other language(s) besides the languages she/he *really* speaks	"[Elia] thinks she is trilingual because we will talk sometimes about 'We are a bilingual family … Our family is in El Salvador.' And we try to talk around this, it is important, and she will get offended and say, 'No! I am not bilingual! I speak three languages, Mama!' And then I am, 'Oh, right she thinks she speaks Chinese!'" Linda, an English-Spanish bilingual mother of Elia (5 years old) and Bella (2 years old)

conscious awareness of being multilingual, was being comfortable and confident while speaking the language. The expression "comfortable speaking the language" came from many parent interviews. Often it appeared as a standalone description of children's attitude toward a language. Monica, a mother of two English-Spanish bilingual sons in their late teens, commented on one of her sons' ability to speak Spanish: "Conversationally, he converses with my parents, his grandparents, in Spanish, and feels very comfortable and very proud of being able to speak in Spanish. So he feels very good about it." Distinct from confidence, comfort appears to add a new shade of meaning to the construct of "confidence speaking the language" that has been linked in the research literature to the motivation to learn a language (Clément, Dörnyei, and Noels, 1994). In our study parents emphasized that while knowing the language (understanding conversations and directions, being able to respond in a language other than English, etc.), children often feel different levels of comfort with multiple languages, even within the same family. The level of comfort did not seem to depend on whether the language was the child's first language or subsequent languages. Nora, a Spanish-English bilingual mother of three daughters ranging in age from pre-teens to early 20s who were exposed to Spanish and English from birth, noticed the difference in their comfort with English: "Alejandra, I think, feels comfortable with both [English and Spanish]. Stefanie, we don't know. Right now she is refusing to speak Spanish." Leonid, a Russian-English bilingual father, who added Russian to his 13- and 11½-year-old sons' linguistic repertoire after they were fluent in English, noticed a similar difference in siblings:

My oldest son, he just doesn't care. He'll speak, and if it comes out in broken Russian, that's fine. He'll just do his best to spit it out. So he just talks … Our first twin is much more tentative. He's much more self-conscious. So he's the one that if he doesn't have sentence ready he will just sit there and stare at you and stumble and refuse to speak Russian.

Understanding of the notion of "being comfortable" when speaking a language is important for parents and educators of multilingual students and society overall. Our study showed that not all children who understood and spoke other languages felt comfortable speaking them. Their refusal to speak their other language and lack of motivation to pursue further knowledge of these languages came from their discomfort. Uncovering the factors that contribute to a sense of comfort when speaking another language may prove to be an important vehicle for fostering multilingualism.

Domain-specific and purpose-specific use of language: refusal to speak a language. Several of the parent comments extended in three additional directions from the theme of comfort level in speaking another language. Specifically, the participants discussed the domain-specific and purpose-specific use of languages they observed in their children. They also hypothesized possible reasons behind their children's frequent refusal to speak languages other than English, even if they were fluent in them. Domain-specific language use or diglossia, where one of the languages is only used in certain situations or contexts and during certain activities, held true across children's ages from toddlers to teenagers and adults. Several mothers noted that their children use languages other than English in the kitchen or around the topics connected with food, while others recalled the use of a different language around self-care. Veronica, the mother of 2½-year-old Andrew, commented,

Andrew speaks German and English.... His receptive language is very strong in German, much stronger than in English, but he responds to both and he answers in both … It is domain centered. So he is with Monica who is his caregiver, friend during the day while I am at school or work, and she does all the cooking and so he says "heiss" which is hot. Those types of words [for cooking] are largely in German, but I get him dressed so he says "shoes" in English.

We inquired if Andrew's use of English and German was person-specific, as is noted in the research on early language differentiation (Köppe, 1996). However, his mother pointed out that rather than being person-specific, Andrew's use of languages was domain-specific, as both his caregiver and Veronica address Andrew in both languages, and he is well aware that both women speak English and German. Mayda, whose children, Vana and Raffi, are trilingual, offered a similar observation:

They don't even know what's cucumber in Armenian. I know it's "heyad" in Arabic. And my kids, for them it is "heyad," and when Vana started going to school she would say, "heyad!" And I said, "Maybe your friends won't understand you because it's not really an Armenian [word]."

Mayda's children's use of Arabic around the kitchen could be explained by her own habits. While being a native speaker of both Arabic and Armenian, Mayda uses primarily Arabic when cooking or talking with her own mother about various recipes. Vana's and Raffi's use of Arabic for various fruit, vegetables, spices and food items could be explained by family habits of using a particular language in a particular context. Fathers also talked about specific domains in which their children used languages other than English. Leonid, the father of English-Russian bilingual 13-year-old Rudy and 11-year-old twins, Elijah and Luis, described the brothers' use of Russian primarily around playing soccer:

I think if I spoke to one of the twins about soccer, for example, I would get less understanding, less response than I would be getting from my oldest son [who loves to play soccer]. So it's domain specific a little bit. It's what I'm comfortable with personally and it's things that do not involve other people like their mother who needs to understand or participate.

In this last quote, the themes of being comfortable and the domain-specific use of language are intertwined, revealing a particular context that provides a sense of comfort for the use of a language. For some children, the domain-specific use of language fostered both curiosity and misunderstanding. Taani, the mother of 2-year-old Mihir, recalled her young son learning the names of animals:

[For example] he would only say the word "elephant" in Hindi … I did not tell [the babysitter] initially that he had learned it in Hindi already, and she would try to get him to say that word, but he would be giving her this other random word. And she could not understand: he would be learning other words, like "cow" and "sheep," but why is this random word for this one particular animal? And I was like, "No, no, no, he actually is recognizing it correctly, and he does understand. He is saying it correctly. He is just saying it in Hindi." It's just interesting how some words in Hindi stuck with him and some words in English stuck with him even though he was getting exposure to both.

Purpose-specific use of a language other than English was another characteristic of multilingual children noted by parents. A few commented that their children would switch to another language when requesting something from the adults who speak the language. Nicole, a native German speaker, noted when her son would switch to German:

Especially if he wants something from me. He is trying to bring it out in German even though it may be completely wrong! You know, the grammar is wrong. Like if he wants a cookie or something or more chocolate he will try and say it in German because I get so happy! He thinks he can get something out of it.

Switching to a particular language to please parents or other family members (especially grandparents) to obtain something desirable was a frequent theme in many participant interviews. The next most common purpose that the parents observed was the use of a language other than English to share a secret. Awareness of the ability to speak a language not generally known by others was typical for children of all ages. Mayda described that her younger son, 6-year-old Raffi, would speak Armenian and Arabic to tell her something that he would not want others to know. Leonid described that his 11- and 13-year-old sons switched to Russian to exchange secrets. Ghodrat, whose adult children had at one time refused to speak Farsi to him, noted the same inclination:

There was one time in Ireland that Zara had a roommate, and she didn't want to say something that the roommate would understand. And you know, she started to speak Farsi with me. And I couldn't stop laughing because it was you know one of the biggest surprises that Zara was talking with me in Farsi. The message was delivered nicely and beautifully, you know. Deep down, there are some roots and then if there is pressure, it comes out. Both Zara and Malik [Zara's brother], they can speak Farsi, you know, if it is in the circumstances that they don't want the third party to know what it is …

Domain- and purpose-specific uses of language add to the idea of language differentiation discussed earlier. It gives another dimension to language differentiation beyond associating language use with a particular person that has been noted by research with young children (Köppe, 1996). We hypothesize that behind the domain-specific and purpose-specific uses of language are motivational mechanisms that explain children's use of languages other than English. These mechanisms are defined as a mixture of language differentiation by domain as well as instrumental motivation. Such sources of motivation are important to understand and utilize in order to promote and encourage the use of multiple languages, especially if children are hesitant or reluctant to use them.

Having established that certain domains and specific purposes propel children to use languages other than English, parents also offered their theories as to why some of the children refuse to speak these languages. The most common reason was the children's desire not to stand out or appear to be different from their peers. Danielle, whose children grew up in France until middle school, hypothesized that this might be due to "Some type of peer pressure. 'Oh you speak an odd language.' Or maybe [feeling as if it is] almost not being polite ... You know, 'why my friends shouldn't understand what my parents tell me.'" Ghodrat recalled that his Farsi-English bilingual children went through a similar stage of not wanting to speak anything but English in early adolescence as well:

When they were in especially middle school, it was hard. They just didn't want to have anything to do with you know anything except American culture or language and all that. But I think when they went to college it all changed. I felt like they would appreciate more that they could actually speak another language.

This refusal to speak languages other than English was reported by several parents as a typical behavior of multilingual children during upper elementary and middle school. Parents, whose children went through a period of refusal and are now adults, told us that many of them went on to study in college the languages spoken in their childhood homes and by their relatives and ancestors. Some even took on leadership roles in their college's L2 cultural clubs and societies. Ghodrat recalled how his son and daughter both turned to Farsi once they became older: "As [Zara and Malik] were in college, they did go back, you know, and tried to just revisit [Farsi]. Malik, who refused to speak it in middle school, did it too. Even in the Persian society, they elected him the president of the society." Many children's initial refusal and eventual embracing of their heritage language can be attributed to the process of becoming not only bilingual, but also bicultural. Grosjean (2009) points out that this process may actually be harder and more complicated than becoming bilingual. It is an identity choice. Research stresses the importance of family and community support of multilingual children and adolescents during the period when they are forming their linguistic and cultural identities (Grosjean, 2009).

School experiences of multilingual children. Another common theme critical to this book, which aims to bring together the voices of parents and educators of multilingual children, is the uniqueness of the schooling experiences faced by multilingual students. For children whose parents were not proficient in English, the beginning of their formal education meant the beginning of their roles as language brokers, that is, their parents' helpers and translators. Bianca, a Spanish-dominant mother of two adolescent bilingual sons, used to be very nervous when she had to go to the doctor. Now she relies on her sons to translate and make sense of doctors' recommendations. Recall also how Dulce, whose 4-year-old son José knows more English than she does, proudly told us that his English helps her communicate with her work friends. Such language brokering by children has been well researched in the last decade. Research links this practice to a child's sense of self-efficacy, enhanced feelings of importance, self-confidence, self-worth, and heightened ability to problem-solve (Morales and Hanson, 2005).

In addition to the narratives about the school experiences of children whose parents do not speak English, our study yielded accounts of multilingual children whose parents spoke primarily English. These children's stories fell into two broad groups. The first group was comprised of children whose parents believed in complete immersion. They spoke to their children exclusively in languages other than English, hoping that they would learn English in school. As a result, the first group of children spoke only languages other than English when they started school. The second group of children was those who spoke languages other than English better than their parents (who were either monolingual or fluent in a different language). The stories from such families can be found at the beginning of the chapter. Here we focus on the most pertinent examples about the experiences of these children during their time in school. Paolo's story serves as a good representation of the experiences of the multilingual children in the first group. Paolo and his sisters Gabriela and Jessica grew up speaking only Portuguese with their parents. Their mother, Tricia, made sure that no English was spoken within her house. In fact, English was forbidden. Tricia described how when first Gabriela and then Paolo went to preschool they both remained silent in class for almost a year. Here is how she describes Paolo's first few months of preschool:

He whispered. He would come out of the class and I would pick him up and I would ask what happened and he would only whisper. "What is your teacher's name?" "Miss what?" He wouldn't even say her name he was … so in awe of her … And then even [the teacher] said he is just super shy, but it is just because he didn't know any words....

Tabors and Snow (2001) describe this non-verbal period as a time when children are silently observing the use of the new language. During this important time receptive understanding of the new language is actively developed. We hypothesize that Paolo's whispering can be attributed to three different factors: being in "awe" of the teacher, feeling that speaking the English language was considered taboo because it was not spoken at home, and his engagement in silently or quietly rehearsing his new language.

Pablo's and Gabriela's experiences in school tell an important story of children whose proficiency in a language other than English and relative lack of fluency in English were mistaken for shyness. We hypothesize that this is a common misinterpretation of multilingual children's social behavior and language skills. Such selective mutism can occur when anxiety, in this instance perhaps uneasiness with speaking a less familiar language in public, is the source of children's lack of verbalization (Muris and Ollendick, 2015). It will be vitally important to untangle selective mutism attributed to multilingual situations as described here, which can be assumed to be temporary until the child acquires the L2, from other situations where unexplained and potentially far graver anxiety disorders are suspected. One irony is that in cases of multilingual children whose parents are not fluent in English, and whose language development is assumed to be weaker in English by association, their lack of fluency is not likely to be attributed to shyness but to a lack of English proficiency. However, in any circumstance, it is important for both educators and parents to be very open and clear with each other when discussing children's language abilities in order for their language development to be appropriately supported at school and home.

Kevin, whose mother, Betty, and housekeeper raised him bilingually in Spanish and English, represents the other group of multilingual children who are more proficient in a non-English language than their parents. Kevin's family was completely monolingual before the pediatrician recommended that they bring up Kevin bilingually, especially since the housekeeper spent the most time with him (see beginning of this chapter for a full account of Kevin's story). Reflecting back on his school years, Kevin recalled having to explain his native sounding Spanish accent:

So I explained to them that both of my parents worked, and [my babysitter] spoke Spanish to me when ... I was a little baby all the time ... I always have to tell that story ...

Despite the need to explain this to people around him, his bilingual abilities always elicited a positive response from others. However, speaking Spanish in a predominantly monolingual family affected his self-perception:

I felt like I was sort of an odd-ball. Unlike most kids who start with another language and then get English (that was sort of the model I had around me), I started with English and got Spanish and that was, I guess, I don't know ... It was just sort of how I perceived the world so I felt strange that way. I guess I was ... I guess I never ... but then after that it was just part of who I was. I didn't separate it in anyway, you know. I just had that as part of my story.

Kevin's self-perception as "an odd-ball" reflects the inner state of a multilingual child who compares himself to others and feels different due to a unique set of skills and the reaction of others. This self-report is important for parents and educators to keep in mind while they support children whose sense of difference might make them vulnerable to both psychosocial as well as linguistic pressures. This seems particularly true in the light of parent reports where many multilingual children at a certain age do not wish to be seen as different to peers and ultimately refuse to speak any language but English.

Parents whose children spoke both a heritage language and English prior to going to school recalled that school experiences in studying both languages often brought the realization that the children were only familiar with the oral modality and colloquial register of their heritage language(s). Formal schooling meant exposure to a formal register of the familiar languages and an awareness that their children were not as proficient in the heritage language as they had thought. Nora recalled the time when her daughter, Caroline, bilingual in Spanish and English, took a Spanish course in school, "thinking that 'Oh, I know Spanish.' And she ended up almost failing the class because it was not all that familiar. It was then that she realized, 'Mom, I was not a Spanish speaker!' "

Additionally, several parents noted that once their children spent some time learning languages, many of them surpassed their parents in language skills in both or all languages. This is due to the fact that not all parents were fully literate or formally educated in the languages that they spoke and passed on in their families. Mayda described her daughter Vana's brief progress in both English and Armenian:

When she first started talking it was in Armenian because all her surroundings of course are Armenian. And once she started going to school, English became her, her first language. She does speak right now English and Armenian, and she reads and writes both languages. Right now she is in second grade and she writes in Armenian better than me.

Parent comments showed that school experiences play a critical role in either maintaining or halting children's multilingual development. School brings in a number of contexts, a hierarchy of social relationships, and new roles for children that are largely beyond a parent's control. These contexts and relationships can promote and nurture children's multilingual abilities or they may hinder them. It is crucial to understand the factors that come into play when multilingual children join the school system. It requires the development of school-home partnerships and common goals to preserve children's abilities to be confident speakers in all their languages and foster a sense of comfort and respect for all languages.

Choosing a culture. Additionally, it is during the school years that these children choose and sometimes change the cultures with which they associate. Here, as with many issues connected with multilingualism, we encounter a continuum of identities. For many multilingual children the choice is predetermined by both their parents' language and culture. Many participants reported making it a priority to create homes where not only a particular language is spoken, but where also parts of the home-language culture (the culture of the parents' or grandparents' home country or the culture of the country where the target language is spoken) are reconstructed through books, music, TV programs, toys and games, and family traditions. In these families, many multilingual children associated themselves with the linguistic minority culture. Tricia, whose family speaks only Portuguese at home, reported that her children "are so proud to be Brazilian and we are always pushing that in them. Like, the Brazilians speak Portuguese." And Bianca, the mother of two teenage sons, described it in the following way:

Since we are in America they often think they are American boys. [But they] were asked once if they think of themselves as Mexicans or Americans. Both of them said proudly they are Mexicans.

A majority of the families fell along the middle of the continuum, where the children identified with both cultures. Other children, who refused to speak languages other than English, preferred to associate with American culture and considered themselves American.

Veronica, English-German bilingual mother of 2½-year-old Andrew and an active member of online multilingual parent communities and multilingual play groups, introduced a group of children that no other parent participant spoke of. Veronica was the parent who talked about "third culture kids" based on her observations and experiences. These are the children of parents who did not grow up in the United States and who did not (initially) speak English. For example, the children of a mother who is a native Vietnamese speaker and a father who grew up speaking Portuguese. With three languages in play, Veronica hypothesized that it may be difficult for third culture children to find a path to self-identity: "They ... don't have a cultural home because their parents aren't at home in the dominant culture. It can be very problematic." Veronica's words echo research findings on third culture children that point to challenges in finding self-identity and the sense of "rootlessness" and "restlessness" associated with not growing up within one clearly determined culture (Pollock et al., 2009). This subpopulation of multilingual children is particularly vulnerable and in need of family and school-based support that would foster the sense of belonging and self-identity (Fail, Thompson, and Walker, 2004).

Parent stories about the unique experiences of multilingual children in school settings provide an important perspective on this population's strengths and vulnerabilities. They prove worth exploring for educators and those who come into contact with multilingual children. In concluding the collective portrait of multilingual children, it is crucial to note that all of the children described here are American children. They belong to the upcoming generation of Americans. Their collective portrait and stories again function to dispel the myth of the

United States as a monolingual nation as discussed in Chapter 3. These children create a contemporary mosaic of America as a multilingual nation.

Multilingualism as the norm. Interestingly, regardless of their beliefs as whether multilingual children are unique or typical children, the majority of parent participants viewed multilingualism as a norm. For many who were multilingual themselves, multilingualism was a reality, a way of life, and a very natural way of being. Mayda, who is raising her daughter, Vana, and son, Raffi, trilingually in English, Armenian, and Arabic, and whose friends and family are multilingual, commented, "When I look for multilingual families around me, it's part of their daily life. You know, you just switch, you don't think about it." Danielle, a native French speaker, and Ultan, whose first language is English, raised their four children fluently speaking both languages. When asked how and when they decided to raise their children multilingually, they spoke of the instinctive use of the first language when addressing the children:

DANIELLE: For me it was something natural. And I think any mother would tell you that. That if you're a mother you're going to speak your mother tongue language to your child.
ULTAN: And a father's tongue [smiles]. So it was natural for us. And it wasn't a decision.

For monolingual parents or parents who learned or planned to learn additional languages later in life, multilingualism within their family represented a goal that they were set to pursue. Linda, an English-Spanish bilingual mother who is raising her daughters bilingually, recalled how the decision about having bilingual children came about:

Once I got to an age where I really thought I do want to have kids I pretty much thought it would be a good thing to raise them bilingually … Kind just off the top of my head, "Yeah I would love my kids to learn two languages" and "Kids are so cute when they speak a different language." And thought that was a really neat thing.

Participants who themselves did not grow up to be bilingual or multilingual saw multilingualism as beneficial for their children. Parents whose first language was English wanted their children to learn additional languages. Parents who did not speak English were planning to raise their children proficient in their own L1 and hoped to learn English from or along with their children. Kelly, a prospective English-dominant mother, who at the time of the interview was expecting her daughter Madison, was planning to raise her bilingually in English and Cantonese. Kelly confessed that her knowledge of Cantonese was comparable to a two- or three-year-old child's language. Nevertheless, Kelly was confident that she and Madison would master the task of becoming bilingual together: "I will know the basic words of what she is trying to say. And hopefully she and I can learn together."

Kelly's sentiment echoes that of other initial monolingual English-dominant parents and similar expectations were expressed by non-English-speaking parents who looked forward to their children mastering the English language and teaching them. For example, we heard earlier from Dulce, the Spanish-dominant mother of 4-year-old Spanish-English bilingual José, that she is learning English along with her son, who is becoming progressively more proficient than she is. These parents viewed their children as potential partners in learning languages or even future teachers of languages that the parents always wanted to learn. It is important to note that regardless of whether they were monolingual or multilingual, all parents within the sample were convinced that multilingualism is a natural phenomenon that exists or that can be created within a family.

Language status. The theme of language status was predominant throughout the parent interviews. We hypothesize that the way society and families position and stereotype certain languages greatly impacts the appeal these languages hold for the children who are learning them. Understanding the mechanisms that create a specific status for a particular language is crucial for planning for successful language acquisition at home and school. As Betty, a mother of adult Spanish-English bilingual sons, eloquently pointed out in her interview,

> The thing that has interested me is how to create circumstances where the second language, the language that is not English actually remains a high status and valued language, so that the kids engage with it. Because kids early recognize it [the unequal status of different languages]. So if can you get it [create such circumstances], so it [the L2] is valued enough that you do it because if you don't do it you are never going to be good [at it].

Earlier, in Chapter 3, we touched upon the dichotomous language status situation that historically formed within the United States (English vs. LOTE), and particularly the status English holds as the dominant language in the United States. Parent interviews revealed an entire hierarchy that pertains to languages other than English. Here we take a brief look at how language status is established and maintained at the local level of schools and individual homes.

Creating language status at the school level. At the school level, language status appears to be formed by educators' and parents' attitudes, and by the importance given to a particular modern language as a college preparatory course. Teachers' attitudes are valued highly and create a long-lasting impression. A few parents talked about the past when, a couple of decades ago, they did not feel comfortable using their home language at school. Monica, a mother of two Spanish-English bilingual teenage sons, recalled, "I went through the public school system and all that we could speak in the public school system was

English. We couldn't use Spanish at all." The fear and uncertainty of whether children should use their home language at school is still present among parents who are not confident English speakers themselves. Nora, who spoke to her daughters in Spanish when they were young, recalled enrolling them in preschool and claiming that they were English-speaking children:

> You know when you sign the Head Start form they ask you which is your home language, I never put Spanish. I use English. So that is my decision ... I prefer them to use the English most of the time because I want them to get used to, especially with academic. I don't want them to feel the pressure sometimes [when/if] they don't understand.... Maybe because I feel that I am not really fluent in English and I don't want them to have the same problem.

Miko and Lilian, bilingual Spanish-English prospective parents in our study, talked about ways this fear and the feelings of linguistic inferiority can be relieved:

> MIKO: I think generally parents need education to know that Spanish is not a lesser language. It is not a language of shame or "just a language within the family." It is something that needs to be taught to the children on an academic level.
> LILIAN: And it's not just with Spanish, it's with any language that parents speak – they should not be ashamed of it. They should do it proudly.

While the use of students' heritage languages in the home is not actively discouraged by schools, Miko and Lilian's suggestion goes further than mere acceptance and tolerance. They are offering ideas for how to change perceived language status within the school system through parent education and by elevating the students' heritage language to the status of an academic discipline.

But even when a language other than English is taught at school as an academic subject, its status is created by its perceived usefulness for students' further education and careers. Lilian and Miko recalled their school years when they had a choice of taking a particular foreign language: "When we were in high school we had a choice of French or Spanish ... These were the options. They offered advanced placement for Spanish and not for French. So you were taking Advanced Preparation (AP) Spanish if you were college bound, or you had an option of French." Both Lilian and Miko considered themselves "college bound" and took Spanish. Lilian briefly mused about learning French because she knew Spanish fairly well already, but in the end decided to further her knowledge of Spanish. In this case, the language status imposed by the high school played a role in Lilian's choice of a "foreign language." For Lilian, Spanish was a heritage language, so it turned out to be a meaningful choice. She told us that studying it was important for forming her self-identity and strengthening the ties with her cultural roots. However, this example of a school providing AP level courses for one language but not the other illustrates how school policy can influence a young person's language choice and creates a different status for different languages. Even for students for whom Spanish might not have been a heritage language, the benefits of taking the AP track would have influenced their choice, thus creating the perception that Spanish is a "more useful language." Research has emphasized the importance of the language status in school, demonstrating that school programs (such as TWI and other dual-language programs), where both minority and majority languages are given equal attention and have equal status contribute to self-confidence and better achievement of minority students, due to uninterrupted language, cognitive, and academic development (Collier, 1995).

Language status within households. Language status is also formed within individual families. In multilingual households, parents who believed that English is key to academic success established practices that reinforced this status. Mayda, whose preteen children were trilingual in English, Armenian, and Arabic and attended an Armenian school where a number of classes were taught in this heritage language, told us, "For me, Armenian homework comes last. First, English language arts, science, math. Definitely, I want them to succeed in English at school first." Through the act of prioritizing homework, English is established as the language of academic success, and thereby accorded a privileged status.

At the family level, deciding whether to encourage languages other than English was considered carefully. The concept of immediate usefulness was one of the factors that influenced parents' decisions whether or not to even teach their children all the languages that they themselves spoke. Hediyeh and Ghodrat, both trilingual in Farsi, English, and German, decided to give up speaking German upon arrival to the United States and did not teach it to their son and daughter: "I always thought you know if anything they would probably need more Spanish than German, you know" (Hediyeh). Mayda, who worked very hard to maintain trilingual daily use of Armenian, Arabic, and English, confessed, "I see Arabic as more important than Armenian. In terms of future success and career-wise, professionally. I definitely I will push them [to master Arabic]." Reflecting the language status within the family, parent interviews yielded salient descriptors used to portray different languages. These included references to a language's usefulness, as well as depicting the feelings associated with speaking a particular language. Table 5.3. illustrates several descriptors for language status found in the parents' interviews.

Overall, the modifiers were overwhelmingly positive, and the children, per parents' reports, succeeded in learning these languages. However, in the context of multiple language use, a child's attitude toward and desire to learn a

Table 5.3 *Language descriptors illustrating language status within households*

Descriptor	Admired language	Number one language for business	Language for the outside world	Cool language	Language of school	Language of our past	Language of comfort
Language	French	Mandarin	English	English, Japanese	English	Farsi	Spanish

language seems to be influenced by his or her parents' perception of the language status.

Language status was not only established by the words parents used to describe the language, but also by family practices, even those not overtly used for teaching the language, unlike some of the practices described earlier in this chapter. The status a language attained through these practices influenced children's mastery of it. For example, several parents reported using a home language or L2 as a "secret parents' language": they used it to discuss matters that they did not intend children to be privy to. As a result of receiving the special status of an "adult" language within the family, many parents noted that children coveted learning it and ultimately succeeded at it. Monica, a mother of two bilingual English-Spanish bilingual sons, recalled using Spanish around her children when they were young so they would not understand the conversation, although this strategy lost value as the children became more bilingual with time: "I'll switch something to Spanish, and Rodrigo says, 'I know what you are saying!' "

The status of a secret language, not only used by adults but also used within the family, seemed to motivate children to learn it. Mayda recalled motivating Raffi to put more effort into Armenian: "This is going to be our family language, our secret language. So at least your friends won't understand what you're saying if you have something secret to tell your parents." This technique worked and Raffi started using Armenian more often. A similar phenomenon was observed by Ghodrat and Hediyeh. Their children, Zara and Malik, resisted speaking Farsi outside their home when they were young. However, as mentioned already both children started using Farsi as they grow older to talk to their parents when they did not want others to understand what they were saying. Overall, 12 out of 26 participants reported using their home language as a "secret language" with their children and the children willingly participating.

Another common practice reported by parents, which was less positive than those discussed above, was using the heritage language for approval, disapproval, commands, and for disciplining their children. Fifteen out of 26 participants reported using languages other than English for such purposes. In her interview, Monica recalled that she and her husband, Gonzalo, used Spanish in different ways: "He spoke more English, and he would use a little bit of Spanish but it was more of the commands in Spanish and just the positive remarks about doing something." An important nuance is that Gonzalo used Spanish not solely to control his children, but also provided them with positive feedback. Both of Monica and Gonzalo's sons perceived Spanish as a "language of comfort" and it was perhaps this balance that promoted the boys' positive attitude toward language. Nora, on the other hand, who tried her best to exclusively use English with her daughters, remembered switching to Spanish only when she was upset:

The only time that I speak mostly Spanish to them is when I am upset ... When I am upset I go back to my home language and it is crazy because they understand when I am telling them these words in Spanish. They are like, "Oh mom, you are angry right now." And I said, "Why?" "Because that is the only time you use full Spanish with us."

Other parents also acknowledged resorting to their heritage language when disciplining their children. Mayda, who speaks English, Armenian, and Arabic to her children, told us, "If I'm really upset, I would definitely address them in Armenian. For sure, you know, just to stop it." Parents may feel more confident and powerful when using the heritage language to regulate their children's behavior. Hediyeh recalled regretting switching entirely to English with her children: "At home we spoke Farsi ... But with kids, the more English became their first language, they kind of mandated us to speak English to them. And that actually I think is a mistake, because it takes away a lot of your authority." The practice of using the heritage language for disciplining children may cut two ways when determining its status. On one hand, the heritage language may be negatively associated with misbehavior. On the other, being the language of discipline and calls to order accords a heritage language considerable power and authority. Research on the subject supports Hediyeh's personal experience. A study by Wong Fillmore (1991) marked the switch from home language to English, the dominant societal language, as a process of a cultural shift in which parental authority breaks down and can have detrimental consequences on children's linguistic and social development and school achievement.

The participant interviews revealed the critical nature of the language status construct as it affects children's language learning. The interview excerpts above illustrated different mechanisms that affect language status at the local levels of individual families and schools. Research on second language acquisition supports parents' perceptions demonstrating that parental attitudes, cultural maintenance within the family, and peer socialization affect students' language learning and sense of identity (Li, 2006; Phinney, Romero, Nava, and Huang, 2001). Having identified parental beliefs as one of the key factors that influence construction of the language status within the family, we turn to parental motivations for raising their children multilingually.

Parents' Motivations

I wanted to give her that gift of communication … I want her to understand various cultures and various people from all different walks of life, and I think one of the best ways and easiest ways to do that is to be able to speak another language. Maybe it's just me as a mom. Just wanting the best for her. And this is something that I can give her, and it's gonna be work on my end but it's worth it in the end. (Tina, Chinese-English bilingual mother of 19-month-old Lilia, explaining her motivation for teaching her daughter multiple languages)

Having taken a look at beliefs of different multilingual households, we now turn to reasons for which the families in our sample decided to maintain multiple languages or raise multilingual children by learning new languages. We look at what the motivation is behind all the hard work, persistence, extra concentration, self-denial in not speaking one's own language, and the occasional doubts and frustration that parents decide to endure to foster multilingualism. Table 5.4 presents the summary of parents' motivations by type, as these emerged from the interviews. This section of the chapter examines each of the types of motivation below.

All of the study participants unanimously felt that multilingualism was a wonderful gift that they were giving their children. Upon examination, this gift was multifaceted and bidirectional. Its complex nature included such motivations as wanting the best for the children, giving them a solid foundation for further language learning and schooling, and opening the world of communication and opportunities. Its bidirectionality was in its focus on benefits for the children and also benefits for the adults/family around them.

Analysis of the parents' motivations revealed two broad clusters of child- and parent-centered motives. The child-centered motivation is focused on increasing their present and future opportunities for success. In this respect, teaching a child another language is a gift of heritage and culture, as well as enhanced social, linguistic, and cognitive development, and favorable conditions for learning and future professional growth. At the same time, some of the interviews revealed additional, parent-centered motivations, such as "not missing the opportunity," "fulfilling parents' dreams," and "feeling good about process and proud of the results." Using analytical lenses that are both child- and parent-centered, we take a closer look at the parents' motivations.

Table 5.4 *Types of motivation in parents' interviews*

Type of motivation	Subtypes
Roots/Heritage/ Identity	Ties with family Ties between generations Strengthens parent/child relationships To keep the language alive To be able to speak with other people of the same heritage Language as an integral part of culture and religion Identity: cultural identification Identity: connection to culture Identity: a way of self-expression Guilt: parental guilt (did not give enough) Guilt: spousal guilt (took the spouse away from the family)
Benefits for the child	Social: Better socialization Better social development Comfort in interaction Helps getting along Promotes the sense of community Multilingual friends To fit into places Cultural integration Cultural enhancement Giving a social choice Linguistic: Opportunity to develop another language Opportunity to value another language Facility/comfort with languages To have a sense of language To enjoy untranslatable nuances of languages Cognitive: Enhanced brain development Enhanced ability to learn Makes kids more able Metalinguistic ability Mental exercise To be better academically Useful academically Economic Benefit Better future
Access	Access to people Access to culture Access to ideas Access to resources Access to the world Language is like another degree

Table 5.4 (*cont.*)

Type of motivation	Subtypes
Catching the right moment	Easier to learn when young
	To avoid stress of language learning as an adult
	Simple and does not take much time
	Natural thing
	Taking advantage of location
	Taking advantage of access to L2 speakers
Perfection	To be a better native speaker
	To have more than peers
	To be unique
Education	School/college readiness
	Not wanting the children to learn L2 at school (spend time on something that can be taught at home)
	To obtain language certificates
	To teach a parent
Business	Trade
	Jobs
	Careers
	Professional advantage
	Access to resources
Travel/Survival in other countries	To defend yourself
	Not to be in trouble
Global awareness, confidence, tolerance, and respect	Bigger sense of the world
	Broadens perspectives
	Expansion of world views
	To appreciate the world
	Break down barriers
	Get global perspectives
	Respect to other cultures
	Promotes open-mindedness
Gift	Wanting the best for the child
	To give a foundation
	Gift of communication
Fulfilling their own dreams	Teach a parent
	Regretting not having learned a language
	Seeing the benefits enjoyed by a bilingual spouse/relative
Positive reinforcement	Positive reaction of others
	Child's successes in other languages
	Sense of achievement
	Pleasure in helping others
	Seeing the benefits enjoyed by a bilingual spouse/relative
	To impress and surprise others
Language is power	Knowing a language is empowering
	Speaking another language makes one a leader
	Better position in the society

Table 5.5 *Motives related to heritage and culture*

Ties within the family	Preserving the language	Identity	Avoidance of cultural/ linguistic guilt
Ties with family Ties between generations Strengthening of parent/child relationships	To keep ancestral language alive Language as a home Conserving a language away from home	Language as an integral part of culture and religion Cultural identification Connection to culture Cultural integration: ability to speak L2 and assimilate with L2 culture A way of self-expression	Cultural guilt: did not teach the language (which is an integral part of culture) Parental guilt: did not give enough Spousal guilt: took the spouse away from the family

Child-Centered Motives: Heritage and Culture

The most common theme that came up when the parents discussed the reasons they were raising their children multilingually was heritage and culture. Eighteen out of 26 participants were fostering their own heritage languages. Parent participants who themselves were not native/heritage speakers of the language that they were teaching to their children were interested in establishing connections between the child and other, "outside-the-family" speakers of the language. They were interested in giving the child access to the L2 culture and the ability to fit in. Within the theme of heritage and culture there were several subthemes which included "ties within the family," "preserving the language," the theme of "identity," and also a theme of "avoidance of cultural/ linguistic guilt." These subthemes were often intertwined. Table 5.5 lists the codes for the motives within each subtheme.

The interviews revealed the multidimensional nature of family ties established and supported by teaching the children's heritage languages. The language connection joined family members between and within generations. For many participants it meant teaching a child the language spoken by the older family members: grandparents, aunts, uncles, and also by the children's peers – their cousins. Tricia, whose young children speak Brazilian Portuguese, told us about the early childhood interactions her son and daughters have had with their cousins in Brazil: "They were singing the songs with their cousins. That was sweet. Their cousins will buy them CDs they like and they all sing the same songs." For families where only one parent was a native speaker of a particular language, speaking the same language was seen as a bond between the parent and child. Veronica, whose husband is from Germany, told us that it was her priority that their son Andrew grows up bilingual: "It is really important that he is able to converse with his grandparents who don't speak anything other than German and to be fluent in his father's mother tongue and culture. I mean that it's important for their relationship, a father-son relationship." Several parents spoke about teaching the children their heritage language as means of creating a special parent-child link that strengthens their relationship. Research supports the benefits of being competent in one's heritage language, as it promotes positive social interactions, a strong sense of ethnic identity, and deeper understanding of cultural values (Cho, 2000; Imbens-Bailey, 1996; 2000).

Another motive connected to raising children to speak heritage languages was to preserve the language often for its own sake. Our study yielded three reasons that made this preservation critical for families: a) saving a nearly extinct language, b) preserving a language as one constant in the context of frequent changes in a family's life, and c) continuing a language tradition far away from home. Taani, the mother of trilingual Mihir, told us about a rare language that Taani's father was teaching his grandson:

My dad speaks to him in another different Indian language, it called Moltani ... it's actually a language that is historically dead now. When the Partition happened between India and Pakistan that state was dissolved, and that's where my dad was from ... my mom also knows this language, but I think their generation is probably the last one to know it ... And my dad speaks it to [Mihir] all the time ...

For Taani and her family, Mihir's progress in this particular language meant sharing a unique part of the heritage, continuing the line of rare speakers, and allowing him to carry on the linguistic legacy. For Mayda, raising her daughter, Vana, and son, Raffi, trilingually in English, Armenian, and Arabic, teaching the children Armenian meant establishing a heritage language in a frequently changing environment:

In a way it's not a choice, you know. It's part of our culture to keep the language alive. Armenians, we do like to keep our culture, tradition, language. Most of us, we do live in diaspora so it's the only way to survive, it's to keep our language alive ... Armenians are very open in terms of learning other languages since they don't live in their homeland. So then they know the only way for them to survive and succeed is by knowing many languages ... Tomorrow I don't know where we're going to be. If war comes up, you know they just, escape, leave and go to another country. We do put a lot of emphasis on languages ...

Mayda's family was used to moving to different countries due to the geopolitical climate of the Middle East. Teaching the children Armenian had a critical way of preserving a heritage language without having a stable home. Finally, for several participants who saw their stay in the United States as possibly temporary, preserving a language meant its conservation within the family, until potential return to their home country. Recall that Dulce, Salvadorian-American mother of Spanish-English bilingual José, told us she was raising her son speaking both languages in case there came a time she decided to return to El Salvador. Even though the motives for preserving the heritage language discussed above were slightly different from one family to another, the common thread that links all the motives together is the preservation of the language for the purpose of connectedness – with family, culture, distant motherland, and the family's past.

A subtheme of teaching the language to children as a means of forming their identity was also prevalent within the larger theme of "heritage and culture." Several parents saw language as an integral part of culture and religion, without which one cannot identify with a particular background. Veronica, whose young trilingual son, Andrew, is growing up speaking English, German, and Hebrew, told us that she and her husband agreed that learning the language and culture are equally important: "Well we wanted him to have both languages, both cultures [Hebrew and German], religion … all those things were conversation before we got married." Parents taught children languages in order to give them an opportunity to connect with the culture of the language. For parents who were raising their children speaking heritage languages, this meant giving them another means of cultural identification. Taani, the mother of Mihir, explained,

I grew up that way myself and to me my native language is a vehicle to culture, so it feels like without the language and especially without the comprehension of the language, it would be really difficult to integrate a lot of my culture that I have grown up with. That is why I want him to know the language and at the very minimum at least to understand the language fully. Because we go back to India often and I think we do primarily identify as being Indian before anything else. So the culture is very important to us, like the values, traditions, and everything else that goes along with that. I think without the language he will be kind of on the outside.

Parents who were teaching children a language that was not necessarily part of their heritage saw it as a way to give their children an opportunity to integrate with another culture, assimilate with it, and feel themselves fitting in. Leonid, whose eldest daughter is bilingual in Russian and English and also speaks French and Spanish fluently, described the perceived benefits of speaking several languages: "I watched my daughter grow up and she's great with languages in general. And if I say what benefits she has obtained by speaking, by being bilingual and speaking four languages, I would say it's great, it's helpful, it's allowed her to travel a lot and fit in in places." The ability for children to associate and possibly feel at home with multiple cultures was a motivation

Table 5.6 *Teaching a heritage language to avoid guilt*

Cultural guilt	Parental guilt	Spousal guilt
"I see language as closely related to culture. So through language, you are passing on that culture … you are valuing your culture, your heritage. I feel that as generations go by, we are more and more detached from … my fear is that as we go on, generation after generation, that [culture] gets lost." (Lilian)	"In my mind, it's mostly about parental guilt. We just want to do the most for our kids so maybe if I don't do it, I'm shortchanging my child and I would never want to do that so I'm going to keep doing more and more things and hope that it's beneficial for them." (Leonid)	"I think there is a lot of guilt when you don't live in your spouse's country. You take someone away from family members." (Tricia)

to teach them another language as a way of self-expression. Mayda pointed out that Vana and Raffi "have the choice to express themselves in many different languages."

Finally, another motive associated with heritage and culture that emphasized the importance of "bettering" the children through teaching them another language was the guilt of the missed opportunity. Parents tried to avoid this guilt by teaching the children the heritage language. Interview analysis yielded three types of motivational guilt feared by the parents if the child did not learn the heritage language: "cultural guilt" of belonging to a culture and not allowing the child into it, "parental guilt" of not teaching the child a language as a useful skill, and "spousal guilt" of taking the heritage language speaking spouse away from his/her family and severing intimate ties with other heritage language speakers within the family. Table 5.6 provides examples of quotes in which the parents expressed feelings of guilt related to not teaching a heritage language to their children.

Table 5.6 illustrates that just as the majority of parent motivations for teaching their children multiple languages, the guilt motivation is bi-directional and focuses on both the child and the parents, within the microcosm of the family, community, and culture. Additionally, all three kinds of guilt are directly connected to two motivation types: instrumental and integrative motivation recognized by Gardner and colleagues (Gardner, 2007; Gardner and MacIntyre, 1994). Not precluding the children from joining the culture, the community of heritage language or L2 speakers, or heritage language speaking family, is closely allied with integrative motivation. However, not teaching the heritage language or L2 to children can also be viewed as not equipping them with

Table 5.7 *Parent motivations: Aiming for enhanced social, linguistic, and cognitive development*

Social development	Linguistic development	Cognitive development
Better socialization	Opportunity to develop	Enhanced brain
Better social development	another language	development
Comfort in interaction	Opportunity to value	Enhanced ability to learn
Helps getting along	another language	Makes kids more able
Promotes the sense of	Facility/comfort with	Metalinguistic ability
community	languages	Mental exercise
Multilingual friends	To have a sense of language	
To fit into places	To enjoy untranslatable	
Cultural integrationCultural	nuances of languages	
enhancementGiving a		
social choice		
"Being multilingual	"In terms of language	"Well, it's all the things
enriches you culturally	development, I would	we read that the brain
… and gives you ideas	love for her to learn	develops. That it's a
about different ways	at least a Romance	more … sophisticated
of communication that	language, because I think	development if
you don't get just from	as long as she learns	people speak multiple
speaking just English,	at least one romance	languages." (Leonid)
those nuances that you do	language, then some of	"I definitely think it's
not get without language	the others will be easier.	shaken up some different
about culture. And I think	Like if she learns Spanish	parts of your brain. So
that directly leads into	early on, then French	it's definitely a plus."
social development.	would be easier, Italian	(Danielle)
The more exposure	would be easier. She'll	"Children who speak two
you have to things that	be able to pick it up, read	languages are better
are different from you,	it, and kinda understand	off than children who
that helps you grow as	a little bit better. And	speak one, and three
a person, and it rounds	I think it'll also help her	languages are better. It's
you out and makes you	too with English even	a mental exercise that
more interesting, a little	later on. I think all these	is very very beneficial
bit more open minded	things will help her with	intellectually. Beyond the
and I think that would	English later on because	communication and the
impact [Mihir's] social	so much of English is	social aspect of it, I think
development in terms of	based in other languages,	it affects their learning,
friendship making and his	based in Romance	their ability to learn
ability to socialize with	languages as well." (Tina)	anything." (Ultan)
people from different		
backgrounds." (Taani)		

valuable tools for obtaining better education, careers, etc., which is part of instrumental motivation (both are discussed further at the end of this section on motivation). The motive of guilt (or attempts to avoid it) demonstrates complexity and multidimentionality of the broader "heritage and culture" motives.

Child-Centered Motives: Enhanced Child Development and Access to Favorable Conditions

In Chapter 2, we discussed research focused on the benefits that multilingualism holds for child development. The interviews revealed that parents were not only aware of comprehensive benefits listed by research but also witnessed them first-hand as they were watching children develop, speak, and think multilingually. This awareness and positive personal experiences served as the most powerful motivation for parents' continuation of multilingual practices. Having heard about the benefits of learning multiple languages, parents anticipated enhancement in their children's social, linguistic, and cognitive development. Table 5.7 shows the different aspects of enhanced child development anticipated and recognized by parents as outcomes of language learning and a multilingual upbringing. It also provides quotations from the interviews that best represented the parents' expectations.

The parent participants were motivated not only by their children's prospects of enhanced social, linguistic, and cognitive abilities. They also believed that multilingualism gives their children unique qualities or characteristics and provides *access to favorable conditions* in children's near and more distant futures. Several parents, especially those who grew up speaking one language, believed that knowing another language will distinguish their children among their monolingual peers and provide their children with better opportunities in school (for example, taking more advanced classes) and deeper understanding of the material taught. For parents who were multilingual, child-centered motivation sometimes lay with the desire to perfect their child's language capabilities: to make sure that their child becomes an excellent native speaker. Tina, a mother of a very young multilingual, Lilia, explained that she would like her daughter "to be able to understand the nuances of another language, which is something that I think you can only get when you learn a language early on. I think that being a native speaker in any language is going to be much better than being a foreign language learner." Overall, between both types of parent the most common motivation was to make their children stand out and be prepared for the competitive world with unique qualities that knowing more than a single language adds to children's knowledge, personality, and methods of social interaction. These qualities that parents perceived as consequences of multilingualism were expected to manifest themselves in children's academic performances and better prepare them for the future. Lilian, a prospective parent in our sample and a teacher, saw it this way:

Learning languages is very important from a very academic point of view. Of course there are cognates and if you are teaching them something, you can make that little connection. "Oh, you say this, and you can remember that if you know that word in

Spanish." I am thinking of 5th grade, you know, the Latin and Greek roots. That very academic language. You can easily tap into Spanish.

Another motivation that many parents shared with us was their belief that knowing another language provided children with access to numerous resources. The parents listed "access to more and different people," "access to different cultures," "access to diverse ideas," and "access to the world." Through this access, parents believed their children would be subjected to more favorable conditions for acquiring knowledge and thus learn better. Parents felt that knowledge of additional language(s) would strengthen their children's school and college readiness. Leonid, whose three sons are growing up speaking English and learning Russian, put it this way: "I still wanted them to have at least the kind of rudimentary knowledge [of Russian] and the base so that in school or college they would at least have the foundation." Some parents also felt that by teaching additional languages to children at home they were saving their children some time. They hoped that this time could be spent at school on other important subjects. Miko, who grew up bilingual and whose parents taught him to speak, read, and write in Spanish at home, planned to continue this practice with his children: "I think we can teach him or her just perfectly fine Spanish in our home. And school should be in English and other important classes."

Parents also hoped that competent knowledge of another language could result in their children earning language certificates that could be used for college credits and studying abroad. Nicole, whose two sons are growing up speaking English and German, had far reaching plans in mind: "When they become teenagers they can also test for the language certificate which then gives them the opportunity to study in Germany if they wanted to. You have to have that language certificate if you went to high school in a foreign country or you have to take it before you go to college there." Additionally several parents saw their children attending colleges abroad as a feasible goal. Nicole continued, "There is another reason why I want my kids to be able to speak German fluently – because college is free in Germany! So if they wanted to eventually just study there that would be an opportunity for them." Some of the parents saw language learning as useful because it could open multiple career opportunities. Taani, whose son Mihir is surrounded by many languages, shared her goals with us: "I definitely want him to be at a minimum bilingual. I am also thinking in terms of when he is older and he has a career, I think being multilingual can be very useful in terms of enhancing the career opportunities."

Parents anticipated that the access provided by languages to resources would result in professional advantage, better careers, and a wider choice of professions. Our findings outlining the values that parents saw in language learning is well aligned with the values recognized by parents globally. A study by Lan, Torr, and Degotardi (2012) surveyed 263 Taiwanese mothers who were teaching English to their preschool children. The authors discovered similar motivations that were provided by our participants, such as school readiness, career opportunities, and access to a global language. Although longitudinal research examining the benefits of multilingual abilities is scarce at the moment, a few studies indicate that bilingual learners who studied in two-way bilingual programs have demonstrated long-term academic success, increased high school graduation rates, and no interference with English (Ramirez, Perez, Valdez, and Hall, 2009). All of the indicators of success listed in the study predict better career options, and, therefore, support parents' beliefs in the socioeconomic benefits of multilingualism.

Child-Centered Motives: Language as Power

Parents also recognized knowing more than one language has power. Tina, who is teaching her young daughter Lilian three languages, stated, "I think understanding foreign language is empowering. And so I think that that will be a gift for her as she goes into school and beyond, and work and beyond." Extending this theme, several parents told us that they witnessed their children take on leadership roles because they were able to speak more than one language. Recalling the time when his French-English bilingual son Georges went to an American high school soon after the family moved to the United States, Ultan told us the following anecdote of Georges' first days in school. In the story below, Georges, who has ASD, became a leader of his ESL class due to his bilingual abilities. He also formed long-lasting friendships:

Knowing several languages is very important, and [Georges] benefitted from it. He was the interpreter, he made friends the first day he went to school and they were in the group of English as a Second Language. And none of the other kids spoke English well, and he was sort of the leader. And this was the first time in his life – he was looked upon as a leader. And that was thrilling for him. He was teased later on for his slow learning and his ways, but I think the first year or maybe two years of high school were thrilling for him. And he still has those friends from various different languages and backgrounds, from Korea and Thailand and Guatemala and things like that, they're still very close friends ...

Knowledge of language allowed multilingual children to translate, make sense, and explain what the speakers of other languages were saying, as well as serve as meaning-makers. This also allowed them to be individuals who had a better understanding of situations and someone to whom their peers and adults had to pay attention. Parents hoped that knowing the languages would also lead their children to a better position in the society. Nora, who is raising her three daughters bilingually, explained the benefits she saw in bilingualism: "I think

Table 5.8 *Ways in which multilingualism promotes the sense of a broader world in children*

Deeper sense of global awareness	Tolerance and open-mindedness	Confidence in knowing more than one language/ culture	Respect for other languages and cultures
"I want them to be multilingual and have a global perspective –what if they want to relocate to a different country." (Lilian)	"Multilingualism helps you grow as a person, rounds you out and makes you more interesting, a little bit more open minded and I think that would impact his social development in terms of friendship making and his ability to socialize with people from different backgrounds." (Taani)	"George was able to start using all his languages and being an interpreter for other kids who arrived from Korea and Guatemala. He had some English, even though he had a French accent, but he was able to really help the other kids around. And that really built up self-esteem, self-confidence, as well as the love for languages. I think when we moved here, all [my children] realized the preciousness of having several languages." (Danielle)	"I want Lilia to understand various cultures and various people from all different walks of life, and one of the best ways and easiest ways to do that is to be able to speak another language. Because the way to get to know other people is to really speak their language. I think it's also a sign of respect for them." (Tina)

when you are bilingual you will be in a better position and I think society wise too. I think you will be able to move not only within this English-speaking population but within the Spanish population as well."

Child-Centered Motives: Increasing Global Awareness, Confidence, Tolerance and Respect

Another child-centered motive was giving the children the gift of a "broader world." It included a deeper sense of global awareness, tolerance, and open-mindedness, as well as confidence and respect for other languages and cultures. Table 5.8 provides participant quotes that illustrate the different ways in which the parents felt multilingualism would broaden the children's world.

Parents wanted to broaden their children's global perspectives and make their world "bigger." They hoped to expand their world views, learn to appreciate different languages and cultures, and to be ready to go and live or work in other countries. Additionally, some parents felt that knowing a language was an excellent tool for traveling: "Whenever it was possible I brought my family to Russia, to Scotland, to Spain and the kids would lust after travel. And this kind of curiosity about other countries, the language is opening the door to a curiosity about other people" (Ultan); and, furthermore, survival in other countries: "Armenians are very open in terms of learning other languages, since many of them don't live in their homeland. So then they know the only way for them to survive and succeed is by knowing many languages" (Mayda). Parents believed that knowing other languages breaks down the barriers between the people and cultures. Several mothers stressed the sense of respect for other cultures that they hoped to instill in their children. Tina, who is raising her little daughter Lilia speaking several languages, explained: "Multilingualism, understanding other people is powerful. I want her to grow up having this gift. And even being able to go out to a restaurant and to speak to everybody, I think is, it's a matter of respect." Summing up the parents' goals and aspirations for their multilingual children, we could say that the study participants saw their sons and daughters as ambassadors of global awareness and multicultural understanding. They wanted the children to move beyond tolerance toward knowledge of languages and cultures, deeper understanding of others, and shared cultural values.

While the majority of motives in this particular subtheme were aimed at the "outside world" with the goal of instilling global awareness and understanding in children growing up within the dominant U.S. culture, the parents whose children were growing up learning English as their additional language had similar goals: to make their children confident and savvy in this language and its culture (see the quotes in Table 5.8). Other sentiments that emerged in the interviews of parents who were not native speakers of English were the motives to learn a language in order to "not get into trouble" and the ability "to defend oneself." Dulce, who does not speak much English herself and who is raising her son José bilingually in English and Spanish, explained her rigorous efforts even though she thought she might return to El Salvador one day:

In the future if he wants to stay here and mom needs to leave, he will know how to defend himself with English. If he only knows Spanish, he will not know how to defend himself. There are people who say, "What's the point of learning English if we will soon leave?" But we don't know, so therefore, they need to learn both languages. I would tell these parents we should not raise them only with Spanish, but also with English and if they have the opportunity to learn yet another language that is even better. [Translated from Spanish]

Parent-centered motives: Catching the right moment. From child-centered
motivations we now turn to the second large group of motives that focused
on parents' interests, dreams, and family priorities. Parent-centered motivations were largely based on their own experiences as language learners.
The majority of the participants, regardless of whether they grew up monolingual or multilingual, had the experience of learning or attempting to learn
a language in adulthood. These motivations combined the parents' experiences with their beliefs about children's language learning. The motives
that we grouped under the subtheme of "catching the right moment" were
largely based on one particular misconception: it is easier to learn a language when one is young (see Chapter 3 for a more detailed description).
The argument that many parents used to support this claim was that it is
hard, extremely time-consuming, and stressful to learn a language in adulthood. Tina used herself as an example, explaining her adamant intent to
teacher her daughter Lilia multiple languages as early as possible: "When
I went back to school and starting taking Chinese, and even before then
I realized what a disadvantage it was to start taking a foreign language as an
adult, how much time and effort it takes, and how much easier it would have
been to start as a child." For children, in the participants' opinion, learning
a language was simpler.

An additional motive many parents used was that for many of them and
their spouses speaking another language to a child was a natural inclination
and was "simple and [did] not take much time" (Kelly, a prospective mother).
Research recognizes this motive as prevalent not only in the United States
but also in other countries. The study by Lan and colleagues (2012) that
surveyed the mothers of Taiwanese preschoolers who were teaching their
children English as an L2 at home revealed that the participants believed
that "the earlier the better" (p. 133). The "catching the right moment" motivation extended beyond the "right time" in the child's and parents' lives to
such motives as "taking advantage of the location" and "taking advantage
of access to L2 speakers." A few families felt that the areas where they lived
were the hubs of access to speakers of the families' heritage languages or
in the case of English-dominant families, their child's L2 and the associated cultural resources of these minority languages. Linda, who lives in Los
Angeles, raising two young bilingual daughters, elaborated this idea in her
interview:

[We need to be] really embracing those cultures [around us]. There is a Latin American
museum and there are book stores and story hours and that is something great that
you can do in Los Angeles that you might not be able to do everywhere or with other
languages but you can do with Spanish. But I think just having fun ... you can kind of
get at it from different avenues from speaking at home to listening to music, all of those
places.

"Hubs of access to the heritage or additional language" included living in another country (19 participant families brought into the family an additional language from places where they grew up, worked, or lived as exchange students), residing either in large multicultural metropolises like Los Angeles, or within or close to linguistic minority communities. Tricia who is raising her children speaking Brazilian Portuguese and who has moved a lot around the United States, gave us a bird's-eye view of multilingual communities: "When I moved to Chicago ... you had the radio in Spanish. You could have turned on the TV in Spanish. You could have gone to the Spanish-speaking neighborhoods!" On a smaller scale, for parents who did not move around and did not set a goal to be connected to the linguistic minority speaking communities, this motivation included living in close proximity to grandparents, who were seen as a powerful factor for developing and maintaining heritage language knowledge and skills in children (see further discussion about the role of grandparents in multilingual upbringing in Chapter 7).

Parent-Centered Motives: Fulfilling the Dreams

Another common motive for teaching children more than one language was coded as fulfilling the parents' aspirations and dreams. Ten out of 26 participating parents told us that they always wanted to learn another language when they were young but did not have a chance to do so (they later learned a heritage language or L2 as teenagers or adults). Tina who comes from a Chinese background recalled,

When my mom came to this country she was first generation. And my paternal grandmother instructed my mother to never speak anything but English to us, because we live in America and it's important for us to speak English. So I did not have the fortune [of learning Chinese] growing up, of listening to that early on, because the dialect and the tones are so difficult.

The parents who dreamed of learning a language during their own childhood saw an opportunity to realize this unfulfilled dream by teaching languages to their children. Tina continued, "I did not grow up bilingual. And that is the reason why I'm so gung ho about teaching Lilia multiple languages." Another source of motivation was seeing the benefits and successes enjoyed by other family members (spouses, siblings, and more distant relatives) and acquaintances who were successful at language learning. These benefits included the ease of understanding of multilingual communication, traveling and studying abroad, and interesting careers. The following quote from Mayda's interview illustrates this point:

Table 5.9 *Seeing multilingual children as language learning partners and teachers*

Tina and 19-month-old Lilia: Language learning partners	Dulce and 4-year old José: Learning together	Tilda and 3-year-old Bryan: Student and teacher
"I'd love for her to learn sign language. I'm actually waiting for her to get a little bit older and then I'm actually gonna go back and take a class in sign language with her."	"I would play with him and he would say, 'Give me the red, give me the red' and I would point to blue and he would say, 'That's not red, that's not red.' He tries to teach me. If I am not able to understand English I will not be able to teach or help him much. Therefore, my goal is to learn English." [Translated from Spanish]	"I would like for him to teach me Spanish and he does. My son is starting to come home and he is telling me the words in Spanish and actually he is also teaching my husband some Swedish."

My nephew, he's just fascinated with the Middle East. When he went to college [overseas] … he specialized in Islamic culture. He learned the language, writing, reading, in college … And now he's [overseas]. He's just fascinated with the culture, with the language.… I want my kids [to be] fluent, you know, definitely reading, writing Arabic. That's my dream, that's my goal for both. In terms of future success and career-wise, professionally. I definitely will push them …

Additionally, a number of parents saw their children as potential future teachers who will later teach them the languages they wanted or needed to learn. This was particularly typical for parents, who themselves were not as swift as their children were at learning languages and who witnessed their children's successful language acquisition. Table 5.9 provides some of the parents' quotes in which they discuss the possibility of learning additional languages with and from their children.

Parent-Centered Motives: External Positive Reinforcement

The motives we discussed all pushed the parents toward engaging in the multilingual upbringing of their children. In other words, most of these motives were present from early on, often even before the children were born. They were shared by people who are currently parents and prospective parents alike. The next subtype of motivation was gained by parents *during* the process of raising their children multilingually and it was based on the multifaceted positive reinforcement they received while doing so. One of the themes present in every interview was the positive reaction of others that parents encountered as they and their children interacted with relatives and strangers in their daily lives. Linda's quote exemplifies the sentiments and experiences of multiple participants in our study: "We often get the 'Oh that is so wonderful! That is such a good thing to do for your kids. I wish I could do it.'" Parents unanimously reported very encouraging comments and the perceived sense of admiration coming from those who witnessed their children's multilingual abilities. Additional motivation came from witnessing their children's successes in language learning. Tina, who was initially worried whether her daughter would be a late speaker due to exposure to multiple languages, told us, "Now that she's a little older and I see that it actually works, it's fine, I'm not worried about that. She's already saying two and three word sentences, which is, you know they don't, aren't actually supposed to start doing two word sentences until age 2, and that inspires me."

Participants also reported feeling the sense of achievement reinforced by external public approbation. This encouraged the parents to persevere with multilingual practices because they felt good about being able to impress and surprise others. Kevin, one of Betty's bilingual sons, who was himself interviewed as a prospective parent in our study, described this type of motivation: "Every now and then it is fun to surprise people. I lived in New York and heard people on the subway discussing in Spanish where they are trying to go and how they are going to get there, so I chimed in and answered. Their jaws dropped to the floor ..." Another motivation was knowing that language is a helpful skill that can be used to assist others. Several parents spoke of it with pride. These parents not only witnessed their children's progress in learning languages, but they also saw them put it to use, and that was a source of powerful motivation for parents. Talking about this, Bianca proudly described her sons' ability to speak Spanish: "For me it is rewarding ... it was easy for them when they met people that don't speak English, and they will help and, going back to my family, they will have more conversations and more freedom away from me without worrying about me translating."

Parents' Motivations: Beyond the Framework of Instrumental and Integrative Motives

Parents' motivations for teaching their children multiple languages were diverse and complex. They did not neatly fit within any one particular motivation framework. Table 5.10 demonstrates the complexity of motivation types that emerged from participants' interviews. While Gardner's (1985) and Dörnyei's (1990) theory of instrumental and integrative motivation for mastering languages systematized the bulk of motives, a number of them seem to have different roots. Having reorganized the motives in this section by type,

Table 5.10 *Classification of parents' motives by types of motivation*

Language learning motivation	Other motivation types				
Gardner (1985), Dörnyei (1990)	Maslow (1943)				Steel and Konig (2006)
	Esteem need	*Safety need*	*Social need*	*Need for self-actualization*	*Temporal motivation*
Instrumental: Language as a tool for obtaining the following "Access"	To increase global awareness, tolerance and respect	To defend oneself and stay out of trouble	Response to positive reinforcement	Fulfilling parents' own dreams	Catching the right moment
Education				A gift	
Career readiness				The best for my child	
Trade					
Business					
Travel					
Language as power					
Cognitive, social, and linguistic advancement of the child					
Perfection of native language abilities					
Integrative: Language as a means of integration into culture					
Getting to know one's roots					
Knowing one's heritage					
Identity					
Integration into culture					

a number of motives discussed above, such as access, education and career readiness, usefulness for trade, business and travel, and even "language as power" fit into the category of instrumental motivation. Parents were teaching children more than one language, so that the children could use these languages to obtain certain benefits. Parents also reported a few motives that fit into integrative motivation, which focuses on belonging to a specific group. Our participants' integrative motivation was based on the goal of associating with the people who speak the same language and share a common linguistic and cultural heritage. The motive of creating an identity of a particular language speaker also can be seen as an integrative motive to join the ranks of people who share identity traits.

The category of "other" types of motives presents a variety of motivation types mentioned in the literature. Maslow's (1943) hierarchy of human needs (which includes physiological, safety, social, and esteem needs, as well as the need for self-actualization) allows for further categorization of remaining motives. "Increasing global and cultural awareness, tolerance, and respect" was one of the leading motives. It can be classified as "esteem needs," which include self-esteem and appreciation of the self by others. Parents' motivation of "response to positive reinforcement" can be categorized as "social needs." "Staying out of trouble" and "learning a language to defend oneself" is a "safety need." "Fulfilling own dreams" through raising multilingual children can be seen as a continued "need for self-actualization." This need is manifested in trying to reach one's own highest potential. If a parent did not succeed in learning a language, they could be vicariously living out this dream through their children. Similarly, the motives of giving the children the "gift of communication" and "giving the best to the child" also fulfill the same need. Finally, Maslow's framework does not fit the motive of "catching the right moment." To explain this, we have to turn to temporal motivation (Steel and Konig, 2006), where the brevity of time perceived as available for learning serves as a motivator. Thus, we had to pull from three motivation frameworks to classify and organize parents' motives for raising their children multilingually. The frameworks are not entirely mutually exclusive and certain parts of the two main frameworks, Language Learning Motivations (Dörnyei, 1990; and Gardner, 1985) and Hierarchy of Needs (Maslow, 1943) overlap. Integrative motivation can be seen as fulfilling the social need. However, the frameworks do not neatly fold into one another, and the challenge of finding one unified motivation framework remains. This perhaps is illustrative of the complexity of motives behind multilingualism within individual families. Understanding this complexity is equally critical for both parents, who might not be aware of the wide range of motivations of other families, and educators, who may not be aware of the mechanisms at play for helping multilingual children develop.

Investment as Motivation

As we analyzed parents' motivation for raising their children bi- or multilingually, we uncovered a complex framework of motives that does not neatly fit into any one single language acquisition motivation theory. This is consistent with previous research findings that propelled research in the late 1990s and 2000s to search for a new theoretical lens to view language learning motivation. The studies of ESL learners' motivation by McKay and Wong (1996) and Norton (1997; 2000) proposed the construct of *investment* as a complex notion that embodies the learner's commitment to language learning. Investment is based on a broad range of desired outcomes, which include but are not limited to such different notions as friendship, education, and financial prosperity (Norton, 2000). It is also linked to the learner's construction of self-identity (Potowski, 2004) and takes into consideration multiple variables of socio cultural context in which the language is learned.

In our study, there is difficulty with fitting this complex network of motives into any existing framework. This is further complicated by the fact that we are examining the motivations of parents and children's families, rather than the language learners themselves. However, as we coded the interviews, the theme of investment clearly emerged in parents' narratives. Therefore, we argue that the framework of investment proposed by McKay and Wong (1996) and Norton (2000) and further developed by Potowski (2004) is an appropriate theoretical stance by which to examine the parents' motivations. In this section, we examine five types of investment that parents reported in their interviews. These include financial and emotional investment, investment in the well-being of the family, investment of time, and investment in a promise of L2 mastery, while faced with current realities of sacrifice of parents' and children's immediate opportunities and comforts. Table 5.11 provides a summary of these five investment types with illustrative examples of each category, as well as the desired outcomes encountered in our study.

Financial Investment

One of the most frequently mentioned types of investment was financial investment. Providing children with complete immersion and opportunities to interact with native speakers of the heritage or additional language did not come at a cheap price for many participants. The parents named three subtypes of financial investment associated with children acquiring more than one language. The first most recurrent expense included visiting target-language countries either to see family or to provide an L2 immersive experience for the child. Often parents brought up how expensive these trips were and discussed their ability or inability to afford such an investment. Veronica and her bilingual

Table 5.11 *Investment types*

Type of investment	Examples/subtypes	Desired outcome
Financial investment	Trips to L2 country Renting a house for vacations in L2 country Hiring helpers who are L2 native speakers A parent staying at home and teaching L2 to children Enrolling children in multilingual programs Paying for private L2 schools "Economic model of bilingualism"	For the children to have better careers in future To immerse children in L2 To have access to cheaper education later To spend now, so that it pays off later
Investment in the family	Visiting L2 speaking grandparents Not raising the child in the dominant culture Following family traditions	To have the children freely converse with L2 speaking relatives To familiarize children with L2 culture Knowing their roots
Emotional investment	Putting up with worries about children's language and social development Struggle to keep children speaking L2 Becoming a family "outcast" Being a very disciplined parent	Children's success in L2
Investment of time	Spending hours teaching children Spending time looking for L2 schools	To provide children with quality L2 education To provide children with access to L2 resources
Investment as a promise of future L2 mastery	Giving up parents' chance to learn English right away Giving up complete understanding of what your child says Risking/giving up the children's sense of comfort	Children's success in L2

2½-year-old son Andrew had just come back from visiting his grandparents in Germany. She shared with us their family plans for continued investment in visits to that country: "We really feel strongly that Andrew is fluent in both cultures as well as both languages. I think when he is older and we can afford … The intention would be to rent a house for the summer and just have him live there."

The next type of expense relayed to us by parents was creating L2-rich home environments by surrounding the child with L2-speaking caregivers. Ten out of 24 participant families hired multilingual babysitters. In six more families, one of the parents stayed at home and interacted in the heritage language or L2 with their child(ren). Tricia, who is raising her children speaking Brazilian Portuguese, explained, "I am not working which is probably costing us a fortune but we are not spending money on teachers. We don't have to spend every Saturday having them go to class to learn a second language. We are doing it pretty economically."

The third subtype of financial investment was creating target-language educational opportunities for children. Six families, nearly a quarter of all of families represented in the sample, enrolled their children in multilingual schools, immersion programs, or afterschool or weekend heritage-language schools, or hired L2 tutors. This did not necessarily depend on the age of the child. When Danielle and Ultan who were raising their children in English and French had to leave France for a brief period of time and moved to Canada, they recalled, "When Georges, the first one, was a baby, he was going to classes, to French classes. In the freezing cold …" The desired outcomes were in the present, as well as in the immediate and more distant future. They included achieving total immersion of children in a heritage language or L2 whether in another country or at home, and gaining skills that would lead to affordable education (e.g., through competitive scholarships to college, eligibility to study for free overseas) or to better career opportunities later. The motto of the financial investment in heritage language or L2 was "spend now, so that it pays off later" (Mayda, a mother of two trilingual children). Monica, a mother of two bilingual sons, explained the "economic model of bilingualism":

Something that I always shared as an educator with other parents is the economic benefit. If you are able to speak in two languages you are able to then communicate with a larger group of people and if you are a doctor that means your clientele has just broaden because of your ability to interact. So if you are a doctor you can have twice the patients because of that. We want them to speak English, [but] we don't want them to lose the Spanish … If you are a writer, you can write in two languages. If you are a teacher you can speak in two languages. There are so many benefits in terms of jobs and employment and opportunities. So many more …

Investment in Family

Investment in family meant keeping ties with family strong through teaching children the heritage language. This included spending time speaking the heritage language with relatives, and particularly grandparents. Twenty out of 23 families in the sample mentioned the importance of staying close with grandparents, demanding that children speak only the heritage language at home with them, and often bestowing major heritage language teaching responsibilities on grandparents. It also meant preserving family traditions, such as celebrating birthdays and holidays only or primarily in the heritage language. For some families, investment in family meant not raising children in the dominant culture. Tricia, whose L1 is English and who grew up in the United States but is raising her children to speak Portuguese, the language of their father and their Brazilian grandparents, reflected on this: "Yeah, it is really pathetic. I mean there are pros and cons. They don't watch the Backyardigans [a children's television show], they don't know any pop culture really. I just really shelter them. I am a little sad but not that sad. They are learning more ..." The payback for the investment in family as seen by parents was threefold. Through this investment, parents hoped that their children will know their roots, converse freely in multiple languages, and be able to confidently navigate multiple cultures.

Emotional Investment

Often strictly adhering to one particular language for the sake of children's mastery of it meant significant emotional investment for the parents who were implementing these practices. This investment manifested itself in overcoming the anxieties connected with myths and beliefs about the impact of multilingualism on children's linguistic and social development, discussed in Chapter 3. It also meant occasional struggles to keep children speaking the heritage language or L2 despite the influences of the outside world. Tilda, who speaks only Swedish to her son, told us, "I never speak to him in English. He asked me to speak to him in English, and I was like, 'No I am not.' I am not going to get into that because that is a very slippery slope." This form of investment demanded being a very disciplined parent and not falling into the habit of speaking the dominant language no matter how convenient. Tina, who speaks English and Taiwanese but who is determined to raise her daughter Lilia multilingually, talked about the challenge of not slipping into English in front of her little daughter, even though her husband does not speak the language. Tina spoke of the self-discipline and the faith it takes on her part: "It's kind of like a religion. You need to decide early on that this is what you want for your child and do it."

Finally, for some families, where only one parent's side of the family spoke the target language, adhering to one language within the family meant significant emotional investment at a cost of losing connections with the one side of the wider family who did not know that particular language or did not believe in the parents' methods of raising their children. A few parent participants brought up the theme of becoming an outcast within their own families. Nora, who decidedly speaks only English to her young adult and two elementary-aged daughters with the hope of improving their chances of succeeding academically, reflected,

Especially when all the family is together, [my daughters'] cousins use Spanish mostly [and not] English; and last time there was a conversation because they say why I don't let my kids, they don't use Spanish ... my husband's family criticized me because I do English even when I am talking with their kids. I don't use Spanish, I use English ... that is the criticism – why you don't use Spanish?

Tricia, whose children went to preschool speaking only Portuguese as it was the only language within their inner-family circle, described how she sensed the feeling of not only going against the wishes of her wider English-dominant family, but also being an outcast from the school community: "But if I am strong and really push it, we might just be kind of outcasts or be known as the family where no one understands anything in our house. I think if I went to a different school people [might have been] more understanding maybe. I don't know ..." This theme of becoming an outcast was present in interviews of parents who refused to speak English for the sake of perfecting their children's heritage language, as well as in the interviews of parents who decided to speak only English for the sake of their children's easier acquisition of the dominant societal language. Both groups of parents shared the experience of wider-family pressure and a lot of emotional stress as a result of their linguistic choices for their children.

Investment of Time

The theme of investment of time for raising children speaking more than one language had two main subtypes. A few parents talked about how time-consuming teaching children another language was. This was characteristic of families where not all family members spoke the target additional languages and one of the parents felt that he/she had to dedicate a lot of time to teaching the child(ren) a target language to counterbalance the lack of interactions in the desired additional language and to compensate for the void in the use of the additional language in regular family conversations. Leonid, whose wife does not speak Russian, described teaching his three sons: "I was the one that had to struggle hours after hours to educate them a little about, you know, 'This is a table,' 'This is a chair,' 'This is a couch,' 'This is a ball.' So literally with them it was like studying a foreign language even though at home, but that's what it was like."

Additional investment of time noted by parents was the time spent on getting to children's schools, language play groups, and other places where the desired additional language was available. At times, distance and time became the factors that stood in the way of children's further language acquisition. Tilda talked about choosing a school for her soon-to-be 5-year-old multilingual son:

There is a trilingual school but it is not close by and he would have to be bussed. So it may not be the best option ... There is a Mandarin school, again not close by, and I only have so many minutes to get to work and get back to pick him up that anything out of the way is not going to work out. Bussing him, it is long days for the kids. They probably get on the bus at 6:30 or 7 and they don't get back until late.

Investment in Future Mastery

In many interviews the theme of investment took on the profile of a sacrifice. Individual parents and families were giving up significant opportunities and changing their ways of life for the sake of their children's success as bi- or multilingual speakers. In some families, one of the parents had to give up a chance to perfect their own English in the name of their children's progress in Spanish, the dominant language of the home and much of the wider family. In Linda's family, two young daughters are growing up speaking Spanish and English. While both parents are bilingual, their Spanish-dominant father feels that he would have benefitted from more practice by speaking English at home. However, the family decided to give up this opportunity, his wife, Linda, reported:

It is a huge trade off because professionally he, you know, started his own business and doing sales ... and he needs to have professional English but we don't do it much at home. We could be doing more English at home for [his] benefit but we both, kind of a no-brainer, decided we want the kids to have Spanish at home.

In other families, parents decided to give up their heritage language for the sake of their children's success in English. As mentioned, Nora, a mother of three daughters, decided to speak only English to them, so that they would succeed in school. For some parents who were not as fluent in the L2 or did not know it, the sacrifice was giving up complete understanding of what their child(ren) were saying. Tina, whose husband does not speak Taiwanese, spoke of their family interactions:

I forget that he doesn't understand a foreign language sometimes. When we go to Taiwan ... we'll be talking, talking, talking in Chinese and I'll just completely forget that he doesn't understand a word that we're saying, you know. So you need a spouse to completely support you.

It turned out that not only parents were sacrificing a lot in the process of multilingual upbringing of their children. A few parents were talking about sacrificing their children's sense of comfort and security. For many of these children brought up without contact with the dominant language or culture, learning a language other than English meant not knowing popular cartoons and games and having a select group of friends and relatives with whom they were meant to interact. Parents reported that in many families children did not have a choice which language to acquire. Tilda, whose young son hears no English at home, told us, "He never had a choice. He has so far not complained about any of this and probably it could be that he started as an infant … It is a little cruel to throw him into his situation maybe but he has not known anything else."

The theme of investment in the future mastery of languages again underscores the difficult choices and the hard work the parents, children, and families at large engage in. Awareness of families' complex and multilevel investment is critical for building the understanding of educators who work with multilingual children and for anyone in the wider society with whom they interact. The state of multilingualism can be a delicate balance and easily destroyed in the face of outside influences. *Would the children who had to give up certain comforts and choices push back as they grow up?* Time will tell. We discuss this further in the next section of this chapter that focuses on challenges and successes of the process of raising children multilingually.

Challenges Perceived by Parents

The picture of a multilingual microcosm of an individual multilingual family would be incomplete if we did not take a closer look at the challenges of daily implementation of multilingualism as perceived by our study participants. Several participants took up the idea of "roadblock" that we had used in the interview schedule and used this metaphor when describing the difficulties they encountered attaining the family's goal of multilingualism. The scope of the roadblocks varied from the societal to the personal and individual. When asked about the challenge of supporting multilingualism, Linda summed it up in the following way:

I guess just, you know, the two things that I am imagining as roadblocks are this overarching English society. English is valued. Spanish is devalued, and Latino is devalued. So that is just tough. You are kind of swimming upstream there, and then I think, "I am so fearful of puberty as a parent."

Similar to Linda's recount of roadblocks, Tricia perceived, "A big roadblock maybe just for me to be like speaking the language and knowing people don't understand it." We analyzed the families' challenges further by grouping them into three distinct categories that emerged in the interviews: 1) fears of outside influences and intra-family insecurities connected with sustaining multilingualism; 2) a closely related category of challenges of finding balance for language use in child-parent and child-siblings relationships; and 3) a category that extends the intra-family dilemmas to challenges connected to family interactions with the educational system.

Intra-family Insecurities and Fears of Outside Influences

This category comprised two central themes. The first of these related to concerns regarding what would happen to the children's language once they began schooling and their world ceased to consist solely of their home lives. The second theme was parental insecurities as to whether their own proficiency in the language(s) that they were teaching to their children was sufficient. Despite the heterogeneity of the parent sample (which included English-speaking parents, parents whose first language was other than English, and varying degrees of parental language and literacy competence) all participants shared uneasiness about their child entering society through schooling and peer interactions. This apprehension can be potentially explained by the sense of losing full control over their children's language development.

Many parent participants felt great apprehension about the moment when their multilingual children would leave their home and begin formal schooling. The parents were concerned about the impact that schooling in English and the influence of peers would have on their children's progress and mastery of other languages. Linda worried about what would happen to her daughters' bilingual abilities in adolescence:

I think at some point my kids will be in a situation where they are valuing their friends' opinions more than their parents' ... So I think that could be a potential roadblock depending on who that peer group is and what is cool.

A group of parents in our study shared the common worry of making the correct school program choice for their children given the multitude of existing choices and past experiences of friends and relatives in a particular program type. Lilian, a prospective parent in our study and a teacher in a bilingual program, told us what guided her sister's choice of an English-only program for her own daughter:

My niece is actually at the school that I work at ... They have an option of the dual literacy but my sister chose to put her in the English only.... My sister is two years older than me, and my mother put her in a program similar to that [dual literacy], and my sister always said that that confused her, that she got behind in English because she was learning Spanish, and so I think this is why my sister decided to put her in an English-only class.

The overall quality of education in schools where these programs were based was another consideration. Leonid, who decided to take on the responsibility of being his sons' only Russian teacher, explained, "We had very good schools in our area so the question would have been, 'Okay, I can raise them bilingual if I move to one of the Russian communities in New York, but am I sacrificing their general education.'"

In several families, an additional complication stemmed from the conflicting opinions of different family members regarding the program choice. Lilian and Miko, both prospective parents in our study, presented two different opinions:

LILIAN: Well, we have differing opinions … at my school, it's dual literacy, not dual language … I would like them to be strong in both reading and writing, but [Miko] has a different opinion.

MIKO: If anything, I would lean towards dual literacy … I think the child will handle it and adjust perfectly fine. But I want my child, our child, to go to school in English, like it's going to be when he or she grows up.

Some parents whose L1 was not English and who, due to their limited English skills, might have encountered school and professional difficulties in the past, wanted to make sure that English instruction would be rigorous enough, so that their children would master the dominant language. Mayda, the mother of Vana and Raffi, for whom Armenian and Arabic heritage language maintenance is very important, told us that she still puts her children's knowledge of English above all languages:

They live where English is the first language. It's the language of school. I pulled them out of the Armenian school and put them in all-English school. That school has very good, strict teachers and is very academic. If they don't know English, they are going to suffer academically in all subjects and have trouble with future careers.

Just like Mayda, many parents within this subgroup were worried that their children would be put into ESL classes and would therefore miss educational and career opportunities to which their English-speaking peers would have access, a very real and documented concern (Estrada, 2014). Nora, who is an English learner herself, put her daughters in an English-only program and did not reveal their bilingual abilities to their school officials. She explained her choice of the educational program:

I did not tell anyone they spoke Spanish. I did not want any ESL for them. I don't believe in bilingual education. Unfortunately that doesn't work, personally. I think it is hard for the kids if your goal for the kids is to be successful in academic [subjects]. So if you want them to succeed you have to give the tools for them to be able to succeed and if everything is in English that is what they have to learn.

The perceived stigma of ESL classes attended by supposedly unsuccessful language learners, experiences of other children who were not able to test out of these classes, and fears that the children would never learn proper English unless they underwent total English immersion were the reasons that parents listed as explanations for not mentioning other languages spoken within their homes as is required at public school enrollment in most U.S. states (Bailey and Kelly, 2013). The excerpts from the interviews above reveal program qualities ("strict," "academic," etc.) that are appealing to parents from very diverse backgrounds. Within this context, it is critical that bilingual programs establish a reputation of academic rigor, so that the families of multilingual children no longer need to hide their linguistic abilities, sacrificing them to perceived if not actual higher quality monolingual English-language education.

A different kind of insecurity was parents' perception of their incompetence or imperfection in language(s) that they were teaching their children to speak. Taani who speaks Hindi fluently exposed her young son to multiple Indian languages and Spanish. The only challenge that she perceived in this process was her own uncertainty whether what she was doing for Mihir linguistically was sufficient and correct:

I think the only roadblock that I am encountering is just sort of how to make sure that he is learning those languages ... just because I am not speaking all of them enough to him at home ... and I do not know all of those languages perfectly ... so just sustaining it.

Although many parents within both groups (English-speaking and LOTE) had decided to assume total responsibility for teaching their children a particular language, many of them worried whether they would be able to teach their children everything within the language and literacy needed to have access to benefits available to competent language speakers.

Danielle, who speaks French, Russian, Spanish, and English, felt natural only about speaking her native French to her children. Even though her children went on and took Russian later at school, she remembered feeling incompetent about reading to them in Russian: "I never read to them in Russian. I showed them the nice drawings and books and things, but no. I didn't feel I was good enough for doing it actually." Parents' insecurity had many facets. Five participants reported being shy about speaking their second or third language outside the comfort of their home. Recalling the beginning of her family's multilingual journey, Tricia for whom Portuguese was not an L1 told us about her initial insecurity: "It is my insecurity ... I went through this when Gabriela was three months, and I am in public speaking a non-native language. You can just feel stupid where you are speaking a foreign language. That is a big roadblock." Other parents told us they or their spouses were shy to speak their non-native language in front of more competent relatives. Bianca remembered:

When [her sons] were little, one or two years old, I only spoke Spanish to them and I did the mistake to change it to English. My husband speaks English, he doesn't speak Spanish. He knows what was happening in Spanish and he understands but he is kind of embarrassed to speak.

This insecurity about speaking a particular language appeared to be transmittable, and several parents reported that their children were similarly shy to speak a language they were still learning when in public. Bianca told us that her sons who started as bilingual toddlers who easily initiated conversations and responded in Spanish in early childhood later became more reticent to speak in Spanish. Bianca said that "they still understand everything" and "talk more when they are in Mexico visiting [Bianca's] family," but they became more shy speaking Spanish as adolescents. Similarly to Bianca's sons, Leonid's Russian-English bilingual sons also went through a stage when they did not speak Russian. However, this happened more outside the home context: "There was a time when my boys were a little reticent and in public would not speak to me in Russian. They would refuse, especially around their friends."

Several parents brought up another critical challenge that possibly contributes to intra-family insecurity and can potentially affect children's desire to communicate in a non-dominant language. This challenge was occasional lack of respect to one of the languages spoken within the family. Veronica, whose son Andrew speaks German and English and is a frequent participant of multilingual play dates, reflected, "I have noticed in some families the parents do not have that same kind of mutual respect for each other's language and or culture and the rift then grows." Sometimes the lack of respect was felt outside the children's homes. Veronica continued, "Kids are often judged [by the mainstream culture] because of their dominant tongue if it is not English." Parents' interviews revealed an understanding of the delicate nature of multilingualism when it is just taking root. They stressed the detrimental impact that a disrespectful commentary or that unwitting jokes may have on young language learners. The interviews revealed that being aware of this impact is critical for maintaining a multilingual inhibition-free environment.

In summary, the themes included psychological challenges caused by social factors within and outside the families as well as insecurities that stemmed from parents' lack of language mastery. Additionally, not all parents felt that they were ready to instruct their children to speak, read, and write in another language, although a majority of parents (75% of the sample) wished that their children would be not only competent in speaking another language, but also literate. *So should parents teach children a language in which they are not completely competent themselves?* Two kinds of pertinent research findings are relevant to the context of this discussion. As discussed in Chapters 2 and 3, research underscores the importance of solid language knowledge in at least one language as a basis for additional language acquisition. If the child's L1 is underdeveloped and/or abandoned in the name of learning another language, he/she runs the risk of further difficulties with linguistic development (Espinosa, 2008). At the same time, if a solid basis for the child's first language is established and maintained, then either concurrent or subsequent exposure to other languages is not only harmless but frequently found to be beneficial (Bialystok, 1991; Dubiner, 2010; Hoff, 2014). Grosjean (2009) directly addresses the issue of parents' insecurity and doubts as to whether or not they should teach their children another language if their own knowledge of a language is less than perfect. He points out that the two critical factors in teaching a child another language are creating the need for the language and maximum exposure to each language. So parents who do not speak a language perfectly "will want to find ways of increasing the child's exposure to that language" (Grosjean, 2009, p. 3).

Challenges of Finding Balance for Language Use in Child-Parent and Child-Sibling Relationships

Apart from the parents' worry about the impact of peers on their children's multilingual abilities and motivations, parents were worried about finding the right balance for using the dominant language and additional languages. Linda's older daughter, who is almost five, is feeling the pressure of using English at school and with friends. She explained the necessity of finding a balance:

There are definitely hard moments where you are thinking, "Okay what is the right balance between really putting the Spanish on her or not the overkill that she is then doesn't like it." So like with reading we don't want her to reject reading just because ... So if she wants an English book that is fine. They go to the library once a week at school and I'll say, "Why don't you pick a Spanish book this week?"

Parents' opinions varied in terms of how much of each language the children should be speaking or should be exposed to. Some parents were absolutely adamant about using one particular language at home (recall Tricia's story from the start of this chapter), while others were more flexible. Many parents reported becoming more at ease with the idea of being flexible when they witnessed their children's continued success in all the languages that they want them to speak. Also when the schooling process was off to a smooth beginning, many parents reported that their worries subsided.

Children's peers and friends who did not speak the language that the parents worked to promote within the family were not the only forces that presented challenges to sustaining multilingualism. Siblings were frequently perceived as a factor potentially undermining the children's desire to speak languages other than the dominant language. Ten out of 17 families with multiple children reported that the siblings spoke English to each other. Fourteen out of 17 families reported that language use depended on the context and the language spoken around them. A factor that could possibly determine whether the siblings were indeed a challenge to multilingual practices within the family was the different language development trajectories of siblings within the family. Several parents reported that children within the same family had grown up with different language proficiencies, sometimes in different languages.

Nicole, who has two German-English bilingual sons, compared their German skills:

The toddler throws in more German words than the older one ... at times the seven year old has a hard time understanding some things because you have a wider vocabulary when speaking to an older child and especially when we do homework. I do it in English because there are certain expressions that he just doesn't understand and so just to make it easier I'll stick to English.

Nora told us that her three Spanish-English bilingual daughters have very different abilities and attitudes toward Spanish:

Alejandra is more fluent in both languages even at a young age. Stephanie doesn't like to speak Spanish. She understands a little bit but as soon as you start talking to her in Spanish she is like "Huh? What?" It is like she refuses to speak Spanish. Caroline, when she was little she did use the Spanish but not like Alejandra. Alejandra loves Spanish. Caroline was kind of forced to use it, but Alejandra, she can read and write it too and that is something!

The two excerpts from the interviews above reveal a number of additional factors that contribute to the differences in siblings' multilingual language abilities: the level of sophistication of conversations with parents, feeling forced or supported in speaking the heritage language, and the predominance of the heritage language or English-language tasks (e.g., homework). In some families, when the older siblings went to school, they came back with an increased amount of English that they then used around the house and in the community. Several parents reported switching to English with older siblings to help them with their studies. In doing so, they set an example for some of the younger siblings, who in turn also started using more English from an earlier age. Research has also documented this effect, with older siblings being the gateway to or source of English language dominance in the household. In some extreme cases within a generation, the oldest offspring are found to be bilingual in the heritage language and English, whereas the youngest siblings may show an almost exclusive English-language preference if not monolingualism by school age (Stevens and Ishizawa, 2007). In some cases, parents decided to be more strategic by using increased amounts of heritage language around the younger children. Nicole's example above illustrates her emphasis on German with her toddler son. Similar to Nicole, Taani shared with us her plans:

I think that when the next baby comes, I may be a little bit better with sticking to Hindi more, because I have gotten lazy about it, especially since he's gone to school, kind of letting English become the predominant language we speak. So, I think with the second baby I will be a little bit more conscious, a little bit more aware of how much Hindi she is learning.

In the families that put more effort in emphasizing the heritage language after the older siblings brought in more English, the younger children spoke the heritage language more fluently than their older brothers and sisters (i.e., Nicole's toddler son, Marta's Alejandra). In a few cases, however, older siblings experienced a resurgence of interest in the heritage language when they began to take it in high school or college. In these cases, their influence on younger siblings was quite positive, and the choice of language among the younger siblings was reversed to the heritage language. Monica who has two teenage Spanish-English bilingual sons gave us an example of a positive influence of an older sibling on the younger one's heritage language use and development,

[My younger son] is a 9th grader and so he started to take Spanish and it is coming back, which is interesting. I see him valuing it much more now and I think it is the influence of the big brother as far as how he has some fluency in Spanish and shows it. [My older son] will purposely switch to Spanish with his grandparents. He was really pushing himself and I think that has an influence on his younger brother.

The interviews revealed that siblings play complex roles in each other's language development and can serve as catalysts as well as inhibitors of multilingual practices within the family. As mentioned, research recognizes the influence of birth order on heritage language retention in families and suggests siblings have a strong effect on each other's language development. A study by Duursma and colleagues (2007) showed that "the language preferred for interaction with siblings had a much larger effect on English proficiency than the language preferred by the parents" (p. 185). Understanding the impact of siblings on language learning within a family and the mechanisms that can turn them into allies rather than an undermining force may enable informed parents to better sustain multilingualism.

Challenges Connected to Family Interactions with the Educational System

Besides anticipated challenges that parents feared in connection with their children beginning formal schooling, they also spoke of the real challenges that they encountered when their sons and daughters went to school. Similar to the intra-family challenges described above, these challenges included both psychological and physical barriers.

The psychological barriers listed by parent participants consisted of a mutual lack of trust between schools and families, a perceived lack of excitement and interest in children's multilingual abilities on behalf of school personnel, and a frequent perception of multilingual children as students who are likely to have issues with academic achievement and even demonstrate potential behavioral challenges. The mutual lack of trust was sensed by a few parents, especially those who felt that they were not familiar with the school system. The parents did not feel that they had enough knowledge about how to successfully navigate the educational system. Nora, a mother of three bilingual daughters who went to both public and private schools, explained her understanding of this lack of trust:

Unfortunately, right now teachers are not so open with parents. I don't know if it is because [they] don't want to step over and talk to the parents, or sometimes [they] are afraid. I noticed that the teachers in private school, teachers and parents can have a little bit more understanding and communication. It is hard when a parent cannot communicate with the teachers what they are feeling. Unfortunately it is, and [teachers] have to be able to understand when a parent comes in. So communication is priceless in a sense. I don't know how to navigate the system.

From Nora's perspective, both parents and teachers are afraid of each other. As a parent who is actively involved in her daughters' education and who is studying to become a teacher herself, Nora observed that multilingual children require "patience and time and effort from the teachers" and in the current climate, teachers feel that "a lot of the parents have power in the school and that can complicate stuff with the teachers." This creates apprehension felt by teachers. At the same time, parents who feel powerless are afraid of being confused by the system. They worry about losing control over their children's program placements, or the length of a particular placement. These worries create uneasiness for parents.

An additional factor that potentially affects the parents' sense of trust is the lack of interest and excitement teachers and staff have regarding a child's multilingual abilities. While parents reported almost universally positive reactions of strangers to the fact that their children spoke more than one language, the picture was dramatically different when it came to reactions of school personnel. Some parents reported that at times their children's teachers showed no interest in children's multilingual abilities. For example, Taani recalled the time when brought her little son Mihir to preschool:

I met kind of sort of puzzled looks whenever I went to his school and said, "These are the words that you would need to recognize when he says them in Hindi because he won't say them in English" ... it seemed that there wasn't any interest or any genuine ... "Oh that's great! Tell me how to teach him other Hindi words," you know, there was more of "Okay, you let us know what he needs to know." The bare minimum that they need to communicate, but nothing beyond that ...

It is possible that the teachers' weariness stemmed from the expectations of spending extra time and effort when they learned that the child spoke little or no English. A few parents mentioned that some teachers even made it clear that they expected the child to experience difficulties with academic success. Nicole shared her thoughts in regards to this:

I think the school board or the teachers have that perception that [my kids'] language development in English, in reading and comprehension, might be different than kids who only speak one language. And somebody who only really speaks German at home possibly could mix up both things and make more mistakes …

Such a pessimistic welcome into a school system caused some parents to be discouraged and then begin speaking English to their school-aged children. Hediyeh told us that such a change occurred in her family when her children went to school:

The switch between from Farsi to English happened totally at school. Once that changed, around the house gradually we also spoke English to them. And that actually I think is a mistake, because they actually speak the language better than you, you know, very quickly. We actually didn't go to school here and our English never became as strong. It's more important to talk your children I think in a language that you're really really good at.

The parents' interviews suggested that it is critical to prepare educators to view multilingual abilities as an asset rather than a deficit. It also seems important to equip educators with effective methods of working with multilingual children. Recognizing the time and effort that it takes teachers to successfully teach this population of learners, it is crucial to provide administrative and systemic support to both families and educators. It is possible that if both parties felt supported and perceived their concerns as being addressed, the sense of distrust noted by several parent participants in our study would dissipate.

Systemic challenges. The systemic challenges for sustaining and developing children's multilingual abilities as perceived by parent participants consisted of limited access to non-dominant language resources within American society. Nearly all parent participants mentioned the scarcity of literacy and language teaching/learning resources (books, educational materials, etc.) in non-English languages. Tina, whose trilingual daughter Lilia is still a toddler, was concerned about the void of multilingual toys (for Spanish and Chinese):

I would love more toys that are multilingual that are also tactile. I want to teach her how to count with something that's tactile. You know things that you can flip, you know. Or a toy like an apple that you squeeze and it says "manzana." And not just the computer. I don't necessarily like the screen thing. I want something that she can touch and she can feel. Like puzzles, blocks, things that are in multi languages.

Taani, who is teaching Hindi to her young son, shared her need of educational bilingual books:

It would be nice to have more resources … It would be nice to have more books that integrate languages … Just having extra resources that would help me teach him languages, just like I have in English – I have lots of educational books in English, to teach him colors, numbers, and shapes, and what not … but I do not have any of that in Hindi.

The shortage of educational resources was true for languages that are quite common in the U. S., as well as languages that are less common. Parents spoke of putting a lot of family effort into getting access to fun heritage language and L2 books to read to children and child- and parent-friendly textbooks that could be useful for teaching children to read and write in the target languages in a systemic way.

Additionally, parents noted the overall absence of within-school L2 literacy and language supports between elementary and high school, even for the most common languages, unless the children attended a dual-immersion program or a heritage-language school. Bianca, two of whose sons spoke Spanish before they went to first grade, told us, "There wasn't a program nearby that would teach them to read and write in Spanish, not until high school when Guillermo took Spanish." Larisa, a mother of Russian-English bilingual Boris, pointed out, "No one was going to teach him Russian outside the family, not to mention reading and writing. He went to parochial Saturday school for 3 years to learn it" [Translated from Russian].

While quite a few elementary schools have dual-immersion programs, middle schools are lacking this kind of language development and maintenance emphasis. Therefore, there exists a significant gap in attention given and importance attributed to learning languages other than English in early adolescence. The language development started in these dual-immersion programs is negatively impacted by a three- to four-year hiatus during the middle school years. This pause may negatively impact further language development when students are able to once again formally study the language in high school (at least higher-incidence languages such as Spanish and Mandarin).

Parent interviews also contained a final common subtheme regarding systemic challenges toward the maintenance of multilingualism. Parents described the shortage of and lack of easy access to diverse language programs, both in public and private schools and tutoring centers. While parents knew of programs that focused on Spanish, Mandarin, Armenian, and French, other school programs for less common languages spoken within the participant families, such as German, Portuguese, Russian, Hindi, Swedish, Korean, Japanese, and Farsi, were hard to find beyond heritage language afterschool and weekend programs. Nicole who ended up sending her German-English bilingual sons to a regular public school told us her story:

There is a German immersion charter school in [town name] and when they first started getting together and trying to hatch out a plan on how to do this, I was in the meetings and very interested and hoping that the school would open up near where I work but then it ended up being in [town name]. We actually had a spot in the lottery for them to go to kindergarten that year but it was just so much out of the way that I figured the commute would just be too much and I didn't think it was worth doing it.

Despite the demand that exists within families for programs offering target languages and despite the parental readiness to be involved there continues to be a void of language-focused educational programs. This means that the needs of large groups of diverse heritage and L2 speakers with great multilingual potential are not met at the societal level. Public schools located within or close to language-minority communities should offer heritage or L2 instruction for children throughout their school years. If this occurred the majority of physical challenges to sustaining multilingualism outside of the family context would be resolved. The school programs could serve as educational, social, and cultural "hubs" for minority language and literacy maintenance and promotion.

Successes of Multilingual Upbringing: Noticing Everyday Progress and Celebrating Achievement

The story of parents' beliefs, motivations, and challenges would be incomplete without an analysis of successes in the multilingual upbringing that participants described in their interviews. In their responses, parents delineated what they saw as successes within the process of multilingual parenting and/or as a result of multilingual upbringing. Twelve out of 26 parent participants focused on recognizing success during the process of raising their children. For example, Nora, who is raising her three daughters bilingually in Spanish and English and who is very proud of their progress in both languages, described it this way: "It is rewarding to see that your kids can succeed in English academics-wise. But at the same time you can see they can communicate with their family back home in Spanish too. So you know, it is important that it's both." Nora focuses on her daughters' bilingual abilities and her recognition of their current successes in both languages. Fourteen parents focused on future successes. For example, Veronica, whose son Andrew is learning German, described the hypothetical advantages that come with knowing this language:

I know that my kid will have the skill that is unique. I mean forget it is another language. It is unique language. My first year of college was in a conservatory of music, German was required ... and the students were struggling so hard with learning this language that they needed for their life, for their talent. I mean my kid could come in and sing opera ... I think that is really cool!

Ten parents evaluated the current successes of their young children who were actively acquiring multiple languages. Taani, whose toddler Mihir is learning his first words in Hindi and Bengali, saw immediate success in the connection established between her little son and his grandparents:

> What's rewarding is that there is a connection to the culture and a special connection to the grandparents also, because they speak only Hindi or in the case of my in-laws Bengali ... When he does say words in our native languages, I can see it's a connection that he has with them that maybe otherwise he won't ... I can see everyone's eyes light up and everyone gets happy, and it's rewarding for me to see that ...

Others, particularly parents who had adult children (n=12), provided more cumulative reports of success. Danielle, whose multilingual children are now in their late 20s and early 30s, explained,

> It's more rewarding now. I think it was just natural at the time. You know we were just speaking those languages[s] at home. Now it's really nice when I see that they pursue these languages. For example, I'm glad that Sylvie works in a bilingual school ... she has to speak French all day. Adele pushed herself because she did a Master's in French, so that was pretty intense ... Andre is using his French with editing and publishing French books ...

It is clear that in many interviews recognition of success was closely connected to the types of motivation that parents revealed in their responses (described earlier in this chapter). Parents who envisioned success within the investment model frequently spoke of future successes (advantages in school and college readiness, access to better careers, etc.). Parents who emphasized that their inspiration for multilingual upbringing was fueled by the positive reactions of others, those who exhibited temporal motivation, and those who were focused on the preservation of language and culture, all tended to provide us with more of the current success definitions.

The leading depiction of success at multilingualism was the description of children's language abilities. This description had two main subtypes. Some parents described a range of language abilities from capability to converse freely in a language other than the dominant language to complete literacy in this language. Leonid, describing his older daughter's accomplishments, provided an overview of her linguistic abilities in four languages: "My daughter is completely bilingual in Russian and English, not only speaking, but also reading and writing and I believe she also speaks French and Spanish conversationally." Others emphasized their children's success in every language they had been learning. Tina, who is determined to raise her little daughter Lilia multilingually, carefully monitors her progress in several languages: "My daughter speaks Chinese, Taiwanese, English, sign language, and we're going to teach her Spanish very soon. She's already saying two and three word sentences, which is, you know, they aren't actually supposed to start doing two word sentences until age two. She's very verbal." For Tina, the measure of Lilia's success goes beyond the number of words she says. Tina is noticing the length of the sentences, advanced overall language development for Lilia's age, and her verbal abilities taken as a whole.

Another important detail to note is that parents' recognition of success went beyond mere linguistic progress. Even though one of the central parameters that parents used to define success was children's multilingual proficiency, the concept of success in this context was not entirely defined within the bounds of language skills. Apart from their children's oral and literacy capabilities in more than one language, many parents recognized the *confidence* and *appreciation* that their children exhibited when using a language other than English as salient forms of successful multilingual upbringing. Nora, whose three daughters are bilingual in Spanish and English, commented that language proficiency results in confidence, and as a result of this confidence Nora's daughters "learned to appreciate the Spanish language too …" Danielle and Ultan moved their family from France to the United States when their French-English bilingual children were in their early teens. During the interview, the parents recalled that their older son, Georges, who also spoke some Spanish, became an interpreter for many students in his high school ESL classes:

… because he had some English. He understood everything in English, even though he had a French accent, but he was able to really help the other kids around. And that really built up self-esteem, self-confidence, and as well the love of really enjoying the two languages. When we moved here they all realized the preciousness of having two languages …

Several parents observed a similar trajectory from the confidence of learning a language to appreciation of languages in their children. They listed the sense of confidence as a standalone indicator of success, and as a desired outcome of their efforts in multilingual upbringing.

Another common theme in parents' discussion of their children's success stories was the theme of children's well-built *sense of identity* and *linguistic and cultural pride* that were strengthened by their language learning. Monica, a mother of two teen boys, told us how her older son's growing Spanish abilities have added to his sense of identity:

His identity … I think language is a part of that identity. I think it is inseparable in some ways because he knows his roots, and language is part of his culture. I don't think that they are separable, and he recognizes the value of that, I think, and appreciates it, and I think that is one of the things for him [that] is so motivating. To be able to, you know, "I am coming to visit my abuelitos [grandparents], and I am speaking to them in Spanish!" It's a different level for him right now because as he is entering adulthood. I mean he is an adult now, and the level of appreciation is far deeper …

For 14 of 26 parents, knowing family roots and culture were the leading reasons for why they embarked upon a multilingual upbringing of their children.

Many of them, like Monica quoted above, noted a qualitative change in children's sense of identity and an increased appreciation for the language(s) they were taught. This appreciation of their heritage felt very rewarding for parents. Therefore, many participants in our sample recognized this language maintenance and fostering aspect of their children's developing identity as a success.

Another characteristic that was positively noted by parents in their children that is closely related to the sense of identity is the *sense of pride* that multilingual children showed when they mastered additional languages. Monica continued describing her older son's attitude toward Spanish:

The 19-year-old has strong receptive skills, and I would say he is like at a level 3 for the age that he is at. Level 3, because he does some reading in Spanish too, but not at the level of fluency that a native speaker would be speaking. Conversationally he converses with my parents, his grandparents, in Spanish and feels very comfortable and very proud of being able to speak in Spanish. So he feels very good about it.

Ghodrat, the father of Malik and Zara, who are bilingual in English and Farsi, recalled a similar transformation of identity and sense of pride that his son began to display in middle school. One of Malik's teachers took interest in his language abilities and in his family story, and Malik "changed his attitude for the point that he liked being Iranian and Iranian language, to the point that he really was proud that he was an Iranian." Many parents noted their children taking pride in language learning and mastery and subsequently (or concurrently) becoming proud of their linguistic abilities and cultural heritage. These two factors – the sense of identity and pride – exhibited by children were rewarding for parents. Bianca, whose two teenage sons are bilingual in Spanish and English, shared with us that the boys proudly perceive themselves as Mexicans: "Because I was born in Mexico, both of them like to be Mexicans, and it makes me happy." The sense of pride and identity also brought the various generations in the families closer together. Monica recalls fostering her sons' Spanish skills for the sake of developing their sense of identity:

My parents can converse in English very well ... but it was about knowing your roots and your heritage. Their great aunts and uncle are in Mexico City and we wanted them to be able to talk with one another ... And [my son] right now the one that would say, "Gosh, I am glad I can understand and it is so important." And it is a part of who he is. His identity, I think language is a part of that identity. I think it is inseparable in some ways because he knows his roots, and language is part of his culture. So I don't think that they are separable and he recognizes the value of that.

The theme of success was also very closely connected to another theme already discussed, namely, to the theme of *perceived benefits of multilingualism* that the parents expected as a result of their hard work. Throughout the strenuous process of raising children multilingually, parents witnessed first-hand the benefits about which they heard and read and that they hoped to achieve. The four types of success enjoyed by their children – 1) heightened linguistic capabilities, 2) confidence, 3) a strong sense of identity, and 4) the children's feelings of pride or accomplishment – were the most frequent types of success noted by parents. The other various instances of success that were mentioned in the interviews were directly related to the benefits that the parents aimed to achieve as a result of multilingual practices. The parents who saw these benefits actualized listed them as successes. These included success in multiple domains of children's lives. Some parents recognized the friendships that were formed on the basis of language learning: "Sylvie makes friends with everybody, so when she went to Italy she had about 10 girlfriends living in Sienna because of them I believe she learned to speak Italian. The other students learned a little, but she was the only one to master the language" (Ultan). Other parents recognized language learning achievements as success in school and in college: "My nephew ... when he went to college [overseas] learned the language, writing, reading ... He excelled in it [Arabic]" (Mayda). Both excerpts above reveal how, similar to college acceptance, successful language learning could also be measured in study or travel abroad. Additionally, effective communication with speakers of other languages was mentioned in multiple interviews as a sign of multilingual success. Nora proudly told us about the time when her 10-year-old daughter, Alejandra, spoke to a group of unfamiliar adults in Spanish: "My husband goes to the [Spanish-only] church meetings and she needed to talk to his [church] group and she asked me, 'But you need to translate,' and I said to her, 'You can do it in Spanish.' But when she started talking to the public she did it in Spanish and it was perfect." The majority of parents who were very aware of the benefits of multilingualism were able to tell several success stories in their interviews. Parents who were not sure about the benefits of multilingualism had a reduced recognition of advantages that came with it. Ironically, due to change in circumstances, sometimes the same parents changed their perspectives on the benefits and usefulness of multilingualism. In such cases, the degree of success in siblings' multilingual upbringing seemed to be comparable to the amount of potential benefits that the parents mentioned. Leonid's story below illustrates this:

I think the parents really need to be committed and see a huge benefit in bilingualism to make that sacrifice because you are giving up other things in the name of bilingualism. My older daughter is completely bilingual. At that time everyone around was eagerly waiting for her to speak Russian. When our boys were born, [I had] a little bit tainted outlook on how useful bilingualism is. I still thought it was great developmentally. I still wanted them to have the kind of rudimentary knowledge so that if later on they decide to pick it up in school or college they would at least have the foundation, but I stopped being fanatical about it. So maybe that's another reason why they are getting by but not, obviously, completely bilingual.

Leonid's story and the stories of families similar to his reveal two mechanisms at work in this context: 1) awareness of the benefits of multilingualism allows parents to persevere and readily notice certain successes in their children's linguistic, cognitive, and social development, and 2) the benefits evident in children's development serve as positive reinforcement and encouragement that propel the parents to continue their hard work, fueling their commitment, which in turn results in greater success. These observations highlight the need for raising parents' awareness of the positive impact of multilingualism on children's development. These also necessitate recognition of children's early successes as an important foundation for continued long-term multilingualism.

Yet another theme that is critical for this study emerged as the parents were describing their own and their children's successes within the context of a multilingual upbringing: "successes should not be attributed to just one person." Parents talked about the impact multiple people – relatives, friends, colleagues, and teachers – had on the favorable outcomes in raising multilingual children. These individuals, each in their own way, helped promote the multilingualism that was started within each individual family and advanced it to a higher level. These people belong to the children's multilingual community. Within it, each member had his or her own range of multilingual abilities, but all stakeholders supported and nurtured the children's multilingualism. Some, whose language proficiency was sufficient, did it through conversing with children in the languages they were learning. Danielle, whose children are completely bilingual in French and English, recalled that family friends took an active role in teaching her sons and daughters Spanish: "We have those friends of the family that always when we see them speak Spanish. So the kids' learning of Spanish was motivated by love for friends and family and country and the fun." Other people expressed their interest and respect in regards to children's language knowledge. Linda told us about asking her older daughter Elia to teach Spanish to her younger sister Bella: "Elia is the first thing that Bella looks for when she gets home, so then we say, 'Elia, you have to teach your sister Spanish.' And we try and encourage that." Allowing children to feel like experts and develop a sense of self-worth was another example of a recipe for success.

Larisa, whose Russian-English bilingual son Boris has ASD and developmental disabilities, told us that his Russian skills allowed him to feel good around the peers who were learning it and gave him a leadership status in a parochial Saturday class: "In everything else, Boris is behind and has a lot of work to do to catch up, but in Russian he is a champion and ahead of everyone. Russian is the only thing he does really well in, and kids looked up to him" [Translated from Russian]. Positive comments provided by people who witnessed multilingual successes inspired the families to build on their progress in order to go further. Monica, the mother of two Spanish-English bilingual teenagers, recalled,

We also were able to connect him [son] with a friend's niece who is totally bilingual and so she said when she came back for the holidays, "You know [your son] speaks really well! I talked to him in Spanish and he is conversing like a native speaker in Spanish." And so she was giving me a compliment, and I said, "What!?" I feel like I needed to do more ...

All of these multilingual community members who approved and supported multilingual families unconsciously were investing in the future of multilingual children and helping them strengthen their sense of individuality, as well as appreciation of diversity, and acceptance of their own diverse backgrounds. As Tina, the mother of 19-month-old multilingual Lilia, pointed out:

Truly it does take a village and it takes so many people. And the support network, whether it is a mom at the park, whether it's your wonderful neighbor you know, whether you're able to have someone to help you, you know, your parents, your grandparents. It takes a village. Because it's not just my love that's gonna help her grow, it's gonna be the love of her teachers. It's gonna be the love of her neighbors. It's gonna be the love of other children. And the more love she's exposed to, the better human being she'll become. You know, because I want her to someday, you know, give a gift back to the world. I want her to make the world a better place at the end of the day. My, that would make me the happiest mother in the world, to see my child make the world a better place for others.

With this, we now turn to describing the perspectives of those who work most closely with multilingual children to formally foster their language development – their educators.

Fostering Multilingualism in Diverse
        Educational Contexts

In this chapter, we outline in detail the existing educational options for supporting multilingualism, including formal language programming offered by schools as well as the opportunities made and taken up by families more informally. The interviews with the 13 educators add first-hand experiences and personal insights into the perceived challenges and rewards of each of these educational options. We specifically report on what the educators' interviews revealed about their views of multilingualism, their beliefs about the effects of multilingualism on students' education and development, and the instructional strategies that they have used to target positive linguistic, academic, and social outcomes for students.

Multilingual Schooling Options

When it comes to schooling, parents who wish to sustain or establish multilingualism for their children face some daunting decisions: Should they place their child in full-time dual-language education? Should they choose a government-funded program if available to them, or a privately supported school? Will part-time classes in the target language(s) alone be suitable for their child? Perhaps a local play-group with children who share the same heritage-language background is the only option available to the family. Is that commitment sufficient for promoting multilingual competencies, building multicultural awareness and cross-cultural friendships, participating in the heritage language of the family and local community, and promoting global sensibilities? Prior research shows that an attempt to sustain linguistic diversity by supporting it solely in the home environment is not a viable option. In their recent review of what they refer to as *heritage and community language education*, Lee and Wright (2014) report findings that show explicit support and instruction of the target language(s) outside of the home are necessary for successful language maintenance or acquisition to occur.

Depending, of course, on where a family is living and the political climate toward multilingualism in their nation or, in the case of the United States, in their specific state, parents may be able to capitalize on options provided to them by government-funded local education agencies (LEAs), most likely the school district of their town or city. In some states (e.g., Illinois, New Mexico) families can access full-time, state and locally funded Spanish-English bilingual programming from the preschool years onwards. In contrast, other U.S. states have had ballot initiatives to reduce the number of publicly funded bilingual education programs (e.g., California, Arizona), thereby rendering formally operated, full-time options for supporting children's multilingual development much harder to come by.

For families facing little support for multilingual development from their state or national educational systems, and who may not be able to afford (or simply not want) to enroll their children in private, often parochial, full-time education, other less intensive options may still be available to them. For example, families may find cultural and religious organizations that provide regular after-school or weekend programs in a heritage language to maintain a local community's language, cultural, and/or religious practices. Below, we describe both the formal and informal options that parents may encounter for schooling children who are already acquiring more than one language, as well as would-be multilingual children at the brink of their formal school careers. For the latter group, entering school around the child's fifth birthday is perhaps the first and quite possibly last realistic chance families have (program options permitting) to begin concerted efforts to develop multilingualism.

Formal Options for Fostering Multilingual Development

Within the range of formal schooling options, we consider not only government-funded programs but also privately funded (independent) schools and part-time programs that provide language instruction. While data on the number of privately funded language programs is limited due to the lack of a central data base collecting this information (Lee and Wright, 2014), we include them here with our description of government-supported programs because they also constitute a formally operated program offering for families. The government-funded programs are predominantly aimed at minority-language students who are still acquiring English language skills and who, if identified as ELL students, are entitled to English language support services in the United States under Title III of NCLB (2001). LEAs are held accountable by their state governments (which are in turn answerable to the federal government under Title III) for student progress in English language proficiency until those students are assessed and determined ready to be reclassified as fluent English proficient (R-FEP) (see Bailey and Carroll, 2015, for review of the U.S. ELL student assessment system).

However, a number of language instruction models available in publicly funded school contexts also service both majority- and minority-language students regardless of their English language proficiency status. These dual-language programs are designed to support both L1 and L2 development. If a language-minority student is identified as an ELL student and is assessed as ready to become R-FEP at any point during his/her enrollment in such a dual-language program, the student may opt to stay in the program rather than move into a mainstream or general education setting. In contrast, minority students who become R-FEP in programs designed to support the acquisition of the majority language only, and if they are receiving services in a program that segregates them from majority-language students, will move to being instructed in English within a mainstream classroom environment (Bailey and Carroll, 2015).

Beyond sources of funding (public or private) and accountability (state or federal), Ortega (2013a) reminds us of an additional crucial contextual distinction between the dual-language learning experiences of majority-language students and the majority-language programming experiences of many minority-language students. For majority-language students, fostering bilingualism is primarily an elective decision on the part of parents. Knowledge of an L2 is not required for accessing school content classes nor is the knowledge of an L2 often thought critical for functioning successfully in the broader society. Minority-language students on the other hand "engage in language learning under conditions of circumstantial bilingualism" (p. 3041). They do not necessarily have any choice but to acquire the majority-language as an L2. If families are reliant on government-funded education, their children will almost universally be enrolled in programs that include some, if not all, of their schooling in the majority language. Attainment of proficiency in the majority language is most often treated as a necessity for successful school achievement. Even in parochial schools independently funded and staffed by a community-language agency or organization, instruction of the majority language may also take up part of the instructional day.

While globalization forces are working to make U.S. society, including schools and the labor market, more appreciative and encouraging of multilingual competencies (Callahan and Gándara, 2014; Rumbaut, 2014), change is slow, so college and career readiness in the United States is still synonymous with needing to speak English even if alongside another (incidental) language; students will still need to learn English to pass college entrance exams or, with the exception of some workplace situations, secure a job. That is not to say that sustaining knowledge of the L1 does not play an important role in educational attainment. Gándara et al. (2013) reported that in their study of the educational needs of Latina students, a key predictor for going to college was the girls' maintenance of their Spanish language abilities. Even more recently, students who speak and are literate in another language have for the first time been shown to have an edge over other students in both school achievement and in the labor market (Callahan and Gándara, 2014). Unfortunately,

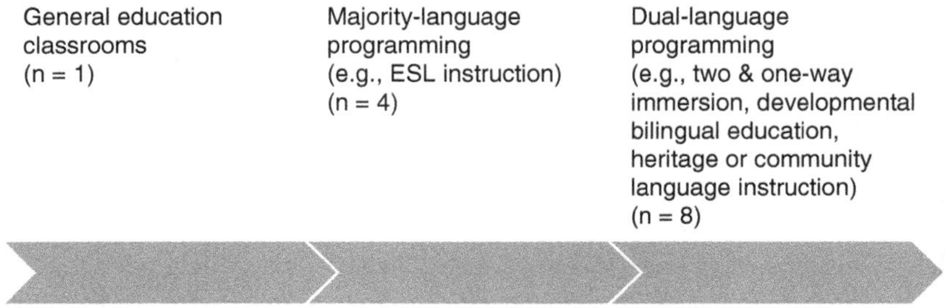

| General education classrooms (n = 1) | Majority-language programming (e.g., ESL instruction) (n = 4) | Dual-language programming (e.g., two & one-way immersion, developmental bilingual education, heritage or community language instruction) (n = 8) |

Figure 6.1 Continuum of multilingual schooling contexts of participating educators

minority-language students, by circumstances of birth, may not have an opportunity to maintain their L1 in a U.S. school setting: they may be located in a state where majority-language instruction (e.g., English-as-a-second-language [ESL] instruction) is the only publicly funded language programming offered to minority-language families.

Language Instruction Educational Program (LIEP) is terminology used by the U.S. Department of Education for two main language program types: (1) LIEP models that focus on developing literacy (and presumably oral language competencies) in two languages, and (2) LIEP models that focus on ultimately developing literacy in the dominant societal language – English (National Clearinghouse for English Language Acquisition [NCELA], 2011). Figure 6.1 presents a continuum of the participating educators' by degree of support their programs can typically give to the multilingual development of students.

We begin with programs that overtly focus on developing two languages but still differ in the degree to which they maintain an equitable focus on the partner languages or adopt an increasingly greater focus on the majority language over time (e.g., a gradual transfer to English).

Dual-Language Programming

Dual-language learning programs in government-funded education are emerging as a distinctive and increasingly prevalent option for families (Espinosa, 2013). The charter school movement in the United States has given educators a degree of latitude over school curricula and philosophical approaches to instruction and consequently appears to be a fertile breeding ground for dual-language programming built on research that suggests students achieve best in literacy when they have first established proficiency in their L1 (Tabors and Snow, 2001). With control over their publicly funded budgets and sometimes receiving supplements from community-based organizations (CBO), these schools can offer dual-language programming where this approach may have otherwise been curtailed by states committed to English-only initiatives in recent years. For example, the Para Los Niños Charter Elementary and Middle Schools in Los Angeles are supported by a CBO to serve the needs of low-income families with predominantly Latino backgrounds, and have grown to include a separate primary center (Grades K-1) offering a dual-language strand in Spanish and English literacy with a wide network of feeder preschool programs across the city (http://paralosninos.org).

Full-time dual-language programs have existed far longer in order to support the maintenance of community languages with private funding from immigrant social welfare organizations or agencies. For example, the Armenian General Benevolent Union (AGBU) has 18 full-time schools found throughout the world wherever Armenians from Armenia and the Diaspora in the Middle East have emigrated, including Sydney, Buenos Aires, Montreal, Detroit, and most recently Pasadena, California. Privately funded programs also exist to support the languages of temporary international residents (e.g., the United Nations International School of New York and the International School of London have stated missions to provide assistance with continued L1 development alongside English, the students' L2). Independent international schools world-wide provide language and academic content instruction in students' L2 (e.g., globally, Lycée Français schools, most accredited by the French Ministry of National Education, offer French and academic content instruction in French to follow the French Baccalaureate college preparation). International schools in non-English language countries also offer instruction partly in the majority language of the country and partly in a selected foreign language that may or may not be the students' L1 (e.g., La Petite Ecole Bilingue in Paris offers parents the option of a trilingual program supporting French, English, and Russian).

Other independent schools that are tied closely to language instruction pro-gramming include cultural organizations and parochial schools that view lan-guage maintenance as important for supporting a community's cultural and/or religious preservation (e.g., the Hellenic Foundation for Culture, which pro-motes the Greek language and culture in major world capitals, and the Greek Orthodox Archdiocese, which funds full-time schools in parts of the world that have seen a large amount of Greek immigration, such as America and Australia). In some countries faith-based schools are supported by govern-ment funds (e.g., the UK, the Netherlands) under mandates to provide equal educational support to students of all religions (e.g., Berkeley and Vij, 2008). In such cases, if the religion is associated with a particular language commu-nity, language instruction may also be part of the curriculum (e.g., Turkish and Arabic in the Netherlands, Jozsa, 2007; even Greek in the one Greek Orthodox government-supported school in the UK, Berkeley and Vij, 2008). In the United States, a faith-based organization, the Two-Way Immersion Network for Catholic Schools, has an initiative to support dual-language programming due to its traditional ties to non-English speaking congregations and its commitment to social justice. Currently the Network's schools provide instruction in Spanish and English or Mandarin and English depending on the location of the school (www.twin-cs.org).

Developing primary and secondary language proficiency and literacy, as well as promoting student academic achievement, are key objectives for students in dual-language schools or dual-language classrooms if a program is a separate strand within a school. In many cases, increasing cross-cultural understanding and global awareness are also objectives (e.g., Bailey et al., 2008; Genesee and Lindholm-Leary, 2008; Howard, 2002). According to the work of the Center for Research on Education, Diversity and Excellence (CREDE), who documented the range and characteristics of language programming during the 1990s and 2000s, (Genesee, 1999; Howard and Sugarman, 2001) there are four key types of LIEP models that fall under the category of dual-language programming, defined broadly as programs that adopt an "enriched" language education model (Howard, Olague, and Rogers, 2003): (1) two-way immersion; (2) foreign language/one-way immersion; (3) developmental bilingual education; and (4) heritage or community language programming.

1.   Two-way immersion (TWI), also known as two-way bilingual immersion

I feel like it really depends on us, you know the adults that are surrounding them. How we approach where they are in their language development.... And to me it's just, it's normal. They're learning two sets of codes for things. The spelling, the reading, the comprehension, ways to express yourself [are] different. (Paola, fifth-grade teacher, Spanish-English TWI program)

This form of dual-language programming involves two partner languages (e.g., German and Italian in Germany, Budach, 2014). The vast majority of TWI programs in the United States have Spanish and English as the partner languages, but Mandarin and English, Korean and English, and Japanese and English as partner languages amongst others are also to be found in cities with local communities that sustain these languages. Ideally, a balance in students is achieved with 50 percent of the class L1 speakers of one of the partner languages and 50 percent of the class L1 speakers of the other partner language. In reality, in our own experiences with TWI programs in the United States, the student composition is more likely to be 33% entering with English as the L1, 33% with Spanish, for example, as the L1, and 33% largely balanced across English and Spanish abilities. The one-third balance across English and

Spanish is most likely a result of some children having had opportunities to acquire skills in both languages due to the pattern of L1 usage in the home and English-language exposure in preschool and other contexts. This was the situation with a number of families in Chapter 5. While challenging to achieve sometimes (anecdotally we hear reports that fewer Spanish-dominant families wish to participate), the relative balance in the composition of students is critical because the students serve as native-speaking models for each other; students with a minority (partner) L1 acquire the majority language as their L2 alongside students who are native speakers of the L2. These students in turn acquire the minority language as their L2.

TWI programming is predicated on research indicating that languages are "best learned as a medium of content rather than as the focus of instruction" (Potowski, 2004, p. 95). In some instances, the partner languages may be alternated equally as the medium of instruction throughout the day, or used on alternate days or even alternate weeks. The pedagogical challenge then becomes whether to repeat the same content in the two languages (risking children tune out when the content is repeated in their L2), to cover some topics within a single content area in one language and other topics in the partner language (at the risk then of having arbitrary gaps in the academic lexicons of both languages), or to cleanly divide the different content areas by the two languages (e.g., teach all mathematics in Spanish and science in English) (Potowski, 2004). Switching between two languages within the same lesson to cover the same material is a sure way to have students stop paying attention when the material is presented in their L2. Clearly, there is no authentic communicative imperative to listen to instruction in L2 if it taxes students more than simply waiting for the content material to be repeated in the L1.

TWI programs may initially begin by exposing all students to the minority language for most of the school day (e.g., a 90/10 model; instruction is split into 90 percent time in the minority language and 10 percent time in the majority language). This is designed on the assumption that students are already highly exposed to the majority language in their daily lives. This could be true of minority-language students as well due to the ubiquitous presence of English in the media of the wider U.S. society. In effect, this initial ratio for the partner languages is closer to a one-way immersion or fully immersive experience for the majority-language students in the program (see below), but may be a necessary antidote to the dominance of the majority language in society and in many of the students' everyday lives. It can be a challenge for TWI teachers to prevent the continued dominance of the societal majority language within the classroom setting to a point that some have questioned the efficacy of TWI for the education of minority-language students (see Palmer and Martínez, 2013, for review). Some teachers in TWI programs may go so far as to fain ignorance of the majority language; still others overtly signal to students with a badge or a piece of clothing (i.e., we have observed brightly colored aprons) that they will only speak and respond to the minority language. With each passing year in the program the ratio of minority-to-majority language exposure typically becomes increasingly balanced so that by fourth and fifth grades TWI programs may operate at close to 50/50 exposure to the two partner languages.

Paola, who teaches in a Spanish-English TWI program in an elementary school, attested to how all-encompassing the majority language can be by the time her students reached her fifth-grade classroom:

Basically because we have about 6 hours with them and half of their day has to be Spanish so it's about 3 hours a day. You know and then you bring in the holidays or pupil free days, and the weekends and the summer vacation, winter vacation, spring break. All of that is English only, for most of the kids. Even the Spanish dominant kids, because their activities outside of school are in English.

In such circumstances, a major pedagogical challenge is how the teacher can motivate students to use the minority language whether it is their L1 or not. Alejandro, a first- and second-grade classroom teacher in the same TWI program speaks directly to this challenge he had encountered in TWI programs:

Especially for a lot of kids who tend not to, who may not be as motivated to learn something that they don't feel good at. And I see that a lot with monolingual English speaking children who want to learn Spanish. If they don't feel good at it already, they're somewhat reluctant to try to take a risk, to speak up.

The gradual shift from L1 dominance to a balance between partner languages in the classroom is designed to first give acquisition of the minority-language a greater chance of occurring, followed by greater preparation of children for academic achievements in the majority language. However, these different instantiations of the TWI model within a single school site at different grade levels were seen as a programmatic challenge. Alejandro reported that "within our program we have four little programs. Because every level [grade] is kind of doing their own thing and there are pros and cons to doing something like that...." Paola confirmed this picture with an explanation of how the languages were being assigned to different amounts of exposure and content areas across the different grades within the school:

We had in the Primary classroom [first and second grades] one teacher trying out to do like one day Spanish, one day English, but I think there were some challenges and the other teachers at that level were having some concerns with how that was working.... At my level [fifth grade], in my classroom we try to maintain 50 percent of the day Spanish, 50 percent of the day English for every single day.

The pressure of trying to get the balance of the partner languages fairly divided across a single day meant that at fifth grade "We haven't done like a personal narrative in Spanish with them this year, or let's say an essay or a non-fiction book. Those, we just don't have enough time. We're always against the amount of time we have. So they do get writing within the reading time, and they get Spanish spelling in there too."

Another design dynamic within TWI models that may cause problems is being a program administrated within a larger school setting. Three-quarters of the TWI programs in the United States registered with CAL are operated as separate strands within otherwise English-medium schools. Alejandro raised this concern with his own TWI program that had about a third of the schools' enrollment. As a strand within the school, the students may have little contact with non-program peers due to different schedules and competing pressures on their time. As a result of this separation of strands Alejandro reported that "when you talk to some kids who are not in [name of program] ... there is some apprehension. There is some confusion about this whole concept of multilingualism, even at our school." Moreover, there was not always buy-in from non-program staff which he found could undermine motivation for Spanish language acquisition by his students:

When they hear that the majority of people on faculty and staff are not bilingual that is an issue because then they really don't see the role models. They don't see that sort of valuing outside of this environment.

Unfortunately the concern with how much reinforcement for their efforts the students in the TWI strand received from the rest of their school was tied to teacher concerns for the long-term outcomes of students. The educators were particularly concerned with the successful acquisition of the minority language (i.e., Spanish) as either an L1 or L2. Alejandro, for example, questioned how successfully students who were graduates of the TWI program were able to retain their Spanish:

When I speak to a lot of my graduated students or you know students that come through here that always say, "I remember learning Spanish 3, 4, 5, 6 years, and I don't remember and I don't speak it. Or I can read it, but I cannot communicate orally." And those are the kids I worry about because obviously they didn't have enough real-life experiences, nor did they have enough time or perhaps people to continue developing and practicing their language with.

In contrast with this TWI program as a program situated within a larger school, was Sarah's report of a school-wide TWI program. Sarah was a fifth-grade science teacher who was temporarily associated with the elementary and middle school TWI program. The school population was approximately half Spanish-dominant and half English-dominant at entry and all Latino ethnicity, so in some sense fulfills the definition of a heritage language program (see below) but at a full-time, school-wide level and with great diversity in exposure to and proficiency in the heritage language.

All the teachers in the school were required to be at least bilingual Spanish-English speakers. The school used an approach that follows a 50/50 language of instruction model at every grade and does not require equal numbers of minority- and majority-language speakers (Gómez, Freeman, and Freeman, 2005). Students received language arts in their L1 (Spanish or English) but other content area instruction is separated by language, so that half of the instruction is in English (e.g., mathematics) and half is in Spanish (e.g., science) even from the earliest grades. At third grade, English language arts is added to the curriculum of all students regardless of L1.

The school alternated daily between Spanish and English for all non-instructional talk, but this switch was a challenge to implement as Sarah explained:

... so that any kind of like conversational language has to be in whatever the language is for that day, like in the passing periods and hallways. You know lunch room conversation. Things like that ...

ANNA: But the announcements for the day are probably in Spanish or whatever.

SARAH: Yeah those kinds of things are in Spanish and then like the person at the front desk will answer the phone in Spanish that day, or will greet the students as they walk in in Spanish. But then the students will respond back in English. I mean it's not.... And even just the signage that they have to visually say the language of the day is, you know it's just on an 8½ by 11 piece of paper that's kind of, you know it doesn't.... There's no like big impact of "okay, today's English!" "Today's Spanish!"

However, adopting different languages for different content areas may have drawbacks when it comes to testing students on federally mandated assessments, because the language of testing may fail to match the language of instruction and create additional challenges for students (e.g., Genesee, Lindholm-Leary, Saunders, and Christian, 2005). Indeed, Sarah described how the TWI program had previously experienced a mismatch between the language of instruction and the language students would be required to use during content assessment:

They had been teaching math in Spanish, and it got to a point where it felt like that that was detrimental to the kids because they were taking the math test in English. And so they just felt that there was probably a disconnect. So now that ... everybody is receiving math instruction in English, they are hoping to see an improvement based on that.

The TWI model being followed also requires strict grade-level instructional arrangements rather than allowing for multi-age groupings, as Sarah explains: "They [researchers] ... in their research, they found that it hasn't been helpful to have the older kids, or those who are above grade level helping because then they're not challenged enough." The theme of heterogeneity in student abilities was also raised by Alejandro. He thought the TWI model he taught with also currently had too great a diversity in English and Spanish language development levels (ELD and SLD) within any one classroom:

... theoretically you could cluster kids by language development level so you have your ELD groupings of first graders and your ELD 2s and so on and so forth. Here we've got ELD 1s with the ELD 5s and SLD 1s and SLD 5s in the same room! So that just [laughs] poses just a huge challenge for anybody, even very experienced teachers.

Furthermore, Alejandro noted that students develop language at quite different rates without obvious reasons for differences:

... they are covering similar material and yet some of the same kids are still stuck in level 1 when they should be approaching level 3 theoretically. Whereas we have other kids that are coming in new to the program at a level 1 and by the end of their first year they are already at level 2 approaching 3 in some cases. Something is going on and I can't quite put my finger on it. I am not quite sure.

This situation led to the adoption of many small group "rotations" to place the students together during content instruction by literacy level of the language of instruction.

In terms of the rewards for teaching in a TWI program, the educators were most obviously struck by the broad linguistic acumen of many students. Early in her interview, Paola enthusiastically stated,

Oh my gosh. I think like ... multilingual students ... I just see their world is so big. They think in different ways, they're able to interact with children in different ways. It's just, it's amazing. I have a student right now, I just had a student that she speaks Chinese, Spanish, and English, so the three most spoken languages in the world. She's set for her future.

Sarah's words strongly echoed Paola's sentiments when she said, "the children that I have encountered who are multilingual do seem to be more easily adaptable to situations. And you know not always, because everybody's a little bit different, but [they] tend to be a little more empathetic and open to some new ideas." Alejandro also noticed this quality of "openness" in the multilingual students he teaches, stating that "... they're able to get to know the world better because of it. And it really does sort of, oh I don't know, early on it helps to open up their minds and they're in some ways I think, I don't want to say more interested in learning but they're more open to different kinds of learning." He ties this to what he believes is their stronger motivation to learn in school.

The earlier theme of insufficient broad exposure from within the schools was connected to the role of parents of students enrolled in TWI programs. Both Paola and Alejandro voiced concerns that their English majority-language students may have needed far more support in the home environment, or at least in out-of-school contexts that were controlled by parents, in order to achieve successful acquisition of Spanish as their L2. Alejandro in an extended exchange on this issue described his concern with first getting parents to see what contributory messages they might be sending to their children. Then he suggested what roles the parents can still hope to play even if they are not currently Spanish speakers:

Well that's interesting because I've been dealing with this issue in the last couple of weeks.... When they [parents]say "yes it's important that my child learn Spanish, yes I want to be supportive, yes I am in agreement with what your approach is and what you're doing, but I don't have anything to contribute. I'm not a bilingual, I don't know the first thing about Spanish, I don't know what I'm doing." And I go "Well, with all due respect, that's part of the problem. Because your child ... does not see the value of learning a second language because it's not valued at home."

ANNA: Your priority, right?

ALEJANDRO: I said, "Now just imagine that if everyone in the family was trying to do this together, how much more the child would be motivated to involve themselves in the learning aspect of this? How motivated would they be to know that mommy and daddy or mommy and mommy or whoever, they're with me on this?" One dad in particular said, "Well, you know I want my child to learn Spanish but if they're not going to learn it I'm going to get them a tutor." I'm like, "Well...." He says, "what's wrong?" and I go, "Well think about that for a minute. I'm not saying getting a tutor is a bad idea because that would give them more exposure."

ANNA: Right, and practice.

ALEJANDRO: "But what's the message that you're sending your child?"

ANNA: "Others will teach you?"

ALEJANDRO: "You're not good enough. You're not making it, so I have to get someone to help you." As opposed to, maybe the tutor is for the whole family. "Maybe the tutor is there to help you help your child learn Spanish, because your child is seeing you trying to learn as well." And with the families where there is some of that, it's great because the father would say, another parent would say, "I had no idea what my child knew until I started trying to speak the language, and then 'no papi' or 'no daddy, that's not how you say it. You say it this way,' and say oh, finally I realize that he is learning something." And I go, "That's right, look at what the message was that you were sending your child, that I'm interested, that I want to learn this too."

As a teacher of the upper elementary grades, Paola felt the pressure of parental concerns over their children's development of English language skills. For those parents who have committed to TWI only while their children are at the elementary level, the expected academic performances necessary for meeting the demands of the middle school years loom large. This concern faces all the families, whether they are primarily speakers of the majority or minority language; the majority-language families take a chance that their children will continue to develop strong English language skills while they get the enrichment of L2 acquisition; the minority-language parents take a chance that time on task is not the mechanism by which their children will acquire English, but rather that the two languages can be mutually reinforcing with the development of high-level language and literacy skills in their children's L1 positively transferring to English literacy (recall in Chapter 3, parent beliefs attached to immersion practices were without contradictory evidence).

As Paola explained further, even in TWI programs the families ultimately have a bias toward the development of English:

They do start getting anxious about it when their child's in fourth grade and you're telling them they're still not writing complete sentences in English. They're not too concerned about the Spanish because they know that eventually their child will be held accountable for English, right? So I worry about that too. We start to think, okay how are we going to support this child to get them further ahead in their English development because come middle school, which is not too far from now, they're ...

ANNA: The expectations?

PAOLA: The expectation is going to be English only, and we need to give them some extra support.

This expectation is likely not only due to the perception that the wider society is still privileging English over multilingualism, but likely also due to the very practical concern that very few families will readily find an accessible TWI program at the middle school level and beyond and so will by necessity be forced to have their children stream into an all-English school environment. This is a realistic concern consistent with the statistics reported by CAL for TWI programming at the higher grades. Moreover, at the higher grades not only programs but materials may not be readily available. Sarah observed teachers in the TWI school struggle with this in the middle school grades. She shared, for example, that the science kits (an inquiry-based science curriculum) purchased for grades K-5 were not translated for all the middle schools grades (the Spanish version is only available for grades K-6).

It is important to note that our interviews with Paola, Alejandro, and Sarah did not always echo Thomas and Collier's (2003) claim that TWI programs "... also provide integrated, inclusive, and unifying education experiences for their students, in contrast to the segregated, exclusive, and divisive education characteristics of many traditional English-only and transitional bilingual programs" (p. 63). Rather, the lived experiences of the educators in our study surfaced a distinct set of challenges also facing TWI programming. While the TWI model may not separate language-minority and -majority children, structural aspects of educational programing can segregate program children from non-program children leading to the potential for isolation from the wider school community for students and staff. The program can also present teachers and administrators with difficulties when it comes to dividing up instructional time to ensure sufficient exposure to both languages, so acquisition can occur either sequentially (with the majority language phased in over an extended number of years) or simultaneously (by attempting to divide up the lesson, day, week, and/or content areas by the two partner languages). None of these program features is likely to be a stable facet. In his program, Alejandro felt he and his colleagues were "always in flux" and as a result of constant changes to the program design were less likely to "delve deeply into things" which we understood to be the pedagogical conundrums he mentioned, such as understanding the causes of different rates of ELD and SLD and how best to group students effectively. Alejandro noted that "every era [new staff, new principal, new curriculum] brings its own set of issues."

TWI programming, if offered by a government-funded LEA, provides majority language families an affordable opportunity to foster multilingualism in their perhaps otherwise monolingual-destined children. For language-minority families it offers the wherewithal to foster the continued development of their children's L1 beyond the home context. For all families enrolled in a program, TWI offers their children a chance at attaining bilingualism and biliteracy and the additional stated objective of TWI programs of "cultural pluralism through increased intercultural competence" (Lyster and Genesee, 2013, p. 1).

Ultimately, despite the many and varied challenges they faced, the educators in our study could not see themselves educating children in any other setting. For Alejandro, it has been a "calling" to be able to teach in an enriched language teaching and learning environment from early on:

I just knew then that was my calling and I have been doing it ever since. I think that as I develop professionally and personally I have come to appreciate bilingualism and multilingualism more as the years have go by.... That this whole idea of bilingualism is just a tool to get them really into a mainstream program. It really wasn't seen as a positive, as an additive to their overall learning trajectory and I always thought that there was something wrong with that and so that is why I said this is what I need to do. This is what I need to be able to support, not only children and their families but along the way myself.

Paola, on the other hand, had to go through a period of self-doubt about the value she placed on multilingualism as a result of external pressures, but ultimately convinced herself of the positive effects of dual-language instruction for students:

PAOLA: But you know, I think there's a lot of pressure from the state, from the government to make sure these kids are performing in English, right? So the principals and the coordinators I think get bombarded you know with all these expectations and so they transferred that to you. And I remember thinking at one point in my career early on, gosh maybe I did study the wrong thing, maybe it's not good to teach the kids two languages at the same time, maybe it is confusing for them. Even though that was going against everything I had learned.

ALISON: So you had a crisis of faith, kind of?

PAOLA: Yeah! I started to feel like well maybe I want to teach English only. You know, this is a little bit too hard. And I don't know what made me get out of that state of mind, but I'm glad that I got back to what I knew was right.

2.   *Foreign language immersion programs (full or partial), also known as one-way immersion programs*

From seeing a child who didn't know any French one year, but seeing him two years later speaking fluent French with no accent. It's really impressive…. Teachers really feel successful and they can do that. They can see how much they can teach someone in a different language. (Sandra, kindergarten teacher, French full immersion program)

These immersion programs primarily enroll students with the majority language as their L1 who learn a target foreign language as their L2, often with no prior exposure to the foreign language. In the case of full immersion, students receive all their academic content instruction through the foreign language as well. Partial immersion involves students receiving some academic content classes in their L1 and some academic content through the foreign language (and in that sense they are more strictly a type of dual-language programming than are full immersion programs that restrict how much they include formal teaching of L1 language and literacy skills). These programs differ from developmental bilingual programming (see below) in that all students have as their L1 the majority language of the wider society rather than the minority language. Moreover, there are no L1 speakers of the target foreign language in classes with these students as there would be in TWI programming, and consequently the teacher is often the sole model of L1 proficiency in the classroom.

CAL also keeps a separate directory of these programs and as of 2011 when CAL last analyzed these data, there were 448 registered foreign language immersion programs in U.S. schools, the majority of them (45%) offering Spanish immersion, followed by French at 22%, Mandarin at 13%, Hawaiian at 6%, Japanese at 5%, German at 3%, and all other languages combined to make up 6% (CAL, 2011). The high number of Spanish programs suggests there is some cross-over (and possibly confusion) between the TWI directory and data maintained by CAL.

Differences between the culture of the majority-language students enrolled in a program and the culture of the target foreign language emerged as both positive and negative forces for Sandra who taught in a French immersion program in the United States. Many staff members at foreign language schools are from the countries where the target language is spoken as the L1 and thus they have largely been prepared according to instructional norms and practices that may be quite alien to the immersion programs' students and their families. Sandra described the distinct differences in cultural orientation toward schooling and teachers that she has encountered as a teacher in the French immersion school, involving both families and teaching staff. Differences in how families socialize students for school settings, she feels, may run counter to the traditional notion of schooling in France: "… American parents always say, 'Have fun in school.' I don't really see French parents really saying that, but more like, 'Do your work!'"

Sandra also reported seeing cultural contrasts in French and American teachers, believing that "French teachers are more strict and more honest and more willing to be helpful in pushing you forward." Whereas American "teachers are more about making sure that you're happy and having a good time." While Sandra never made an explicit judgment about which orientation she felt was more effective for teachers and student learning, she did relate that the French orientation may have positive results in terms of student attitudes and behaviors in school:

I have noticed the way the students react in front of their French and English teachers and they seem to be more respectful and more stay out of trouble around the French teachers.

Regardless of whether the immersive experience of students is with TWI or a foreign language/one-way immersion program, Lyster and Genesee (2013) in their review of both international and U.S. research studies report that "immersion students attain the same levels of achievement in all aspects of the L1 as students attending non-immersion programs, although they may experience short-term lags in literacy development during grades when the L2 is used as the exclusive language of instruction. They also demonstrate the same levels of achievement in academic domains as students in non-immersion programs" (p. 1).

Despite these reported successes and the fact that the vast majority of students she witnessed first-hand went on to develop French-English bilingualism as a result of their foreign-language immersion experience, Sandra did have some lingering doubts. First, as a bilingual herself, she was conscious of not having the vocabulary knowledge equivalent to two monolinguals:

I've heard this said before and I think it's somewhat true and with me speaking languages; I think sometimes the more languages you know, the less your vocabulary can only be, like you have so much vocabulary split between two languages. That the vocabulary from one language is never as big as someone who only speaks one language, maybe.

Sandra's understanding of the configuration of a bilingual's vocabulary knowledge was consistent with the research studies we reported in earlier chapters. Research by Pearson and colleagues (1997), for example, suggests that the distribution of words across the two languages of bilinguals is not the same as for monolingual speakers of the two languages, but rather most bilingual individuals have knowledge of some words in one language and not the other and a third set of words that are known in both languages. This is thought to represent the division of their daily lives such that some activities are only ever conducted in one language and others in another, so either the need to know vocabulary in both languages for such activities is not necessary or no opportunity to become exposed to the same vocabulary in the other language may ever even arise.

Sandra mentioned this notion of "one language is never as big" because of her concerns with a subset of struggling students in the school who showed difficulty in acquiring French alongside English. She attributed their difficulties with their L2 to also having difficulties with their L1, stating that:

I don't know if going to school trying to learn two languages is good for children who already have a problem with one language on their own ... there's so much pressure for them, for us to expect them to do well in two languages. Sometimes it can be confusing.... The only reason why I mentioned that is because I know a couple of students who have a hard time learning one language and then see how stressful it is when they're not doing well in both languages. They don't have that much time to concentrate on just one.

In such circumstances, the immersion school does not council families to drop out if they wish their children to continue in the program. While Sandra reports that the "school does try to figure out ways to help the students" (including an example of a child with a developmental disorder), she is concerned that "It's just that they [the school] might not always be equipped." Ultimately, however, Sandra was convinced of the positive effects of the bilingual track her elementary students were on, stating of multilingualism that it "shows you what the human mind can do at such a young age. I think it's just very impressive."

3.   *Developmental bilingual education programs (DBE), also known as late exit or maintenance bilingual education programs*

We're also trying to do is really good ... programs, by giving the students other opportunities aside from just the traditional classroom setting. (Gael, K-12 district dual-language administrator)

DBE is an approach to dual-language instruction by which students who have a minority language as their L1 are initially taught academic content through their L1 to prevent students from falling behind in their academic learning.

Increasingly, the L2 (e.g., English) is taught and gradually students transition to also learning academic content through L2. However, instruction of L1 literacy and oral language are maintained to foster L1 development alongside L2. In the United States, eventually students may transition to an all-English instructional environment. For families in the Southwestern United States, where many language-minority families reside, this kind of dual-language programming was targeted for removal from state-funded schools by English-only immersion initiatives at the state level (Lindholm-Leary and Howard, 2008). Currently, in some states (California, for example, where previously most families had automatically been offered bilingual education options for their children), families of ELL students must now obtain a waiver in order for their children to enter bilingual programs.

Gael, an administrator of ELL services, explained the process of how he came to also be directing dual-language programs for students in his Californian school district:

"... Many of the parents in our district, they want children to continue to develop and learn their primary language, so that's why I offer the dual program. They say it reinforces the belief to our parents that being bilingual, or [...] all kind of language is important ... Also the fact that, in regards to our parents, obviously these parents have selected our program because they believe in the program and they want certain outcomes of the program. And many of our parents you know, not only do they want their child to know English, but also to be able to be biliterate, and also have greater opportunities in the future."

Even with the English-only initiative, approximately nine percent of California's ELL students statewide still receive dual-language programming of some kind through the action of a parental waiver to request it. In some cities like San Francisco with a highly diverse ethnic and linguistic population, 30 percent of ELL students receive dual-language instruction in English and one of a number of other languages including Spanish, Cantonese, Mandarin, and Korean. Students also are given the option to acquire Filipino, Italian, Japanese, or Spanish at the elementary level and additionally Cantonese, French, Hebrew, Italian, Latin, and Russian at the secondary level, as a foreign language that might also be a student's L1, or added to their linguistic repertoire as an L2 or an L3 (www.sfusd.edu).

After more than 17 years of restrictions on bilingual education, however, and perhaps as a sign of the changing times and attitudes toward multilingualism in California and elsewhere in the United States, a new ballot initiative is slated for 2016. This state bill is designed to remove the legal restrictions on the dual-language programming that LEAs can currently offer students (Ash, 2014).

In the meantime, meeting the needs of minority-language students in the United States so that they can acquire English without the abject loss of their

L1, and supporting and building literacy in both English and the L1, has been a struggle for educators like Gael who believed that bilingualism and biliteracy are important assets for minority-language students. Gael's interview was dominated by the theme of commitment from all involved in a dual-language program aimed at enabling those assets. The following excerpt is representative of this focus on commitment:

I think you know it requires a long-term commitment. It's not a 1 year, 2 year thing you know. This we started 12, almost 11 years ago. It requires a big commitment from the students, from the parents, for the district office, for the school site. And along the way there's ... you know we've had our obstacles. Our conversations that we've had. And you had to know it wasn't easy, but it requires a commitment to the program. And so it's always easier to give up and do something new, than to fix something and make it better.

He went on to add the commitment of classroom teachers to this mix, stating that because they ultimately are the ones who inspire student commitment, teachers' interactions are perhaps amongst the most critical:

... One of the things that really will motivate and is a challenge to develop is where the school site, the commitment from the school site, and also the specific teacher that's involved in the program. Because if this teacher for example is just teaching the subject matter without really supporting the program, it can be more detrimental than someone who maybe doesn't have the subject matter but really believes in the kids and also the program.... Because the teachers, remember the teachers are the ones interacting with the kids day in and day out, and how they interact with the kids will determine the motivation or the desire that the kid would have at the end.

Pablo, a middle school teacher who teaches in the same district, confirmed the positive impact of the program teachers on student's commitment to bilingualism and their educational outcomes more generally. When prompted to describe how these behaviors and attitudes are caused, he described a mechanism by which teachers' own self-esteem is first raised by being part of the DBE program and that this in turn has a positive effect on students:

Another benefit is that more than anything the kids in this program, they tend to be more self-motivated and more in tune with the education and the goals in the future. And then....
ANNA: What do you think causes it?
PABLO: I think it's because of the fact that everyone is involved in things like community in the school. And they are also, I think that they themselves, they know they're being looked at for that, for what they are. This is a program that it is for those students who not only speak one language but two. The way teachers ... how they are raised in their own self esteem with everything, engaged in providing that support for them.

The scrutiny under which these dual-language programs come because they buck the wide-spread utilization of English-only programming for minority-language students surfaces in Pablo's response to the prompt too. He overtly states that "being looked at for that … for what they are [bilingual]. This is a program that it is for those students who not only speak one language but two." This brings home the pressures that the program students (and presumably their teachers) are under to make sure they do acquire both English and the L1.

Emily, a secondary-level teacher in the same school district, spoke of the rewards of working in the program when she sees "the students speak in Spanish and to see how proud they are of speaking two languages." She also acknowledged the motivation shown by the students: "They already come in motivated to us: They know the purpose of the program, and they deliver. It's so easy to teach them." Emily also invoked the broader commitment that Gael spoke of when she mentioned the parents' motivation to have their children in the program: "I think that's why they really want their students in the program, because they want their students to be able to be bilingual."

The DBE program is not without its challenges though. As a high school teacher, Emily reported that the "biggest roadblock at the high school and probably the middle school is not enough Spanish materials, textbooks, CDs, etc." Much as the parents reported to us, the availability of L1 materials at more advanced levels of proficiency can be a challenge to find for schools as well. For example, Scholastic, the educational publisher, has "Club Leo en Español" that supplies Spanish-only and Spanish-English bilingual books but virtually no selections in Spanish at the middle school level and none marketed for high school classes. Clearly, in trying to sustain dual-language programs, teachers' hands are tied by the lack of availability and quality of educational materials. This situation is true even in a high-incidence language such as Spanish that is the target of most DBE programming in the United States.

4.   *Heritage (community) language programs*

So I kind of encourage that and making fun of why Chinese is not hard. It is just, I try to encourage them and if you work, if you can be successful in learning a language you can translate [it] to better grade maybe. It is hard. It is like anything else, you practice." (Jake, director and instructor, Mandarin heritage-language program)

Heritage or community language programs mainly enroll students whose L1 is the majority language in the society at large but whose parents, grandparents, or other ancestors spoke a minority language as their L1. In just two generations families may not have a common language by which to communicate (Alba, Logan, Lutz, and Stults, 2002; Portes and Hao, 1998, 2002). In some cases even within a generation, older children in a family may be bilingual whereas the youngest sibling may be monolingual in the majority language of a society

(Ellis, Johnson, and Shin, 2002; Wong Fillmore, 1991; see also Gathercole, 2014, for review of factors impacting childhood bilingualism). It is the L1 of family members or ancestors that is the target language of the heritage or community language program. Often students may have some oral-language skills in the heritage language but have not developed literacy skills. Literacy is a much greater investment for families raising children to acquire a heritage language (Imbens-Bailey, 2000), and so it makes sense that it is often a stated target of these programs. Moreover, NCELA (2011) also includes *indigenous language programs* taught in American Indian educational communities under this category. These programs are designed to support endangered indigenous languages in which "students may have weak receptive and no productive skills" (p. 1) in the heritage language. There is clearly some overlap in program types when we take the perspective of the child into account, for presumably, a child enrolled in a one-way immersion program may consider the objective to be the acquisition of his/her heritage language if the target language is also the L1 of other family members or ancestors.

Heritage language programming is reported in the popular press to be on the rise (Wides-Munoz, 2013). Although the need has long existed, in part because of "the events of September 11, 2001, heritage students' knowledge has become increasingly valued in the U.S.A. as the federal government has become mindful of the need for competent speakers of foreign languages, especially languages considered vital for national security" (Kagan and Dillon, 2008, p. 44).

As de Jong (2011) points out, "In most cases, however, heritage language maintenance efforts for school-age children are community-based and hence fall outside the realm of federal or state educational policies. The growth in the number and range of heritage language programs or community-based language schools (including in Chinese, Japanese, and Korean) illustrates the value and the importance that parents and ethnic communities continue to place on native language and cultural maintenance" (p. 130). In fact, the AGBU which, as mentioned earlier, supports Armenian heritage language programming, opened a new privately funded full-time school in Pasadena, California, as recently as 2006. It is remarkable that there is demand for full-time Armenian-English dual-language programming when there has been no new immigration to the United States from the Armenian Diaspora since the two main events which precipitated the second wave of Armenian immigration to the United States: the Armenian earthquake of 1988 and the fall of the Soviet system more than 25 years ago. We have to assume that the demand is coming from the parents of subsequent generations who still wish their children to acquire Armenian as a heritage language.

Jake, as director and instructor in a Mandarin language after-school program, had his own hypothesis about the popularity of the Mandarin program

– the number of mixed-ethnicity marriages. The children of such ethnically and linguistically blended families "speak like five different languages and those kids are really smart." The parent whose L1 is the minority language may enroll their children in a heritage language program in an attempt to foster not only oral language development but also the acquisition of literacy skills in the L1.

Heritage or community language programming differs from the dual-language programing we have outlined thus far in terms of pedagogy, content, and scheduling. According to Potowski (2001) and Kagan and Dillon (2008) teachers in heritage language classes can capitalize on most students' intimate knowledge of the culture in which the language is embedded and if sensitized to students' linguistic and cultural capital educators can best serve students' unique linguistic needs and strengths by taking their familiarity with the language into account. Authentic texts, for example, can be used from students' daily lives – texts in the heritage language that come through contact with family and friends who are L1 speakers of the heritage language. In terms of scheduling, heritage-language instruction can be given as a single course or a class over a period of just a few weeks, and is supplemental to a student's academic content learning and language arts education in the majority language (e.g., English language arts/literacy). In fact, in a survey of over 1000 college students by the National Heritage Language Resource Center (NHLRC) the third most common reason students had for enrolling in a heritage language course was to *fulfill a school language course requirement* (after the reasons *learning about their roots* and *communicating better with friends and family*, NHLRC, 2009).

Recently several states in the U.S. have given high-school students yet further reason to pursue their heritage language study. Fast gaining currency with both educators and parents is the Seal of Biliteracy. This is a special endorsement placed on the high school diplomas of eligible (i.e., proven biliterate) graduating seniors. The intention is to get employers and colleges to notice a new breed of high school student who can not only speak but also read and write in two (or more) languages. The Seal of Biliteracy initiative was started in California in 2011 and has spread quickly to seven other states including New York, Texas, New Mexico, and Illinois amongst others (sealofbiliteracy.org). Many more have it under consideration. It is not yet clear whether employers and colleges have begun to value this indicator of a twenty-first-century global competency. Certainly educational think-tanks and agencies that have influenced reforms in curricula in the United States and elsewhere have earmarked multilingual competencies as characteristics of students who will be effective communicators meeting the challenges of a globalized future. For example, the Partnership for 21st Century Skills expects students to "Communicate effectively in diverse environments (including multilingual and multicultural)" (National Education Association [NEA], 2011, p. 14).

While these documents do not elaborate on the kinds of multilingual skills expected of students in the new century, multicompetencies have been articulated in the educational and applied linguistics fields (Cook, 2008). For example, translanguaging practices are good candidates as instantiations of this twenty-first-century communication skill. Translanguaging involves students in using their knowledge of two or more languages to act as language brokers between monolingual individuals (e.g., family or friends speaking the L1 interfacing with government officials or healthcare workers speaking only the L2), and codeswitching skillfully and deliberately between two languages for reasons of emphasis, identity, or affiliation with other speakers (Bailey and Orellana, 2015). Studies will be needed to see if communicative competencies prized for the twenty-first century are merely aspirational on the part of the education-standards writers and policy-makers responsible for the Common Core State Standards for English Language Arts/Literacy and Mathematics (CCSSO, 2010a; 2010b) and the Next Generation Science Standards (NGSS Lead States, 2013), or if indeed such competencies are being sought in the workplace. In fact, multilingual students may excel in all four of the competency areas identified by NEA and taken up in the CCSS initiative (CCSSO, 2010a; 2010b). These are *critical thinking, communication, collaboration, and creativity* (NEA, 2011). Regardless, the positive face value and social desirability of the Seal of Biliteracy are undeniable as an increasing number of states take up this goal for their multilingual high school seniors.

Motivation of students to pursue the acquisition of a heritage language is a major challenge of this type of dual-language programming, and was a major theme throughout the interview with Jake. He indicated that "A lot of them just don't want to do Chinese. If you have strict teachers [inaudible]. I think I have kids like that. We used to have really strict Chinese teachers and then kids would complain." And yet for Jake the rewards of heritage language learning for his students were evident in the students' enhanced academic performances across the board. He told of several cases of former students who had gone on to excellent colleges. He believed their achievement was due in some ways to their bilingualism, as he explained in the case of his former student Bobby:

I mean those kids learn Chinese really quick and pick up stuff really quickly. I mean if you know Chinese really well obviously.... I see the relation between if you can learn the language really well I think you can be successful in learning different things. I see the relation now.... I have one kid who ... one of the kids [inaudible] Bobby, who used to come here, he is going to [an Ivy League institution].

An additional program that is described by NCELA (2011) as developing students' literacy in two languages but one that CREDE does not count amongst the four dual-language LIEP models is *transitional bilingual education (TBE)* or *early exit bilingual programs*. We also hesitate to include TBE along with the previous four LIEP models discussed in this chapter because it is not designed with the intention of fostering dual-language competencies in students; rather it is a stop-gap measure to use the students' L1 in content instruction until they have acquired sufficient English to transition to an all-English instructional environment. For the child to maintain the L1 and become literate in the L1 is not the objective. TBE programming was ubiquitous prior to the anti-bilingual education initiatives that curtailed bilingual educational offerings in many U.S. states. It was condemned for failing students' educational needs and indeed research suggests that it may very well have been less than pedagogically sound, not because it was a form of bilingual education but because the model did not allow for instruction to *build* on students' L1 language resources. TBE functions as a form of *subtractive bilingualism*, whereby the L1 is replaced by the L2 rather than leveraging L1 knowledge and abilities to grow not only the L1 itself but to successfully promote L2 language and literacy as well (Bialystok, 2013; Castro, Páez, Dickinson, and Frede, 2011).

Also as an important reminder for *all* dual-language program initiatives, as long ago as 1993, Landry and Allard were cautioning the educational field that arguments for the effectiveness of bilingual programming were (and may still be) "socially naïve." They came to this conclusion because few programs have taken account of the socio- and ethnolinguistic contexts within which the programs are embedded. Thus when they fail (or succeed) they may do so because of how the program languages are situated within the communities they serve. Their research found that it is the vitality of a language's social network (i.e., the amount and quality of linguistic contact between speakers of a language) that is most crucial for predicting key program outcomes such as students' social integration with the L1 and L2 communities, their linguistic identities, their own perceptions of their L1 and L2 oral proficiency, as well as cognitive and academic outcomes in the L2. The observations of Landry and Allard (1993) explain why students speaking an L1 with a large degree of vitality (e.g., a dominant societal language) can experience L2 immersion as an additive experience, whereas students with an L1 considered to have less vitality may not, and consequently experience L2 immersion as subtractive bilingualism.

It is critical to also point out that as a major (and growing) pipeline to any one of the schooling models designed to support the education and development of multilingual children, preschool programs must be available that can support children's multilingual development. With increasing numbers of children starting their educational experiences far in advance of the traditional years of schooling between ages 5 and 18, the availability of such multilingual preschool experiences is critical. Students who go into all-English preschool environments at ages three or four may rapidly lose their L1 during the process of learning their L2 (Castro et al., 2011), the danger being not only that the

L1 is lost for its own sake but that a strong oral language base in a child's L1 may be important for later literacy in L2 (e.g., Bialystok and Martin, 2004). However, contrary to past fears that early exposure to the all-encompassing dominance of the majority language will lead to L1 loss (Wong Fillmore, 1991), there is evidence that children who experience "true bilingual education" in the preschool years acquire the majority language as an L2 while managing to maintain their L1 (Winsler, Díaz, Espinosa, and Rodríguez, 1999). By "true bilingual education" Winsler and colleagues mean bilingual education comprising exposure to "high-quality" experiences in both the majority and minority languages. This is a finding also supported by a more recent study by Barnett, Yarosz, Thomas, Jung, and Blanco (2007), who conducted a rare randomized trial of TWI and English-language programming and found that the language-minority preschoolers who spoke Spanish not only maintained their L1 in the TWI program, but they also made gains in English, their L2, on par with children in the English-language program. The language outcomes were equally favorable for the majority language preschoolers in the TWI program.

The review by Castro and colleagues (2011) of early childhood care and education programming for language-minority children suggests strong evidence of the benefits of dual-language programming. These authors advocate that such programming be incorporated more systematically into federally and state-funded preschool initiatives and the standards that guide early childhood care and education programming. Furthermore, pedagogically sound approaches to language immersion in the early years require far more research and policy attention. This field is still in its infancy, and Hickey and de Mejía (2014) have cautioned that those working with preschoolers will need training in immersion strategies that address the needs of both minority-language and majority-language preschoolers. Moreover, they raise the issue of the availability of resources for immersion approaches for early childhood programs especially those offered for less commonly spoken languages.

Majority-Language Programming

We turn now to programming that focuses on the singular development of literacy in the dominant societal language, including content-based/sheltered language programs, structured immersion, and pull-out/push-in language development programs (NCELA, 2011). We include these LIEP models here despite our intent to describe programming that is overtly designed to foster multilingual development because the educational experiences of many language-minority children may fall outside the explicit multilingual programming we reviewed above. Rather, students may be enrolled in formal schooling contexts that are ostensibly monolingual but have characteristics and strategies that nevertheless may help to foster multilingual outcomes. Most importantly, as our interviews with educators revealed, students may encounter teachers who see the students' acquisition of English as part of a broader multilingual repertoire to which the students are adding. We further divide the discussion of the programs into: (1) English-language instruction; and (2) acquisition of English as an L2 in general education classrooms.

1.   *English-language programs*

If you look at the world economy, and the global economy, if they want to be twenty-first century employable people, you have to be multilingual and therefore, for them to come here and learn English at such a young age is beneficial beyond a dollar amount. (Elena, middle school ESL specialist)

With *content-based language programs,* subject matter instruction is given in English to minority students of various language backgrounds. For all students, English is the L2 (or an additional language). A common ESL version of content-based programming is the *specially designed academic instruction in English* or SDAIE approach. Students who have the potential to be multilingual in the United States may find themselves placed in content-based ESL programs that use their L1 only as necessary (and if available), along with use of *total physical response* (TPR) techniques (e.g., using non-verbal forms such as gesture, actions), realia (objects from real life) to connect language use to activities in the classroom, and visual aids (e.g., pictures, graphics) to support comprehension of the content areas (e.g., mathematics, science) that they are being taught. Such numerous ways of representating the same content/material through different media facilitate students' comprehension and are defining characteristics of the SDAIE approach.

Other SDAIE strategies include thematic instruction and frequent opportunities for meaningful peer interaction focused on lesson material, such as cooperative group work and small group instruction with an emphasis on learning strategies and scaffolding of academic language acquisition with occasional use of students' native language(s) (Moughamian, Rivera, and Francis, 2009). Teaching techniques include explicit direct and interactive instruction, chunking and webbing information, increased wait time for responses, use of expansion of students' responses in lieu of correction, and building on students' prior knowledge (e.g., Cline and Necochea, 2003; Coleman and Goldenberg, 2009). Learning strategies include word analysis, context clues analysis, creating personal definitions for academic vocabulary, and self-monitoring strategies for reading comprehension (Klingner, Boardman, Eppolito, and Schonewise, 2012).

Structured English immersion (SEI) involves teaching content in English adjusted to students' levels of proficiency, so typically only ELL students are taught together. Ideally teachers have receptive skills in the students' L1 or have a bilingual aide so they can assist students. However, Lyster and Genesee (2013) have referred to SEI programs as *submersion* rather than *immersion* because while they may have the trappings of the one-way immersion programs that do lead to bilingualism as discussed above, SEI programs may result in a subtractive language learning experience; language-minority students do not get to enrich their linguistic experiences with the continued development of their L1 as they learn English, unlike their majority language counterparts in foreign language immersion programs who add an L2 to the continued development of their English. In the second situation, the L1 continues to prosper because it is supported by the wider society.

Language development programs (*ELD* is the term typically used at the elementary level; *ESL* is typically used at the secondary level) are supplementary to mainstream (i.e., general education) programming. All content classes are taught in the target L2 and students are either taken out of their mainstream classroom for language instruction (e.g., pull-out ESL or ELD) or they remain in the mainstream classroom with language support given to them as needed by an ESL instructor or the general education classroom teacher (e.g., push-in ESL or ELD). No L1 support is expected, in part because in contexts where there are several different languages spoken by students or where ELL students are in small numbers in their communities, general education teachers and ESL specialists cannot be expected to know each of their students' home languages.

Elena voiced her frustration with the wider population, school administrators, and other educational entities having the power to disempower her ELL students by restricting their access to bilingual education. In the following excerpt she even levels this frustration at her fellow teachers:

… Even though the constitution of California dictates that every student should be educated, there necessarily isn't that belief. If you don't have that belief, how much are you going to do as a teacher beyond what you believe your job description requires you to do. That's beyond [name of school district]. That's statewide, nationally. That's all teachers. When we're talking about an economy where there isn't very much money, who has the voice? The kids don't have the voice. The people that do have the voice are the ones who are advocating for the funds and use of the funds and dictating how those are distributed through the school site council, and the PTA [parent teacher association], and the school board. That is statewide, that's national.

One of the key criticisms leveled at majority-language programming, such as SEI in the United States is the segregation of ELL students from their English-speaking peers (e.g., Valdés, 2004) as a result of the structure of the programming. This segregation is pernicious for several reasons; not only may it lead to a lack of opportunity to learn (OTL) in high-quality content classes and impact students' social integration in the school setting, but it also restricts students' access to models of the English language. David, a high school ESL specialist, spoke directly to the latter issue. Within his linguistically mixed classroom he reported that:

My Korean kids would always be with Korean kids; my Chinese kids would always be with Chinese kids. And as soon as I gave them like a, let's say I gave them a five minute break in class, no one is going to venture out to actually practice their English. They go right back to their....

ANNA: Default native language.

DAVID: And I say, "English! Let's try to do English in this class, okay. And actually, how about at lunch today, when you go out to lunch, why don't we see how many people are going to speak English."

The four educators in the study who are ESL teachers in English-language program settings presented a complex portrait of both positive and less positive attitudes toward multilingualism, as well as individually holding sometimes contradictory viewpoints of their ELL students. With an optimistic view of multilingualism, Camila, a middle school ESL specialist spoke of the advantages to being a bilingual individual as a teacher even in the SEI setting, stating, "I think that anyone with two or more languages has a definite advantage and immediately from a teaching point of view, too."

Melanie, who is an ESL specialist with experience teaching students from pre-kindergarten through the middle school levels, provided a concrete example of a time that her own impressive multilingualism (three European languages and two African languages) served to break through the resistance of a fifth-grade class, when she was their temporary teacher in a school she regularly substituted in, by winning the trust of a key student through language:

I think a lot of it is relating to the students on a level that they can understand. For example, I have been in the classroom for the past five days, I'll be there six days total. I've had phenomenal success with the students that I can relate to personally. One girl came up to me and said her grandmother was from Mauritania and she didn't know how to speak the language. I told her how. I wrote down the greetings.... She went home with the greetings and greeted her grandmother. Since then she has adored me and gets order in the classroom for me. The whole class respects me.

Elena, however, worried that her middle school students needed to know the instrumental value of English or they would not be motivated to learn the language. It is interesting that she views this from a multilingual perspective and not one of replacing the students' L1 with English. Elena uses the term "multilingual" in her work as an ESL specialist because she sees her teaching as taking her students from monolingualism in their L1 to at least bilingualism with their newly acquired knowledge of English. This is not a point of view commonly seen in the literature evaluating English-focused programs, where students very often do not achieve high levels of literacy in either language when English is the only language being supported in the classroom (Callahan and Gándara, 2014). Elena does not raise this as a criticism, but rather she has conceptualized her ESL instruction as a positive influence in her students' educational lives.

Elena said she has stopped short of pointing out to her students what she feels is the most critical connection between language-learning outcomes and her students' futures – their employment opportunities: "I haven't yet said, 'if you want a job, you need to be multilingual.'" However, in lieu of this very direct approach, she has explained that she has managed to focus her students on appreciating the need for English for successfully completing high school and going on to college:

I've noticed that they are very motivated to do well. I think what I've been able to do is draw the connection between what they are doing now and high school and then college. That's usually where I need to make it visible in their world because, you know, they are talking about video games and toys. If I don't put it in front of them, they don't make that connection. So, I have put it that way …

The ESL specialists voiced other concerns about their ELL student population including concerns for gender differences in language development and the isolation of ELL students they witnessed. David raised the issue about gender differences. He sees the ELL boys in his classes struggling to keep up with the girls in terms of L2 development:

Girls are testing out [of the program]. Girls are working harder. They seem to have more sense of the future than the guys are.... this may be a stereotype but you have boys, the girls out-achieve the boys always. And you have a certain percentage of the boys who really don't care and they're [not] doing their homework.
ANNA: So that's a changing stereotype, you're thinking because before the male....
DAVID: Well, I don't know, I hate to make, no, it's not a changing stereotype. I hate making a stereotype but, in general, girls are much more diligent at learning English than their boy counterparts.

In this observation David may be correct. On at least one major standardized assessment of English language proficiency (ELP) used in the United States to initially identify and to annually monitor students continued ELP development, ELL boys are reported to lag behind girls. This is the case in the listening, speaking, and reading domains until the later high-school grades. Boys' English writing performances were found to lag those of girls across their school careers (Taylor et al., 2007). However, as the interview progresses and further questions probe this situation, David revealed an additional dimension – classroom behaviors that differentiate boys from girls:

ANNA: Well, let me ask you this. Do you think it's because girls are also more talkative and, you know, there's this other stereotype in terms of …
DAVID: They're much more verbal.

ANNA: More verbal. So do you think that comes into play or do you think it's just something, you know, just about girls being studious or do you think….

DAVID: It's interesting. Actually, I think girls are much more verbal and they do better verbally, but in terms of like talkativeness or the squeaky wheel, I think the boys overwhelm the girls like that.

David speculates about the origins of these differences between boys and girls in both language development and their classroom behaviors, and had a couple of hypotheses he shared with us; one was that the boys are perhaps not pushed as hard at home as the girls or that the boys are more socially isolated than the girls. He spoke from specific experiences, giving for instance one example of a group of six boys with Korean as their L1 in his class who "just always were together and they were always talking and they sat next to each other. All the socialization would be with each other."

Isolation of ELL students was in fact a theme throughout the interview with David and was part of a broader theme of isolation we found in the interviews of other ESL teachers as well. First, the report of isolation in students: David and Camila both spoke of the social and cultural isolation of their ELL students. David suggested:

… Part of this learning thing too and the socialization thing and then this language. I've come across a lot of these kids who are incredibly isolated here. They're dumped with their grandma or something like that…. They just, they feel isolated and you try to be a good teacher and you try to keep wanting them to get integrated into stuff.

He said "I find it hard" and "It's really difficult" to work with students who are so isolated. The fact they did not respond to his attempts to integrate them into English-language interactions made him wonder aloud if "A big thing could be that these [desires to learn English] are their parents' dreams, but maybe not their dreams." However, Camila may have the solution. She had an explicit goal for the social integration for her ELL students and it comes from wanting to foster confidence in and reasons for using both English and their L1 whenever they can in school:

The goals I have for them [are] to be, as you said, to socially be integrated, converse with other students at the school and with their teachers. I want them to be prepared for the academic English that they're going to be required to use in their classes. I want them to have an understanding of American culture as well. I want them to continue with the self-esteem, the pride that comes with having two backgrounds or three backgrounds.

Reports of teacher isolation were also made by David and Camila. Each spoke of how the structure of ESL instruction literally placed them out of the mainstream along with their students so that they had little contact with or collegiality with the general education teachers in their schools. Specifically, Camila said that due to the lack of involvement of other teachers, "Believe it or not, with this diversity, I'm the only one on campus who is really fluent in Spanish or has the ability or willingness to find a way to communicate [with students and families]." David reported similar sentiments and compared the isolation of the ESL instructor to special education teachers. He felt the ESL instructors were in a less favorable situation because the special education teachers had classroom aids for company. He did not only blame the situation on the disinterest of the general education teachers though. He also identified the students themselves as contributing to his own feelings of isolation, particularly when in some years his class enrollment was predominantly made up of ELL students reluctant to talk due to certain cultural backgrounds "... Typically I think of the Asian kids that I've dealt with are so much less engaging. So I told you about being isolated. I'm feeling even more isolated when you feel like you're the only [one] talking in the classroom." A final challenge mentioned by the ESL instructors was their lack of interaction with the parents of their students. David accounted for this as a difference between cultures, and not because parents do not care to establish as close a home-school connection as parents of non-ELL students. In fact he compared parents of ELL students to their non-ELL counterparts favorably:

I think they care as much or more, but I don't know think they know what to do and they, and sometimes they respect the educational program so much that they don't question it or they don't even talk to you. And it's like, you know, when you're teaching, the squeaky wheel gets the grease.

However, educators' comments could reveal orientations toward their students' families that were less than positive or may have been stereotypic, while they did acknowledge the challenges of immigrant life and were intended to explain why certain supports were not in place for language development in the home. For example Camila had her own "theory." She stated, "I think the parents, in their situation, the parents are working so hard to just make a living. There isn't much time spent in building relationships or language at home. They speak in incomplete sentences." She was not alone in this belief. David also stated, "But I also think there's this thing where a lot of parents just think, 'Oh, the teacher will do it. The teacher will handle that. And I can just worry about making money or what's going to happen next.'" Elena also spoke of the immense challenges of forging home-school connections with her ELL students' families:

When I'm dealing with parents and unfortunately, my experience with Chinese and Korean parents, any class that seems like it's a help is in their view a crutch. So, even though there's a huge gain and they can see a huge gain, all they can see is my son or daughter is not in regular English. It doesn't matter how much growth there is or how much the child sees it himself or herself, but there's still this cultural bias against getting any type of assistance. It's taken me, well this is year three here. To gain credibility here and rapport with the families has taken three years to build a group of parents that have seen the transitions and then understand what I'm doing. The same with the kids. I think what has helped is that because I was already at the high school, the siblings are coming through. I know the parents. This added another level of trust there. But I did have to build a new one.

While there may also be stereotypic beliefs expressed in this account (parents not wanting ESL services because these were perceived as a "crutch"), Elena explained what she explicitly termed "a cultural bias" and how she has worked over a period of years to build trust with families whose cultures she did not share. Parents have responded positively to her, rewarding her patience and the onus she placed on herself to build credibility with them.

2.   English acquisition in the general education classroom

The school where I am at does not have an ESL program. And so the, you know, all the students are in the mainstream English classes, even when many of them could benefit from being in a different English class. (Thomas, high school history and government teacher)

In Chapter 2, we reported on teacher demographics in the United States with the vast majority (82%) of public school teachers being non-Hispanic White and with great variation in how many speak a language other than English. This does not necessarily bode well for the multilingual development of those students who do find themselves as language-minority students receiving supplemental ELD in mainstream classrooms. This situation is unfortunate for at least two reasons. First, the linguistic and academic success rate of students in these English-focused programs is poor (e.g., Slama, 2012). Second, the restrictions placed on the use of a student's L1, sometimes its subjugation, means there may be little to no encouragement of its further development in publicly funded school settings. Moreover, students may receive instruction from a teacher who currently has little or no training in the teaching of ELL students (NCELA, 2008).

Only 12.5% of the close to 3 million U.S. school teachers report having received eight or more hours of recent training in teaching students with limited English proficiency (NCES, 2002), although, 41.2% of them reported having taught students with limited English proficiency in their classrooms. More recent figures from NCES could not be found, but from reports of more recent smaller-scale surveys of teachers (e.g., Rubinstein-Avila and Lee, 2014) and with increased numbers of ELL students over the past 10 years, we have reason to believe that the gap between the number of teachers with adequate preparation and the number of ELL students enrolled in mainstream classrooms has only grown. At the secondary level, the situation may be especially acute with as many as 90% of single-subject teachers reporting that they have never received any training for working with ELL students (Reeves, 2006, cited in Rubinstein-Avila and Lee, 2014). Furthermore, researchers such as Stoddart, Pinal, Latzke, and Canaday (2002) and Lee, Hart, Cuevas, and Enders (2004) in the field of science education for example, report that most classroom teachers are not sufficiently prepared to integrate content instruction and English language instruction. Teacher education is woefully in need of articulating the kinds of preparation general education teachers need for meeting the needs of ELL students (Lucas, Villegas, and Freedson-Gonzalez, 2008; NCELA, 2008).

At the heart of the issue is the concern that content material OTL may be reduced if ELL students are taught at a slower pace, miss content classes for language instruction, or are not taught to the same depth of knowledge as English-speaking students. Performance may also be impacted when students lack exposure to or experience teaching that does not make accessible the crucial academic uses of English (e.g., content-specific vocabulary and grammar, and academic language functions such as description, explanation, prediction) (Bailey and Martínez, 2010).

In a small-scale survey focused on the preparation of 85 general education teachers for teaching ELL students, Coady, Harper, and de Jong (2011) found that educators who were also multilingual rated themselves as more prepared to teach ELL students. Coady and colleagues interpret this finding to suggest that "teachers' personal experiences learning additional languages may provide them with unique insights into language structure and language-learning strategies and can help them to develop empathy and respect for ELLs facing the challenge of learning language and content simultaneously in school" (p. 234). However, the teachers did not report that they were any more effective than those teachers who were monolingual. Although not mentioned in the study, it is possible that the languages spoken by the teachers did not match those of their students, thus they did not have more of an advantage in the day-to-day interactions of classrooms than a monolingual English teacher working with ELL students.

Despite these pessimistic findings about the preparation and/or effectiveness of mainstream teachers working with ELL students, there are reports of monolingual English teachers in mainstream classrooms who do create environments for their students to foster their multilingualism. Hawkins (2004) for example describes a number of different ways in which educators who do not share a common language with students and who are working in all-English classroom settings can nevertheless support students' language growth. Here she describes Lynn, the teacher of a kindergartener, Shousa, who speaks Hmong as her L1 and is at the earliest phases of English language acquisition:

Lynn had always felt that her role as teacher was to provide scaffolding for language and learning during instructional time.... Teacher scaffolding of language practice and social interaction is appropriate throughout all the events of the school day, and may be necessary to help move emergent English speakers from the periphery to the core of the classroom community. (p. 16)

Hawkins explains that this effort by general education teachers is especially important in the case of students who may be reticent to have any kind of interaction with their peers and who also may have little contact with English outside the school context.

Our prior research has also made monolingual English teachers in mainstream classrooms a target of observation to better understand what strategies they use to effectively teach ELL students. Our observations of Mrs. Troy teaching science in her fourth-grade general education classroom showed her support of content and language learning for the two ELL students placed in her otherwise all-English-speaking classroom of 30 students. Through ELL strategies to scaffold student understanding of content material (e.g., use of graphics, making representations), through academic language strategies that model desired language structures and scientific uses of vocabulary, and by providing opportunities for student-teacher interactions that encouraged elaborated responses, she was able to support the ELL students without calling special attention to them (Bailey and Martínez, 2010). Indeed, Mrs. Troy reported that she made no distinctions in her teaching practices between ELL and others students (Bailey, 2010). In fact, Mrs. Troy herself was not distinct from the bilingual teachers we also observed who did share the languages of the ELL students in their classrooms in terms of the repertoire of instructional strategies to ensure OTL for ELL students. Mrs. Troy's teaching emphasized the necessity for all students to communicate basic science facts, as well as the expectation and support for all students to use the challenging language associated with higher-order thinking skills (e.g., inference making, causal reasoning, and hypothesis generation). As Bailey (2010) reports, it is not surprising to learn that Mrs. Troy teaches in a school that has far exceeded the academic achievement targets required by its state for NCLB accountability.

Lynn, teaching in her kindergarten classroom, and Mrs. Troy, with her fourth graders, share something in common: despite their monolingualism, both exhibit a keen sense of the interconnected nature of language and academic content. While neither could use the L1 of their ELL students to support their content learning, these educators worked to find ways to have them participate meaningfully in instructional interactions well before their language skills would have traditionally been considered up to the task; anywhere from four to seven years (e.g., Hakuta, Butler, and Witt, 2000) if such proficiency estimates were to be used as a gauge. These kinds of efforts were also reflected in our interview with Thomas, a high school history and government teacher.

When we asked how he approaches the "situation" for teaching one student he had described as "not an English Speaker at all," he first notes that "it is very challenging for him and for me." While Thomas does know some Spanish, he is also perceptive enough to know that his Spanish is "not good enough to give him academic instruction in Spanish." His use of L1 support is more for building rapport with his students rather than for effectively teaching content. However, Thomas goes on to describe how he strategically employs the proficient bilingual students in his classes to aid in instruction: "I do have him working with another student who is a ... also a Spanish speaker but he is also fluent in English. They are working as a team which is you know the ... solution...."

When we asked Thomas for his opinion on the efficacy for English language acquisition of the classroom environment he had created for the ELL student he had paired with a proficient bilingual student, he responded:

I think he is going to pick up English slower in this the situation just because he rarely, if ever, is using English in the classroom. And I mean if he was in an ESL classroom, I think they would ... I think it will help him transition better than the situation in which he is now.

This view of the situation contravenes much of what L2 acquisition scholars and policy reformers are currently touting as effective practices and would raise their fears about a lack of OTL and engagement in authentic discipline practices in English for ELL students. Thomas's first-hand experience with an ELL in his classroom leads him to conclude that his student will develop English more slowly than had he received ESL instruction. What he is describing, of course, is the language *submersion* experience described by Lyster and Genesee (2013). Thomas implies a period of time before the transition to a mainstream classroom may be more optimal for his student. Ironically, Thomas instinctively does strive to provide his ELL student access to deep disciplinary content knowledge at the same time creating meaningful language learning experiences within his mainstream classroom despite his beliefs that the student would be better off first acquiring English in an all ESL environment. The following excerpt relays the efforts he has gone to in order to connect language and content learning:

Well, realia, you see, I do not have any, but I would always try to use songs and auditory/audio [support]. Just for example, when I was teaching the War of 1812 as eighth graders, I would ... when I was a kid, my dad used to sing this song, he taught it to us, I guess it was a song from 1960s. It was this twangy country song that was called the Battle of New Orleans, and there is just from listening to the song ... and the kids loved listening to it – not because it was their kind of music, but because it was new and different in the classroom, but just from listening to the words of song, you get so much history content. It talks about Colonel Jackson, and it calls him by his nickname Ole Hickory, and it talks about the Battle of New Orleans and the tactics that he used.

And when I am done with it, the students remember all of those things.... Also in that unit, even though that wasn't in the standards anywhere, The Star Spangled Banner comes from the Battle of Fort McHenry, or the bombardment of Fort McHenry, even though the standards do not say anything about it, but in my mind, I always try to connect history to our lives today, and they are all sports fans, they all hear Star Spangled Banner sung before every single game – and so you know I talk about that and where it comes from ... And I gave the kids an opportunity to sing if they wanted to in class, and each time when I taught eighth-grade history, there were probably 5–10 students that all wanted to sing. They may not have learned CA standards during that time, but it helped them make a connection between their lives and the history of the things.... so that the ones who could not read, they could hear it. They could hear me talking about it, but they could see the pictures, the words, vocab next to pictures, and I hope it helped.

Apparently, while he does not personally think ELL students are best served in his general education classroom, Thomas's account clearly reveals how a mainstream classroom teacher teaching in a disciplinary area like history can modify his instruction to meet the language needs of ELL students while not compromising the deep discipline learning to which ELL students also need access. The interconnected nature of language and disciplinary learning so vividly painted in the interview with Thomas, as well as others earlier in the chapter, is a theme repeated in several reviews and policy recommendations of effective teaching of multilingual students. We now turn to these hallmarks of effective teaching, along with the characteristics of effective teachers themselves.

Effective Teaching of Multilingual Students

First, we consider dual-language instructional situations. Howard, Sugarman, and Coburn (2006) expressly adapted the existing *sheltered instruction observation protocol* (SIOP) model, which lists teacher behaviors and strategies for making content comprehensible for ELL students while they are acquiring their L2, to the TWI context to create the TWIOP. The SIOP Model itself has come under increasing criticism for not demonstrating effectiveness under rigorous research conditions and for including a cacophony of teacher behaviors and strategies from differing approaches and theories of L2 acquisition (e.g., Krashen, 2013). Nevertheless, the SIOP was adapted to TWI instruction and shares many of the language instructional features already mentioned above for English-language programming. Additionally, the TWIOP emphasizes coordinated instruction in the partner languages to promote language and literacy development in both languages (including the transfer of skills between languages). To achieve an effective level of coordination, the authors recommend that educators use similar instructional strategies and assessments across the partner languages, coordinate language learning objectives, develop awareness of cognates (a strategy that is *only* applicable if the specific languages partnered have linguistic roots in common of course) and avoid switching to the L1 to translate content for the majority-language students because "It is essential for teachers not to switch to English during instructional time in the partner language because doing so encourages students to use English when they should be using the partner language" (p. 13).

TWIOP is also designed to capitalize on two additional characteristics of TWI programs; namely the cultural awareness these programs can foster in students and the intended peer modeling they allow for. In terms of cultural awareness, the authors recommend cultural objectives to accompany language and content objectives that are also complementary across the partner languages, so learning can transfer from one language to another. They also recommend peers be taught how to support each other's learning of the partner languages by explicitly teaching students SIOP strategies, such as wait time, slower speech, and use of gestures and visual aids (Echevarria, Vogt, and Short, 2004) ostensively to create comprehensible input for one another.

In terms of English-language instructional situations, all too often mainstream teachers are not given the wherewithal to teach the ELL students they encounter in their classrooms. Instead, they are told to "adapt" what new material they have learned about to their ELL students without further elaboration. Alejandro shared his frustration with this less-than-adequate approach from his wife's perspective:

Why does my wife who is still in a public school system, when she goes to a training.... Mind you a training she probably could have sat in 20 years ago. They are still saying the same things and at the end of trainings, "Oh! By the way, if you have an English learner modify it." "Oh! Of course. Why not!" Why are we still dealing with those issues?

The Stanford Understanding Language initiative (ELL.Stanford.edu) addresses this paucity of instructional preparation through its focus on supporting educators to make content accessible within the disciplinary practices of language arts/literacy, mathematics, and science. The initiative's principles for effective instruction of ELL students could largely pertain to high-quality instruction for any student, multilingual or otherwise, but they additionally include ELL-specific instructional moves and strategies to meet the unique language-related needs of students with emerging English-language abilities. These are: (1) leveraging ELL students' home languages and cultures as assets to be used in bridging between prior knowledge and new content knowledge; (2) providing "deliberate and appropriate scaffolds" so students can participate in activities aligned with the educational standards for language arts/literacy, mathematics, and science (CCSSO, 2010a; 2010b; NGSS Lead States, 2013) even as their L2 is still emerging (as Lynn, Mrs. Troy, and Thomas in our examples above all demonstrated); (3) "taking into account English proficiency level(s) and prior schooling" in order to design instruction accordingly; (4) equipping ELL students with strategies necessary to "comprehend and use language in a variety of academic settings," ultimately with autonomy; and (5) employing assessments for learning that can "measure students' content knowledge, academic language competence, and participation in disciplinary practices" (Understanding Language, 2013, p. 1; see also Saunders, Goldenberg, and Marcelletti, 2013, for guidelines specific to the ELD instruction of ELL students).

Regardless of LIEP model, educators need to be effective instructors of language and content for all their students. Summarizing the literature on factors that affect the quality of instruction Gándara, Maxwell-Jolly, and Driscoll (2005) highlight the qualities that educators themselves need to have, including "knowledge of teaching and learning, deep content knowledge, experience, and full certification in the field" (p. 3). More specifically the knowledge and skills that their review found to contribute to effective ELL teaching include the "ability to communicate with students, ability to engage students' families, knowledge of language uses, forms, mechanics, and how to teach these, and feelings of efficacy with regard to teaching English language learners" (Gándara et al., 2005, p. 3).

Thomas, as we mentioned above, intuitively had a sense of the interconnection of language and history content and described how he supported content learning using techniques he ascribes to the SDAIE approach, employing these whether he has ELL students in his classes or not. He believed all students are having to learn the language of the history discipline and can benefit from such an approach:

When you know I am using the graphic organizers, that we use, that helps all the students to organize, whether they need that or not.

ANNA: What else do you use?

THOMAS: Well, I mean ... The first thing I do in any unit, I preview all the vocabulary that we are going to do. And that's when we get into the sections, and we start using the words, I make sure you know that they know what all the vocabulary that we are going to use. And history is, it's most of the vocabulary words we use are history-based you know it's not just standard academic vocabulary. So even English [-speaking] learners, they do not know history vocabulary, like they do not know who Hatshepsut was or any of these other people, and so you know the fact that I preview it, is good regardless. And I always do that. We do our work in history journals so that they can see how their work has changed over time. You know, I do my best to try to make sure that you know ... all sixth graders in my experience are extremely disorganized, and so trying to teach them how to be organized, you know.... You know I think they help me with my English learners, but you know I think they help even more because sixth graders are so disorganized.

ANNA: You know you mentioned peer support for one of the students who ... speaks very little English. At that level, for students whose language you do not always speak, are there any other things that you are doing – or even for older students, for your twelfth graders what do you do [to support them]?

THOMAS: Well, I try to show them a lot of visuals ... So you know, we do do reading in class, but I would reinforce everything we read with ... make PowerPoints, with a lot of pictures in them. Vocabulary will be on there, so that we could reinforce the words that we've learned....

However, not all general education teachers develop these intuitive strategies for integrating language and content learning on their own. We can apply the lens of investment to the prior research and our own study with educators, as we did with families and see a need for society to invest in educators' adequate preparation for working with diverse multilingual students; or even for educators to invest time in their own training. The investment may need to come in the form of more time and expense to allow for the necessary collaboration between educators to meet the educational needs of multilingual students. For example, schools may find it more costly but it may be more advantageous to not attempt to have one teacher take on both the roles of the ESL specialist and the content specialist, but rather invest in having these two types of teachers work together. Collaboratively, they may meet the needs of multilingual students in the mainstream classroom more effectively (Martin-Beltran and Peercy, 2014).

Differentiating instruction for students at different levels of language development was also a theme that cut across the programs. Elena providing ELD instruction, and Alejandro in his TWI program, each had vivid accounts of how they modified instruction. Elena explained:

You have a responsibility to differentiate the curriculum and that would require modifying assessments, modifying the manner in which material is delivered. Even in term of instructional materials that are used. Modifying class work and homework assignments. Allowing choice so that you have a variety of ways to demonstrate learning. They need to make the information comprehensible. And that would be something you would take the time to check for understanding frequently during the lesson or during independent practice or during collaborate groups in class.

Similarly, Alejandro faced with "rotation" in the TWI program in order to group students by SLD and ELD levels would differentially work with the individual groups, facilitating their language learning at a specific, more homogeneous level, as he taught geography concepts, for example.

Teachers who happened to be bilingual themselves regardless of program also reported that they were able to flexibly capitalize on their students' different language and cultural experiences during instruction. Paola (a TWI teacher) shared how she can utilize her students' multilingual and multicultural knowledge with the following examples from her classroom in which the varieties of

Spanish found across Latin America offered students an opportunity to notice geographic differences and make connections in word usage:

... they just think in different ways. They'll say like "oh that's like Spanish." They'll make these connections between languages. Or in class when we're talking about you know a specific book and a word comes up and I have students from South America, Central America, and Mexico so the language can vary a lot, so we talk about that. And they have so much fun with that and how they're able to understand and say like "oh you're Argentinian, you say it this way." "You know you use this accent." And they're just so lively I feel.

Alejandro also described how the contact between Hispanic and U.S. mainstream cultures can prime students to be open to considering the possibilities of additional contrasting cultures in a much less superficial way than the "culture of the month" activities typically found in school curricula and criticized as an approach to introducing students to cultural diversity in the United States (i.e., rather than fostering social justice) (McDonald, 2005). In this next example, the class had been preparing for Day of The Dead, a Mexican tradition that honors deceased ancestors, when Alejandro was able to extend discussion of the concepts further afield to include an understanding that the traditions of honoring ancestors are practiced more widely than in Hispanic cultures alone:

... the time that we were ... talking about traditions and not the "culture of the month" type of thing but trying to bring it into the curriculum. And this one particular year we were talking about ancestry. And we looked at all of the children's ancestry, but there was one particular way that this Mexican, or Latin American culture because it's more than just Mexican, honor their loved ones who have passed. And same thing we find in Japan, we find in Africa, we find in other countries that there are traditions to honor the memory of loved ones.

Not surprisingly, Melanie, our polyglot educator, reported providing strong support of L1 usage by her ELL students:

Whenever I find another student who speaks another language at home, I always encourage them to speak their family's language. There was one girl today who was telling me that in her family they speak a language but she understands it and responds in English. I encouraged her to speak to her parents in their native tongue so that at school she's getting English and at home she's getting a different language. So I try to encourage it.

Camila, an ESL instructor, also described how she incorporates the students' multilingual background into her interactions with her students to build rapport for instruction. Specifically, she described this as "building a relationship with them and then engaging them." She wants her students "to continue with the self-esteem, the pride that comes with having two backgrounds or three backgrounds. I also talk with them about helping to break stereotypes.... Here's lesson number one today, 'We come in all shapes, sizes, colors, races.' Then I'll start speaking Spanish and they say, 'Oh, she does!'"

These strategies of capitalizing on students' multilingual backgrounds for instruction need not, however, be confined to the classrooms of teachers who are bilingual. In fact they are similar to those of Ms. Chang, the ESL teacher described in a study by Palmer, Chen, Chang, and Leclere (2006). Ms. Chang actively sought ways in which to continue to build the L1 Mandarin skills of her second-grade students Zongyou and Xiaowei alongside their acquisition of English without herself knowing Mandarin. This teacher used the students' native language to gauge how much they understood when they read by enlisting the help of her bilingual paraprofessional to conduct reading comprehension checks. But importantly, the authors reported that she looked for ways to support the boys continued reading development in Mandarin itself.

"Ms. Chang encourages the students to read in Mandarin at home and encourages their parents to continue speaking Mandarin to their children (Fu, 2003). Finally, Ms. Chang has built a classroom library filled with appropriate materials to support her Mandarin-speaking students' literacy development" (Palmer et al., 2006, pp. 254–255). "Appropriate materials" not only means bilingual books to support both Mandarin and English reading development, but also books that are culturally responsive: that is, books that are written in English with Chinese themes that the students can relate to or will find familiar. This latter aspect will allow students, at the early stages of L2 acquisition especially, to more readily transfer their familiar knowledge of topics and concepts in the L1 to the unfamiliar English language, rather than having to learn unfamiliar concepts simultaneously with learning English language.

Informal Options for Fostering Multilingual Development

We have focused exclusively on the formal educational options of parents until this point. However, parents also have informal options available to them to either supplement the formal educational programs their children are enrolled in or as the only mechanism for fostering their children's multilingualism outside the home context. As already mentioned, there are no central databases that maintain a log of such informal community offerings (Lee and Wright, 2014), and certainly no census of the activities and opportunities for language learning that parents themselves generate for their children amongst their family and networks of friends. Consequently, the best source of information we can offer on these informal options can be found in Chapter 5 and with the 23 families themselves. Their interviews were replete with stories about play groups/parent support groups they had joined or had established when their children were young; parent-organized informal classes;

community-sponsored language enrichment classes; recreational, scouting, and sports groups that might be attached to organizations hoping to support the maintenance of the heritage language, sometimes for religious reasons; and summer camps. The latter especially might be organized by religious organizations that could pull together in central locations sufficient numbers of children during summer vacations. Religious activities, more generally, often presented exposure to the heritage language (e.g., Sunday schools and church services in the L1). Perhaps the most ubiquitous practice was spending vacations with family, often in the parents' country or countries of origin. A variant of this was to send older children alone to spend summers with family. In both cases the infusion of an immersive vacation was frequently revealed as the only way families could sustain their children's L1.

From our extensive examination of the formal options open to families, we noted how formal and informal language-learning settings may be more closely aligned to provide stronger support of multilingualism. We see possibilities for forging closer ties between the formal and informal options in three key ways: (1) through a child's interactions with peers; (2) by identifying activities and programs that can serve as transitional spaces between informal and formal language leaning; and (3) increasing teacher awareness of students' out-of-school translanguaging practices so they can be leveraged for student learning in the classroom.

First, there is evidence that school is important for language learning but not simply because of the formal instruction provided by teachers, but also because of encounters with other children. In the earliest years, the home environment and preschool peers, in addition to the child's preschool teachers, are found to be predictive of a child's English language outcomes among young Spanish-speaking children (Palermo et al., 2013). The importance of informal language exposure from peers in school continues even into adolescence. Carhill, Suárez-Orozco, and Páez (2008) found the single best predictors of English language proficiency outcomes in high school were the informal language of the students and their opportunities to acquire English by interacting with their peers in informal contexts such as at recess, in hallways, and during out-of-school contact (e.g., interactions with peers in their neighborhoods).

Second, encouraging more "transitional" spaces like the public library-sponsored bilingual music and play classes reported by Alvarez (2014) can create a bridge between informal community schooling and formal school-based language and literacy learning environments for young children. This echoes the call by Palmer and Martínez (2013) more generally for educators to challenge the hegemony over the curriculum even within dual-language programs. Alvarez describes the library initiative as an out-of-school institution that responded "to detrimental language ideologies by creating positive spaces which can nurture and foster bilinguals' practices" (p. 16). Specifically, the library was able to foster "moments in which the children exhibited *felicidad* (joy) in participating in both of their linguistic repertoires" (p. 3). They accomplished this by employing "play as a community schooling practice, which may increase students' self-esteem and self-awareness in being bilingual and bicultural" (p. 3).

Another recent example of a space that can bridge the informal everyday practices of families and the literacy demands of school, this time using technology, shows families to be no longer constrained by the physical location in which they are raising their families. Compton-Lilly, Kim, Quast, Tran, and Shedrow (2014) in a study of transnational literacy practices found immigrant families from Mexico and Morocco, among other parts of the world, using digital technologies to foster the heritage languages of their children. With technology, families no longer have to wait for the summer vacation with family to get the life-preserving "infusion" of exposure to their heritage languages. The technologies families adopted included face-to-face video-conferencing (e.g., Skype, FaceTime), social media (e.g., Facebook), and other online resources (e.g., informational websites and chat rooms). The authors also saw use of transnational religious literacy practices taking place via digital technology, thus documenting a twenty-first-century incarnation of the role religion has played for the preservation of multilingualism.

Third, closer ties between informal and formal supports for multilingualism may be brought about by increasing teacher awareness of everyday language practices. Bailey and Orellana (2015) argue that "Rather than fostering the idea that everyday and academic literacies are distinct (a message that is conveyed by well-meaning teachers who say such things as 'That kind of language is fine at home, but in school …'), teachers can help adolescents to see how things they do every day can help them in school, as well as how what they learn in school can support their everyday language work" (p. 22). Fostering the translanguaging practices that can tie informal learning contexts to formal schooling contexts is important because adolescent multilingual students are especially vulnerable to the prejudices of a monolingual-centric society and may view their multilingualism competencies as deficits rather than seeing the strengths in what they can do with language (Martínez, 2010).

Ortega's (2013b) notion of the *bi-/multilingual turn* in the L2 acquisition field has placed emphasis on an assets oriented view of multilingual students and expanded the traditional dichotomous contrast between bilingualism and monolingual L1 acquisition to also include connections between L2 acquisition, bilingual L1 acquisition, successive monolingualism, early L2 acquisition in children, and delayed L1 acquisition among other language-learning contexts. As an antidote to the deficit orientation that educators may have of students or their families who speak an L1 other than the majority language, educators might be encouraged to view students' multicompetencies as "untapped resources." This should be the goal of all educators whether or not they are bilingual or teach in TWI, DBE, or SEI programs. The first step is for educators of multilingual students "to acknowledge everyday competencies in order to help students to see the relationship between what they do every day and what is asked of them in school" (Bailey and Orellana, 2015, p. 23).

Common and Distinct Programming Experiences

We conclude the chapter by briefly highlighting some of the themes we uncovered that were common across the different programs as well as those that were more distinctive of certain programs. A number of the educators raised issues about instability in their programs. The contexts of their teaching situations regardless of program type often kept shifting. For example, Paola spoke at length of the changes in the ratio of time given to L1 and L2 instruction as well as to the division of content areas across the partner languages of her elementary TWI program. Similarly, Sarah spoke of the change in instructional models that had recently taken place in the TWI school. Both Alejandro, an elementary TWI teacher, and David, a high school ESL specialist, spoke of changes in teachers, aides, curriculum, and other school policies.

The educators in our study felt that school resources for multilingual instruction were severely limited. For example, most programs suffered the frustration of finding materials at the right grade level and of high quality for their multilingual students. Both Sarah, researching TWI elementary and middle school levels, and Emily, teaching in a high school DBE program, thought this was particularly pronounced for educators working at the middle- and high-school levels, stages when even the Spanish-language textbook market has shrunk in size, let alone adequate availability of academic publications in core content areas in lower incidence languages. There are certainly far fewer ELL students at these higher grade levels and fewer dual-language programs existing beyond the elementary grades as well.

Several educators reported feeling isolated in their programs. This was not unique to just one program. The middle and high school ESL specialists Camila and David teach in English-language programs that follow an approach to language instruction already known and critiqued in the literature to be a socially isolating experience for the program students (Lyster and Genesee, 2013). In addition, one of the TWI teachers (Alejandro) reported feelings of isolation. This can likely be explained by the fact that this particular TWI program was a strand within a larger school. The other classrooms offered English-only instruction and the day-to-day language of the school was entirely English.

Subsequent to our interview, the place of the TWI program has been given more visibility within the school. School-wide there has been greater adoption of Spanish-language signage, student work in Spanish is hung in the corridors and, the most radical change, a half-hour Spanish enrichment is required of the entire student body each day. It remains to be seen whether these efforts to validate the presence of the TWI program will manage to ameliorate the isolating effects of being a separate strand within the school.

Another theme that is worth reiterating because it cut across most interviews with the educators was the positive attitude they had toward the multilingualism of their students. We heard this expressed as admiration numerous times, for example, "it's amazing" (Paola), "openness" (Alejandro), "easily adaptable" (Sarah), "really impressive" (Sandra), "self-motivated" (Pablo), "come in motivated" (Emily), "pick up stuff really quickly" (Jake), and "very motivated" (Elena).

All the educators regardless of program also mentioned the importance of the parents' role in the successful education of their students. Gael, the director of district-wide dual-language programming, spoke of the need for on-going commitment and close collaborations with the families of students, and all of the educators strongly emphasized the school-home connection. For just a small subset, the lack of parent-teacher contact was a cause for concern. Without the parents to explain their situations, educators could start to make assumptions that they were too busy or even disinterested to get involved with their children's education. In some cases (occurring in both dual-language and English-language programming) the perception was that parents could not (the parents of ELL students) or were not inclined to (the parents of TWI majority-language students) support their children's language development in the home environment.

A final theme is the educators' perceptions of their own abilities to meet the needs of their students. On the whole, they talked at length about the different teaching strategies and techniques that had enabled them to teach a wide variety of language ability levels within classrooms, including how they implemented differentiated instruction and ESL techniques to meet the diverse needs of students. However, several of the educators talked of improvements to their own repertoire of practices for working with multilingual students knowing their own learning was never complete. We conclude with this comment by Paola as illustrative of these sentiments, as she reflects on her teaching and strives to keep up with the individual language-learning experiences of students in her TWI classroom:

For me there is always, 'How can I do this better? You know, "What would ... how can my students get more out of this?" So it's never, I don't feel like I ever have definite answers for anything. I know how to teach to a second language, but I always feel like there must be a better way, you know? Because not everybody understands, and not everybody gets it, and not everybody perfects it the way you want. So you as a teacher, you're always thinking there has to be something better, you know, what else can I do. So I'm always looking for that. Like what else can I do? How can I enrich this?

7 How Families and Schools Can Develop Together

This chapter draws conclusions from the study's findings and prior research, making salient the key connections between the families' and the educators' perspectives in an attempt to shift from a piecemeal approach to multilingual supports to a more systematic or collectivist outlook on multilingualism. After key findings are summarized, a student "portrait" combines the perspectives of both parents and educators. Next, we consider the advice parents and educators wished to relate to each other. The chapter also compiles a wide array of parent-reported strategies and practices used to promote multilingualism within the family context. We conclude with recommendations for families, schools, and future research in the areas of multilingual development and education.

Linking Families to Each Other and to Educators

This study of multilingualism is extremely timely given the rapid growth in the numbers of children who speak more than one language, be that from necessity (e.g., learning the majority language of wider society alongside an L1 acquired in the home and local community) or because more parents are deliberately choosing to raise children speaking languages other than the majority language of their society. Understanding multilingualism first-hand from families in their individual contexts can highlight commonalities and differences across their different situations. This is important because multilingualism is typically seen as leading to *additive* experiences and outcomes for children (i.e., becoming proficient in L2 without the loss of L1, Lambert, 1974) from higher socioeconomic backgrounds but often not for children from lower socioeconomic backgrounds. Thus, recognizing the unique potential of all children, including vulnerable and often educationally at-risk children, allows for new connections to be made across diverse social and economic backgrounds, as well as highlighting what new educational and social policies need to be explored. Importantly, it also allows educators and researchers to shift from a deficit perspective of multilingual children to a viewpoint that acknowledges and capitalizes on children's linguistic resources as crucial assets in their development and education.

221

222   How families and schools can develop together

Our research suggested some parents beginning to articulate the need for a more systematic and unified approach to raising and teaching multilingual children whose unique linguistic and socio-emotional potential requires joint home and school nurture, as well as forging ties to other parents across a variety of backgrounds. It is critical that from two of the most important spheres in children's lives (family and school settings) key individuals emerge who will recognize common goals, share successful strategies, overcome the divide in responsibilities, and bridge the two environments of home and school as resources for children's linguistic development.

Lee and Wright (2014) have recently called for initiatives that will "cultivate broad-based support" (p. 145) for heritage- and community-language learning in the United States. We extend this further to include all manner of language-learning situations, not just heritage and community languages, so that families and teachers of children who are acquiring more than one language in any circumstance can adopt a collectivist approach to the education and development of their children.

To date, Lee and Wright (2014) paint a pessimistic picture of the existence of wider support from U.S. society for children's acquisition of heritage and community languages: "Public awareness of and interest in HLs/CLs [heritage and community languages] have been minimal. As such, societal efforts from outside academia to document the existence of such programs or to explore these venues as potential resources for building language capacity in the United States have been meager ..." (p. 145). The interviews with parents and educators that were analyzed for this volume as well as the review of language education policies across the U.S. highlight the vulnerability of multilingualism as a notion within a society and as a set of skills within an individual child. On a societal level, the interest and commitment to multilingualism is undermined by the lack of open and ongoing dialogue between families, schools, and policy-makers. On the level of an individual child who enters a school system speaking a minority language, linguistic and literacy skills are vulnerable if the L1 is not supported and nourished throughout the school system on multiple levels: academic, motivational, etc. A student's languages need to be recognized, respected, and nourished. Lee and Wright (2014) go on to argue that "To cultivate broader support, public awareness of HL/CL programs must be raised by establishing a strong understanding of the local contexts of language communities and the relationship between the HL/CLs and the broader society" (p. 146).

Likewise, we recommend that a broad base of support be built to assist families and educators in their work with children, but rather than focus on raising public awareness and waiting for society at large to respond, we believe we can achieve such a broad base of support sooner by calling attention to the need to create initiatives right now that forge closer connections between multilingual families, between families and educators, and between educators themselves. Although the families we interviewed came from immensely diverse backgrounds in terms of languages spoken, languages that had minority and majority status, numbers and ages of children, schooling choices, culture, religion, immigration status, and socioeconomic situations, our findings revealed striking similarities in outlook, attitudes, and common experiences. These shared parental experiences and understandings of multilingualism can be the cornerstone of the broad-based support initiative, and include needing to forge connections with schools and their children's classroom teachers specifically, confronting issues with other family members, dealing with lack of linguistic resources, and navigating their children's puberty, which can bring with it peer influences that undermine the long-standing multilingual efforts of the family. On just some or all of these issue families can be united. Even as we enlist wider society's support, we can be highlighting and building on what families might achieve by finding ways to work together for all of their children's multilingual prospects.

First we consider the key findings from our study of families and educators and the combined portrait of the multilingual child or student that emerges. We then examine the advice they had for each other and reference the research literature throughout as it may support or refute this advice. Next we report an extensive catalogue of parent practices for supporting multilingual development documented in the interviews, and finally return to specific implications for supporting a collectivist approach to fostering multilingualism.

Key Findings

While raising and/or teaching multilingual children, parents and educators frequently encountered persistent myths about negative academic, linguistic and developmental effects of introducing children to more than one language. The most common beliefs that we came across in our study are presented in Chapter 3 and included: "learning more than one language is detrimental to children's language development," "multilingualism negatively affects academic achievement," "one-parent-one-language is the only approach that works to foster acquisition of two languages," and "children with disabilities should not be exposed to multiple languages." Like other recent reports on bi- and multilingualism, our review of the literature did not find strong empirical support for these beliefs, rather they persist as myths that may even stymy the efforts and best intentions of families and educators to support the multilingual development of children.

Our analysis of the parents' and educators' interviews also revealed expectations that they hold for each other. In Chapter 5, parent participants *parents* expressed their hopes that educators would have a lot of patience in working with multilingual children. They also exhibited trust in educators' ability to give their children all they needed for mastering English and achieving academic success. Many parents reported being ready/willing to assume sole responsibility for maintaining languages other than English in their homes, and indeed they saw multilingualism as an "investment," as we had anticipated from the existing literature. They also spoke of financial, time, and emotional investment, as well as other types of investment in the context of multilingualism, such as investment in the well-being of the family and investment in the promise of their children's eventual linguistic attainments. The educators in Chapter 6, on the other hand, spoke of their hopes for improved home-school communication, the need to understand the families' needs and values, and lack of parent involvement in the academic life of multilingual children, especially in cases where parents were not fluent in the target L2.

Parent participants listed some deliberate and some happenstance strategies that families utilize to successfully sustain the different languages in their homes. Many parents spoke of "infusing" children with their home language with trips to visit family in the United States or in the country of origin. Educators showed great admiration of their students' multilingual abilities, openness to others, and motivation for learning more broadly. They emphasized the importance of showing respect and acceptance for all cultures, as well as bringing parents who speak languages other than English into their classrooms and allowing parents to share their expertise, skills, and experiences.

The study unveiled questions, needs, and fears of parents as their multilingual children move into puberty, start to take on the views and language of their peers, and show a waning interest in maintaining their linguistic heritage. Participants shared how hard it is to support more than one language and how important it is to strike a balance, so that the parent-child and sibling relationships do not suffer even if parents insist on using two or more languages. Parents' reported needs included access to communication and friendships in languages other than English as their children grew older. For educators, the lens of "investment" could be applied to the necessity by society to provide for their adequate preparation and on-going support in the diverse instructional settings in which they teach multilingual students. There was also overlap in the needs and concerns of parents and educators. Many parents and educators spoke of much-needed community venues to share rich linguistic and cultural heritage. All participants spoke of their ongoing search for quality resources that could help sustain and develop multilingual children's unique linguistic and socio cultural potential.

Portrait of the Multilingual Child/Student

While acknowledging that there are great individual differences across children, in Chapter 5, we attempted to compose an extensive portrait that included several characteristics of multilingual children from the parents' perspectives. Here, we briefly reiterate key facets of the parents' portrait of their children to combine these with the educators' views and create a joint summary portrait. In terms of children's social development, from parents we heard that their children were very often "outgoing" individuals, which they attributed to their multilingual experiences with a wide range of different people. This is something that was echoed by the educators who mentioned their students' sociability, although they were also aware of children who could be socially isolated from others in school, but these cases were attributed to multilingual language skills taking time to emerge. This could be true of students who spoke minority and majority languages as the L1 alike, but, in the case of minority-language students, being compelled to learn English in school, and, in the case of majority-language students, electing (or their parents electing for them) to learn and be schooled in a minority language in TWI programs. At the intersection of social and cognitive development, parents also remarked on the empathy for others evident in their children. The educators articulated this as being "open" or having a terrific sense of "openness" to other people, ideas, and cultures. Alejandro eloquently articulates these sentiments for the majority of the educators thus:

I think that in many ways being multilingual is a lot like being a reader. It really opens up your world. It opens up the world. It opens up a multitude of possibilities in terms of how you see the world. How you interact with the world. How the world interacts with you. When you are multilingual and you are in a social situation that may be new or unfamiliar, and yet you run into people that are multilingual themselves, it makes for I think an easier social interaction because people recognize immediately that you are someone, maybe not speaking their particular language but the fact that you come with a particular perspective that is open and engaging and validating and valuing other peoples and other cultures and other perspectives. I think it just really enriches not only that situation, those conversations, but yourself as well.

In terms of linguistic abilities, the parents especially singled out their children's heightened "conversational" abilities for mention. Teachers reported some instances where they encountered students who were challenged by the acquisition of an L2 but again these were students who appeared to be in the early stages of development and felt most comfortable speaking with students who were speakers of their L1. Teachers, not surprisingly, gave us the clearest picture of the children's academic abilities and were almost unanimous in speaking of the perseverance of multilingual students and strong motivations of most to succeed. Teachers described how students would readily make connections across content/topics/people and appeared eager and largely engaged in school. The outcomes in academic performance were mixed though, with educators citing a bilingual advantage in helping, for example, to put some former students into the Ivy League, whereas in other cases, mostly boys who were learning English as their L2, students were singled out who were struggling with both language and school work.

Home, School, and Community Connections

The connection between the child's home and school has long been identified in the general education literature as a key factor in school success. Along with community as a third sphere of influence in students' lives, the continuity in learning activities and communication between the home and school environments is argued to have positive effects on academic outcomes (e.g., Epstein, 2001; Epstein and Sheldon, 2006). The relationships that schools foster with families are therefore paramount in their joint efforts to support the multilingual development and academic achievement of school-age children (Schechter and Cummins, 2003). However, the nature of the home-school relationship needs to be respectful of the different ways that families of multilingual children might choose to connect with and participate in the school lives of their children. Language-minority families may have been marginalized by the dominant U.S. society and have specific linguistic and cultural considerations that require schools to rethink issues of power relations between schools, community, and families, including the need to recognize (1) different ways for parents to be engaged, (2) differences in expectations for school performance, and (3) the range of values of different communities within which schools are embedded (Baquedano-López, Alexander, and Hernandez, 2013). Anything less can lead to deficit views by school personnel of the support families and communities provide students for their learning and school achievements.

Communication (or the lack thereof) between the home and the school emerged as one of the cross-cutting themes in the parent and educator interviews. This may have its roots in the reported beliefs by several parents that teaching their child a language other than English (as either the child's L1 or L2) was the sole responsibility of the family. Many parents reported a resistance to even telling their children's schools about the language(s) spoken in the home. This is likely to contribute to a disconnection with families that several of the educators in our study reported they were feeling. As we reported in Chapter 6, educators could on occasion view parents as a problem when it came to connecting with the school over their children's progress, supporting homework completion, and providing information on the (in)stability of the home environment (e.g., parental seasonal immigration patterns). We heard that connecting with parents could be "hard" and that there was a strong need to impress upon parents the necessary commitment to dual-language programming for its success.

Research by Crosnoe (2009) suggests contact between families and schools is related to student academic achievement, however, such achievement is also influenced by how much educators talk to one another. In particular, he found that students "started high school in higher-level math [classes] when parents, middle school personnel, and high school personnel were in contact with each other and when middle school personnel bridged the other two" (p. 1061). Moreover, this kind of meaningful continuity in the communication between families and different school personnel at this key transition period in student lives was related to a reduction in achievement gaps attributed to income and language differences.

In their recent review of parent and community involvement in schools, Baquedano-López et al. (2013) stress that "Recognizing the social and cultural distance between homes and schools within many low-income urban school districts, new proposals for a relational approach to parent involvement include identifying community-based organizations to serve as intermediaries between the schools and local families" (p. 167). The authors advocate "… models that push past traditional involvement paradigms to develop meaningful collaborations between educational stakeholders and to bring about a shift in the culture of schools so that they are better aligned with the families they serve" (p. 167).

For dual-language program planning specifically, Howard and Christian (2002) have found that "… it is also important to have a community of parents that is committed to the program and will work collaboratively with teachers and staff to strengthen it" (p. 15). Of keen concern with TWI programming specifically, and taking note of the concerns raised by Baquedano-López and colleagues (2013) on structural inequalities in parental involvement, these authors go on to caution:

Make certain that both the parents of the language minority students and the parents of the native English speakers participate in the TWI program in similar ways. Because TWI programs are intended to help equalize the status of the two languages and the two groups of students, it is important to pay attention to this at the level of parent involvement, as well as in the classrooms. Both groups of parents should have equal access to information and be equally involved in activities that exert the most power and influence over the program (such as participation in curriculum committees and holding PTA officer positons). This is one way to help equalize the status of the two languages and the two groups of students, and of ensuring that the academic needs of all students are being met. (p. 15)

Echoing Crosnoe's study findings, communication between teachers is highlighted by Howard and Christian (2002):

As many respondents indicated, strong teachers and other staff form the cornerstone of a strong TWI program…. Suggestions were made that project staff should meet at least once a month for staff development and coordination, and that teachers should meet on a regular basis to plan lessons and work cooperatively. Such frequent communication and collaboration is likely to result in a TWI program that is more cohesive, and where the needs of students are being served both within a given grade level and across grade levels. (p. 15)

In the next sections, we augment these findings and recommendations found in the current literature with the advice parents gave to educators and that educators offered to parents during the course of their interviews. These comments offer a rare opportunity to assemble the broad range of concerns and issues of the two spheres of influence on students' lives in a systematic way. As part of the interview protocols we had deliberately requested that the participants share advice with other parents or educators of multilingual students that was informed by but could be extended beyond the specific circumstances of their own home-school relations.

Parents' Advice to Educators

The parents' advice to educators ranged from the very specific instructional approaches they wanted teachers to practice in their classrooms, practical requests that teachers provide more information about the L1 acquisition process for example, to more prosaic advice about adopting a certain orientation and mindset when working with multilingual children. We highlight some of the advice here to show this wide range of input. Appendix F provides a full list of comments along with information on the parents who offered the advice and example excerpts from the interviews to provide greater context.

In terms of the specific practices they suggested educators might adopt, parents included use of the L2 to make connections to academic language, the use of songs and rhymes, learning some words in the children's languages, creating structure and consistency in their adoption of a language program model, and having books of authentic children's literature and other high-quality support materials in all relevant languages so children and parents can read together in the parents' L1 as well. Along with more information about L1 acquisition processes, amongst the practical advice, parents told educators to communicate with them and get families involved. They counseled patience and treating their children the same as they would treat other students in their classes. They advised letting children use both (all) their languages in school to express themselves fully and meaningfully. This last piece of advice is consistent with the recommendations of Bailey and Orellana (2015) to leverage children's out-of-school language practices such as language brokering and codeswitching for learning within the classroom. This is a transformative practice for the home-school-community connection that has drawn on the 'funds of knowledge' of families (e.g., Moll et al., 1992, cited in Baquedano-López et al., 2013). Specifically, the family's social and intellectual knowledge should also be "recognized as viable resources to be leveraged in the classroom" (Baquedano-López et al., 2013, p. 167).

More abstractly, parents wanted educators to "embrace language differences," "see the bigger picture and the long term process," "point out to children they are rich with two cultures, two languages," and "talk about other cultures, emphasize their value." We interpreted these comments in effect as parents advising educators to play a more engaged role on their children's behalf as advocates for and visionaries of what multilingual education can achieve for their children. As Ortega (2013a) has noted, there is a benefit to increasing a teacher's capacity for advocacy "particularly in cases when teachers can support students and parents in asserting their rights to language education" (p. 7). Such a teacher advocacy role will be critical to the creation of a grass-roots community to support multilingualism.

Educators' Advice to Parents

Educators in all program types mentioned encountering challenges with school-home interactions. Much like the parent forms of advice, we can place the educators' comments on a continuum from concrete actions educators thought parents might take to foster their children's multilingual education to the more abstract suggestions educators had for parents. Appendix G provides the advice the educators offered arranged by program type along with information on the educators and example excerpts to provide context for the given advice.

Educators suggested parents could support their children by establishing a daily routine to check their child's performance (through online grading tools for example), to talk to their children about any struggles and successes, and to even make the effort to learn the target L2 their children are learning. This last piece of advice is consistent with Howard and Christian's (2002) survey of TWI programs that found many programs provided ESL classes for the minority-language parents and classes in the program partner language (i.e., minority language) for the majority-language (i.e., English-speaking) parents. For minority-language parents with children in other types of dual-language programs and in English-language programming, family literacy programs have also provided a way to learn the L2 and are believed to also support the L2 acquisition and academic outcomes of minority-language students. Two-generation programs involve families in ways to support their children's literacy development at home that are aligned with school approaches (e.g., parent education on how to read to children and strategies to support their independent reading) as well as involving parents in ESL and adult education classes of their own. However, family literacy programs need to be culturally relevant to families and be empowering experiences, or they run the danger of imposing deficit views of the literacy practices of families from non-dominant segments of society (Baquedano-López et al., 2013). Educators in the present study actually saw the value in parents' learning the target L2 (whether the L2 was the majority or a minority language in society) as a signal to children of how important it was to know the language.

A common theme in the advice educators addressed to parents included the general appeal for parents to communicate with them regularly. One educator spoke in frustration of only hearing at infrequent parent-teacher conferences that communication on homework had broken down. Educators needed parents to realize they (the educators) cannot handle everything. Rather, educators needed parents to be committed to the language program and to have high aspirations for their children to work for. However, at least one educator advised parents to be realistic about their expectations for L2 language development, especially that these be commensurate with the amount of effort they put into supporting and exposing children to L2 input outside the school setting. The difference in these two views may be explained by program type; the former piece of advice was in the context of dual-language programming that as a developmental bilingual education program serviced ELL students who needed to meet mandated annual progress and proficiency in English language as their L2. In the latter case, the educator taught in a TWI program and the advice was addressed to majority-language parents who needed to temper their expectations for the speed of L2 development given the school was often the only source of L2 input. At the more abstract level, parents were advised to be dedicated to the preservation of the children's L1 and to be reassured that schools would be in a position to affirm their children's backgrounds.

Parent Strategies and Practices for Fostering Multilingualism

In regard to the ways in which they sustain, foster, and nourish multilingualism within the context of their households, parent participants shared numerous strategies and practices. In our discussion of multilingual family experiences, we differentiate the concepts of strategies and practices. Strategies are defined as methods purposefully used within the family with a particular goal in mind, for example, multilingual abilities in their children. Family multilingual practices are more in line with family traditions and customs. It is an engagement with language that is less goal-oriented, yet nevertheless supports multilingualism. First we discuss parent strategies before turning to multilingual family practices and traditions.

Parent Strategies for Achieving Multilingualism

In total, the parents offered nearly fifty different strategies that they used to promote their children's multilingual development. Table 7.1 is a summary of these strategies. In this section we offer a detailed overview of these approaches. They are grouped into five categories: Language "infusion" and/ or "immersion," Literacy strategies and educational activities, Approaches to language teaching, Use of technology, and "Fun" activities.

Language "infusion" and/or "immersion." Several parents believed in full immersion within their households or during vacation/family trips to target language countries. Linda, whose young daughters Elia and Bella grew up speaking primarily Spanish and were about to return to a dual-language program, talked about boosts of full Spanish immersion: "We are planning a trip to El Salvador for August, … so we want to get her kind of infused with Spanish before going back to school."

In talking about the importance of full immersion, these parents used vivid metaphors of "submerging" and "infusing" their children with languages other than English. Mothers who decided to raise multilingual children reported listening to L2 music and talking in L2 to their future babies during their pregnancy. Dulce, the mother of four-year old José, recalled playing songs in both languages while she was pregnant: "Since I was pregnant I would have him listen to music in Spanish and English, so that he would start listening not only to Spanish but also to English …" When the infants arrived, many parents reported starting their multilingual upbringing by giving them bilingual names. Bianca, who lives in the United States but whose parents live in Mexico, remembered, "The reason I named them William is because it is Guillermo, and Tim is Timoteo [in Spanish]. I wanted to have bilingual names that are easy to pronounce in both languages." The majority of parents in the sample believed in immersion and did everything they could to create immersion conditions for their children. Research on second language acquisition indicates that immersion (which often refers to domestic immersion programs) is a powerful tool for language learning, especially if it combines some formal language instruction with a variety of interactive activities in L2 (Freed, Segalowitz, and Dewey, 2004). Freed and colleagues showed that learning a language in an intensive summer immersion context leads to significant gains in oral language performance, including the total number of spoken words, turn length, rate of speech, and in speech fluidity. Students in full immersion condition outperformed their peers who learned L2 in regular classroom settings or in a study-abroad program. In this context, it is also important to note our discussion in earlier chapters that it is the quality of language interactions, and not necessarily their length or setting, that are critical for successful acquisition of more than one language (Grosjean, 2009).

Table 7.1 *Types and examples of strategies used by participants to foster multilingualism*

Type of strategy	Examples of specific strategies
Language "infusion" and/or "immersion"	Speaking only L2 within the household: Spanish channel
	Speaking L2 to young children and babies
	Giving children bilingual names
	Having a lot of L2 conversations
	Surrounding children with L2 speakers: visits of L2 speaking relatives (special role of grandparents), hiring L2 caregivers
	Trips to L2 country
	Using environment for L2 learning
	L2+ culture or just L2
Literacy strategies and educational activities	Books: looking at books together and labeling pictures
	Reading books together
	Choosing books that promote conversations
	Going to the library
	Bedside stories
	Educational games
	Nursery rhymes
	Phonemic awareness in 2 or more languages
	Sign language
	Pen pals in L2
	Journaling in L2
	Taking Latin
Approaches to language teaching: persistence, balance, support, role models	"Pushing"
	Practice-practice-practice
	Consistence and methodicalness
	"Use it or lose it"
	Do not give up
	Have time and will
	Keep L2 to keep the authority
	Translation, cues, correction
	"Focus on the message"
	Balance
	Making a list of words for others
	Role models: L2 speakers and bilinguals
Use of technology	Skype
	CDs
	DVDs
	TV vs. no TV
	Radio stations
	Films
"Fun" activities	Music: songs, concerts,
	Doing authentic cultural things
	Play dates/play groups
	L2 games
	Diverse toys
	L2 culture toys
	Exchanging skills

Note: For brevity in this table, we use L2 to refer to any target language (i.e., home, heritage, additional) that parents aimed to foster.

Many parents emphasized focusing on total immersion for young children. The parents believed that it was crucial to "infuse" the children with the target language before they enrolled in the school system, as they recognized that the influences of English-dominant school and English-dominant peers would be hard to control. Therefore, a lot of family efforts were concentrated on using as much home language or L2 as possible during the early childhood period. Even while the children were not actively using a language, the parents made sure that they heard the language at all times. Veronica, who is raising 2½-year-old Andrew to speak German and English, commented that he is included in all family conversations: "Andrew is never excluded when we eat dinner. He eats at the table with us and so he is always present in conversation." The parents emphasized the importance of creating a rich language environment and stressed that they were constantly engaging their children in conversations. Research shows that encouraging not merely children's exposure but their participation in conversations promotes their vocabulary development and conversational abilities (Hoff, 2006). Additionally, research shows that multilingual identity is shaped in the multilingual family context (Quay, 2008).

Once the children began to acquire language, their parents tried to make languages other than English more concrete and explicit. They use the one-person-one-language-approach, domain-specific use of languages, and some other strategies they invented. Linda provided us with a description of her family practice to support her daughters' Spanish:

Spanish is something that we will definitely have to support and push ... We do a lot of "Really you have to answer us in Spanish," "We are on the Spanish channel!" And we do a little gesture and a click. And a lot of reminding because Elia just knows that we both speak English and understand it and it comes quicker so it is just easier ... She is a four-year-old that has important things to say ...

Here Linda reports the "Spanish channel" strategy that is parent-invented. Other parents established rules of speaking only the target language in their household. Tricia, a mother of young pre-kindergarten children, whose story we showcased in the introduction of Chapter 5, reported that the rule of no English in the house is fairly common: "I have a friend who said that they had rules in their house where they were not allowed to speak English in their house. I followed that rule ... we only speak Portuguese."

Another group of strategies is aimed at surrounding children with multiple target language speakers. The parents talked about visiting and hosting heritage-language speaking relatives, including grandparents, aunts and uncles, and cousins. A particularly significant role was given to the grandparents in this context. In families where parents were maintaining or reviving a heritage language, grandparents were the primary carriers of that language and often the only ones who spoke it. Taani, 2½-year-old Mihir's mother and a graduate student, reports mixing languages when talking to Mihir. However, Taani's parents "speak only Hindi to him and that other language I mentioned … 90% [of the time] they speak to him in our native languages." Many parents who had full-time jobs hoped the grandparents who cared for their children would teach the family's heritage language to them. Kelly, a prospective mother, shared her plans about teaching her soon-expected daughter Cantonese: "[My husband's] parents are going to be our caretakers for her, while both of us are at work. His parents pretty much speak only Cantonese, so she will be completely submerged." Several families had grandparents who lived in another country. Visiting them and speaking the language was another common strategy. Research supports the importance of the role that grandparents play in heritage language acquisition. Grandparents' presence is critical for creating proper environments for heritage language development and initiation into the heritage culture: within the tri-generational families, interacting with grandparents necessitates the use of honorifics and provides linguistic and social contexts that are different from the interaction with parents (Kondo-Brown, 2006). Ishizawa's research findings (2004) indicated that the presence of grandmothers had a stronger effect on children's heritage language use than the presence of grandfathers.

Apart from strategically using the heritage-language speaking relatives, the parents talked about hiring heritage-language or L2 speaking caregivers who could continue to provide bilingual or multilingual immersion. As the children grew older and were ready to travel, many families talked about taking trips to home language or L2 speaking countries, both to visit relatives and further the experience of total immersion. Parents also spoke about using the home and community environment to teach the home language or L2 to their children. Miko, a Spanish-English bilingual prospective father, discussed tapping into the many Latino cultural resources of Los Angeles.

Other parents talked about having books, dishes, toys, decorations, and other L2 culture specific household items. Nicole, a native German raising her two young sons in the United States, mentioned a few German toys her children have:

My friend is German and she actually is the Godmother of my [older son]. She brought a couple of things from Germany like a SpongeBob plush toy that speaks German when you pinch its nose or arm … around Christmas they have the advent calendar that counts down until Christmas. When I first moved here they didn't have that here. The first year when my first child was born I had somebody send one to me. I think my Mom brought it and I started that tradition here.

Some parents also mentioned "infusing" the environment with home language or L2 music. Mayda, who is raising her children trilingual in Armenian, Arabic, and English, talked about the importance of music in her daughter Vana's upbringing:

Table 7.2 *Continuum of integration of cultural practices along with home language or L2 teaching*

"Only teaching the language"	"Teaching the language and selectively using some cultural practices"	"Total immersion in language and culture"
"It is a different culture and they have different ways of parenting and I just ... yeah I don't want that." (Tricia)	"I don't want to pressure them to choose one language or culture or the other. I think they can make the conscious call on that." (Nora)	"And so it would be very important to me to foster that love of the language and what it means is not only being able to read, write and speak in Spanish, that would mean that their culture is also engraved in them too, and the appreciation of the language too." (Lilian)

With language you just don't acquire the language, the alphabet or words, you understand culture as well. Music, appreciation for music. My daughter, she loves listening to Arabic music. When she was like two or three, I would listen to Arabic music. It touches me and now it touches her.

Interestingly, when talking about total immersion, parent participants differed in their intentions about "infusing" their family life with the home language or L2 culture. They were divided on a continuum of only teaching the language, teaching the language and selectively using some cultural practices, to total immersion in the language and culture as it is reconstructed within the family and the minority-language community, if possible. Table 7.2 provides participant statements to highlight different areas of the continuum.

We suggest that multiple factors are at play when it comes to the wide range of opinions that parents have regarding the inclusion of culture. The parents who decided to focus only on language were very diverse. This included parents who were teaching their children multiple languages. Tina, for example, who is fostering six different languages in her young son Bryan, did not feel that she could easily adhere to one particular culture. The situation is complicated because her husband's family is Portuguese and her family is Swedish. The difference in parents' cultures was mentioned by at least one-fifth of our participants as a factor contributing to their decision not to follow cultural practices or to teach select aspects of both parents' cultures. Monica, whose family is from central Mexico, reported being a bit shocked by the cultural differences in talking to children typical for northern Mexico, where her husband was from:

Their way of being endearing to children is to use some foul language and for me it was a bit of culture shock with how they talk. They are not mad when they say things. They don't use foul language when they are upset, they use it when they are being loving. It is very weird. It's interesting.

Another factor that affected parents' use of cultural practices was the availability and ease of access to cultural resources and artifacts: festivals, restaurants, concerts, books, and toys. Often, participants whose families decided to embrace both the language and culture either grew up within the culture or were living in areas where the family had access to the target language community.

Literacy strategies and educational activities. The next category introduces the literacy strategies that parents used as a method to foster multilingualism. One of the most common strategies that parents of very young children used was sign language. This was seen as both a strategy that promotes multilingualism and a way to promote early communication. Some parents named sign language as one of several languages their children were learning. Tina, a mother of 19-month-old Lilia, told us that she started teaching her daughter sign language from "early on. Sign language is actually considered a language for [infants] as well." Others saw it as a way to support infants whose language development may have been delayed due to their simultaneous acquisition of languages. The belief in benefits of teaching children symbolic signs is supported by research. In a study by Goodwyn, Acredolo, and Brown (2000) that examined the implications of teaching symbolic signs to hearing, typically developing children, the treatment group of infants in the "sign training group" outperformed the control group that was exposed only to verbal training in the majority of language acquisition tests. The authors concluded that symbolic gesturing aids verbal language development.

Parent participants in our study recalled many literacy activities using books written in the home language or L2 that were suitable for children of all ages. For example, parents of younger children talked about early literacy activities that included looking at books together and labeling pictures, reading and reciting nursery rhymes, and telling bedtime stories in the home language or L2. A few parents talked about playing bilingual phonological (rhyming, segmenting and blending words) and phonemic awareness (naming words that start with the same letter) games with their children. Research of phonological awareness in bilingual preschool children provides evidence that phonological awareness in one language is highly correlated with phonological awareness in the child's other language(s) (Dickinson, McCabe, Clark–Chiarelli, and Wolf, 2004), thus empirically supporting the benefits of such strategies.

As their children grew older, several parents reported taking them to the library to pick out books in the home language or L2. They talked about reading books together and the importance of selecting books that promote conversations. Monica, whose teenage sons are bilingual in Spanish and English, named reading to them as the number one strategy even at times when the other practices were less consistent:

I read to them in Spanish and I also read to them as many books that were bilingual. That was one of the things I did do. I had books in Spanish at home and I had them accessible. And there were books at different levels, so they were fairly easy to pick up and so that was part of the regular book shelf but it wasn't something they necessarily self-selected except for the bilingual books. The bilingual books they did go for. I remember "Nacho, Tito y Miguel" [book title], the story of the three pigs. They liked those kinds of stories that would have some words in Spanish ... there is this story called "Arturo y Clementina" [book title]. It is two turtles ... and the male turtle is giving Clementina a lot of things to carry, and she is carrying it all on her shell and so finally in the end she is like "I am done with this!" So I was thinking, "God, that would be a great book to read to [my sons] in Spanish!" ... whatever the reading is that it's something that can provoke conversation with them on some points. You know, what a great opportunity to talk about these things.

Parents talked about playing other educational games, including word-finding games, charades, and pretend play with cultural references. Eighteen out of 26 participants, nearly 70% of the sample, wanted their children to grow up not only multilingual but also multiliterate. Many hoped their children would grow up with the ability to read and write in their languages. Miko, a prospective parent bilingual in Spanish and English, stressed literacy skills by naming these even before the speaking skills (that go without saying): "I would definitely want to see our child to read, write and speak Spanish very well."

Home language or L2 writing activities that were mentioned by parents included corresponding with family members, writing birthday cards, corresponding with pen pals, and journaling. About one-third of the parents thought heritage language or L2 literacy was important and planned to send their children to heritage weekend schools, full immersion bilingual schools, or to study abroad as an exchange student or to attend college. Three of the families had a unique strategy for maintaining home languages even if their teenage children had temporarily refused to study or speak the home language. These families encouraged their children to take Latin at school. The parents felt that this way, while their children were not studying Spanish or French, they were still acquiring a strong base in vocabulary with Latin roots and developing an understanding of concepts such as noun gender, declension, and conjugation. Research on the subject supports these parents' beliefs. Sparks, Ganschow, Fluharty, and Little (1995) suggested that studying Latin had positive effects on both native language vocabulary and on foreign language aptitude, especially on semantics (i.e., word meaning).

Approaches to language teaching. Parent philosophies toward language teaching are summarized in four concepts: persistence, supports, maintaining a balance, and role-modeling. Aware of the influence of the dominant language from English-speaking peers, school, and the children's desire to fit in, all the parents emphasized the importance of persistence, consistency, and methodicalness. Linda, whose two young daughters started speaking Spanish while in El Salvador, recalls having to become a lot more systematic in order to preserve Spanish when the family moved to America,

Yeah, since coming here we have been much more consistent and adamant about buying books in Spanish and tried to be strategic about everything. Like at bed time Elia usually picks books from the bookshelf ... So we don't want to say "You can't choose English books" because we also want her to feel like reading is fun. Sometimes we will say, "Mom's going to read an English book. That is okay, but Dad's going to read a Spanish book."

The metaphor of "pushing" for home language or L2 use was present in several interviews. Ultan recalled the childhood years of his son Georges who grew up speaking French and English, but also studied Spanish: "He has a Spanish Godmother with whom he's stayed on occasion. And although she's multilingual, she always wanted him to speak Spanish, and pushed it." Acknowledging the *push back* from a society with a different dominant language, the parents encourage families embarking on the journey of raising multilingual children not to give up. Parents talked about practicing the home language or L2 constantly with their children. Tina, a mother of multilingual 19-month-old Lilia, advised, "If you don't use it you lose it. So that's the advice I would give other parents: do it and keep it up. And when your child tries to speak to you in English, push back. Because they'll speak English just fine." As mentioned at the start of the book, "use it or lose it" was a motto several participants mentioned. They advised other parents to plan on dedicating will and time to language learning. Several parents who gave up pushing and persisting regretted switching to English because going back to another language was very hard. This was particularly true for parents for whom English was not their L1. Giving up their household language and watching their children quickly master English at school and through peer interaction, these parents sometimes felt their English skills were inadequate. Thinking back to when she and her husband switched to English, Hediyeh commented,

Well at home we still speak Farsi [with each other]. But with kids, you know the more English became the first language, they kind of mandated us to speak English to them.... Because they actually, they speak the language better than you, you know, very quickly. And then like whenever you're mad at them, they kind of try to pick at your English.

Discussion of supports ranged from a very strict adherence to speaking only the chosen language to a more flexible practice that considers the children's wishes and choices of language and identity. Compare Nora presenting the position of one of her relatives who "often corrects [the children], 'That's not how you say it!'" to her own views on this matter: "I made the conscious call for my kids that our Spanish is just going to be at home. Spanish is going to be their second language. But on the other hand it is up to them to really develop [their] own language now that they are older. [They] know the basics, so now it is up to them." The proponents of a strict adherence to L2 use in the home, similar to Nora's relative quoted above, reported using immediate translation, feedback, and supporting cues as strategies for language learning. Linda shared with us her strategies:

With Bella particularly I'll translate what she produces in English into Spanish. With Elia, I'll help her a lot. I'll give her stems and I ask Ubaldo too more because he will, I think, while he is insistent about asking her to speak Spanish when she is starting to stumble and not thinking of a word in Spanish he will kind of just let her stumble ... One of the things that makes Spanish hard for her is she can't think of it as quickly, I am more like let's give her some of those stems and then she will just keep going in Spanish.

Opposite to the recommendations of immediate correction, some parents (like Linda's husband, Ubaldo) tended to focus on the message conveyed in the target language and less on their grammatical correctness. Ghodrat, the father of Zara and Malik who are bilingual in English and Farsi, told us he was always focusing on the meaning of what his children were saying, and their messages were usually "delivered nicely and beautifully, you know. But you know the point is just uh, deep down there are some roots and then if there is [a need] to speak it, it comes out and both Zara and Malik, they can speak Farsi ... Correcting will only stifle the message." Similar to Ghodrat, this group of parents felt that correcting their children frequently would discourage them from speaking the target language. They preferred recasting and restating the messages, instead of explicitly making children conscious of their errors. So which group of parents is adhering closer to the research-recommended methods: the parents who focus on the message or the parents who provide immediate correction? In this case research provides an interesting finding: language learners' perceptions of feedback differ depending on the language domain that is being corrected. For example, a study by Mackey, Gass, and McDonough (2000) found that lexical feedback and phonological feedback are usually recognized as corrective feedback and taken into consideration, whereas morphosyntactic feedback is frequently not recognized by learners accurately as feedback that focuses on grammar. Therefore, the authors suggest that while it may be beneficial to supply the children with new vocabulary and explain word meanings, it may not be as productive to explain grammatical rules to them, as this may lead to cognitive overload. Overall, recasts are recommended as a form of interactional feedback.

The group of parents who tended to have more moderate views on instilling home language or L2 in their children talked about the importance of maintaining a balance and being sensitive to the children's right to self-define, enjoy reading, and communicate with their friends and peers in the language of their choice. Linda provided an example of trying to find linguistic balance for her daughters:

Just this weekend Elia really wanted to watch [TV] in English, and there were tears involved, so we were like, "Okay we can watch it in English, but we will say next time it is going to be in Spanish." So there are definitely hard moments where you are thinking, "Okay what is the right balance between really pushing the Spanish on her and not the overkill that she then doesn't like it." And with reading we don't want her to reject reading just because it [is in Spanish] … if she wants an English book that is fine. I mean I'll say, "Why don't you pick a Spanish book today?" … I just noticed last week all of her friends got really traditional fairytale books. So that was more important getting the Beauty and the Beast type book rather than a Spanish book.

These parents maintain open attitudes and hope that their children will turn back to the heritage language or the L2 when they feel the need and importance of it. Another method of maintaining children's interest in speaking and learning in more than one language is participating in culturally relevant practices that we will discuss further.

A prominent theme in parent interviews in the discussion of their approaches to teaching language is bringing in multiple heritage language or L2 speaking role models into the children's life. This approach included pointing out speakers of the same language and speakers of any language other than English in an effort to promote an understanding of linguistic diversity. Several parents considered bringing in multilingual role models for their children to observe and learn from to navigate the community using more than one language. Betty pointed out that the quality of bilingual role models is very important, "[It is critical] to get language models that are good. Like [one of the children's caregiver's] language was not elevated, and to start with it is fine wherever it is, but eventually if you keep on you want kids to have educated language." Overall, parents recognize that the participation in multilingual practices by relatives, friends, caregivers, and educators is crucial for maintaining children's multilingual abilities. Parents would ask people in their close circles to use a particular language when talking to their children. Parents of young children who had mastered a few words in more than one language also created lists for people who came in contact with these children to help them feel understood. Taani recalled using this strategy when her little son Mihir went to daycare:

I would really like him to sustain some of that Hindi that he knows, so I have to tell his childcare providers, these are the words that he only speaks in Hindi. Because what happens is that if he wants milk or if he wants water, he will only ask for that always in Hindi, he will never ask for it in English. Or if he is saying, "I am tired, I want to go to sleep now" or "nap time." If you say "nap time" for him in English, he does not necessarily understand that, but if you tell him "nap time" in Hindi, he will completely understand, so I had to kind of prepare everybody for that. I had to make the list; these are the words that he says only in Hindi so that when he says it they can understand what he wants.

Use of technology. Parents reported using technology as means of promoting multilingualism and creating a multilingual environment in their homes. They saw technology as a way of keeping themselves and their children current with the language of their culture, which included following the news, watching films and cartoons, and following the latest music trends. The participants talked about using Skype to call distant heritage-language speaking relatives and friends (Tricia: "We got Skype right after [my daughter] was born so they are always talking to the family. They are always hearing Portuguese."). Ortega (2013a) reports that such high technology is transforming formal foreign-language instructional approaches through distance learning programs bringing "the possibility of multilingualism to students who can form language-learning communities dispensing with the need to be gathered in the same physical classroom" (p. 7). Similarly, we would argue along with Compton-Lilly et al. (2014) that high technology is transforming the informal spaces in homes and in communities to support multilingualism in hitherto unexplored and unexpected ways.

The purchase of CDs and DVDs with games, educational language programs (Plaza Sesamo), and films (Nicole: "They [watched German] cartoons, and we actually had a Dora the Explorer version in German, and there was some other German cartoons and movies.") were all additional forms of technology that families utilized to support their children's language development. The families also reported playing L1 and L2 radio stations at home and in the car (Tina: "In the car when I listen to music, I buy foreign language music. So I have Chinese CDs in the car. And so I listen to the Chinese CDs in the car because I sing to [my daughter].").

Parents' opinions varied vastly when they discussed the use of television in the process of fostering multilingualism. Many parents saw the merits of TV in creating an atmosphere of a multilingual home. For many multilingual families, watching TV in a target language was a family practice. Tricia told us that she knows "a lot of families [who] only watched Univision, the Spanish channel, and the ones who kept the Spanish TV on it was kind of like part of the culture of their home." Other parent participants displayed adamant opposition to the use of TV. They saw TV as a source of the dominant language and culture. Veronica, a mother of trilingual Andrew, explained her reasons for not having TV: "I think that people often use TV as a babysitter and then it is hard to have multilingualism because the TV is very dominant." While research does not recognize TV as a universal evil, as it was perceived by many participants, it does not support the educational value or feasibility of learning a language through TV input. Grosjean (2009) discussed the importance of the nature of language input for language learning. In this discussion the author stressed the necessity of human input and posited that children learn language through the need to communicate, which is void in child-TV interaction.

Fun activities. The final category of strategies used by parents included a wide range of "fun activities." Parents talked about listening to music with their children and singing songs together in the target languages. When the children got older, the parents bought them CDs of their choice and went with them to the concerts of popular music stars and bands. Monica, the mother of two teen-age sons bilingual in Spanish and English, told us about her family strategies of enhancing the boys' motivation to study Spanish:

My dad he sings songs in Spanish. And Rodrigo does because he loves to sing. So my dad when we travel to Mexico together one of the things he did was to buy DVDs of Pedrito because he wanted him to sing "La Canción de la Mochila de Azul" and he teaches him songs of my father's time. So my father explains to him what the song means and then Rodrigo learns the song. Maná [Mexican rock group] is another one. Rodrigo really likes Maná and so does [his brother], and so we went to a Maná concert together."

Besides apparent motivational appeal of attending concerts of favorite heritage language or L2 performing groups, research recognizes the beneficial effects of incorporating music into language instruction. An experimental study by Lowe (1995) enhanced foreign language learning classes with music instruction while emphasizing similarities with pronunciation, oral grammar, vocabulary, and reading comprehension. Instruction resulted in better oral grammar outcomes and stronger reading comprehension.

Additionally, parents invested in creating home language or L2 friendships for their children by taking them on play dates and enrolling them in target language playgroups. Parents formed their own parent communities online and in real life to preserve a robust communication in a home language or L2. Several participants in our study belonged to the informal group "German Speaking Moms and Dads of the Valley." According to their website, their mission is "… to raise their kids speaking both languages, English and German. Teaching our children two languages by surrounding them with both is an easy and fun way to do so. Let's get together and stay connected with parents facing the same challenges in a country thousands of miles away from home" (http://www.meetup.com/German-speaking-Parents-of-the-Valley/).

Parents frequently cited the membership in a community of L1 or L2 speakers as a source of support and as a fun strategy. They reported doing authentic cultural activities together with other home language or L2 speaking families. Another type of fun strategy centered on home language or L2 culture toys and games. Parents observed that these activities promote the use of the home language or the L2. Some of the toys and games did not have an English equivalent and it was also easier to convince children to use a home language or the L2 while playing with authentic toys. One family had a different fun activity for older children. When they got to high school, Bianca's English-Spanish sons became interested in learning more Spanish. While they took Chinese and French, they started to ask their mother to teach them Spanish. In response, Bianca invented a game that was called an "exchange of skills." She told her children that she would gladly teach them Spanish in return for them teaching her computer skills. She turned learning into a fun and useful activity for herself and for her sons, giving the boys the opportunity to show their skills in another area and feel good about themselves. In Bianca's story we witness an extension of dynamic learning principles at work in which the roles of the "expert other" and novice can be reversed, with the children scaffolding their mothers' learning as well as she theirs (Eksner and Orellana, 2012). The exchange of skills is not limited to just language learning.

Multilingual Family Practices and Traditions

In addition to the use of strategies that parents reported using on a daily or weekly basis, they also spoke of family practices and traditions. These included family celebrations, household language and literacy practices, religious traditions, and cultural festivals. For example, family celebrations included special ways of celebrating children's birthdays and birthdays within the family. Parents spoke about singing home language or L2 birthday songs, such as 'Mnogia Leta' (Многия Лета, Russian), 'Joyeux Anniversaire' (French), and 'Las Mañanitas' (Spanish). For example, Monica shared that "Spanish isn't lost. It is valued. It is intrinsic to the family relationships and to who we are and so is singing Las Mañanitas. It is a birthday, so you sing Las Mañanitas. Those traditions are a part of [my sons'] life." Monica also spoke of her family's tradition of writing birthday cards in Spanish:

My parents write messages to the kids in Spanish. And [son's cousin] said some very nice words to my parents to Spanish. So there are influences still ... It is more in the context of the family: the love that the grandkids are able to express to their grandparents in Spanish is getting some wonderful lessons with that.

Other participants spoke about visiting special places that required the heritage language around family holidays (recall Lilian and Miko's family practice to visit the Hollywood Forever Cemetery on El Dia de Los Muertos that we discussed earlier).

Household practices included domain-specific use of the home language or L2. This involved reading and writing in particular situations only in the home language or L2. For example, many mothers used their heritage language when cooking, shopping, and to preserve family recipes. As their children became familiar with these household tasks, they began to use the heritage language within the same activities. Some families read the Bible in languages other than English, and parents reported that at times younger members of the family were asked to read the Bible and other books, newspapers, and magazines to their elderly relatives. When asked about whether her daughters read in Spanish, Nora, the mother of three Spanish-English bilingual daughters, told us, "My mom has mostly magazines, and even with the Bible she tends to do it in Spanish. So Alejandra reads some stuff in the Bible in Spanish [for her]." Some parents reported the family practice of talking on the phone or writing each other notes in their home language. Nora continued, "Alejandra … writes to her relatives in Spanish. I think she likes to write notes, she tends to do it a lot with my mom and dad. So with my mom she does it in Spanish. Birthday cards and stuff I tell them to do it in Spanish." The parents reported that they found this to be a very private and endearing manner of communication.

Observing religious holidays and participating in cultural celebrations is another category of family practices. Parents reported going to church and listening to services in their home language, as well as enrolling children in Sunday schools to study catechism and language. They follow Lenten traditions, observing religious holidays while speaking the heritage language and participating in religious rituals, such as Las Posadas (a Mexican Christmas tradition celebrating Mary and Joseph's journey to Bethlehem), naming ceremonies, and keeping Mezuzahs in the children's rooms (a Jewish tradition of affixing Hebrew verses to the doorframe of rooms and houses).

More secular practices involved celebrating holidays associated with the culture of the heritage language or the target L2, such as the independence or national days of the heritage language or L2 countries (e.g., commemorating the Day of Bastille in French), country-specific Mother's Days (on different dates from the U.S. Mother's Day), as well as adding home language or L2 cultural nuances to the celebration of holidays observed in the United States. Nicole, a German mother of two young bilingual sons, for example, explained that in her family, following the German traditions, the children get their Christmas presents on December 24, and that for Easter, they decorate an Easter tree with Easter eggs. Traditions and cultural practices promote social construction of identity, which is recognized as a critical part of heritage-language learning (Leeman, Rabin, and Román-Mendoza, 2011). Strong sense of identity is a developmental asset which in turn promotes investment in language learning (Norton, 2010) and successful socialization (Leffert et al., 1998). Therefore, "fun" strategies described in this section that focus on culture also contribute to successful language acquisition.

We also examined the educators' strategies and practices for fostering multilingualism and presented a summary of these in Chapter 6 with an emphasis on students who are acquiring the majority language as their L2 and whose successful multilingualism is particularly vital for their future academic achievement. Rather than repeat that discussion here, in the next section we focus on the implications of key findings for making recommendations for future work with families and schools and for the field of education research.

Recommendations and Resources for Families and Schools

In this concluding section, we discuss several connections across family and educator perspectives that have implications for more coordinated efforts to sustain children's linguistic resources in the future, and we highlight future research needs in these areas. These recommendations go beyond calling for closer home-school connections – such ties go without saying given the extensive prior research on parent involvement and student academic outcomes. Rather, we use the findings of the current research as the catalyst to enumerate specific and, wherever possible, culturally relevant direction for future practice and research efforts.

1.   A Continuum of Language Skills and Learning Context for Students Requires a Continuum of Practices and Program Offerings on the Part of Educators and School Systems

The interviews with parents and educators in this study described a continuum of multilingual children's language skills across ages, settings, and activities – from knowing some words in a language spoken at home or in the local community for instance, to being multilingual and multiliterate, functioning proficiently in more than one language in a variety of contexts. Such a continuum of language and literacy skills requires not only a deep awareness of a student's present levels of performance and potential on behalf of the teacher, it also necessitates a continuum of age-appropriate instructional strategies and practices that take into consideration the whole child with his/ her academic, linguistic, socio-emotional, and cognitive needs. The increased availability of one type of educational offering that parents especially called for was second and foreign language programming in elementary schools.

Furthermore, the research suggests educators need to be attuned to and able to monitor students' evolving proficiency in multiple language domains (i.e., listening, speaking, reading, and writing) (Bailey and Heritage, 2014). However, educators will also need to be aware that not all domains will be relevant to a student's multilingual circumstances; literate uses of a student's heritage language, for instance, may not be aspired to nor readily supported by families. Expectations by educators and educational systems will need to be adjusted to the local conditions of families and communities accordingly.

2.   *A Fair and Accurate Accounting of Student Linguistic Resources*
        Requires an Overhaul of the Initial Identification Practices by Schools

Recent efforts to revise the Home Language Surveys (HLS) that are used by most U.S. states to identify students who may need specialized services in English for accessing the academic curriculum have come as a result of close examination of the constructs represented on the surveys (Bailey and Kelly, 2013). One of the concerns has been that asking parents to state their child's first or primary language has been too vague (do these terms refer to a child's first language learned or to a language they currently speak most frequently?). The HLS have also restricted parental responses to just one language ignoring the possibility that children may be native bilingual speakers. These features of current surveys have led to parental responses that may either under- or over-identify students as potential ELL students.

Previous studies of parent reports of their children's language abilities suggest they may not always judge language proficiency very well. Parents may have a fair sense of their children's abilities in the L1 they share with their children but may overestimate their children's L2 performances relative to researchers' independent assessment of the children's languages (Duursma et al., 2007). Possibly, parents may only get to witness their children's use of the L2 in casual talk outside of an academic context and such use may not equate with the academic language demands placed on children's L2 in school settings. This restricted range of contexts by which parents were judging their children's L2 may have led to less consistency with the researchers' assessment of children's L2. Moreover, Schwartz and Moin (2012) in their study of young Russian-Hebrew bilingual children in Israel found parents' assessment of their children's language abilities likely to be influenced by their choice of "family language policy" (i.e., maintaining a bilingual household). These parents were unable to accurately detect the length of their children's utterances and overestimated their language abilities. The authors interpreted the overstated language skills as the justification by parents for choosing to send their children to bilingual preschool programs.

In government-funded schools in the United States completing a HLS is typically a family's first encounter with officialdom over the languages they speak with their children. Getting survey responses to be completed as accurately as possible is no trivial feat. This is the first stage in the ELL assessment system in which enrolling students are identified as either potential ELL students or not. Potential ELL students (those whose families indicated that a language(s) other than English is spoken in the home environment) are then assessed using an English language proficiency screener or assessment instrument to make the definitive classification of being an ELL student and placed into services as applicable (See Bailey and Carroll, 2015, for further discussion of this process). To date, we have no empirical study of the efficacy of current HLS for identifying the right potential ELL students; identifying too many potential ELL students for further evaluation is an unnecessary cost to LEAs and may be unnecessarily distressing to students and families, whereas identifying too few potential ELL students means students who may benefit from English language services may not be getting assessed for them in the first place. Currently many states are in the process of revising questions on HLS to better address the most relevant constructs of student current language usage and exposure with the intention of enhancing the effectiveness of the surveys (Linquanti and Bailey, 2014).

Given that parents have found it difficult to judge their children's language proficiency, one thing is clear: HLS will not be revised to directly ask parents to make such a determination. However, findings from the present study can inform how best to conceive of the constructs of student language usage and exposure, as well as ways to best word questions that will resonate with parents' perspectives on language.

First, a possible enhancement to existing HLS is the expansion of the range of contexts that can be considered when contemplating children's development of linguistic resources. *Home* language survey may in fact be a misnomer in the twenty-first century. According to Michael Erard of the New York Times (2012), the U.S. Census Bureau's question about languages spoken at home is not equivalent to asking whether one speaks more than one language. Additionally, many Americans speak a language other than English outside of home: at work, nurses, doctors, teachers, retail personnel, and court employees often use other languages, as the parents and educators in our research frequently reported to us. A growing number of Americans work, or study abroad for a time, thus learning and becoming fluent in a language other than English, and this may be a third language that also differs from the language that they speak at home within their family. In other parts of the world, such cases of trilingualism due to linguistic differences in work, home, and wider societal contexts are becoming the norm. For example, in Europe, Ortega (2013a) reports that most language learning that takes place during later childhood and adulthood involves individuals learning a third language or even more. Questions on the HLS therefore, should more realistically ask about languages spoken *inside* and *outside* respondents' homes.

Second, in our study of multilingual families, many parents reported feelings of *confidence* or *comfort* as deciding factors in their own and their children's use of a language. However, no HLS to our knowledge have used this terminology in the wording of questions about children's language preferences and usage. For example, Nora stated, "I think with **confidence** she [her daughter, Alejandra] has learned to appreciate the language too, Spanish ... Alejandra, I think, feels **comfortable** with both [English and Spanish]." Monica mentioned, "Conversationally, he [her son, Rodrigo] converses with my parents, his grandparents, in Spanish, and feels very **comfortable** and very proud of being able to speak in Spanish. So he feels very good about it." She went on to later say, "When I think back to when he was three, I remember we went [to Mexico] during the holidays and he was able to get along with kids and all of that because it was his language of **comfort**." Hediyeh continues this theme with:

And then little by little, English became the first language. And when we moved here, because we thought Malik ... has to learn English quickly, we started him off in a Montessori school right away. And he was miserable for I think it was like six months or so ... I think after a while he kind of picked up the language and he was more **comfortable,** but it took a long time.

Confidence is a construct that is recognized in prior research as a dimension of motivation that is closely related to language competence (Clément, Gardner, and Smythe, 1977). *Confidence* and *comfort* also allow children to recognize the value and the equal status of their home language and their L2. Therefore, future questions of the HLS could address the construct of current language knowledge by asking questions about the child's and the parent's confidence and/or comfort in speaking the different languages in the child's different environments. As American states and researchers develop new HLS and empirically test them for the first time, including such constructs and wording could be part of establishing the efficacy of the HLS and identifying the most meaningful questions, that is, questions that capture those students who after further testing will prove to need English language services and avoid capturing the majority of those students who do not.

3.   *Recognition that Multilingual Adolescents May Experience Feelings of Increased Distance from Multilingualism, and that Families and Schools Should Plan Accordingly*

When multilingual children reached puberty, their parents reported a decline in their interest in speaking the language(s) that are not dominant in the wider society. Some parents of even quite young children anticipated this stage of their children's development with some trepidation. For example, as we reported in Chapter 5, Linda explicitly identified the peer group and the pressures of "what is cool" as a source of influence during her children's future adolescence that could derail her current efforts to have her children develop language skills in both English (the wider societal language) and Spanish (the father's heritage language and the language spoken in the home).

Concern with the decline in preference for the minority and increasingly marginalized languages (in terms of authentic contexts for use) that are in a child's linguistic repertoire is not the purview of families alone, nor should it be their burden to combat this decline alone. There is a great paucity in the area of educational supports for multilingualism with older students (Budach, 2014; Grosjean, 1982). The nature of multilingualism in school and wider society may change over the course of childhood. Budach (2014) has argued that "multilingualism as an educational resource undergoes a fundamental meaning shift" (p. 525). In Germany, where her work was conducted, in the "primary years multilingualism is drawn on as a *capital for social inclusion*" (p. 526) such that children's linguistic resources are used educationally and socially to ensure they can access the official school curriculum and social aspects of the schooling context. In contrast, she finds that secondary-level educational systems "value languages as *capital for social distinction* and an indicator of individual achievement" (p. 526), such that adolescents find that their language knowledge is useful for meeting foreign-language school and university requirements for example, but not necessarily useful for participating in the school curriculum more widely and not, as we heard from parents and educators in the current study as well, valued as useful for participation in the wider social life of their schools.

The plethora of myths and misunderstandings around the notion of multilingualism discussed in Chapter 3 is a striking illustration of the vulnerability of multilingualism within society. Convinced by these misconceptions, parents in the study reported abandoning multilingual practices for a while or for good. Believing that they will not get enough buy-in from families at the secondary levels, many schools are not providing K-12 multilingual support. Meanwhile, our findings have shown that availability of such programs is seen as desirable by families. The existence and persistence of anti-multilingualism myths leads to abandoning of multilingual ways on personal and societal levels. In this context, the myths may unfortunately function as rationales for families deciding to drop multilingual practices.

Motivation for maintaining an L1 alongside English as well as acquiring English as an L2 amongst high school students were also major concerns of parents and educators in the current study. One way in which LEAs in a small number of states have attempted to combat the decision to drop multilingualism by individual students at this critical point in their school careers and multilingual development is through such grass-roots initiatives as a *Seal of Biliteracy* mentioned in Chapter 6. This *Seal* allows multilingual students to graduate high school with an additional endorsement on their diplomas that states they are literate in two (or more) languages. Research is needed to determine if universities and employers are taking note of this accomplishment, and if, in turn, such recognition is beginning to motivate high school students more forcefully.

Such initiatives also speak to the need for adopting a broader definition of success by which we can more comprehensively evaluate the efficacy of dual-language programming, as we have argued elsewhere (Bailey et al., 2008). Educators support children's development not only academically but also in terms of children's linguistic, cognitive, and socio-affective outcomes. Consequently, educators' efforts could and, we would argue, should be measured and acknowledged in these areas as well. The additional information that this notion of dual-language programming efficacy yields can also serve to provide educators with crucial feedback for further improvements in meeting the wide-ranging needs of their multilingual students.

All the educators in our study who worked at the secondary level reported an extreme lack of materials for language instruction in both the majority language, English, being acquired as an L2 during adolescence and the myriad minority languages encountered in dual-language programming of all stripes in the United States. The latter included Spanish which despite it being the L1 of 85% of ELL students and the most common partner language of TWI programs still suffered from a paucity of pedagogical materials at the secondary level. To redress this situation, we can appeal to textbook and trade publishers to anticipate the increased demand for language instructional texts and authentic children's and young adult literature and non-fiction texts in high-incidence languages and other curricular materials that will inevitably occur in the near future for Spanish and for several Asian languages. According to the Pew Research Center reporting in 2013 on U.S. Census Bureau data, Spanish, with more than 37 million speakers, has increased its number of speakers by 233% since 1980. This number is projected to rise to 40 million by 2020. The number of Vietnamese speakers while smaller in absolute size (just over 1.25 million) grew fastest of all language groups, by 599% over the same time period (http://www.pewresearch.org/fact-tank/2013/09/05/what-is-the-future-of-spanish-in-the-united-states). Other recommendations for increasing the breadth and quality of materials in the range of partner languages as well as effective and age-appropriate ESL materials for the secondary level are mentioned in the Resources section below.

4.   *Biases Need to be Confronted to Overcome Fears of Failed Multilingualism, Especially for Students with Disabilities*

The findings from the parent and educator interviews in our study are in alignment with the previous research regarding the overall language development and academic progress prospects of multilingual children with disabilities, and support the recommendations that parents and educators have received from the research field (Paradis et al., 2011). Recent studies with children with a wide range of disabilities, including learning disabilities, Specific Language Impairment (SLI), language delays, cognitive disabilities, and ASD (Kremer-Sadlik, 2005; Paradis et al., 2011) show an overwhelming support for continuing home language communication (see Chapter 3 for a more detailed discussion). Providing evidence that children with disabilities are capable of learning more than one language, research recommends not merely maintaining, but actively promoting and supporting children's first language instruction and literacy activities (Paradis et al., 2011), as the children master English or any other additional language(s).

One of the most important findings in this literature is that often bilingualism is a life necessity for children with disabilities. These children often need to maintain and develop L1 because their families are often their leading source of social and emotional development. Learning the majority language, on the other hand, is critical for multilingual children with disabilities as a vehicle for integration into wider society. Therefore, limiting children with disabilities to one language is detrimental to their well-being. Another key finding is that bilingual children with disabilities perform just as well academically as their monolingual peers with disabilities in English-only programs (Paradis et al., 2011). This finding underscores the fact that bilingual programs hold no harm for multilingual children with disabilities and that their families should not be counseled out of enrolling their children in multilingual programs simply as a matter of course. Studies indicate that a large variation in children's L2 learning outcomes can be explained by such factors as their individual phonological short-term memory, analytic reasoning, L1 typology (e.g., L2 outcomes may be more positive in cases where L1 and L2 are in the same language family, such as Spanish and Italian, which share linguistic features due to having Latin as their common root), length of exposure to L2 and the richness of L2 environments (Paradis, 2011).

Research also recommends paying particular attention to challenges exhibited by multilingual children in their L1 (Erdos, Genesee, Savage, and Haigh, 2014). These difficulties exhibited early on serve as predictors of challenges that children with disabilities might experience later in the additional languages they learn. This information is critical for educators and schools and has important implications for instructional practices and academic supports for this vulnerable population. While we did not find biases against the multilingual raising of children with disabilities in parents in the current study, except for worries that multilingual practices may slow down or "confuse" their children (possibly due to the self-selection that occurred with families who, committed as they were to multilingualism in one form or another, agreed to be participants in the research), we did hear from a small number of educators across different program types who felt that multilingualism would not be beneficial and could even be harmful for the development of students with disabilities. For example, Sandra, an elementary teacher in a French immersion program stated:

SANDRA: I also think for children who have language difficulties in the first place I don't know if going to school trying to learn two languages is good for children who already have a problem with one language on their own.
ANNA: Why do you think that?
SANDRA: Because if you have this problem where English is, you know, slower learning, there's so much pressure for them, for us to expect them to do well in two languages. Sometimes it can be confusing.

Specific strategies outlined in research as beneficial for multilingual support of students with disabilities in school environments include the use of dynamic assessment (Gutierrez-Clellen and Peña, 2001), support of children's communication in both languages (Kohnert and Derr, 2004, as cited in Paradis et al., 2011), use of team approaches in which interpreters, para-educators, and parents are involved, as well as the use of peer-mediated approaches (Kohnert, Yim, Nett, Kan, and Duran, 2005).

It is of course not only for students with disabilities that biases against multilingualism can occur and potentially adversely affect academic performances and school outcomes. One of the persistent erroneous approaches within the school system and within the society is the practice of comparing multilingual children with a monolingual "norm." In such practice, children whose language skills in *two or more* languages are actively developing, often come out at a disadvantage and/or are penalized by the school system (Grosjean, 2009). Anecdotally, we are aware of families who have children enrolled in a publicly funded Spanish-English TWI program who received notices to sign and return acknowledging that their majority-language children were at risk for grade retention (i.e., required to repeat the same grade during the next school year) because they had not reached Spanish-language milestones by the middle of the first school trimester. This school district has a policy of assessing students in Spanish only during the early grades. Only once the students have received three years of Spanish and the program shifts closer to a 50/50 split in Spanish and English is the district willing to assess the students' English language skills. While this seems a sensible policy (assessing students in the language in which they receive instruction), the threat of retention was particularly demoralizing for the families who had relatively recently taken a chance on TWI programming for their children – the letters went home to families after just 12 weeks of enrollment in kindergarten!

Since research indicates notable differences in multilingual children's cognitive and socio-emotional development (see Chapter 2), be they minority- or majority-language students learning an L2, comparisons to monolingual peers are erroneous and school districts, researchers and society at large need to realize that multilingual children constitute a unique population that is in need of development of its own language norms (Ortega, 2013b).

5.   *Identifying and Creating Multilingual Resources*

We recommend that states and LEAs, individual schools, educators and families advocate for the increased breadth and quality of materials for ESL instruction as well as for instruction of and instruction *through* a range of minority languages (i.e., texts in content areas such a mathematics, science, and social studies, as well as age-appropriate high-quality literature by native-speaking authors). This advocacy can take a pragmatic stance by pointing out the increasing number of TWI programs and the increasing number of households in which parents are raising a child with a language other than English. Publishers may stand to gain by the shifts in linguistic demographics we enumerated in Chapter 2 and earlier in this chapter and take note of the most commonly spoken minority languages in the United States (e.g., Spanish, French, Russian, Korean, Mandarin, Vietnamese, Armenian, and Arabic) in their production of core content and leisure reading materials for K-12 students.

Another concrete action that might be taken up by linguists, families, and multilingualism advocacy groups in the United States is to promote the creation of a system comparable to the Common European Framework of Reference for Languages (CEFR), or perhaps to adopt an extension of this initiative that has as its main aim a common elaboration of language syllabi, curricula, etc. The framework has six levels of language proficiency for 39 different languages and is recognized across Europe and beyond. It is used by language professionals and other educators to coordinate efforts across nations such that a student deemed to be at level A1 (the starting level) will have the same linguistic skills in German for instance in the UK as a student deemed A1 in France or the Czech Republic or anywhere else in Europe that subscribes to the CEFR. The framework was designed with the aspiration that it will facilitate "European mobility" (www.coe.int/lang-CEFR).

We see such an effort working in tandem with and perhaps taken up by other organized educational reform efforts in the U.S. such as the Partnership for 21st Century Skills. This initiative is intended to provide guidance to the states to better prepare their students for the globalized labor market and life skills confronting students in the twenty-first century. Specifically, Essential Element 3: A New Approach to Language Instruction advises states to,

Institute a statewide dual language/immersion plan that begins in elementary school and continues through high school,

and,

Refocus traditional high school credit world language courses to include a greater emphasis on the study of global and international affairs and the economies, societies and cultures of other nations and on survival language skills. (http://www.P21.org)

Nothing could come closer to meeting the educational hopes and desires of the parents and educators we studied here. These guidelines are echoed in the recommendations of Espinosa (2013) in the early childhood care and education field who suggests new policies should

Support bilingualism for all children whenever possible; dual language programs are an effective approach to improving academic achievement for DLL [dual-language learner] children while also providing many benefits to native English speakers. ... We can improve the educational outcomes for DLL children as well as the social and economic health of our diverse communities. (p. 20)

In the U.S. context, efforts similar to the CEFR specifically may serve a number of functions not least making university World Language requirements across the states comparable and importantly making more uniform the educational experiences of ELL students in different states. Different language standards and assessments are used by states to first identify and then monitor the English language development and proficiency of ELL students. Unfortunately, the inconsistancies between states in their policies and practices continue to be an area of much educational policy concern, and research is needed to determine how equitable these practices are and what happens to ELL students who cross state lines during their school careers (Linquanti and Cook, 2013).

While we await these systemic approaches to be built or adapted to a U.S. context, there are resources that families and educators can consult and that may be useful in determining how best to address one another's needs and concerns. We list in Table 7.3 several organizations, all dedicated to fostering multilingualism in different countries and offering further cross-national comparisons. Such organizations or newly formed ones can help families connect beyond the specific communities they geographically abide in or beyond the specific educational programs their children attend. Linked by the commonalities we surfaced in the interviews (e.g., the challenges of connecting with schools and teachers, issues with extended family, peer influence) families can

Table 7.3 *U.S. domestic and international resources for families and educators of multilingual children*

Organizational name	Description	Website URL

In the United States:
Colorin Colorado
Multilingual Children's
  Association
Multilingual Living
	Colorin Colorado: for families
	  and educators of ELL
	  students
	Multilingual Children's
	  Association and
	Multilingual Living: both
	  are for families raising
	  multilingual children in
	  a wide range of contexts
	  (e.g., linguistically mixed
	  marriages, work abroad
	  situations, etc.)
		www.colorincolorado.org
		www.multilingualchildren.org
		www.multilingualliving.com

In Australia:
Bilingual Families
	Servicing Western Australia,
	  mission to support families
	  and communities who are
	  fostering more than one
	  language
		www.bilingualfamilies.net

In the European Union:
Multilingual Families
	EU Commission sponsored
	  project to help multilingual
	  (incl. immigrant) families
	  and students as well
	  as educators and other
	  stakeholders
		www.multilingual-families.eu

In the UK:
Bilingual Immersion
  Education Network
  (BIEN)
	A network for schools,
	  policy-makers, parents,
	  researchers and others
	  on the topic of bilingual
	  immersion education
		elac.ex.ac.uk

garner resources and exchange ideas to create networks that are built on these shared experiences.

Concluding Remarks: A Return to "Cultivating Broad-Base Support" for Multilingualism

Even with the many recommendations made above, several additional factors will need to be in place and better understood in order to "cultivate the broad base" of support that Lee and Wright (2014) spoke of and that families and educators of multilingual children will need in order to unify and magnify their efforts. Home-school-community connections will still be paramount, and Espinosa (2013) has specific recommendations based on her review of the research for strengthening such ties, including:

Family engagement policies and practices need to be examined through the lens of diversity. Traditional models may need to be expanded to include a focus on developing meaningful relationships with extended family members and a better understanding of family expectations for their children's development and learning. Family partnerships that are mutually respectful, engage in two-way communication and incorporate important cultural and family background information offer promise for stronger home-school connections. (p. 19)

Edwards (2004, cited in Pandey, 2004) specifically reminds educators of the "hidden literacies" that linguistically and culturally diverse communities engage in. These practices, such as songs, folk and family lore, recitations, religious readings, etc. may go unnoticed by educators who do not share their students' linguistic and cultural backgrounds, but should be brought to the fore of their interactions with and evaluations of multilingual students. Knowing and understanding that such literacies may play a valuable role in student's language and literacy learning both of the minority language and majority language is important because the linguistic and cognitive abilities they help rehearse may transfer to and be deliberately leveraged by educators for use in mainstream literacy practices (Bailey and Orellana, 2015).

These recommendations shift not only the rhetoric but suggestions for future research from a deficit paradigm to an "assets" paradigm. Pandey (2004), for example, suggests that in order to "yield a truly inclusive pedagogy" (p. 757) the work on the "how" of minority-language students' home-school connections begun more than ten years ago by Schechter and Cummins (2003) as a school-community-university collaboration in Canada, needs to be expanded to "include ... information on peer group interactions, specifically student-student, student-sibling, student-parent, and student community member interactions." In particular, it would seem critical to know how the amount and quality of these interactions contributes to the notion of ethnolinguistic vitality that Landry and Allard (1993) argue is so important to understanding the success of dual-language education. Student-sibling interactions would seem to be a high priority for such research given that schools may currently implement sibling policies, allowing younger siblings automatic entry into selective language instruction programs. Most obviously, such a policy may hope to garner parental buy-in and student retention through the convenience and continuity this policy offers to families. However, such sibling policies may also prove an effective pedagogical tool if student-sibling interactions are found to play a role in language development and attrition prevention by helping to build a requisite social network or critical mass of speakers with whom young language learners can engage.

We see an examination of multilingualism at its root – within the home and school environments – as a critical and timely contribution to the fields of education and social science, but only as a preliminary step. While our research has contributed to a richer and more nuanced understanding of parents and educators in a wide range of multilingual home and instructional situations, future research must also address the agency of students throughout the course of their multilingual development in their homes, schools, and community contexts.

As we close, we can also reflect on what the families and even the educators obtained from of their participation in this research project specifically. Parents and educators were eager to share their successes, needs, concerns, and efforts with us. Most were articulating these aloud in an extended way for the first time and felt they learned from the experience. Furthermore, for the parents, many had a message to share with their children's schools which, due to various reasons (e.g., keeping their children's ELL status secret, lack of time, lack of trust, assumed role of the sole L1 teacher, etc.) they may have never been able to share directly. With the notion of investment particularly, it appeared that parents were disputing the perception of parental non-involvement. On the contrary, we found how much they were invested and what an arduous task this could be. Similarly, the educators found an outlet in the interviews to express their concerns with the educational systems they worked within; they had not necessarily been able to voice these directly to their administrations or other teachers before. They expressed a need for organization, consistency, resources, investments of time and preparation, and innovative yet proven models of effective language instruction. Finally, parents (and educators too) loved to talk about their children and the world needs to hear about them and understand better just what is involved in their upbringing. In the introduction, we stated that the education field must "be ready to greet this new multilingual student population" and the parents and educator in this study provided us with concrete examples of how to be ready.

The research we reported here allowed for a closer examination of multilingual contexts of development from early childhood into adulthood. Such an examination raises society's and the research community's awareness of the difficult challenges families and educators can face but also an awareness of their persistence, strategies, and triumphs with children who have distinctive linguistic, cognitive, and social profiles and who will make up the majority of the next generation of students. This awareness should serve to promote future research of the ways in which multilingual children preserve and develop their various competencies. Such research will help reveal commonalities across different contexts of multilingualism that may prove useful in fostering a systematic approach to sustaining multilingualism that takes account of the following: promoting closer home-school connections; promoting a collectivist approach amongst families with disparate backgrounds and reasons for sustaining multilingualism; identifying effective language instruction methods; and encouraging second/foreign language programming from the start of elementary schools. Such a coordinated approach to sustaining multilingualism also has the potential to change the United States' image as a monolingual nation.

Even as we find ways to enlist wider society's support for multilingualism, we can also be building a solid base of connections between families, between families and educators, and between different educators. We do not need to wait to hear from others in society that they acknowledge and will support the fact that we live in a multilingual nation; we see that families and educators have already begun the task of working for the advancement of all children's multilingual prospects.

Appendix A: Parent Interview Schedule

I. Tell Me a Little about Your Family:

1. What languages does your child speak?
2. How old is your child?
3. When your child started to talk, what language did he/she speak?
4. How early did your child become multilingual?
5. Are there other multilingual family members in your family?
6. What do other people say when they learn that your child speaks several languages?

II. Language Development History:

7. When your child started to talk, what language did he/she speak? Why?
8. When did you decide that you would like your child to grow up speaking many languages? Why?
9. Did your views and values in regards to multilingualism change as your child was growing up?
10. What happened (will happen) when your child starts going to school?
11. Were there any changes in your child's language development that were very noticeable?

III. Why Multilingualism?

12. When did you decide that your child should grow up speaking several languages?
13. Why did you decide that your child should grow up speaking several languages?
14. What do you see as benefits of multilingualism?
15. What do you see as main challenges of multilingualism?
16. Do you consider it hard or easy to raise a child speaking many languages? Why?
17. What is rewarding about raising a multilingual child?

18. What are your goals for your child in terms of language development, communication, and social development?

IV. Strategies:

19. What made your child successful at acquiring several languages?
20. What were some strategies that worked?
21. Were there any specific methods that you involved in raising your child?
22. What advice would you give other parents who aim to raise multilingual children?
23. What advice would you give teachers who work with multilingual children?

V. Roadblocks:

24. What are some roadblocks in the way of raising a multilingual child?
25. Is there anything that worries you in this process?

VI. Gaps/Needs/Questions:

26. Is there anything that you would still like to know about raising multilingual children?
27. What are some venues through which you would like to learn about it?
28. What are some of your needs, as a parent of a child who speaks several languages?
29. What do you think the needs of other parents like you are?
30. Is there anything else you would like to share about your experiences of bringing up a multilingual child?

Appendix B: Educator Interview Schedule

I. **Multilingualism in the Context of Teaching:**

1. How many students in your classroom (in an average classroom in your school) speak more than one language?
2. How do you find out that they speak more than one language?
3. What do you see as benefits of multilingualism?
4. What do you see as main challenges of multilingualism?
5. Do you consider it hard or easy to teach children speaking many languages? Why?
6. What is rewarding about teaching multilingual students?
7. What are your goals for your students in terms of language development, communication, and social development?

II. **Background Information:**

8. What languages do the students in your classroom/school speak?
9. Do you speak any of these languages?
10. How old are your students?
11. What training do you have for working with multilingual students?
12. What comes to mind when you learn that your student speaks several languages?

III. **Student Language Development Trajectories:**

13. When yours students came to your classroom for the first time, what language(s) did they speak?
14. What language did you speak to them? Why?
15. What do you notice about language, social and academic development of such students?
16. Do you think they will grow up speaking many languages? Why?
17. What do you value about multilingualism?
18. Did your views and values in regards to multilingualism change as you worked with multilingual students?

19. Were there any changes in your students' language development that were very noticeable?

IV. Strategies:

20. What made your students successful at acquiring several languages?
21. What were some strategies that worked?
22. Were there any specific methods that you involved in teaching multilingual students?
23. What advice would you give other teachers who work with multilingual students?
24. What advice would you give parents who are raising multilingual children?
25. What are some ways in which you communicate with families of multilingual children?

V. Roadblocks:

26. What are some roadblocks in the way of teaching multilingual students?
27. Is there anything that worries you in this process?

VI. Gaps/Needs/Questions:

28. Is there anything that you would still like to know about teaching multilingual students?
29. What are some venues through which you would like to learn about it?
30. What are some of your needs, as a teacher of students who speak several languages?
31. What do you think the needs of other educators like you are?
32. Is there anything else you would like to share about your experiences of teaching multilingual students?

Appendix C: Parent Interview Coding Scheme and Examples

Thematic categories/meta themes and examples of subthemes/codes	Example excerpts from transcripts
Parental Beliefs about Multilingualism: multilingualism as a norm [MULTNorm]; multilingualism as a natural phenomenon [MULTNat]	"In their school there are a lot of bilingual kids who speak Russian or Farsi so it is fairly normal that kids speak another language." [MULTNorm] (Nicole, a mother of 2 German-English bilingual sons, 2½ and 8 years old) "It's natural for children to speak their mother's language and another language spoken in the country …" [MULTNat] (Danielle, a mother of 4 multilingual children in their 20s)
Myths about Multilingualism: U.S.A. as a monolingual nation [MYTHMonLing]; children with disabilities cannot/should not learn more than one language [MYTHDis]	"the language that is most spoken here is English" [MYTHMonLing] (Dulce, a mother of a 4-year-old son) "Raising a child bilingually is very challenging when your kid has a disability." [MYTHDis] (Kelly, a prospective mother)
Parental Motivation for Multilingual Upbringing: connection to family roots [MOTRoots]; access to resources [MOTRes]	"… knowing your roots and your heritage. Understanding what that heritage was." [MOTRoots] (Monica, a mother of 2 teenage sons bilingual in Spanish and English) "for me [bilingualism] is just access to people and culture and ideas" [MOTRes] (Linda, a mother of two Spanish-English bilingual daughters, 8 and 5 years old)
Investment: financial investment [INVFin]; emotional investment [INVEm]	"We could be doing more English at home for [my husband's job] benefit but we both decided we want the kids to have Spanish at home." [INVFin] (Linda, a mother of two Spanish-English bilingual daughters, 8 and 5 years old) "[My husband] is incredibly supportive. Because I forget that he doesn't understand a foreign language sometimes." [INVEm] (Tina, a mother of 19-month-old multilingual Lilia)

Thematic categories/meta themes and examples of subthemes/codes	Example excerpts from transcripts
Strategies Used by Families to Promote Multilingualism: immersion [STRATImmer]; literacy strategies [STRATLit]	"Full immersion ... If some people ask, 'Why are you speaking Spanish all the time?' – keeping it very clear to our families and friends that we are making a conscious effort in raising the child bilingually." [STRATImmer] (Lilian, prospective parent) "On a family road trip, I'll be in the backseat and I'll read to her ... Because I don't like her just sitting in the back staring at herself, even though she's beautiful, in the mirror." [STRATLit] (Tina, a mother of 19-month-old multilingual Lilia)
Challenges and Roadblocks to Multilingualism: family-level roadblocks [RDBFam]; systemic roadblocks [RDBSys]	"Well, we have differing opinions ... at my school, it's dual literacy, not dual language ... I would be interested in maybe dual language, because I would like[my children] to be strong in both reading and writing, but [my husband] has a different opinion ..." [RDBFam] (Lilian, prospective parent) "Kids are often judged [by the mainstream culture] because of their dominant tongue if it is not English." [RDBSys] (Veronica, a mother of a 2½-year-old, Andrew, trilingual in German, Hebrew, and English)
Portraits of Multilingual Children: multilingual children are unique [MULTCHUn]; social development of multilingual children [MULTCHSocD]	"I think bilingual children are in a unique place where they are a step ahead of children who are not bilingual." [MULTCHUn] (Miko, a prospective parent) "maybe they are more social? [They are] in the position where [they have] to translate a lot ... so you have to be more social. You have to be okay with talking to adults ..." [MULTCHSocD] (Lilian, a prospective parent)
Factors Contributing to Success of Multilingual Upbringing: family support [SUCFACFam]; multilingual supports within the community [SUCFACCom]	"My sister who saw him regularly is very competent in Spanish ... and she use to speak to him in Spanish regularly." [SUCFACFam] (Betty, a mother of a Spanish-English bilingual son in his 30s) "With the community school where they went, most kids actually come in speaking Spanish to start with and not English." [SUCFACCom] (Betty, a mother of a Spanish-English bilingual son in his 30s)

Thematic categories/meta themes and examples of subthemes/codes	Example excerpts from transcripts
Parents' Advice for Schools: instructional strategies [ADVInstr]; school-family communication [ADVComm]	"Allow kids to respond in two languages … let them express themselves, and then you scaffold it and say it in English." [ADVInstr] (Kelly, a prospective mother) "Be really clear about what the goals are." [ADVComm] (Linda, a mother of two Spanish-English bilingual daughters, 8 and 5 years old)
Parents' Needs: resources [NEEDRes]; unanswered questions [NEEDQuest]	"It would be nice to have more resources … It would be nice to have more books that integrate languages." [NEEDRes] (Taani, a mother of a 2-year-old, Mihir, trilingual in Hindi, Spanish, and English) "… exposure to four different languages when he was just starting to formulate language, I am still curious to know if that was in any way involved in his language delay …" [NEEDQuest] (Taani, a mother of a 2-year-old, Mihir, trilingual in Hindi, Spanish, and English)

Appendix D: Educator Interview Coding Scheme and Examples

Thematic categories	Example excerpt from transcripts
Beliefs about the roles of multilingualism in the classroom: aides in academic learning [POSAcad]; positive social development [POSSoc]; negative impacts [NEGImp]	"I think what I've been able to do is draw the connection between what they are doing now and high school and then college…. So, I have put it that way, although I haven't yet said, 'if you want a job, you need to be multilingual.'" [POSAcad] (Elena, ESL specialist) "I think they have a broader perspective of the world and the issues and people and culture and I think that's an experience and a perspective that a native speaker or someone who has never traveled can even, they can't begin to understand. They can compare science in the United States to science in another country." [POSSoc] (Elena, ESL specialist) "And you have a certain percentage of the boys who really don't care and they're [not] doing their homework." [NEGImp] (David, ESL specialist)
Beliefs about the roles of multilingualism in the home/community: multilingualism helps child connect with family [CONwFAM]; connect with local community/culture [CONwCULT]	"I think it is so dependent on the family and the values they place on education and in keeping the connections. The more Americanized, you know the studies, with every generation, they lose the native language and customs. I think it really requires a dedication and an effort." [CONwFAM] (Camila, ESL specialist) "… because they don't have that connection. They don't have that relationship and I think that is so, so important." [CONwCULT] (Alejandro, TWI teacher)
Beliefs about the roles of multilingualism in the wider U.S. society: value of multilingualism for U.S. [VALforUS]	"So I think if everybody speaks multilanguage I think it makes a better world, better society." [VALforUS] (Jake, after-school program tutor and director)

266

Thematic categories	Example excerpt from transcripts
Experiences with challenges: difficulties with children [DIFwChi]; with administrators [DIFwAdmin]; with parents [DIFwPar]; with resources [DIFwRes]; with feelings of isolation [DIFwIso]	"My Korean kids would always be with Korean kids; my Chinese kids would always be with Chinese kids. And as soon as I gave them like a, let's say I gave them a five minute break in class, no one is going to venture out to actually practice their English." [DIFwChi] (David, ESL specialist) "… my superiors were telling me 'okay they have to perform in English,' but the Spanish was never really talked about as much or embraced. You know and I felt like many of them were looking at it as a problem that they speak Spanish as their primary language." [DIFwAdmin] (Alejandro, TWI teacher) "It's definitely challenging. My theory. I think the parents, in their situation, the parents are working so hard to just make a living. There isn't much time spent in building relationships or language at home." [DIFwPAR] (Melanie, ESL Specialist) "Now on the flip side of that is as a school community we have very limited what I would call linguistic resources for children who do not speak either English or Spanish, but who may need that other support. That's a challenge for us." [DIFwRES] (Alejandro, TWI teacher) "So, yeah, seeing individual accomplishment, but there's also as a teacher, there's a feeling of isolation … You're not really interacting a lot with your peers in terms of what you're doing in the classroom. You're sort of on your own trying to find your way." [DIFwIso] (David, ESL specialist)
Experiences with instructional practices that foster growth of multilingualism [POSPrac]	"… I think, to helping students to use what they have, to use their background experience, their culture, to help them succeed in school. Now I think there is more of a political bent to the things I do and why I choose to do them." [POSPrac] (Alejandro, TWI teacher)

Thematic categories	Example excerpt from transcripts
Prognoses for the future: positive [POSProg]; negative [NEGProg] Other themes: concern that ELD/ESL focus ignores L1 potential [ELLFoc]	"And even my bilingual students that don't get to travel so much because their socioeconomic background is just, doesn't allow it, they just think in different ways. They'll say like oh that's like Spanish. They'll make these connections between languages." [POSProg] (Paola, TWI teacher) "… from seeing a child who didn't know any French one year, but seeing him two years later speaking fluent French with no accent. It's really impressive. It also shows you what the human mind can do at such a young age." [POSProg] (Sandra, one-way immersion teacher) "Because if this teacher for example is just teaching the subject matter without really supporting the program, it can be more detrimental than someone who maybe doesn't have the subject matter but really believes in the kids and also the program." [NEGProg] (Gael, district dual-language administrator) "And many of our parents you know, not only do they want their child to know English, but also to be able to be biliterate, and also have greater opportunities in the future." [ELLFoc] (Gael, district dual-language administrator)

Appendix E: Information about Individual Families in the Study

Language profile of the family	Parent participant (pseudonym)	Role	Participant's country of origin (mother/father)	Occupation	Languages spoken within family in order of dominance	Immigrant status (mother/father)	Number and gender of child(ren)	Age of child(ren), or adulthood	Parent perception of success in multilingualism
Bilingual (includes initially monolingual English or LOTE families)	Linda	Mother	U.S.A./El Salvador	Graduate student	Spanish and English	Non-immigrant/1st generation	2 daughters	2 yrs and 5 yrs	High
	Monica	Mother	Mexico/Mexico	Elementary school administrator	English and Spanish	Non-immigrant/non-immigrant	2 sons	14 yrs and 19 yrs	High
	Betty*‡	Mother	U.S.A.	Higher education administrator	English and Spanish	Non-immigrant	1 step-daughter, 2 sons, 1 step-son	Adults (late 20s–30s)	High (for subset of children)
	Kevin	Prospective father	U.S.A.	Medical professional	English and Spanish	Non-immigrant	None, prospective parent	N/A	N/A
	Nora	Mother	El Salvador/El Salvador	Domestic worker	Spanish and English	1st generation/1st generation	3 daughters	7 yrs, 9 yrs and adult (early 20s)	Medium
	Bianca	Mother	Mexico/U.S.A.	Cafeteria worker	English and Spanish	1st generation/non-immigrant	2 sons	14 yrs and 16 yrs	Low
	Lilian (wife)	Prospective mother	Mexico/Mexico	Elementary school teacher	English and Spanish	2nd generation/2nd generation	None, prospective parent	N/A	N/A

Language profile of the family	Parent participant (pseudonym)	Role	Participant's country of origin (mother/father)	Occupation	Languages spoken within family in order of dominance	Immigrant status (mother/father)	Number and gender of child(ren)	Age of child(ren), or adulthood	Parent perception of success in multilingualism
	Miko (husband)	Prospective father	Mexico/Mexico	Graduate student	English and Spanish	2nd generation/2nd generation	None, prospective parent	N/A	N/A
	Dulce*	Mother	Salvador	Domestic worker	Spanish	1st generation	1 son	4 yrs	Medium
	Tricia	Mother	U.S.A./Portugal	Stay-at-home parent, former finance professional	English and Portuguese	Non-immigrant/1st generation	2 daughters and 1 son	4 yrs, 5 yrs and 17 mos	High
	Veronica	Mother	U.S.A./Germany	Graduate student	English and German	Non-immigrant/1st generation	1 son	2 yrs	Medium
	Nicole	Mother	Germany/U.S.A.	Travel agent	English and German	1st generation/non-immigrant	2 sons	3 yrs and 5 yrs.	Low
	Kelly‡	Prospective mother	U.S.A./U.S.A., Taiwanese descent	Graduate student	English and Taiwanese (Mandarin)	Non-immigrant/2nd generation	None (was pregnant with daughter)	N/A	N/A
	Kimberly	Mother	Korea/Korea	Higher education lecturer	Korean and English	2nd generation/2nd generation	1 daughter, 1 son	6 mos and 5 yrs	Medium
	Hediyeh (wife)	Mother	Iran/Iran	Home designer	English and Farsi	1st generation/1st generation	1 daughter, son	Adults (early 30s)	Low
	Ghodrat (husband)	Father	Iran/Iran	Higher education professor	English and Farsi	1st generation/1st generation	1 daughter, 1 son	Adults (early 30s)	Low
	Sonia*	Mother	Russia/Russia	Science laboratory assistant	Russian	1st generation/1st generation	1 son	Adult (mid 20s)	High
	Larisa*	Mother	Russia/Russia	Stay-at-home parent	Russian	1st generation/1st generation	1 son	Adult (early 20s)	High
	Leonid	Father	U.S.A./Russia	Software professional	English and Russian	Non-immigrant/1st generation	1 daughter and 3 sons	Adult (early 20s), 13 yrs and 11 yrs (twins)	High and Low

Trilingual								
Mayda	Mother	Jordan/Soviet Armenia	Graduate student	Armenian, Arabic, English	1st generation/1st generation	1 daughter, 1 son	8 yrs and 6 yrs	Medium
Danielle (wife)	Mother	France, Russian descent/U.S.A., Irish descent	Substitute teacher	French, English, Russian	1st generation/non-immigrant	2 daughters and 2 sons	Adults (early–late 20s)	High for French, medium for Russian
Ultan (husband)	Father	France, Russian descent/U.S.A., Irish descent	Retired film critic	French, English, Russian	1st generation/non-immigrant	2 daughters and 2 sons	Adults (early–late 20s)	High for French, medium for Russian
Taani	Mother	U.S.A., Hindi descent/U.S.A., Bengali descent	Graduate student	Hindi, English, Spanish, Bengali (father only)	2nd generation/2nd generation	1 son	2 yrs	High
Polyglot (4 or more languages)								
Victor‡	Father	Japan/U.S.A.	Pastor	Japanese, English, Korean, Russian, Italian	1st generation/non-immigrant	2 daughters	14 yrs and 12 yrs	Medium
Tilda	Mother	Sweden/U.S.A.	Fashion designer	Swedish, English, Spanish, Mandarin, Portuguese, French	1st generation/non-immigrant	1 son	3 yrs	Medium
Tina	Mother	U.S.A., Taiwanese descent/U.S.A.	Stay-at-home parent	Taiwanese, Mandarin and English, American Sign Language	2nd generation/1st generation	1 daughter	19 mos	High

* Family initially monolingual in English; ‡ English-dominant parent; ‡ Family initially monolingual in a LOTE.

Appendix F: Parents' Advice to Educators

Advice	Participant	Example
Create structure and be consistent about the model	Linda	"They really do. But for other schools, you know, other teachers it is the flip. They are trying to promote the English and really get kids…. Maybe be really clear about what the goals are and then structure accordingly and really clear about who your family base is."
Embrace language differences	Taani	"Any advice … I would say that I think to really embrace the fact that … I would not say that I met any resistance per se to it but I met kind of … sort of puzzled looks whenever I went to his school and said, 'Look, these are the words that you would need to recognize when he says them in Hindi because he won't say them in English'; you know … it seemed that they were like 'Oh, okay, we will write them down and try to remember that but there wasn't any interest or any genuine 'Oh that's great! Tell me how to teach him other Hindi words,' you know, there was more of 'Okay, you let us know what he needs to know.' Like the bare minimum that they need to communicate, but nothing beyond that … like 'We are done.' But I think now his current particular daycare provider is definitely on the end of being more progressive and a little bit more culturally more oriented because on their intake interview forms, their assessment process, they asked us in the questionnaire questions like 'How does your child ask for milk or blanket' and things like that. They asked about other languages. I think that's definitely atypical, I do not think it is the norm for most other child care providers or daycare centers, I think. So even though they are probably much further ahead of the game than most, I still think that there can be more in terms of embracing the cultural differences and language differences."
Be aware	Tina	"Well I think I'd like to make them aware that she does speak many languages, but I, mostly likely if she were to go her teacher would only speak English to her."

"Stop when they stop"	Tina	"You know um, I don't think they need, no I don't think they need to be careful at all. I think they need to, I think the thing that I would tell her teachers 'you know she's brilliant, you know she's bright and she can understand everything you throw at her. I mean, you know test her. You know give her more than you think she's capable of and let her decide the limit. You know because I think what I've learned from her is that we are the limiting factor. We as parents are the limiting factor. They are capable of everything. So you know I think just letting the teacher know that she is smart, that she can understand things that you think you just don't, don't just follow you know, go beyond the textbook. You know, just throw everything you have at her, you know? And then if she needs more time on something then we'll spend more time on it. But just, don't just do the 1-2-3s today because you think that that she can only learn three, the first three numbers today, you know. Hey, go up to 100. Stop when you think, stop when they stop you know?'"
Get family's involvement	Leonid	"So, the teachers I would say, you know, evaluate what it is that you are trying to do. If you try to raise a bilingual child then you've got to have families' huge involvement and commitment in that respect. Otherwise, I would say it's a fool's errand. You will never do it and then best you can hope for is that it will be just like another subject."
Communicate with the family	Bianca	"If the parents don't speak English they are all Spanish speaking, it would be good for the teacher to find some ways to communicate with the parents or have a conference with the translator or somebody from the school but not to ignore that family or that issue or whatever it is because if the teacher knows the family doesn't speak English, it is the same thing with the other kids, they get in trouble they get bad grades. Or even if the child doesn't understand a few words in English but it would be better to have somebody to translate for them and since they get better and better."
See the bigger picture and the long term process	Monica	Monica: "I think that that's the advice. To see the long term, the bigger picture. That it is a long term commitment. It is actually a lifelong commitment is what it is. Yeah I think it is probably changing that in a sense that it is not five to seven years it is a lifelong commitment and I wish I would have done more. That that be communicated to parents who are starting. 'Look there is this great opportunity for you to connect the experience that you had been an example.' Like 'this is what you can do.'"
		Alison: "But since that you are also saying that, 'Don't prematurely give up because you are not seeing results yet because the results might not show up for years.'"
		Monica: "Yes"

Advice	Participant	Example
Counter example: it did not occur to me to speak to a teacher about multilingualism	Veronica	Anna: "Now, when he goes to school would there be advice you could give his teachers?" Veronica: "You know a parent has never brought it up to me as a teacher." Anna: "But you, so you are bringing Andrew to school…" Veronica: "I don't know? It shouldn't be an issue. I don't see why it would be an issue. Frankly, I don't think he will be around other German speakers. It is just the way it is and his English should be fluent enough. We are assuming that it will be an English dominant school. It never occurred to me that I would even speak to the teacher about multilingualism."
Patience, treat the students the same, learn a bit of a child's language	Bianca	"First, not to get mad or frustrated with them because the kids sense it when the teachers get mad about anything they don't understand. I think if you are going to be a teacher you are going to have a lot of kids with different languages. It would be good for you to know a little bit of the language for the teacher. Instead of getting mad or frustrated. I would like not to ignore that kids because the teacher doesn't know what the kid is say in their language and I would like you to treat him like all the kids, give the papers and talk to them in English like they are not different. They are even more special in my opinion because they are learning another language. Not to make difference of the kids and trying to do the same things they do with the kids that speak English to the kids that don't speak English. That is what I would told the teachers to treat them the same and to be patient with them because they are lost. I was lost too!"
Give reassurance and clarity. They also want to know what happens in school after they drop their children off	Bianca	"Yes, I like it a lot [that teachers spoke Spanish] because it was kind of times for me when they were going away from me and even though they went to preschool I was scared. I really was scared because Steven was going to preschool." "Because he was crying and crying for every single morning I drop him off and I had Christopher and he was one year old and I was scared to leave my first baby in preschool every day. So that was kind of, for me it was a hard transition to let it go. It was." Anna: "So it was comforting that somebody spoke Spanish" Bianca: "Yes and the two teachers he have there that speak Spanish so they always 'Oh after you left two minutes later he find a toy and he was happy and he forget about it.' 'Oh good!' And sometimes I had to drop him and run and disappear and I don't like to do that. Yeah that was one of the things that I have kind of issues for that some words I didn't get it with doctors and other places.

Use L2 to make connections to academic language	Lilian	I had to ask them twice or three times. In the beginning it bothered me but after that I say why. There are other ways for to explain me I don't get it. I am sure there is another way I will understand. But I used to call my husband a few times I would give the telephone to my husband to the doctor talk to my husband." "I mean from a very academic point of view. Of course there are cognates and if you are teaching them something, you can make that little connection. 'Oh, you say this' and you can remember that if you know that word in Spanish. I do not know. I am thinking of 5th grade, you know, the Latin and Greek roots. That very academic language. You can tap into Spanish. So that helps, I think."
Treat my child as the rest of the class	Miko	"I would not. I would say please treat and teach my child like the rest of the class and have the same expectations in English. I would not want the teacher giving a child a break because oh, here she is speaking English and Spanish."
Be careful with what you say; do not devalue my child's language	Lilian	"I am just trying to take a broader perspective. I am trying to think what if they have the most horrible teacher that might not be supportive or in agreement with the way we are trying raise our child bilingually … it would not happen if the teacher is cool, but what if this teacher is does not like bilingualism or does not like the fact that we are raising her in Spanish, what if she decides to make comments, like I do not know … Because I remember in 1st grade I had this teacher who was very very old and she did not hide that she was a Republican or that she was a Pete Wilson's supporter and at that time for us that was the time when bilingual education was being debated in the 90s … and she was not afraid to say things that were offensive and things that would devalue our language. So if that were the case, then I would say 'be careful with what you say,' but this would not be really specific just to working with our child, that would be important for everyone."
Teach that the past is important and so is where you come from	Lilian and Miko	Miko: "I would hope that the teacher maybe teaches the children about culture and how important it is to know all about your past and where you come from and how language is a part of it." Lilian: "That it's valued and it's important to keep it." Miko: "That the second language that your mom and dad speak is very important to who you are. Because I would say that honestly that for the children who go into school speaking Spanish and English and come out speaking only English, I think it is for the parents of the children who are bilingual, like us, me and Lilian, to nurture that language so that they can continue speaking it when they come out of the school."
Value the L2	Lilian	"I guess then if we know that it is valued in the school, then we are in good shape. But I do not know.…"

Advice	Participant	Example
Have books and other support materials in all target languages so children and parents can read and preserve literacy	Betty	"[School district name] this is supposed to be a dual language program and they know most of the kids come in speaking Spanish but the library for the elementary children, only in English. I was like 'What are you doing!' They have stock books and that is it. But the kids couldn't even read it and the parents couldn't read it too either. It is crazy."
Teach L2 so that it can be internalized and understood	Kevin	"Well, let's see, I have thought about that kind of thing and I imagine that if I were to have a child right now in this world the way it is I would absolutely want them to have more than one language, hopefully more than two but our educational system is not really set up that way, at least public education. I feel like it is difficult to get quality education in English, let alone another language. Part of it is not just about being taught it, you have to live it to really, I think, internalize and understand the language. Otherwise it is just kind of knowledge that you recall or methods that you repeat as opposed to something that is inside you that you use. So I would never want my child to be deprived of some advantage I had. I would want to do at least as good for them as I had and hopefully better. So yeah I would want to give them that if they would accept it."
Create authentic experiences (for L2 teachers)	Kevin	"Well, okay, let's see. Well things are probably different now than when I went to school because multimedia has a whole new meaning. I think using many different media is helpful in your class. I am thinking of language class. I am imagining Spanish classes that were good for me. So listening to songs and singing about or writing about the lyrics or trying to write down the lyrics, watching television reading actual newspapers. Things like that are helpful. Actual children's books rather than worksheets."
For English teachers: engage the brain, tap into kid's L2 knowledge	Kevin	"And then for other teachers of other subjects, English and then whatever what have you, if you know that you've got a bilingual kid in that classroom and you can do something with it then I think it is helpful to both engage that part of their brain and sort of flip more switches for learning if you can. But then also use it as an access point to teach them better. Like in an English class, I was talking about vocabulary although that requires a lot of knowledge on the teacher's part ... [sound fades out] I just think, I just had that idea. That's all."

Listen to what parents want	Tricia	"Oh my gosh! Okay, when Gabriela started preschool they decided that since she wasn't talking that she didn't understand. She totally understood and she could speak English because she speaks English to her cousins. She speaks English. I am like, 'it is a mind game it is not an English issue' and then they didn't listen to me so then they started speaking Spanish to her. Like the word for red in Portuguese it is vermelho. In Spanish is is rojo. They are like yelling at her rojo, rojo! And then I am like, butterfly it is borboleta and in Spanish it is mariposa so they are like 'mariposa!' I am like 'Okay! Spanish is not Portuguese! And you are only totally confusing her!' Listen to what the parents want. Well, it depends on how much the parents know. They are sending them to an English speaking school because they want them to learn English so it is going to be hard for the kids. They need to get immersed."
Use songs and little rhymes	Nicole	"For teachers, I don't know I am not a teacher. I think the easiest way to learn language is through songs and little rhymes or what have you."
Give assignments that tap into preserving and reminding kids of their culture	Nicole	"Oh yeah! I see what you mean. So it is not a language teacher it is a teacher in general. My son's class has a lot of bilingual kids. I guess they could promote multiculturalism in general and actually our school does that a lot they have the Iranian new year's day and last year they had African American history month they had a day were they present stuff and if you have different cultures, I think there was a day for the Russians cultural at one point, that can teach the kids that there cultural that they extend from is valuable.

Another thing that I really, really liked the project my son did was create a flag with a family crest that you come up with yourself that represents your family and could be anything like if you go camping a lot you can have, you know how the crest is often divided by four areas, and you can have a tent or we put water and the beach with the son and the German flag and I actually saw another family who the dad's side is German. They also have the German flag there. Yeah, and we put a basketball because we love sports, the kids love sports. So that would be another way of preserving or reminding kids about their culture. If you do it in elementary school it requires the parents to participate too because they are actually the ones who do the project with them. Then you can get into geography and you can talk about other countries and languages and maybe even food that people eat in other countries if they even come from that country but you know their parents usually do or their grandparents." |

Advice	Participant	Example
Know that parents like multilingualism and request it	Dulce	"That I like it, and I request it. The teacher of a child that I take care of speaks two languages, three, Hebrew. Is that what this language is called?. "Aha. It is a great opportunity for him, so I congratulate her and I am happy because it will help the children very much."
Have patience and know the child	Dulce	"For example, if she speaks no Spanish she should have a little bit of patience because if he will speak to her in Spanish she will not be able to understand anything so she may act meanly. Then the child will be scared. So she should be patient and know, know her students."
Give parents L2 support information	Dulce	Anna: "Do you have any other questions about something you would like to know about regarding the process of raising multilingual children?" Dulce: " … When they have asked me this question at the school, I always request information about English, about how I can help my son, but for his English."
Include hands-on experiences	Kelly	"I think just to be good teachers. I see so many bad teachers … Just to be good teachers and I like teachers who use more hands-on, creative approaches, visual experiences. Not just worksheet after worksheet after worksheet."
Let children use both languages and express themselves; scaffold; involve families	Kelly	"Allowing kids to respond in two languages. I know that is sometimes frowned upon, because we do not do bilingual programs anymore, unless it is a dual immersion or something like that. Cause I know many teachers do not let kids speak Spanish to them even though they speak Spanish themselves. So I think letting them express themselves, and then you scaffold it and say it in English. And … just using a lot of visuals, generalizing the language to different situations, if they speak the language. Things like that."
Teach about multiculture, be open-minded	Larisa	"I think mainly what we want definitely is to, is teachers to be taught about multiculture, multilingual and you know they have to be open-minded and appreciate."
Emphasize connections	Ultan	"That they were welcomed as stars. I mean, they took Adele, I think it was Adele and they took her for a weekend sleepover the first day she arrived and they were put into 'we need something to be the Statue of Liberty because the Statue of Liberty came from France.' And all the different things. But that was the progressiveness of that area and of the teachers."

Teach in different ways, so that children are challenged more	Ultan	"Exactly. And we're at the bridge of cultures, the computer age limiting people's knowledge of acquiring knowledge because it's so available easily and they, we haven't learned how to teach this generation or the coming generation to adapt their life to the computer age. We're still teaching them the same way as we did before they had the abuse of the internet and things like that. This is something that I don't see being discussed. They discussed it, but the schools are not even teaching different ways. And they should be because children don't – I had to memorize, and you going to Russian schools had to memorize things, and memorize poetry and have vocabulary, and the things like that. And have knowledges of history and things like – none, none, none. We have bright kids, but they're not forced to know anything because all they have to do is that."
Consider bilingualism a virtue	Ultan	"Only to consider their bilinguality a virtue rather than anything else. And I mean it, they tried to pass a law here that they would only teach Mexican immigrants uniquely in Spanish for the first three grades and then they would begin to teach English. On the basis of the fact that you can never learn a second language unless you know the first one well. And these children were coming uneducated Spanish working families and so it was necessary. That lasted two years and they threw it out because they, it was un-American. And I was with the teachers that were broken hearted because they knew they were doing something right, and had proven in France how to teach languages and share multi languages. But there is still an attitude in this country, not the coasts, but in the great American middle, and you hear it in the election and the politics of it all is America is wonderful and the language is English and we don't, we expect the Spanish to only speak – why don't you learn English for crying out loud? Without realizing that they have this wonderful rich language of their own, and the fact that their coming and trying and making the effort. So to say is to, ideally tell teachers what a wonderful gift these children have and to somehow perhaps use them as examples to other children, in teaching to say you know."
Teach appreciation of culture	Larisa	"That high school teacher, she was doing high school and middle school. So somehow they took summer school the first, we arrived in April so they took summer school. And she organized trips to little museums and every day they were doing that so that, she was really good and nice. And she was appreciating the culture, and you know. Her background was mainly English and Spanish, but you know she was teaching all the other kids ESL too. Like Korean, Italian, all that stuff."

Advice	Participant	Example
Change children's attitudes; alleviate the sense of responsibility for the L2 nation	Hediyeh/ Ghodrat	Hediyeh: "Yeah I think I needed to add something to that. As Malik was in middle school, he was not pleased he is Iranian. And he had a teacher by the name of Mr. F. and he was just African American, and later on I found out that he was nominated for the best teacher in the county, so he did actually have profound effect on Malik. that changed his attitude for the point that it is like Iranian and Iranian language, to the point yeah that he really was proud that he was an Iranian. Because it just yeah the teacher that in my opinion translating differently from the point that he was Iranian to that the point that he was proud of that."

Anna: "Do you know what he did?"
Ghodrat: "I don't know really."
Hediyeh: "I think through his own experience as an African American he taught them you know if you speak another language, if you have another culture, you're better rather than being worse, you know. And I think he also, I'm not really sure because like you never know how they do it, but he also I think kinda told them that whatever happens anywhere else, it's not your fault." |
| Point out to children they are rich with two cultures, two languages | Ghodrat | "I think he was also more into that you know because Malik's competitive. I believe again yeah, all of that talk is crucial for kids, but I think it came to his mind that you are by far better than the guy that's next to you because you can speak another language, you have another culture that they don't have it. You have more than the other people have. You know you are whatever they have it here and some more because of the background and culture or whatever it is. And maybe I said there are nobody here who could appreciate the flavor of the food, of Persian food. You know that people see I cook is [unintelligible] and so on, but you enjoy that, you know. I think it is just a multitude of things that a good teacher translated, and a good teacher communicated effectively to a person that changed the personality. And to me it is the most important thing is just, if you are lucky to have a good mentor, good teacher in the age or stage of your life that you are very receptive to something new and your character is starting to form and become solid. If you are lucky at that time having a mentor, it can be your parent, it can be a teacher, it could be the coach [recording stops]." |
| Concentrate on the language of the society | Ghodrat | "I think just to concentrate in the one [language] that you are in the environment. But that's me you know." |

| Talk about other cultures, emphasize their value | Hediyeh | "I think in school they should have like, they should talk about other cultures. And they should actually teach children not to be, you know like in this country everyone says America is the best country in the world? The reason for it is because they don't know anything about any other countries. I think actually if from the beginning children would be brought up to actually look at other cultures, not as enemies, not as peoples you wanna destroy them or you know like steal their culture, as far as like equals. And also not as like inferior to them. It will actually bring up a better society. Like children who grew up that way, I think they are less prone to start wars, or less prone to be hostile to you know like people who don't speak the language, or they are not from the same culture.

"I think in school they should have like, they should talk about other cultures. And they should actually teach children not to be, you know like in this country everyone says America is the best country in the world? The reason for it is because they don't know anything about any other countries. I think actually if from the beginning children would be brought up to actually look at other cultures, not as enemies, not as peoples you wanna destroy them or you know like steal their culture, as far as like equals. And also not as like inferior to them. It will actually bring up a better society. Like children who grew up that way, I think they are less prone to start wars, or less prone to be hostile to you know like people who don't speak the language, or they are not from the same culture. Because, and in this country I mean everybody comes from somewhere. If we have actually embraced that rather than having to make people all like be proud of the one thing, being American, which you know like each one of us would understand differently, it would actually bring up a you know a more open-minded society altogether. Rather than just like really blind nationalism, or you know?" |

Appendix G: Educators' Advice to Parents by Program Type

Program	Advice	Participant	Example
TWI	Adopt realistic expectations of language development (commensurate with amount of parent support given)	Paola	"So they're very, quite proactive in putting their kids in bilingual program, trying to find activities that are in Spanish. They do have expectations that are a little bit skewed though. They don't necessarily take into account developmental stages of acquiring a second language. So once they're in the bilingual program, by the end of that first year when they're 4 years old, they want them to be speaking in full sentences, you know and it's like it doesn't really work that way. So it's hard to help them understand. Because we do get some parents saying things like, well by this time they should be speaking in full sentences, or you know having conversations or. And you know it depends on the child, it depends on how much exposure they've had, it depends on the support you're providing at home too. It's like a combination of things."
	Become a language learner too (signal importance of L2 to children)	Alejandro	"When they say 'Yes it's important that my child learn Spanish. Yes I want to be supportive. Yes I am in agreement with what your approach is and what you're doing, but I don't have anything to contribute. I'm not a bilingual. I don't know the first thing about Spanish. I don't know what I'm doing.' And I go, 'Well, with all due respect, that's part of the problem. Because … your child does not see the value of learning a second language because it's not valued at home.'" Anna: "Your priority, right?" Alejandro: "I said 'Now just imagine that if everyone in the family was trying to do this together, how much more the child would be motivated to involve themselves in the learning aspect of this? How motivated would they be to know that mommy and daddy or mommy and mommy or whoever, they're with me on this?' One dad in particular said, 'well you know I want my child to learn Spanish but if they're not going to learn it I'm going to get them a tutor.' I'm like, 'Well…' He says, 'What's wrong?' and I go, 'Well think about that for a minute. I'm not saying getting a tutor is a bad idea because that would give them more exposure….'" Anna: "Right, and practice." Alejandro: "'But what's the message that you're sending your child?'" Anna: "Others will teach you?"

Alejandro: "'You're not good enough. You're not making it, so I have to get someone to help you.' As opposed to, 'Maybe the tutor is for the whole family. Maybe the tutor is there to help you, help your child learn Spanish, because your child is seeing you trying to learn as well.' And with the families where there is some of that. It's great because the father would say, another parent would say, 'I had no idea what my child knew until I started trying to speak the language, and then 'no papi or no daddy that's not how you say it. You say it this way,' and say 'Oh. Finally I realize that he is learning something.' And I go 'That's right. Look at what the message was that you were sending your child. That I'm interested. That I want to learn this too.' So that would be my advice to parents is that if you want your child to be multilingual, then you be multilingual. If you are multi – then another parent for example is multilingual, but he is multilingual in Hindi and French, not so much in Spanish. And I said 'Well there's, there's a good and bad there. One is the great thing is he is being raised in a multilingual environment. Very literate household. But your child isn't seeing you helping them with the Spanish.' He says 'You're right. You're absolutely right but I don't have time.' I said 'Well who picks the child up from school?' 'I do.' 'Get yourself a CD in Spanish, listen to it on the way home. Listen to songs on the way home.'"

| Developmental Bilingual Education | Need parent commitment and aspirations for children's success | Gael | "From my point of view I think if they're committed to the program, the program will have results.... " "Well I think just like any other family, depending on the family background, what the family desires, you know will determine I guess the amount of emphasis that the child will place into their dual program or the primary language instruction. So if you have for example, if you have a family geared toward a college education and making the necessary steps to ensure that the child goes to college, the child themselves will have a greater awareness also." |
| structured English Immersion | Need to check on child's day-to-day performance Do not think teacher must handle everything | David | "I think they have to be much more involved in their kids' lives and they have to think of this as ... themselves too. It's not like, it's like, 'Okay, you walk out the door and I'm wishing you luck but I don't even know what the hell is even happening with your American education.' And I don't think there is a lot of that. And, you know, you don't have a lot of parents being diligent about looking at ARIES [online student grading system] and saying, 'Well, why is my kid getting this' or ... It's very weird. I don't get the parent contact that I get in a regular classroom." |

Anna: "How interesting. You mean less?"

David: "Yeah, I get much less. I get much less and so I think sometimes there's a couple of things going on. Sometimes some people, parents, think 'Oh, the teacher's God' and they never say anything against the teacher but I also think there's this thing where a lot of parents just think 'Oh, the teacher will do it. The teacher will handle that. And I can just worry about making money or what's going to happen next.' So I don't really think there's a lot of involvement in their kids' education."

Program	Advice	Participant	Example
	Be consistent in support of child; communicate with teachers	Camila	"I am very consistent because what I noticed is that the students need consistency. They need consistency from home as well as from school and they know I'm going to check every single week to see, 'Did your parents sign this? Are you following through on things?' Come time that we meet for conferences 'Well, he said he's doing it.' I said, 'I'm showing you that he's not. I think that has hindered his progress.'"
	Success depends on families' values placed on education and keeping connections		"In a nut shell, I think it's the communication between parents and home and that's one of my jobs here with this particular class is to strengthen that and to be the communication."
	Need dedication to L1 preservation		"Again, I think it is so dependent on the family and the values they place on education and in keeping the connections. The more Americanized, you know the studies, with every generation, they lose the native language and customs. I think it really requires a dedication and an effort."
	Parents should know the school will affirm child's background	Cristina	Cristina: "I think schools can do something, not everything." Anna: "Like what?" Cristina: "I think they can continue to affirm the child's background."
	Communicate with teachers; use online grade book to check performance	Elena	"The parents I would say make sure that you communicate with the teachers. That you gain access to the technology that is available, access to the grade book, access to the course syllabus, to the homework assignments, grading scale, checking to see what your student … having conversations with your kids daily or weekly about what they're learning. What they're struggling with and what they're successes are for the week or the day.
	Talk to children about struggles and successes daily/weekly		
	Preview week's work with children before classes		And then I would say in terms of time management, depending on their level, they might need significant amount of time after school. If you go over the material to review the material, but they also need to preview the material. They need to know, next week we're going to do chapter eight, they should be doing chapter eight the week before, or the weekend before. By the time they get the information, it's not when the teacher tells them in a 50 minute lecture and they don't understand. They need to be going through, using their electronic dictionaries or their book dictionaries and going through the chapters and pulling out all the vocabulary. So that they have a context for what's being said to them."

Glossary

Academic language
A register or style of language used in school contexts; in contrast with language used in other contexts, it is often characterized by precise or technical vocabulary use, complex sentence structures (especially in the written variety), and language functions suited to acquiring and displaying content area knowledge (e.g., explanation, description, argumentation, etc.) (see also pp. 207 and 208).

Balanced (or native) bilingualism
Proficient knowledge and use of two languages; often bilinguals do not need to use their two languages in the same context so one language may be dominant in a given context.

Bilingual first language acquisition
Language learning situation in which two (or more) languages are learned simultaneously or successively very early in life; the individual acquires two *first* languages.

Codeswitching
The act of switching between languages either within a sentence or across sentence boundaries; parallel codeswitching can occur across speakers (e.g., child maintains English in reply to Korean-speaking parent; each comprehends the other) (see also p. 21).

Circumstantial bilingualism
Two or more languages may be acquired not from choice but because the dominant societal language (acting as input for a second language) differs from an individual's first language (e.g., Ortega, 2013a; see also p. 177).

Dual-language programming
Instruction designed to foster literacy and content learning in two languages. An alternative to the term bilingual education; this term is increasing in popularity in the United States possibly in response to the controversial status of bilingual education that has been perceived to offer substandard education.

Extended discourse
Language that is organized beyond the level of the sentence into conventional or predictable formats such as narration (i.e., storytelling), conversational routines, expository (i.e., informational) structures.

Foreign language
An additional language acquired without exposure to the society speaking the language; learned primarily from exposure to instruction in a classroom context.

Heritage language
A language acquired as either a first or second language and spoken by family or, in some instances, that was spoken by more distant ancestors.

Immersion
An approach to language instruction that requires the learner to be extensively (sometimes exclusively) exposed to the target additional language rather than learning the additional language through instruction in a first language.

Immigrant language
A language spoken by individuals who originate from countries whose citizens speak first languages that differ from those of citizens in the receiving country.

Indigenous language
A language spoken by individuals whose ancestors were the original inhabitants of a country.

Instrumental motivation
An orientation to or rationale for language learning that focuses on the gains to the individual in terms of occupation, societal position, wealth etc. (e.g., Gardner, 1985; see also pp. 13 and 148).

Integrative motivation
An orientation to or rationale for language learning that focuses on interpersonal gains such as affiliation with the speakers of a language and their culture (e.g., Gardner, 1985; see also pp. 148–150).

Investment
An extended metaphor for understanding the rewards to language acquisition that may come at personal cost in terms of time, money, effort, emotional commitments etc. in return for perceived benefits such as greater job and income opportunities, personal enrichment such as cultural capital, travel, and academic, cognitive, and metalinguistic advantages (e.g., Norton, 2010; see also pp. 10 and 151–153).

Lingua franca
A language that different communities or societies may utilize in order to communicate when in contact with each other but which may not be the first language of either.

Linguistic repertoire
The collection of languages a child or family knows and uses, as well as the individual's skills in different modalities (e.g., listening, speaking, reading, and writing), and knowledge of how to use language in different contexts (e.g., pragmatics).

Majority language
The language of the dominant group in a society; either a numerical dominance or a political dominance.

Metalinguistic abilities
The ability to reflect on language; consciously manipulate features of a language.

Metacognitive abilities
The ability to reflect on one's own thinking, beliefs, and knowledge states.

Minority language
The language of a non-dominant (politically, numerically) group in society; can be an indigenous or immigrant language.

Monolingualism
Knowledge and use of a single language (e.g., English-only speakers).

Multilingualism
Knowledge and use of two or more languages (see also pp. 11 and 74).

Pragmatics
The socially appropriate use of language (i.e., language conventions) in different contexts.

Phonology
The sound system of a language.

Polyglot
An individual who knows and uses multiple languages (used in the study reported here to denote children or parents who speak more than three languages).

Sequential bilingualism
The acquisition of an additional language after the acquisition of the first language is (largely) completed.

Social justice
An orientation toward civic life that shows an awareness of and commitment to diversity, inclusion, and redressing inequities in modern society due to differences in race, ethnicity, immigration status, religion, wealth, etc. (see also pp. 3 and 214).

Submersion
Like immersion, the language learner is exposed largely or exclusively to the second language, but the individuals' first language has a minority status and the second language erodes the first language resulting in a *subtractive* rather than an *additive* form of bilingualism (e.g., Lyster and Genesee, 2013; see also pp. 201 and 209).

Successive monolingualism
The first language is lost to be fully replaced by the second language; individuals function as monolinguals knowing and using only one language by the time their first language is replaced by the second language.

Syntax
The structure of sentences; required word order of a language.

Transitional Spaces
Use of out-of-school institutions that may bridge the distance between community language practices and formal schooling language practices (e.g., Alvarez, 2014; see also pp. 216–217).

Translanguaging
A set of practices in which individuals can use their knowledge of two or more languages for complex, strategic purposes (e.g., interpret or translate for others, switch between languages for emphasis) (see also p. 197).

Trilingualism
Knowledge and use of three languages.

References

Adesope, O. O., Lavin, T., Thompson, T., and Ungerleider, C. (2010). A systematic review and meta-analysis of the cognitive correlates of bilingualism. *Review of Educational Research*, 80, 207–245.

Alba, R., Logan, J., Lutz, A., and Stults, B. (2002). Only English by the third generation? Loss and preservation of the mother tongue among the grandchildren of contemporary immigrants. *Demography*, 39(3), 467–484.

Alvarez, S. P. (2014). Nuestros Sonidos: A Case Study of Bilingual Music and Play among Primary-school Age Heritage Language Learners. Master's thesis. University of Kentucky, Lexington, Kentucky.

Ardasheva, Y., Tretter, T. R., and Kinny, M. (2012). English language learners and academic achievement: Revisiting the threshold hypothesis. *Language Learning*, 62(3), 769–812.

Ash, K. (March 5, 2014). Calif. Bill would repeal bilingual-education restrictions. *Education Week*.

Au, T. K. F., Oh, J. S., Knightly, L. M., Jun, S. A., and Romo, L. F. (2008). Salvaging a childhood language. *Journal of Memory and Language*, 58(4), 998–1011.

Baker, C. (2011). *Foundations of Bilingual Education and Bilingualism* (5th ed.). Bristol, England: Multilingual Matters.

Bailey, A. L. (2010). Implications for instruction and assessment. In M. Shatz and L. Wilkinson (Eds), *The Education of English Language Learners* (pp. 222–247). New York: Guilford Press.

(2011). Unpublished data. University of California, Los Angles.

Bailey, A. L., and Carroll, P. (2015). Assessment of English language learners in the era of new academic content standards. *Review of Research in Education*, 39, 253–294.

Bailey, A. L., and Heritage, M. (2014). The role of language learning progressions in improved instruction and assessment of english language learners. *TESOL Quarterly*, 48(3), 480–506.

Bailey, A. L., and Kelly, K. R., (2013). Home language survey practices in the initial identification of English learners in the U.S. *Educational Policy*, 27(5), 770–804.

Bailey, A. L., and Martínez, F.-J., (2010). How do English-only and Bilingual Teachers Facilitate the Science and Language Learning of ELL Students? Paper presented at the American Educational Research Association Annual Conference, Denver, CO.

Bailey, A. L., and Orellana, M. F. (2015). Adolescent development and everyday language practices: Implications for the academic literacy of multilingual learners. In D. Molle, E. Sato, T. Boals, and C. D. Hedgspeth (Eds), *Multilingual Learners and Academic Literacies: Sociocultural Contexts of Literacy Development in Adolescents* (pp. 53–74). New York: Routledge.

Bailey, A. L., Osipova, A. V., and Kelly, K. R., (2015). Language development. In E. Anderman and L. Corno (Eds), *Handbook of Educational Psychology* (pp. 199–212). American Psychological Association.

Bailey, A. L., Moughamian, A. C., and Dingle, M. (2008). The contribution of Spanish language narration to the assessment of early academic performance of Latino students. In A. K. McCabe, A. L. Bailey, and G. Melzi (Eds), *Spanish-language Narration and Literacy: Culture, Cognition, and Emotion.* (pp. 296–331) New York: Cambridge University Press.

Bailey, A. L., Zwass, R., and Mistry, R. (2013, April). *Characterizing Language Attitudes of 4–5-Year-Old Dual-Language Immersion Students and Their Peers in English-Only Instruction.* Poster presented at the Biennial Conference of the Society for Research on Child Development, Seattle, WA.

Bain, B., and Yu, A. (1980). Cognitive consequences of raising children bilingually: One parent, one language. *Canadian Journal of Psychology/Revue canadienne de psychologie*, 34(4), 304–313.

Ball, M. J. (Ed.) (2008). *Clinical Sociolinguistics* (Vol. 15). New York: John Wiley and Sons.

Baquedano-López, P., Alexander, R. A., and Hernandez, S. J. (2013). Equity issues in parental and community involvement in schools: What teacher educators need to know. *Review of Research in Education*, 37(1), 149–182.

Barkley, R. A. (1997). Behavioral inhibition, sustained attention, and executive functions: Constructing a unifying theory of ADHD. *Psychological Bulletin*, 121, 65–94.

Barnett, W. S., Yarosz, D. J., Thomas, J., Jung, K., and Blanco, D. (2007). Two-way and monolingual English immersion in preschool education: An experimental comparison. *Early Childhood Research Quarterly*, 22(3), 277–293.

Barron-Hauwaert, S. (2004). *Language Strategies for Bilingual Families: The One-Parent-One-Language Approach* (Vol. 7). Clevedon, England: Multilingual Matters.

Barth, R. (2003). *Lessons Learned.* Thousand Oaks, CA: Corwin Press.

Baum, S., and Titone, D. (2014). Moving toward a neuroplasticity view of bilingualism, executive control, and aging. *Applied Psycholinguistics*, 35(05), 857–894.

Ben-Zeev, S. (1977). The influence of bilingualism on cognitive strategy and cognitive development. *Child Development*, 1009–1018.

Berkeley, R., and Vij, S. (2008). Right to divide. *Faith Schools and Community Cohesion. London: The Runnymede Trust.*

Bialystok, E. (1991). *Language Processing in Bilingual Children* (1st ed.). Cambridge University Press.

(1997). The structure of age: In search of barriers to second language acquisition. *Second Language Research*, 13(2), 116–137.

(2001). *Bilingualism in Development: Language, Literacy, and Cognition.* New York: Cambridge University Press.

(2013). The impact of bilingualism on language and literacy development. In T. K. Bhatia and W. C. Ritchie (Eds), *The Handbook of Bilingualism and Multilingualism* (pp. 624–648). New York: John Wiley and Sons.

Bialystok, E., Luk, G., and Kwan, E. (2005). Bilingualism, biliteracy, and learning to read: Interactions among languages and writing systems. *Scientific Studies of Reading*, 9, 43–61.

Bialystok, E., and Martin, M. (2004). Attention and inhibition in bilingual children: Evidence from the dimensional change card sort task. *Developmental Science*, 7, 325–339.

Bialystok, E., and Peets, K. F. (2010). Bilingualism and cognitive linkages: Learning to read in different languages. In M. Shatz and L. C. Wilkinson (Eds), *The Education of English Language Learners: Research to Practice* (pp. 133–151). New York: Guilford Press.

Bialystok, E., Peets, K. F., and Moreno, S. (2014). Producing bilinguals through immersion education: Development of metalinguistic awareness. *Applied Psycholinguistics*, 35(01), 177–191.

Bialystok, E., Craik, F. I., Green, D. W., and Gollan, T. H. (2009). Bilingual minds. *Psychological Science in the Public Interest*, 10(3), 89–129.

BI-SLI Poland Studies. Website retrieved August 1, 2013, from http://psychologia.pl/bi-sli pl/studies.html

Bird, E., Cleave, P., Trudeau, N., Thordardottir, E., Sutton, A., and Thorpe, A. (2005). The language abilities of bilingual children with Down syndrome. *American Journal of Speech-Language Pathology*, 14(3), 187–199.

Bjork-Willen, P. (2008). Routine trouble: How preschool children participate in multilingual instruction. *Applied Linguistics*, 29(4), 555–577.

Brown, D. H. (2000). *Principles of Language Learning and Teaching* (4th ed.). New York: Addison Wesley Longman, Inc.

Bruner, J. (1985). *Child's Talk: Learning to Use Language*. Oxford University Press. (1990). *Acts of Meaning*. Harvard University Press.

Budach, G. (2014). Educational trajectories at the crossroads: The making and unmaking of multilingual communities of learners. *Multilingua*, 33(5–6), DOI: 10.1515/multi-2014-0027.

Bunch, G. C. (2013). Pedagogical language knowledge preparing mainstream teachers for English learners in the new standards era. *Review of Research in Education*, 37(1), 298–341.

Callahan, R. M., and Gándara, P. C. (2014). Contextualizing bilingualism in the labor market: New destinations, established enclaves and the information age. In R. M. Callahan and P. C. Gándara (Eds), *The Bilingual Advantage: Language, Literacy and the US Labor Market* (Vol. 99) (pp. 3–15). Clevedon, England: Multilingual Matters.

Camarota, S. A. (2012, August). *Immigrants in the United States, 2010: A Profile of America's Foreign-Born Population*. Center for Immigration studies. Website retrieved September 5, 2013, from: http://www.cis.org/2012-profile-of-americas-foreign-born-population

Carhill, A., Suárez-Orozco, C., and Páez, M. (2008). Explaining English language proficiency among adolescent immigrant students. *American Educational Research Journal*, 45(4), 1155–1179.

Carlo, M. S., August, D., Mclaughlin, B., Snow, C., Dressler, C., Lippman, D., and … White, C. E. (2008). Closing the gap: Addressing the vocabulary needs of English-language learners in bilingual and mainstream classrooms. *Journal of Education*, 189(1/2), 57–76.

Carroll, J. B., and S. Sapon. (1959). *Modern Language Aptitude Test (MLAT)*. New York: The Psychological Corporation.

Carroll, J. B. (1962). The prediction of success in intensive foreign language training. In Glaser, R. (Ed.), *Training Research and Education*. (pp. 87–136) University of Pittsburgh Press.

Castro, D. C., Páez, M. M., Dickinson, D. K., and Frede, E. (2011). Promoting language and literacy in young dual language learners: Research, practice, and policy. *Child Development Perspectives*, 5(1), 15–21.

Center for Applied Linguistics (2011). *Directory of Two-Way Bilingual Immersion Programs in the U.S.* Retrieved September 28, 2013, from http://www.cal.org/twi/directory

Cheatham, G. A., Santos, R. M., and Ro, Y. E. (2007). Home language acquisition and retention for young children with special needs. *Young Exceptional Children*, 11(1), 27–39.

Chen, D., Klein, M. D., and Osipova, A. V. (2012). Two is better than one! In defense of home language maintenance and bilingualism for young children with disabilities. In R. M. Santos, G. A. Cheatham, and L. Duran (Eds), *Supporting Young Children Who are Dual Language Learners with or at-risk for Disabilities (Young Exceptional Children Monograph Series No. 14)*, (pp.133–147). Missoula, MT: The Division of Early Childhood of the Council for Exceptional Children.

Cheng, L. R., and Butler, K. (1989). Code-switching: A natural phenomenon vs language 'deficiency'. *World Englishes*, 8(3), 293–309.

Chevalier, S. (2013). Caregiver responses to the language mixing of a young trilingual. *Multilingua: Journal of Cross-Cultural and Interlanguage Communication*, 32(1), 1–32.

(2012). Active trilingualism in early childhood: The motivating role of caregivers in interaction. *International Journal of Multilingualism*, 9(4), 437–454.

Cho, G. (2000). The role of heritage language in social interactions and relationships: Reflections from a language minority group. *Bilingual Research Journal*, 24(4), 369–384.

Churchill, E. (2008). A dynamic systems account of learning a word: From ecology to form relations. *Applied Linguistics*, 29(3), 339–358.

Clément, R., Dörnyei, Z., and Noels, K. A. (1994). Motivation, self-confidence, and group cohesion in the foreign language classroom. *Language Learning*, 44(3), 417–448.

Clément, R., Gardner, R. C., and Smythe, P. C. (1977). Motivational variables in second language acquisition: A study of Francophones learning English. *Canadian Journal of Behavioural Science/Revue canadienne des sciences du comportement*, 9(2), 123–133.

Cline, Z., and Necochea, J. (2003). Specially designed academic instruction in English (SDAIE): More than just good instruction. *Multicultural Perspectives*, 5(1), 18–24.

Coady, M., Harper, C., and de Jong, E. (2011). From preservice to practice: Mainstream elementary teacher beliefs of preparation and efficacy with English language learners in the state of Florida. *Bilingual Research Journal*, 34(2), 223–239.

Cobo-Lewis, A. B., Eilers, R. E., Pearson, B. Z., and Umbel, V. C. (2002). Interdependence of Spanish and English knowledge in language and literacy among bilingual children. In D. K. Oller and R. E. Eilers (Eds), *Language and Literacy in Bilingual Children* (pp. 118–134). Clevedon, England: Multilingual Matters.

Coleman, R., and Goldenberg, C. (2009). What does research say about effective practices for English learners? Introduction and part I: Oral language proficiency. *Kappa Delta Pi Record*, 46(1), 10–16.

Collier, V. P. (1989). How long? A synthesis of research on academic achievement in a second language. *TESOL quarterly*, 23(3), 509–531.

(1992). A synthesis of studies examining long-term language minority student data on academic achievement. *Bilingual Research Journal*, 16(1–2), 187–212.

(1995). Acquiring a second language for school. *Directions in Language and Education*, 1(4), 1–14.

Collier, V. P., and Thomas, W. P. (2004). The astounding effectiveness of dual language education for all. *NABE Journal of Research and practice*, 2(1), 1–20.

Common Core State Standards Initiative (2010a). Common core state standards for English language arts and literacy in history/social studies, science, and technical subjects. Retrieved from http://www.corestandards.org/assets/CCSSI_ELA%20 Standards.pdf

Common Core State Standards Initiative. (2010b). Common core state standards for mathematics. Retrieved from http://www.corestandards.org/assets/CCSSI_ Math%20Standards.pdf

Compton-Lilly, C., Kim J., Quast, E., Tran, S., and Shedrow, S. (2014). Transnational Literacy Practices in Immigrant Families. Conference paper presented at National Council of Teachers of English, Washington, DC.

Cook, V. (2008). Multi-competence: Black hole or wormhole for second language acquisition research. In Z. Han (Ed.), *Understanding Second Language Process*, 25 (pp. 16–26). Clevedon, England: Multilingual Matters.

Cooper, T. C. (1987). Foreign language study and SAT-Verbal scores. *Modern Language Journal*, 71 (4), 381–387.

Costigan, C. L., and Dokis, D. P. (2006). Relations between parent-child acculturation differences and adjustment within immigrant Chinese families. *Child Development*, 77, 1252–1267.

Crawford, J. (2003). *Making sense of census 2000*. Retrieved March 30, 2010, from http://www.languagepolicy.net/excerpts/makingsense.html

(2000). *At War with Diversity: US Language Policy in an Age of Anxiety* (Vol. 25). Clevedon, UK: Multilingual Matters.

Crosnoe, R. (2009). Family-school connections and the transitions of low-income youth and English language learners from middle school into high school. *Developmental Psychology*, 45(4), 1061–1076. DOI:10.1037/a0016131.

Cummins, J. (1979). Cognitive/academic language proficiency, linguistic interdependence, the optimal age question and some other matters. *Wording Papers on Bilingualism*, 19, 197–205.

(1998). Immersion education for the millennium: What have we learned from 30 years of research on second language immersion? In M. R. Childs and R. M. Bostwick (Eds), *Learning through Two Languages: Research and Practice. Second Katoh Gakuen International Symposium on Immersion and Bilingual Education* (pp. 34–47). Katoh Gakuen, Japan.

(2000). *Language, Power, and Pedagogy: Bilingual Children in the Crossfire*. Clevedon, England: Multilingual Matters.

de Bruin, A., Treccani, B., and Della Sala, S. (2015). Cognitive advantage in bilingualism: An example of publication bias? *Psychological Science*, 26(1), 99–107.

De Houwer, A. (2007). Parental language input patterns and children's bilingual use. *Applied Psycholinguistics*, 28(3), 411–424.

de Jong, E. D., and Howard, E. (2009). Integration in two-way immersion education: Equalising linguistic benefits for all students. *International Journal of Bilingual Education and Bilingualism*, 12(1), 81–99.

de Jong, E. (2011). *Foundations for Multilingualism in Education*. Philadelphia, PA: Caslon Publishing.

DePalma, R., and Teasley, C. (2013). Constructing Spanish. In D. B. Napier and S. Majhanovich (Eds), *Education, Dominance and Identity* (pp. 101–118). Rotterdam, the Netherlands: SensePublishers.

Dickinson, D. K., McCabe, A., Clark–Chiarelli, N., and Wolf, A. (2004). Cross language transfer of phonological awareness in low-income Spanish and English bilingual preschool children. *Applied Psycholinguistics*, 25(03), 323–347.

Directorate General for Education and Culture. (2006). Europeans and their Languages. *Eurobarometer, 243*. Brussels: European Commission.

Dixon, Q. L., Zhao, J., Shin, J.-Y., Wu, S., Su, J.-H., Burgess-Brigham, R., Unal Gezar, M., and Snow, C. (2012). What we know about second language acquisition: A synthesis from four perspectives. *Review of Educational Research*, 82, 5–60.

Döpke, S. (1992). A bilingual child's struggle to comply with the 'one parent-one language' rule. *Journal of Multilingual and Multicultural Development*, 13(6), 467–485.

   (1998). Can the principle of 'one person – one language' be disregarded as unrealistically elitist? *Australian Review of Applied Linguistics,* 21(1), 41–56.

Dörnyei, Z. (1990). Conceptualizing motivation in foreign-language learning. *Language Learning*, 40(1), 45–78.

Dubiner, D. (2010). The impact of incipient triinguality on the socio-affective development of Jewish elementary school children in Israel. *Journal of Multilingual and Multicultural Development*, 31(1), 1–12.

Duursma, E., Romero-Contreras, S., Szuber, A., Proctor, P., Snow, C., August, D., and Calderón, M. (2007). The role of home literacy and language environment on bilinguals' English and Spanish vocabulary development. *Applied Psycholinguistics*, 28(01), 171–190.

Echevarria, J., Vogt, M. E., and Short, D. (2004). *Making Content Comprehensible for English Language Learners: The SIOP Model* (2nd ed.). Boston, MA: Pearson/Allyn and Bacon.

Edgin, J. O., Kumar, A. A., Spanò, G. G., and Nadel, L. L. (2011). Neuropsychological effects of second language exposure in Down syndrome. *Journal of Intellectual Disability Research*, 55(3), 351–356.

Eksner, H. J., and Orellana, M. F. (2012). Shifting in the zone: Latina/o child language brokers and the co-construction of knowledge. *Ethos*, 40(2), 196–220.

Ellis, N. C., and Larsen-Freeman, D. (2009). *Language as a Complex Adaptive System*. Malden, MA: Wiley-Blackwell.

Ellis, R., Johnson, K. E., and Shin, S. J. (2002). Birth order and the language experience of bilingual children. *TESOL Quarterly*, 36(1), 103–113.

Epstein, J. L. (2001). *School and Family Partnerships: Preparing Educators and Improving Schools*. Boulder, CO: Westview Press.

Epstein, J. L., and Sheldon, S. B. (2006). Moving forward: Ideas for research on school, family, and community partnerships. In C. F. Conrad and R. C. Serlin (Eds), *The*

SAGE Handbook for Research in Education: Engaging Ideas and Enriching Inquiry (pp. 117–138). Thousand Oaks, CA: Sage Publications, Inc.

Erard, M. (January 14, 2012). Are we really monolingual? *The New York Times.*

Erdos, C., Genesee, F., Savage, R., and Haigh, C. (2014). Predicting risk for oral and written language learning difficulties in students educated in a second language. *Applied Psycholinguistics,* 35(02), 371–398.

Espinosa, L. (2013). Assessment of young English-language learners. In. C. A. Chapelle (Ed.), *The Encyclopedia of Applied Linguistics.* Oxford: Blackwell.

Espinosa, L. M. (2008, January). *Challenging Common Myths about Young English Language Learners* (Policy Brief No. 8). New York: Foundation for Child Development.

—— (2013). PreK-3rd: Challenging common myths about dual language learners: An update to the Seminal 2008 Report. (Policy to Action Brief No. 10, August). New York: Foundation for Child Development.

Esposito, A. G., Baker-Ward, L., and Mueller, S. T. (2013). Interference suppression vs. response inhibition: An explanation for the absence of a bilingual advantage in preschoolers' Stroop task performance. *Cognitive Development,* 28(4), 354–363.

Estrada, P. (2014). English learner curricular streams in four middle schools: Triage in the trenches. *The Urban Review,* 46(4), 535–573.

Fail, H., Thompson, J., and Walker, G. (2004). Belonging, identity and third culture kids' life: Histories of former international school students. *Journal of Research in International Education,* 3(3), 319–338.

Faulkner-Bond, M., Waring, S., Forte, E., Crenshaw, R. L., Tindle, K., and Belknap, B. (2012). *Language Instruction Educational Programs (LIEPs): A Review of the Foundational Literature,* Washington, DC: U.S. Department of Education, Office of Planning, Evaluation and Policy Development, Policy and Program Studies Service.

Fenson, L., Dale, P. S., Reznick, J. S., Bates, E., Thal, D. J., and Pethick, S. J. (1994). Variability in early communicative development. *Monographs of the Society for Research in Child Development,* 59 (Serial No. 242).

Feuer, A. (2009). School's out for the summer: a cross-cultural comparison of second language learning in informal settings. *International Journal of Bilingual Education and Bilingualism,* 12(6), 651–665.

Fitzgerald, J. (1995). English-as-a-second-language learners' cognitive reading processes: A review of research in the United States. *Review of Educational Research,* 65(2), 145–190.

Freed, B. F., Segalowitz, N., and Dewey, D. P. (2004). Context of learning and second language fluency in French: Comparing regular classroom, study abroad, and intensive domestic immersion programs. *Studies in Second Language Acquisition,* 26(02), 275–301.

Friedman, N. P., Haberstick, B. C., Willcutt, E. G., Miyake, A., Young S. E., Corley, R. P., and Hewitt, J. C. (2007). Greater attention problems during childhood predict poorer executive functioning in late adolescence. *Psychological Science,* 18, 893–900.

Gabryś-Barker, D., and Otwinowska, A. (2012). Multilingual learning stories: Threshold, stability and change. *International Journal of Multilingualism,* 9(4), 367–384.

Gándara, P., Maxwell-Jolly, J., and Driscoll, A. (2005). *Listening to Teachers of English Language Learners: A Survey of California Teachers' Challenges, Experiences, and Professional Development Needs.* UC Berkeley: University of California Linguistic Minority Research Institute.

Gándara, P., Oseguera, L., Huber, L. P., Locks, A., Ee, J., and Molina, D. (2013). *Making Education Work for Latinas in the US.* Commissioned by the Eva Longoria Foundation. Los Angeles: Civil Rights Project, UCLA. Retrieved Jan 12, 2014 http://civilrightsproject.ucla.edu/research/college-access/underrepresented-students/making-education-work-for-latinas-in-the-u.s/gandara-longoria-report-2013.pdf

Gardner, R. C. (1985). *Social Psychology and Language Learning: The Role of Attitude and Motivation.* London: Edward Arnold.

Gardner, R. C. and MacIntyre, P. D. (1991). An instrumental motivation in language study. *Studies in Second Language Acquisition,* 13(01), 57–72.

Gardner, R. C. (2007). Motivation and second language acquisition. *Porta Lingarium,* 8, 9–20.

Gathercole, V. C. M. (2014). Bilingualism matters: One size does not fit all. *International Journal of Behavioral Development,* 38(4), 359–366.

Gathercole, V. C. M., and Thomas, E. M. (2009). Bilingual first-language development: Dominant language takeover, threatened minority language take-up. *Bilingualism: Language and Cognition,* 12(2), 213–237.

Genesee, F. (1998). French immersion in Canada. In J. Edwards (Ed.), *Language in Canada* (pp. 305–327). Cambridge University Press.

(Ed.) (1999). *Program Alternatives for Linguistically Diverse Students.* Santa Cruz, CA: Center for Research on Education, Diversity and Excellence.

(Ed.) (2006). *Educating English Language Learners: A Synthesis of Research Evidence.* Cambridge: Cambridge University Press.

(2008). Early dual language learning. *Zero to Three,* 29, 17–23.

(2008), Dual language in the global village. In T. W. Fortune and D. J. Tedick (Eds), *Pathways to Multilingualism: Evolving Perspectives on Immersion Education* (Vol. 66) (pp. 22–58). Clevedon, England: Multilingual Matters.

Genesee, F., and Gándara, P. (1999). Bilingual education programs: A cross-national perspective. *Journal of Social Issues,* 55(4), 665–685.

Genesee, F., and Lindholm-Leary, K. (2008). Dual language education in Canada and the USA. In *Encyclopedia of Language and Education* (pp. 1696–1706). Springer US.

Genesee, F., Lindholm-Leary, K., Saunders, W., and Christian, D. (2005). English language learners in US schools: An overview of research findings. *Journal of Education for Students Placed at Risk,* 10(4), 363–385.

Genesee, F., Lindholm-Leary, K. J., Saunders, W., and Christian, D. (2006). *Educating English Language Learners: A Synthesis of Empirical Evidence.* New York: Cambridge University Press.

Genesee, F., Nicoladis, E., and Paradis, J. (1995). Language differentiation in early bilingual development. *Journal of Child Language,* 22(03), 611–631.

Goldenberg, C. (2008). Teaching English language learners: What the research does – and does not – say. *American Educator,* 32(2), 8–23 and 42–43.

Goldring, R., Gray, L., and Bitterman, A. (2013). Characteristics of Public and Private Elementary and Secondary School Teachers in the United States: Results from the 2011–12 Schools and Staffing Survey. First Look. NCES 2013–314. *National Center for Education Statistics.*

Gómez, L., Freeman, D., and Freeman, Y. (2005). Dual language education: A promising 50–50 model. *Bilingual Research Journal,* 29(1), 145–164.

Goodwyn, S. W., Acredolo, L. P., and Brown, C. A. (2000). Impact of symbolic gesturing on early language development. *Journal of Nonverbal Behavior*, 24(2), 81–103.

Grosjean, F. (1982). *Life with Two Languages: An Introduction to Bilingualism*. Harvard University Press.

(2002). An interview of François Grosjean on bilingualism. *Retrieved September 10, 2013, from* http://www.francoisgrosjean.ch/interview_en.html

(2009). What parents want to know about bilingualism. *The Bilingual Family Newsletter*, 26(4), 1–6.

(2011). Myths about bilingualism. Retrieved September 5, 2013 from www.francois-grosjean.ch/interview_en.html

Gutierrez-Clellen, V. F. (1999). Language choice in intervention with bilingual children. *American Journal of Speech-Language Pathology*, 8, 291–302.

Gutierrez-Clellen, V. F., and Peña, E. (2001). Dynamic assessment of diverse children: A tutorial. *Language, Speech, and Hearing Services in Schools*, 32, 212–224.

Gutierrez-Clellen, V. F., Simon-Cereijido, G., and Wagner, C. (2008). Bilingual children with language impairment: A comparison with monolinguals and second language learners. *Applied Psycholinguistics*, 29, 3–19.

Gutierrez-Clellen, V. F., Simon-Cereijido, G., and Sweet, M. (2012). Predictors of second language acquisition in Latino children with specific language impairment. *American Journal of Speech-Language Pathology*, 21, 64–77.

Hakuta, K., Butler, Y. G., and Witt, D. (2000). *How Long Does It Take English Learners to Attain Proficiency?* University of California Linguistic Minority Research Institute Policy Report 2000–1. University of California, Santa Barbara.

Hambly, C., and Fombonne, E. (2012). The impact of bilingual environments on language development in children with autism spectrum disorders. *Journal of Autism and Developmental Disorders*, 42(7), 1342–1352.

Harris, J. (1995). Where is the child's environment? A group socialization theory of development. *Psychological Review*, 102(3), 458–489.

Hawkins, M. R. (2004). Researching English language and literacy development in schools. *Educational Researcher*, 33(3), 14–25.

Hickey, T. M., and de Mejía, A. M. (2014). Immersion education in the early years: a special issue. *International Journal of Bilingual Education and Bilingualism*, 17(2), 131–143.

Hoff, E. (2006). How social contexts support and shape language development. *Developmental Review*, 26(1), 55–88.

(2009). *Language Development* (4th ed.). Belmont, CA: Wadsworth Cengage Learning.

(2014). Introduction to the special section: Language development in multilingual environments. *International Journal of Behavioral Development*, 38(4), 307–308.

Hoffmann, C., and Ytsma, J. (Eds) (2004). *Trilingualism in Family, School, and Community* (Vol. 43). Clevedon, England: Multilingual Matters.

Hornberger, N. H. (1998). Language policy, language education, language rights: Indigenous, immigrant, and international perspectives. *Language in Society*, 27(04), 439–458.

Horwitz, E. K. (1999). Cultural and situational influences on foreign language learners' beliefs about language learning: a review of BALLI studies. *System*, 27(4), 557–576.

Howard, E. R. (2002). Two-way immersion: A key to global awareness. *Educational Leadership*, 60(2), 62–64.

Howard, E. R., and Christian, D. (2002). *Two-Way Immersion 101: Designing and Implementing a Two-Way Immersion Education Program at the Elementary Level.* Educational Practice Report. Santa Cruz, CA, and Washington, DC: Center for Research on Education, Diversity and Excellence.

Howard, E. R., and Sugarman, J. (2001). *Two-Way Immersion Programs: Features and Statistics* (ERIC Digest EDO-FL-01-01). Washington, DC: ERIC Clearinghouse on Languages and Linguistics. Retrieved from http:/www.cal.org/eric1/digest/0101twi.html

Howard, E. R., Olague, N., and Rogers, D. (2003). *The Dual-Language Program Planner: A Guide for Designing and Implementing Dual-Language Programs.* Santa Cruz, CA, and Washington, DC: Center for Research on Education, Diversity and Excellence.

Howard, E. R., Sugarman, J., and Coburn, C. (2006). *Adapting the Sheltered Instruction Observation Protocol (SIOP) for Two-Way Immersion Education: An Introduction to the TWIOP.* Washington, DC: Center for Applied Linguistics.

Imbens-Bailey, A. L. (1996). Ancestral language acquisition implications for aspects of ethnic identity among Armenian American children and adolescents. *Journal of Language and Social Psychology*, 15(4), 422–443.

    (2000). Language background and ethnic identity: A study of bilingual and English-only speaking children of Armenian descent. In E. Olshtain and G. Harenczyk (Eds), *Language, Identity and Immigration* (pp. 255–269). Jerusalem: Magnes.

Ishizawa, H. (2004). Minority language use among grandchildren in multigenerational households. *Sociological Perspectives*, 47(4), 465–483.

Jozsa, D.-P. (2007). Islam and education in Europe. With special reference to Austria, England, France, Germany and the Netherlands. In R. Jackson, S. Miedema, W. Weisse, and J.-P. Willaime (Eds), *Religion and Education in Europe. Developments, Contexts and Debates* (pp. 67–85). Münster, Germany: Waxmann.

Kagan, O., and Dillon, K. (2008). Issues in heritage language learning in the United States. In N. V. Deusen-Scholl and N. Hornberger (Eds), *Encyclopedia of Language and Education, Volume 4: Second and Foreign Language Education.* (pp. 143–156): New York: Springer.

Kirkpatrick, A. (2008). English as the official working language of the Association of Southeast Asian Nations (ASEAN): Features and strategies. *English Today*, 24(2), 27–34.

Klingner, J. K., Boardman, A. G., Eppolito, A. M., and Schonewise, E. A. (2012). Supporting adolescent English language learners' reading in the content areas. *Learning Disabilities – A Contemporary Journal*, 10(1), 35–64.

Kohnert, K., and Medina, A. (2009). Bilingual children and communication disorders: A 30-year research retrospective. *Seminars in Speech and Language*, 30, 219–233.

Kohnert, K., Yim, D., Nett, K., Kan, P. F., and Duran, L. (2005). Intervention with linguistically diverse preschool children: A focus on developing home language(s). *Language, Speech, and Hearing Services in Schools*, 36(3), 251–263.

Kondo-Brown, K. (Ed.) (2006). *Heritage Language Development: Focus on East Asian Immigrants* (Vol. 32). Amsterdam: John Benjamins Publishing.

Köppe, R. (1996). Language differentiation in bilingual children: The development of grammatical and pragmatic competence. *Linguistics*, 34(5), 927–954.

Krashen, S. D. (1981). *Second Language Acquisition and Second Language Learning*. Oxford: Pergamon.

Krashen, S. (2013). Does SIOP research support SIOP claims? *International Journal of Foreign Language Teaching*, 8(1), 11–24.

Krashen, S., and Brown, C. L. (2005). The ameliorating effects of high socioeconomic status: A secondary analysis. *Bilingual Research Journal*, 29(1), 185–196.

Kremer-Sadlik, T. (2005). To be or not to be bilingual: Autistic children from multilingual families. In J. Cohen, K. T. McAlister, K. Rolstad, and J. MacSwan (Eds), *Proceedings of the 4th International Symposium on Bilingualism* (pp. 1225–1234). Somerville, MA: Cascadilla Press.

Kroll, J. F. (2009). The consequences of bilingualism for the mind and the brain. *Psychological Science in the Public Interest*, 10(3), i–ii.

LaFromboise, T., Coleman, H. L., and Gerton, J. (1993). Psychological impact of biculturalism: evidence and theory. *Psychological Bulletin*, 114(3), 395–413.

Lambert, W. E. (1974). Culture and language as factors in learning and education. In F. E. Aboud and R. D. Mead (Eds), *Cultural Factors in Learning and Education*. Bellingham, WA: Fifth Western Washington Symposium on Learning.

(1975). Culture and language as factors in learning and education. In A. Wolfgang (Ed.), *Education in Immigrant Students*. Toronto: Ontario Institute for Studies in Education.

(1987). An overview of issues in immersion education. In *Studies in Immersion Education: A Collection for U.S. Educators* (pp. 8–30). Sacramento: California State Department of Education.

Lan, Y. C., Torr, J., and Degotardi, S. (2012). Taiwanese mothers' motivations for teaching English to their young children at home. *Child Studies in Diverse Contexts*, 2(2), 133–144.

Landry, R., and Allard, R. (1993). Beyond socially naive bilingual education: The effects of schooling and ethnolinguistic vitality on additive and subtractive bilingualism. In L. Malave (Ed.), Annual Conference Proceeding of the *National Association for Bilingual Education* (pp. 1–30). Washington DC. National Association for Bilingual Education.

Lanza, E. (1997). Language contact in bilingual two-year-olds and code-switching: Language encounters of a different kind? *The International Journal of Bilingualism*, 1(2), 135–162.

(2001). Bilingual first language acquisition: A discourse perspective on language contact in parent–child interaction. In J. Cenoz and F. Genesee (Eds), *Trends in bilingual acquisition* (pp. 201–230). Amsterdam: John Benjamins.

Larsen-Freeman, D. (2011). A complexity theory approach to second language development/acquisition. In D. Atkinson (Ed.), *Alternative Approaches to Second Language Acquisition* (pp. 48–72). London: Routledge.

Leaper, C., Anderson, K. J., and Sanders, P. (1998). Moderators of gender effects on parents' talk to their children: A meta analysis. *Developmental Psychology*, 34, 3–27.

Lee, O., Hart, J. E., Cuevas, P., and Enders, C. (2004). Professional development in inquiry-based science for elementary teachers of diverse student groups. *Journal of Research in Science Teaching*, 41(10), 1021–1043.

Lee, S. J., and Wright, W. E. (2014). The rediscovery of heritage and community language education in the United States. *Review of Research in Education*, 38, 137–165. DOI: 10.3102/0091732X13507546.

Leeman, J., Rabin, L., and Román-Mendoza, E. (2011). Identity and activism in heritage language education. *Modern Language Journal*, 95(4), 481–495.

Leffert, N., Benson, P. L., Scales, P. C., Sharma, A. R., Drake, D. R., and Blyth, D. A. (1998). Developmental assets: Measurement and prediction of risk behaviors among adolescents. *Applied Developmental Science*, 2(4), 209–230.

Li, G. (2006). Biliteracy and trilingual practices in the home context: Case studies of Chinese-Canadian children. *Journal of Early Childhood Literacy*, 6(3), 355–381.

Lindholm-Leary, K. J., and Howard, E. R. (2008). Language development and academic achievement in two-way immersion programs. In T. W. Fortune and D. J. Tedick (Eds), *Pathways to Multilingualism: Evolving Perspectives on Immersion Education* (pp. 177–200). Oxford: Blackwell.

Linquanti, R., and Bailey, A. (2014). *Reprising the Home Language Survey: Summary of a National Working Session on Policies, Practices, and Tools for Identifying Potential English Learners*. Washington, DC: Council of Chief State School Officers.

Linquanti, R., and Cook, H. G. (2013). *Toward a "common definition of English learner": Guidance for states and state assessment consortia in defining and addressing policy and technical issues and options*. Washington, DC: Council of Chief State School Officers.

Lowe, A. S. (1995). *The Effect of the Incorporation of music learning into the second language classroom on the mutual reinforcement of music and language*. Doctoral dissertation, University of Illinois at Urbana-Champaign.

Lucas, T., Villegas, A. M., and Freedson-Gonzalez, M. (2008). Linguistically responsive teacher education preparing classroom teachers to teach English language learners. *Journal of Teacher Education*, 59(4), 361–373.

Luk, G., and Bialystok, E (2008). Common and distinct cognitive bases for reading in English Cantonese bilinguals. *Applied Psycholinguistics*, 29, 269–289.

Lyster, R., and Genesee, F. (2013). Immersion education. In C. A. Chapelle (Ed.), *The Encyclopedia of Applied Linguistics* (pp. 1–7). London: Blackwell.

Mackey, A., Gass, S., and McDonough, K. (2000). How do learners perceive interactional feedback? *Studies in Second Language Acquisition*, 22(04), 471–497.

Malakoff, M., and Hakuta, K. (1991). Translation skill and metalinguistic awareness in bilinguals. In E. Bialystok (Ed.), *Language Processing and Language Awareness by Bilingual Children* (pp. 141–166). Oxford University Press.

Martin-Beltran, M., and Peercy, M. M. (2014). Collaboration to teach English language learners: opportunities for shared teacher learning. *Teachers and Teaching*, (ahead-of-print), 1–17.

Martin-Rhee, M. M., and Bialystok, E. (2008). The development of two types of inhibitory control in monolingual and bilingual children. *Bilingualism: Language and Cognition*, 11, 81–93.

Martínez, R. A. (2010). Spanglish as literacy tool: Toward an understanding of the potential role of Spanish-English code-switching in the development of academic literacy. *Research in the Teaching of English*, 42(2),124–149.

Maslow, A. H. (1943). A theory of human motivation. *Psychological Review*, 50(4), 370–396.

Mayberry, R. I., and Nicoladis, E. (2000). Gesture reflects language development evidence from bilingual children. *Current Directions in Psychological Science*, 9(6), 192–196.

Mayer, J. (2007). Policy Needs: What Federal and State Governments Need from Language Research. In A. L. Bailey (ed.) *The Language Demands of School: Putting Academic English to the Test* (pp. 50–67). New Haven, CT: Yale University Press.

McCabe, A., Tamis-LeMonda, C. S., Bornstein, M. H., Cates, C. B., Golinkoff, R., Guerra, A. W., ... and Song, L. (2013). Multilingual Children. *Social Policy Report*, 27(4).

McCormick, L., Loeb, D., and Schiefelbusch, R. L. (2003). *Supporting Children with Communication Difficulties in Inclusive Settings* (2nd ed.). Boston: Allyn and Bacon.

McDonald, M. A. (2005). The integration of social justice in teacher education: Dimensions of prospective teachers' opportunities to learn. *Journal of Teacher Education*, 56(5), 418–435.

McKay, S. L., and Wong, S. L. C. (1996). Multiple discourses, multiple identities: Investment and agency in second-language learning among Chinese adolescent immigrant students. *Harvard Educational Review*, 66(3), 577–609.

McLaughlin, B. (1992). *Myths and Misconceptions about Second Language Learning: What Every Teacher Needs to Unlearn*. Santa Cruz, CA: National Center for Research on Cultural Diversity and Second Language Learning.

McWayne, C. M., Fantuzzo, J. W., and McDermott, P. A. (2004). Preschool competency in context: an investigation of the unique contribution of child competencies to early academic success. *Developmental Psychology*, 40(4), 633–645.

Mora, J. K. (2008). *Metalinguistic Transfer in Biliteracy Instruction: Theory, Research and Effective Practice*. CABE Two-way Bilingual Immersion Conference, Newport Beach, CA.

Morales, A., and Hanson, W. E. (2005). Language brokering: An integrative review of the literature. *Hispanic Journal of Behavioral Sciences*, 27(4), 471–503.

Morton, J. B. (2014). Sunny review casts a foreboding shadow over status quo bilingual advantage research. *Applied Psycholinguistics*, 35(05), 929–931.

Moughamian, A. C., Rivera, M. O., and Francis, D. J. (2009). *Instructional Models and Strategies for Teaching English Language Learners*. Portsmouth, NH: RMC Research Corporation, Center on Instruction.

Mundy, P., Kasari, C., Sigman, M., and Ruskin, E. (1995). Nonverbal communication and early language acquisition in children with Down syndrome and in normally developing children. *Journal of Speech and Hearing Research*, 38(1), 157–167.

Muris, P., and Ollendick, T. H. (2015). Children who are anxious in silence: A review on selective mutism, the new anxiety disorder in DSM-5. *Clinical Child and Family Psychology Review*, 1–19. Online. DOI: 10.1007/s10567-015-0181-y

Mushi, S. L. P. (2002). Acquisition of multiple languages among children of immigrant families: Parents' role in the home-school language pendulum. *Early Child Development and Care*, 172, 517–530.

National Center for Education Statistics. (2002). *1999–2000 Schools and Staffing Survey: Overview of the Data for Public, Private, Public Charter and Bureau of Indian Affairs Elementary and Secondary Schools.* Washington, DC: U.S. Department of Education, Office of Educational Research and Improvement.

National Center for Education Statistics. (2014). Common Core of Data (CCD), "Local Education Agency Universe Survey," 2011–12. Digest of Education Statistics 2013, Table 204–20. Percentage of public school students who are English language learners (ELL), by state: 2011–12. *The Condition of Education 2014* (NCES 2014–083). Retrieved from http://nces.ed.gov/programs/digest/d13/tables/dt13_204.20.asp

National Clearinghouse for English Language Acquisition (2008). *Educating English Language Learners: Building Teacher Capacity.* Washington, DC: Author. Retrieved from http://www.ncela.us/files/uploads/3/EducatingELLs BuildingTeacherCapacityVol1.pdf

National Clearinghouse for English Language Acquisition (2011). What language instruction educational programs do states use to serve English learners? *NCELA Fact Sheet.* Washington, DC: Author. Retrieved from http://www.ncela.us/files/uploads/5/LIEPs0406BR.pdf

National Collaborative on Diversity in the Teaching Force (October, 2004). *Assessment of diversity in America's teaching force: A call to action.* Washington, DC: National Education Association. Retrieved from http://www.ate1.org/pubs/uploads/diversityreport.pdf

National Education Association (2011). *Preparing 21st Century Students for a Global Society: An Educator's Guide to the "Four Cs."* Retrieved from http://www.nea.org/assets/docs/A-Guide-to-Four-Cs.pdf

National Heritage Language Resource Center. (2009). *The Heritage Language Learner Survey: Report on the Preliminary Results.* University of California, Los Angeles. Retrieved from http://www.international.ucla.edu/media/files/paper.pdf

NGSS Lead States (2013). *Next Generation Science Standards. For States, by States.* Washington, DC: The National Academies Press.

Nicoladis, E., Pika, S., and Marentette, P. (2009). Do French–English bilingual children gesture more than monolingual children? *Journal of Psycholinguistic Research,* 38(6), 573–585.

Norton Peirce, B. (1995), Social identity, investment, and language learning. *TESOL Quarterly,* 29, 9–31.

Norton, B. (1997). Language, identity and the ownership of English. *TESOL Quarterly,* 31(3), 409–429.

(2000). *Identity and Language Learning: Gender, Ethnicity and Educational Change.* Harlow: Pearson Education.

(2010). Language and identity. In N. Hornberger and Mackay, S. (Eds), *Sociolinguistics and Language Education* (pp. 349–369). Clevedon, England: Multilingual Matters.

Office of Head Start (2010). *Revisiting and Updating the Multicultural Principles for Head Start Programs Serving Children Ages Birth to Five.* Washington, DC: Administration for Children and Families, retrieved from http://eclkc.ohs.acf.hhs.gov/hslc/hs/resources/ECLKC_Bookstore/PDFs/Revisiting%20Multicultural%20Principles%20for%20Head%20Start_English.pdf

Oh, J. S., and Fuligni, A. J. (2010). The role of heritage language development in the ethnic identity and family relationships of adolescents from immigrant backgrounds. *Social Development,* 19(1), 202–220.

Oller, D. K., Cobo-Lewis, A. B., and Pearson, B. Z. (2004). Profiles in early bilingual learning: Vocabulary acquisition and the distributed characteristic. Lafayette, LA: International Clinical Phonetics and Linguistic Association.

Oller, D. K., and Jarmulowicz, L. (2009). Language and literacy in bilingual children in the early school years. In E. Hoff and M. Shatz (Eds), *Handbook of Language Development* (pp. 368–386). Oxford: Blackwell.

Oller, D. K., and Eilers, R. E. (Eds) (2002). *Language and Literacy in Bilingual Children*. Clevedon, England: Multilingual Matters.

Ong, A. D., and Phinney, J. S. (2002). Personal goals and depression among Vietnamese American and European American young adults: A mediational analysis. *The Journal of Social Psychology*, 142(1), 97–108.

Orellana, M. F., Reynolds, J. F., Dorner, L., and Meza, J. (2003). In other words: Translating or "para-phrasing" as a family literacy practice in immigrant households. *The Reading Research Quarterly*, 38(1), 12–34.

Ortega, L. (2013a). Language learning and teaching: Overview. In C. A. Chapelle (Ed.), *The Encyclopedia of Applied Linguistics* (pp. 3041–3048). Oxford: Blackwell.

(2013b). SLA for the 21st century: Disciplinary progress, transdisciplinary relevance, and the bi/multilingual turn. *Language Learning*, 63(1), 1–24.

Ostler, N. (2005). *Empires of the Word: A Language History of the World*. New York: HarperCollins.

Ovando, C. J. (2003). Bilingual education in the United States: Historical development and current issues. *Bilingual Research Journal*, 27(1), 1–24.

Oyama, S. (1976). A sensitive period for the acquisition of a nonnative phonological system. *Journal of Psycholinguistic Research*, 5(3), 261–283.

Pagett, L. (2006). Mum and Dad prefer me to speak Bengali at home: code switching and parallel speech in a primary school setting. *Literacy*, 40(3), 137–145.

Palermo, F., Mikulski, A. M., Fabes, R. A., Hanish, L. D., Martin, C. L., and Stargel, L. E. (2013). English exposure in the home and classroom: Predictions to Spanish-speaking preschoolers' English vocabulary skills. *Applied Psycholinguistics*, 35(6), 1163–1187. DOI:10.1017/S0142716412000732.

Palmer, B. C., Chen, C. I., Chang, S., and Leclere, J. T. (2006). The impact of biculturalism on language and literacy development: Teaching Chinese English language learners. *Reading Horizons*, 46(4), 239–264.

Palmer, D., and Martínez, R. A. (2013). Teacher agency in bilingual spaces: A fresh look at preparing teachers to educate Latina/o bilingual children. *Review of Research in Education*, 37(1), 269–297.

Pandey, A. (2004), Review of *Multilingual Education in Practice: Using Diversity as a Resource. TESOL Quarterly*, 38(4), 756–757. DOI: 10.2307/3588300.

Pandya, C., McHugh, M., and Batalova, J. (2011). *Limited English Proficient Individuals in the United States: Number, Share, Growth, and Linguistic Diversity*. Washington, DC: Migration Policy Institute.

Paradis, J. (2011). Individual differences in child English second language acquisition: Comparing child-internal and child-external factors. *Linguistic Approaches to Bilingualism*, 1(3), 213–237.

Paradis, J., Genesee, F., and Crago, M. B. (2011). *Dual Language Development and Disorders. A Handbook on Bilingualism and Second Language Learning* (2nd ed.). Baltimore: Paul H. Brookes.

Pearson, B. Z., Fernández, S. C., Lewedeg, V., and Oller, D. K. (1997). The relation of input factors to lexical learning by bilingual infants. *Applied Psycholinguistics*, 18(01), 41–58.

Phinney, J. S., Romero, I., Nava, M., and Huang, D. (2001). The role of language, parents, and peers in ethnic identity among adolescents in immigrant families. *Journal of Youth and Adolescence*, 30(2), 135–153.

Pollock, D. C., Van Ruth, E. R., and Van Reken, R. E. (2009). *Third Culture Kids: Growing Up among Worlds*. Nicholas Brealey Publishing.

Portes, A., and Hao, L. (1998). E pluribus unum: Bilingualism and loss of language in the second generation. *Sociology of Education*, 269–294.

(2002). The price of uniformity: Language, family and personality adjustment in the immigrant second generation. *Ethnic and Racial Studies*, 25(6), 889–912.

Potowski, K. (2001, May). Educating university foreign language teachers to work with heritage Spanish speakers. In *Research and practice in language teacher education: Voices from the field. Selected papers from the First International Conference on Language Teacher Education CARLA Working Paper* (Vol. 19). Available at http://carla.acad.umn.edu/workingpapers

(2004). Student Spanish use and investment in a dual language classroom: Implications for second language acquisition and heritage language maintenance. *The Modern Language Journal*, 88, 75–101.

Pratt, M. L. (2003). Building a new public idea about language. *Profession*, 1, 110–119.

Prevoo, M. J., Malda, M., Mesman, J., Emmen, R. A., Yeniad, N., Van Ijzendoorn, M. H., and Linting, M. (2013). Predicting ethnic minority children's vocabulary from socioeconomic status, maternal language and home reading input: Different pathways for host and ethnic language. *Journal of Child Language*, 1–22. *First view* DOI:10.1017/S0305000913000299.

Puig, V. I. (2010). Are early intervention services replacing home languages and cultures "at risk"? *Early Childhood Research and Practice*, 12(1), 1–19.

Quay, S. (2008). Dinner conversations with a trilingual two-year-old: Language socialization in a multilingual context. *First language*, 28(1), 5–33.

Ramirez, M., Perez, M., Valdez, G., and Hall, B. (2009). Assessing the long-term effects of an experimental bilingual-multicultural programme: implications for drop-out prevention, multicultural development and immigration policy. *International Journal of Bilingual Education and Bilingualism*, 12(1), 47–59.

Razakowski, J., McElvany, N., Ohle, A., Gebauer, M. M., Hardy, I., and Cinar, M. (2013). *The potential of the L1 for vocabulary learning in L2. Results of an intervention study in grade 4.* Unpublished manuscript. Technical University of Dortmund.

Reyes, I. (2004). Functions of code switching in schoolchildren's conversations. *Bilingual Research Journal*, 28(1), 77–98.

Rodríguez, M. V. (2010). Pathways to bilingualism: Young children's home experiences learning English and Spanish. *Early Childhood Research and Practice*, 12(1), 1–8.

Roosa, M., O'Donnell, M., Cham, H., Gonzales, N., Zeiders, K., Tein, J., and … Umaña-Taylor, A. (2012). A prospective study of Mexican American adolescents' academic success: considering family and individual factors. *Journal of Youth and Adolescence*, 41(3), 307–319.

Rubinstein-Avila, E. and Lee, E. H. (2014). Secondary teachers and English language learners (ELLs): Attitudes, preparation and implications. *The Clearing House: A Journal of Educational Strategies, Issues and Ideas*, 87(5), 187–191.

Rumbaut, R. G. (2014). English plus: Exploring the socioeconomic benefits of bilingualism in Southern california. In R. M. Callahan and P. C. Gándara (Eds), *The Bilingual Advantage: Language, Literacy and the US Labor Market* (Vol. 99) (pp. 182–210). Clevedon, England: Multilingual Matters.

Ryan, C. (2013). *Language Use in the United States: 2011*. Retrieved from: http://www .census.gov/prod/2013pubs/acs-22.pdf

Saunders, W., Goldenberg, C., and Marcelletti, D. (2013). English language development: Guidelines for instruction. *American Educator*, 37(2), 13–25.

Schechter, S. R., and Cummins, J. (2003). *Multilingual Education in Practice. Using Diversity as a Resource*. Portsmouth, NH: Heinemann.

Schiffman, H. F. (1996). *Linguistic Culture and Language Policy*. London: Rouledge.

Schwartz, M., and Moin, V. (2012) Parents' assessment of their preschool children's bilingual development in the context of family language policy. *Journal of Multilingual and Multicultural Development*, 33(1), 35–55, DOI: 10.1080/0143 4632.2011.638078.

Schwarzer, D., Haywood, A., and Lorenzen, C. (2003). Fostering multiliteracy in a linguistically diverse classroom. *Language Arts*, 80(6), 453–461.

Seung, H. K., Elder, J. H., and Siddiqi, S (2006). Intervention outcomes of a bilingual child with autism. *Journal of Medical Speech-Language Pathology*, 14, 53–63.

Skutnabb-Kangas, T., Phillipson, R., and Rannut, M. (1994). *Linguistic Human Rights: Overcoming Linguistic Discrimination* (Vol. 67). New York: Walter de Gruyter.

Slama, R. B. (2012). A longitudinal analysis of academic English proficiency outcomes for adolescent English language learners in the United States. *Journal of Educational Psychology*, 104(2), 265–285.

Sparks, R. L. (2006). Is there a "disability" for learning a foreign language? *Journal of Learning Disabilities*, 39(6), 544–557.

Sparks, R., and Ganschow, L. (2001). Aptitude for learning a foreign language. *Annual Review of Applied Linguistics,* 21, 90–111.

Sparks, R. L., Ganschow, L., Fluharty, K., and Little, S. (1995). An exploratory study on the effects of Latin on the native language skills and foreign language aptitude of students with and without learning disabilities. *Classical Journal*, 165–184.

Steel, P., and Konig, C. J. (2006). Integrating theories of motivation. *Academy of Management Review*, 31 (4), 889–913.

Stein-Smith, K. (2013). *The US Foreign Language Deficit, and Our Economic and National Security: A Bibliographic Essay on the US Language Paradox*. Lewiston, NY: Edwin Mellen Press.

Stevens, G., and Ishizawa, H. (2007). Variation among siblings in the use of a non–English language. *Journal of Family Issues*, 28(8), 1008–1025.

Stoddart, T., Pinal, A., Latzke, M., and Canaday, D. (2002). Integrating inquiry science and language development for English language learners. *Journal of Research in Science Teaching*, 39(8), 664–687.

Strauss, A., and Corbin, J. M. (1990). *Basics of Qualitative Research: Grounded Theory Procedures and Techniques*. Thousand Oaks, CA: Sage Publications, Inc.

Tabors, P. O., and Snow, C. E. (2001). Young bilingual children and early literacy development. *Handbook of Early Literacy Research*, 1, 159–178.

Tamura, E. H. (1993). The English-only effort, the anti-Japanese campaign, and language acquisition in the education of Japanese Americans in Hawaii, 1915–40. *History of Education Quarterly*, 33(1), 37–58.

Taylor, A., Bailey, A., Cooper, P., Dwyer, C., Kramarae, C., and Lieb, B., (2007). Gender differences in reading and communication skills. In S. S. Klein (Ed.), *Handbook for Achieving Gender Equity through Education* (pp. 281–303). Mahwah, NJ: Lawrence Erlbaum Publishers.

Thomas, W. P., Collier, V. P., and Abbott, M. (1993). Academic achievement through Japanese, Spanish, or French: The first two years of partial immersion. *The Modern Language Journal*, 77(2), 170–179.

Thomas, W. P., and Collier, V. P. (2003). The multiple benefits of dual language. Dual language programs educate both English learners and native English speakers without incurring extra costs. *Educational Leadership*, 61(2), 61–65.

Trimbur, J. (2006). Linguistic memory and the politics of U.S. English. *College English*, 68(6), 575–588.

Understanding Language (2013). Key principles for ELL instruction. Stanford, CA: author. Retrieved from http://ell.stanford.edu/sites/default/files/Key%20 Principles%20for%20ELL%20Instruction%20with%20references_0.pdf

U.S. Census Bureau (2011). *American Community Survey, Table 1: "Detailed Languages Spoken at Home by English-Speaking Ability for the Population 5 Years and Over: 2011."* Retrieved from http://www.census.gov/prod/2013pubs/acs-22.pdf

U.S. Census Bureau (2014). *American Community Survey: 2009–2013, Young Adults: Then and Now.* Retrieved from http://www.census.gov/newsroom/ press-releases/2014/cb14-219.html

Valdés, G. (1997). Dual-language immersion programs: A cautionary note concerning the education of language-minority students. *Harvard Educational Review*, 67 (3), 391–429.

——— (2004). Between support and marginalisation: The development of academic language in linguistic minority children. In J. Brutt-Griffler and M. M. Varghese (Eds), *Bilingualism and Language Pedagogy* (pp. 102–132). Clevedon, England: Multilingual Matters.

Valdés, G., and Figueroa, R. A. (1995). *Bilingualism and Testing: A Special Case of Bias*. Norwood, NJ: Ablex Publishing.

van Goor, R., and Heyting, F. (2008). Negotiating the world: Some philosophical considerations on dealing with differential academic language proficiency in schools. *Educational Philosophy and Theory*, 40(5), 652–665.

van Lier, L., and Walqui, A. (2012). Language and the common core standards. In K. Hakuta and M. Santos (Eds), *Understanding Language: Commissioned Papers on Language and Literacy Issues in the Common Core State Standards and Next Generation Science Standards* (pp. 44–51). Palo Alto, CA: Stanford University.

Verhoeven, L. (2000). Components in early second language reading and spelling. *Scientific Studies of Reading*, 4(4), 313–330.

Vu, J. A., Bailey, A. L., and Howes, C. (2010). Code-switching in narrative story-completion tasks in Mexican-heritage preschoolers. *Bilingual Research Journal*, 33, 200–219.

Vukelich, C., Christie, J. F., and Enz, B. (2008). *Helping Young Children Learn Language and Literacy*. Boston, MA: Allyn and Bacon.

Vygotsky, L. S. (1978). *Mind and Society: The Development of Higher Mental Processes.* Harvard University Press.

Wan, Y., and Ramsey, A. (2014). Shaping our global future: Advocating for bilingualism and multilingualism. *Perspective*, 36(1), 5–8.

Weaver, S. W., and Kim, S. Y. (2008). A person-centered approach on the linkages among parent–child differences in cultural orientation, supportive parenting, and adolescent depressive symptoms in Chinese American families. *Journal of Youth and Adolescence*, 37, 36–49.

Wen, Z. (2012). Foreign language aptitude. *ELT Journal*, 66(2), 233–235.

Werker, J. F., Weikum, W. M., and Yoshida, K. A. (2006). Bilingual speech processing in infants and adults. In P. McCardle and E. Hoff (Eds), *Childhood Bilingualism: Research on Infancy Through School Age* (pp. 1–18). Clevedon, England: Multilingual Matters.

Wharton, R. H., Levine, K., Miller, E., Breslau, J., and Greenspan, S. I. (2000). Children with special needs in bilingual families: A developmental approach to language recommendations. In S. I. Greenspan and S. Wieder (Eds), *The Interdisciplinary Council on Developmental and Learning Disorders Clinical Practice Guidelines* (pp. 141–151). Bethesda, MD: ICDL. Retrieved September 30, 2013, from http://www.icdl.com/graduate/documents/Chapter7.pdf

Wides-Munoz, L. (Sept 26, 2013). University Heritage Language Programs on the Rise. Associated Press.

Winsler, A., Díaz, R. M., Espinosa, L., and Rodríguez, J. L. (1999). When learning a second language does not mean losing the first: Bilingual language development in low-income, Spanish-speaking children attending bilingual preschool. *Child Development*, 70(2), 349–362.

Wong Fillmore, L. (2000). Loss of family languages: Should educators be concerned? *Theory into Practice*, 39(4), 203–210.

——— (1991). When learning a second language means losing the first. *Early Childhood Research Quarterly*, 6(3), 323–346.

Worthy, J., and Rodríguez-Galindo, A. (2006). "Mi hija vale dos personas": Latino immigrant parents' perspectives about their children's bilingualism. *Bilingual Research Journal*, 30(2), 579–601.

Wright, S. (Ed.) (1996). *Monolingualism and Bilingualism: Lessons from Canada and Spain.* Clevedon, UK: Multilingual Matters.

Yi, Y. (2007). Engaging literacy: A biliterate student's composing practices beyond school. *Journal of Second Language Writing*, 16(1), 23–39.

Yoshida, H. (2008). The cognitive consequences of early bilingualism. *Zero to Three*, 29(2), 26–30.

Zentella, A. C. (1997). *Growing Up Bilingual: Puerto Rican Children in New York.* Malden, MA: Blackwell.

Zhou, M., and Kim, S. S. (2006). Community forces, social capital, and educational achievement: The case of supplementary education in the Chinese and Korean immigrant communities. *Harvard Educational Review*, 76(1), 1–29.

Zhou, Q., Tao, A., Chen, S. H., Main, A., Lee, E., Ly, J., and … Li, X. (2012). Asset and protective factors for Asian American children's mental health adjustment. *Child Development Perspectives*, 6(3), 312–319.

Author Index

Abbott, M., 56
Acredolo, L.P., 236
Adesope, O.O., 14, 18
Alba, R., 194
Alexander, R.A., 226, 227
Allard, R., 198, 256
Alvarez, S.P., 216
Anderson, K.J., 40
Ardasheva, Y., 56
Ash, K., 3, 192
Au, T.K.F., 44

Bailey, A.L., 15, 17, 19, 21, 56, 159, 176, 177, 180, 197, 203, 207, 208, 217, 218, 228, 246, 247, 250, 256
Bain, B., 65
Baker, C., 20, 75
Baker-Ward, L., 20
Ball, M.J., 112
Baquedano-López, P., 226, 227, 229, 230
Barkley, R.A., 19
Barnett, W.S., 199
Barron-Hauwaert, S., 64
Barth R., 8, 77
Batalova, J., 13
Baum, S., 6, 14
Ben-Zeev, S., 57
Berkeley, R., 179
Bialystok, E., 14, 18, 19, 20, 57, 161, 198, 199
Bird, E., 53
Bitterman, A., 14
Bjork-Willen, P., 14
Blanco, D., 199
Boardman, A.G., 200
Breslau, J., 52
Brown, C.A., 236
Brown, C.L., 58
Brown, D.H., 70
Bruner, J., 8, 17, 77
Budach,G., 180
Bunch, G.C., 14

Butler, K., 64
Butler, Y.G., 208

Callahan, R.M., 177, 202
Camarota S.A., 28
Canaday, D., 207
Carhill, A., 216
Carlo, M.S., 58
Carroll, J.B., 49
Carroll, P., 176, 177, 247
Castro, D.C., 198, 199
Chang, S., 215
Cheatham, G.A., 41
Chen, C.I., 215
Chen, D., 52
Cheng, L.R., 64
Chevalier, S., 4, 75
Cho, G., 136
Christian, D., 17, 184, 227, 229
Christie, J.F., 40
Churchill, E., 17
Clark–Chiarelli, N., 236
Clément, R., 118
Cline, Z., 200
Coady, M., 207
Cobo-Lewis, A.B., 41, 58
Coburn, C., 210
Coleman, R., 200
Coleman, H.L., 63
Collier, V.P., 56, 129, 187
Compton-Lilly, C., 217, 241
Cook, V., 197
Cook, H.G., 254
Cooper, T.C., 56, 203
Corbin, I.M., 80, 82
Costigan, C.L., 62
Crago, M.B., 52, 62, 251
Craik, F.I., 19
Crawford, J., 13, 28
Crosnoe, R., 227
Cuevas, P., 207
Cummins, J., 17, 18, 67, 226, 256

Subject Index

academic language, 54, 56, 141, 200, 207, 246, 274
  definition of, 285
affective filter, 20, 43, 63, 113, 114
African American, 14, 277, 280
African languages
  treatment of, 31
AGBU, 179, 195
America
  as a monolingual nation, 26
  as the "melting pot," 28
American
  identifying as, 125
American accent, 115
American Indian, *see* Native American/
  Alaska Native
American Indian/Alaska Native, 14
American Sign Language, 39, 42, 87, 107, 111, 271
Ana Cecilia Zentella, 66
Arabic, 15, 39, 47, 69, 78, 84, 85, 87, 89, 119, 120, 126, 129, 131, 136, 147, 159, 172, 179, 234, 235, 253, 271
Arizona, 3
Armenian, 8, 36, 39, 43, 47, 69, 78, 84, 85, 87, 89, 119, 120, 124, 126, 129, 130, 131, 136, 159, 167, 179, 195, 234, 253, 271
Armenian Diaspora, 195
Armenian earthquake of 1988, 195
Armenian General Benevolent Union, *see* AGBU
Arturo y Clementina 237
ASD, 52, 53
Asia, 27
Asian American, 14, 21, 62
Association of Southeast Asian Nations (ASEAN), 4
autism spectrum disorder, *see* ASD

Basque, 4
Bengali, 39, 84, 85, 87, 169, 271

bi-/multilingual turn, 217
bilingual education, 2, 192
bilingual upbringing, 69, 104
bilingualism
  additive forms of, 221, 288
  and attitudes, xiv, 6, 14, 21, 26, 28, 31, 35, 67, 127, 131, 163, 190, 192, 193, 202, 223, 240, 280
  and balanced bilinguals, 75, 285
  and contested cognitive effects, 19
  and dementia, 6
  and emergent bilinguals, 75
  and executive functioning, 6, 14, 19, 20
  and identity, 6
  and metacognitive abilities, 7
  and metalinguistic abilities, 7, 14, 18
  and simultaneous acquisition, 18, 43
  andnative bilinguals, 75
  circumstantial forms of, 177, 285
  cognitive benefits of, 6
  neurocognitive effects of, 6
  sequential forms of, 43, 44, 48, 287
  subtractive forms of, 16, 198, 288
Brazil, 104, 105, 106, 135
Britain, 4

CAL, 1, 13, 183, 187, 189
California, xii, 3, 13, 14, 22, 26, 30, 176, 179, 192, 195, 196, 201
Canada, xi, 4, 51, 65, 153, 256
Cantonese, 15, 50, 87, 89, 126, 192, 234
Castilian, 4
Catalan, 4
CCSS, 21, 197, 211
CEFR, 253, 254
Center for Applied Linguistics, *see* CAL
Center for Research on Education, Diversity and Excellence, *see* CREDE
Central America, 104, 214
charter schools, 167, 178
Cherokee, 31
Chicago, 146

313

multilingualism (*cont.*)
  and phonological development, 44, 70
  and puberty, 9, 44, 157, 223, 224, 248
  and roads to, 92
  and sibling interactions, 5, 256
  and sibling relationships, 162
  and social development, 20, 56
  and teacher attitudes, 219
  and vocabulary, 44
  as a continuum, 25, 75
  as the norm, 126
  definition of, 287
  importance of, 11
  linguistic benefits of, 18
  metalinguistic benefits of, 18
  norms for, 253
  promoting systematic approaches to, 23,
    222, 257
  systemic challenges to, 166
  teachers as advocates of, 229
  vulnerability of, 12, 16, 24, 71, 222, 249
  vulnerability.of, 161

Nacho, Tito y Miguel, 237
National Center for Education Statistics,
  see NCES
National Clearinghouse for English Language
  Acquisition, *see* NCELA
National Education Association, *see* NEA
National Heritage Language Resource Center,
  see NHLRC
National Public Radio, *see* NPR
Native American languages
  eradication of, 30
  treatment of, 31
Native American/Alaska Native, 29, 30
NCELA, 178, 195, 197, 199, 206, 207
NCES, 13, 206
NCLB, 3, 176, 208
NEA, 196, 197
Nelson Henriquez, 2
Netherlands, the, 3, 179
New York, 66, 148, 158, 196
New York Times, The, 4, 247
Next Generation Science Standards, *see* NGSS
NGSS, 21, 197, 211
NHLRC, 196
No Child Left Behind Act of 2001, *see* NCLB
non-verbal period, 122
North Americans, 4
NPR, 2

one-parent-one-language method, 64, 65,
  72, 223
opportunity to learn, *see* OTL

Oregon State press law, 31
OTL, 201, 207, 208, 209

Para Los Niños Charter Schools, 179
parochial schooling, 9, 167, 173, 176,
  177, 179
Partnership for 21st Century Skills, 196, 253
Pedrito, 242
Persian, *see* Farsi
Poland, 4
Polish, 4
polyglot, xvii, 76, 83, 106, 214
Portuguese, 26, 34, 42, 55, 67, 69, 84, 85, 87,
  104, 105, 106, 107, 108, 109, 115, 122,
  125, 135, 146, 153, 154, 155, 160, 167,
  233, 235, 241, 271, 277
preschool programming, *see* early childhood
  care and education programming
Proposition 227 in California
  ballot initiative, 3
Puerto Rican, 66
Pulaar, 86, 88

Question 2 in Massachusetts
  ballot initiative, 3

Russian, 15, 26, 39, 45, 46, 48, 71, 85, 87, 89,
  95, 96, 98, 99, 111, 114, 116, 118, 119,
  120, 137, 141, 155, 158, 160, 161, 167,
  169, 172, 173, 179, 192, 243, 246, 253,
  263, 271, 278
Rwanda, 86

Salvadorian-American, 26, 137
SDAIE, 200, 212
Seal of Biliteracy, 196, 197, 249
second language, *see* L2
selective mutism, 123
  and anxiety disorder, distinct from, 123
Seneca, 31
Senegal, 86
sensitive periods, 44
Sheltered Instruction Observation Protocol,
  see SIOP
siblings, 30
sign language, 109, 110, 114, 147, 169, 232,
  236, *see also* American Sign Language
SIOP, 210, 211
SLD, 185, 188, 213
SLI, 4, 53, 251
social justice, 3, 7, 214, 288
Society for Research in Child Development's
  Social Policy Report, 2
Southern California, 1
Southwestern United States, 192

CPSIA information can be obtained
at www.ICGtesting.com
Printed in the USA
LVHW02s1623210818
587659LV00019B/372/P

9 781108 449274